TABLE DES MATIÈRES

	Pages
Table des Matières.	5-8

PREFACE : *Objectif. Organisation générale du Cours. Plan détaillé des Units. Conseils aux autodidactes utilisant* The Language of Business.. .. .. — **9-15**

Signes phonétiques (tableau). .. .. — **16**

GENERAL INTRODUCTION : THE HISTORY OF THE COMPANY.. — **17-26**
Word Study p. 17-20 ; History of the Company p. 21-23 ; Notes and Practice p. 24-26

UNIT 1 : NEW MARKETS ARE VITAL.. .. .. — **27-42**
   I. Introduction (Word Study p. 27-30 ; Summary p. 31)
   II. Conversation and Documents (Conversation p. 31-33 ; Letters 35-36)
  III. Notes and Practice (*Grammaire* p. 37-40 ; *Exercices* p. 41-42)

UNIT 2 : A VISIT TO THE FACTORY .. .. — **43-56**
   I. Introduction (Word Study p. 43-45 ; Summary p. 45)
   II. Conversation and Documents (Conversation p. 46-48 ; Letters p. 51-52)
  III. Notes and Practice (*Grammaire* p. 52-54 ; *Exercices* p. 54-56)

UNIT 3 : AN EMERGENCY IN THE SALES OFFICE .. .. — **57-74**
   I. Introduction (Word Study p. 57-61 ; Summary p. 61-62)
   II. Conversation and Documents (Conversation p. 63-66 ; Business letters p. 67-68)
  III. Notes and Practice (*Grammaire* p. 69-72 ; *Exercices* p. 72-74)

UNIT 4 : TROUBLE WITH A SPECIAL ORDER.. .. .. — **75-88**
   I. Introduction (Word Study p. 75-78 ; Summary p. 78)
   II. Conversation and Documents (Conversation p. 78-82 ; Letters p. 82-84)
  III. Notes and Practice (*Grammaire* p. 84-86 ; *Exercices* p. 87-88)

UNIT 5 : THE FACTORY EXTENSION MEETING .. .. — **89-100**
   I. Introduction (Word Study p. 89-92 ; Summary p. 92)
   II. Conversation and Documents (Conversation p. 92-95 ; Minutes of meetings p. 96)
  III. Notes and Practice (*Grammaire* p. 97-98 ; *Exercices* p. 99-100)

UNIT 6 : APPOINTING THE NEW ADVERTISING MANAGER   101-113

    I.   Introduction (Word Study p. 101-104 ; Summary p. 104-105)

    II.   Conversation and Documents (Conversation p. 105-108 ; Advertisements p. 109)

    III.   Notes and Practice (*Grammaire* p. 110-112 ; *Exercices* p. 112-113)

UNIT 7 : COMPLAINT FROM AN ANGRY CUSTOMER   114-127

    I.   Introduction (Word Study p. 114-117 ; Summary p. 117-118)

    II.   Conversation and Documents (Conversation p. 118-122 ; Letters p. 123)

    III.   Notes and Practice (*Grammaire* p. 124-125 ; *Exercices* p. 125-127)

UNIT 8 : AN ACCIDENT IN THE FACTORY   128-141

    I.   Introduction (Word Study p. 128-131 ; Summary p. 131-132)

    II.   Conversation and Documents (Conversation p. 132-135 ; A Memo p. 136)

    III.   Notes and Practice (*Grammaire* p. 136-139 ; *Exercices* p. 139-141)

UNIT 9 : PRODUCTIVITY — A WORK STUDY SURVEY   142-155

    I.   Introduction (Word Study p. 142-145 ; Summary p. 145-146)

    II.   Conversation and Documents (Conversation p. 146-149 ; Memo p. 150)

    III.   Notes and Practice (*Grammaire* p. 151-153 ; *Exercices* p. 153-155)

UNIT 10 : THE PENSION FUND MEETING   156-170

    I.   Introduction (Word Study p. 156-159 ; Summary p. 159-161)

    II.   Conversation and Documents (Conversation p. 161-164 ; Memo p. 165)

    III.   Notes and Practice (*Grammaire* p. 165-168 ; *Exercices* p. 168-170)

UNIT 11 : THE CASE OF THE MISSING FILE   171-183

    I.   Introduction (Word Study p. 171-173 ; Summary p. 173-174)

    II.   Conversation and Documents (Conversation p. 175-177 ; Payment by cheque p. 178)

    III.   Notes and Practice (*Grammaire* p. 179-181 ; *Exercices* p. 181-183)

UNIT 12 : A LABOUR DISPUTE   184-199

    I.   Introduction (Word Study p. 184-187 ; Summary p. 187-188)

    II.   Conversation and Documents (Conversation p. 189-192 ; Personnel management p. 193-194)

    III.   Notes and Practice (*Grammaire* p. 195-197 ; *Exercices* p. 198-199)

UNIT 13 : RISK OF A TAKEOVER   200-217

    I.   Introduction (Word Study p. 200-206 ; Summary p. 206-207)

    II.   Conversation and Documents (Conversation p. 207-211 ; Letter p. 212)

    III.   Notes and Practice (*Grammaire* p. 213-215 ; *Exercices* p. 215-217)

BRITISH BROADCASTING CORPORATION

The Language of Business

A L'USAGE DES CADRES DE L'INDUSTRIE ET DU COMMERCE

TEXTE ANGLAIS D'ANGELA MACK
CO-PRINCIPAL OF PADWORTH COLLEGE
AVEC LA COLLABORATION DE HENRY BEST

Méthodologie de
PIERRE VIREY
Agrégé de l'Université

PUBLIÉ EN ASSOCIATION AVEC
BRITISH BROADCASTING CORPORATION
PAR ÉDITIONS-DISQUES B.B.C. — FRANCE
8 RUE DE BERRI - PARIS (8e)

*Ce cours est accompagné de 2 cassettes C 60
et d'un livret (appendice) contenant la traduction
des conversations et le corrigé des exercices.
Cassettes et livret sont disponibles séparément.*

ISBN : 2 - 85294 - 004 - 3

UNIT 14 : THE ADVERTISING MANAGER AT WORK   218-234

    I. Introduction (Word Study p. 218-222 ; Summary p. 222-223)

    II. Conversation and Documents (Conversation p. 223-227 ; Press release p. 227-228)

    III. Notes and Practice (*Grammaire* p. 229-232 ; *Exercices* p. 232-234)

UNIT 15 : DEALING WITH AN IMPORTANT NEW MARKET   235-249

    I. Introduction (Word Study p. 235-241 ; Summary p. 241)

    II. Conversation and Documents (Conversation p. 241-245 ; Sightseeing programme p. 245-246)

    III. Notes and Practice (*Grammaire* p. 246 ; *Exercices* p. 246-249)

UNIT 16 : TRANSPORT PROBLEMS   250-265

    I. Introduction (Word Study p. 250-253 ; Summary p. 254-255)

    II. Conversation and Documents (Conversation p. 255-258 ; Memo p. 259)

    III. Notes and Practice (*Grammaire* p. 259-262 ; *Exercices* p. 263-265)

UNIT 17 : THE NEW BOARD OF DIRECTORS   266-280

    I. Introduction (Word Study p. 266-268 ; Summary p. 269)

    II. Conversation and Documents (Conversation p. 270-274 ; Letters p. 274)

    III. Notes and Practice (*Grammaire* p. 275-277 ; *Exercices* p. 277-280)

UNIT 18 : THE TRIALS OF A SALES REPRESENTATIVE   281-297

    I. Introduction (Word Study p. 281-284 ; Summary p. 284-285)

    II. Conversation and Documents (Conversation p. 285-288 ; Circular and complaint p. 289-290)

    III. Notes and Practice (*Grammaire* p. 920-294 ; *Exercices* p. 294-297)

UNIT 19 : AUDITING THE ACCOUNTS   298-314

    I. Introduction (Word Study p. 298-303 ; Summary p. 303-304)

    II. Conversation and Documents (Conversation p. 305-308 ; Directors'report p. 308-309)

    III. Notes and Practice (*Grammaire* p. 309-311 ; *Exercices* p. 311-314)

UNIT 20 : IMPROVING METHODS OF TRAINING   315-329

    I. Introduction (Word Study p. 315-318 ; Summary p. 318-319)

    II. Conversation and Documents (Conversation p. 319-323 ; Applications p. 323-324)

    III. Notes and Practice (*Grammaire* p. 325-327 ; *Exercices* p. 327-329)

UNIT 21 : DEBTORS AND CREDITORS   330-342

    I. Introduction (Word Study p. 330-332 ; Summary p. 332-333)

    II. Conversation and Documents (Conversation p. 333-336 ; Demands for payment p. 337-338)

    III. Notes and Practice (*Grammaire* p. 339-340 ; *Exercices* p. 340-342)

UNIT 22 : PATENTS AND TRADE-MARKS   343-354

    I.   Introduction (Word Study p. 343-345 ; Summary p. 346)

    II. Conversation and Documents (Conversation p. 346-349 ; Market research p. 350)

    III. Notes and Practice (*Grammaire* p. 351-352 ; *Exercices* p. 352-354)

UNIT 23 : INSURANCE   355-370

    I.   Introduction (Word Study p. 355-357 ; Summary p. 358)

    II. Conversation and Documents (Conversation p. 359-361 ; Applying for cover p. 362-363)

    III. Notes and Practice (*Grammaire* p. 364-367 ; *Exercices* p. 367-370)

UNIT 24 : THE FIRM EXPANDS   371-383

    I.   Introduction (Word Study p. 371-373 ; Summary p. 373-374)

    II. Conversation and Documents (Conversation p. 373-377 ; Companies in England p. 377-378)

THE NEW BRITISH CURRENCY   379

    III. Notes and Practice (*Grammaire* p. 379-380; *Exercices* p. 380-382)

Verbes Irréguliers   384

GLOSSAIRE GENERAL   385

Abréviations usuelles de l'anglais commercial   397

PRÉFACE

OBJECTIF

THE LANGUAGE OF BUSINESS constitue une introduction à l'anglais du commerce et des affaires. Il s'adresse au grand public des autodidactes qui travaillent dans le commerce et les affaires, et à tous ceux qui plus généralement éprouvent le désir et le besoin de dominer la langue que parlent, écrivent et lisent les hommes d'affaires d'aujourd'hui dans leur existence quotidienne, et plus particulièrement dans le cadre de leurs activités professionnelles. Il s'adresse également aux grands élèves et étudiants des Lycées (B.T.S.), des I.U.T., E.S.C., Préparations à la Chambre de Commerce Britannique et Cours d'Interprétariat et de Traduction, préparation à l'entrée à de Grandes Ecoles des Affaires, etc.

Lorsqu'il aura terminé ce COURS, l'étudiant devrait pouvoir participer sans difficulté à une conversation ou débat de caractère général, économique ou commercial ; rédiger correctement une correspondance ou document d'affaires ; lire sans peine la presse et les revues ou ouvrages professionnels anglo-américains.

ORGANISATION GÉNÉRALE DU COURS

THE LANGUAGE OF BUSINESS comporte 25 chapitres : une INTRODUCTION GENERALE et 24 UNITS, qui font vivre devant nous les divers membres d'une entreprise moderne en pleine expansion dans leurs tâches et activités particulières, avec leurs problèmes, leurs ambitions, leurs difficultés et leurs réussites.

Chaque UNIT est centré sur une importante CONVERSATION entre les membres d'un service particulier de l'entreprise, précédée d'une introduction dans la langue écrite, illustrée d'études de vocabulaire, de rappels phonétiques et grammaticaux, complétée par des lettres et documents commerciaux divers, et renforcée de nombreux exercices oraux. On trouvera à la fin de l'ouvrage un GLOSSAIRE GENERAL suivi d'une liste des abréviations anglaises courantes.

Le contenu des CONVERSATIONS comme celui de tous les TEXTES et définitions, etc... répond bien entendu aux exigences d'authenticité les plus rigoureuses. L'objectif est d'entraîner d'abord à l'expression orale et à la compréhension, sans jamais négliger les niveaux « écrit » et « lu » qui ont souvent plus d'importance qu'on ne croit dans le monde des affaires.

PLAN DÉTAILLÉ DES UNITS

Après une INTRODUCTION GENERALE (non enregistrée), on trouvera donc 24 UNITS qui se composent tous des trois parties suivantes :

PART I : INTRODUCTION, composée de :

1. WORD STUDY :

Vocabulary : *liste alphabétique* du *vocabulaire général* ou *spécialisé* pouvant poser quelque · difficulté dans l'ensemble des textes (Summary, Conversation, Documents) de l'Unité.
A quelque endroit de l'Unité que l'étudiant se trouvera, il pourra toujours retrouver le terme qui l'embarrasse en tête de chapitre.

Explanations and Other Useful Terms : *liste alphabétique* de *termes spécialisés figurant* dans l'Unité, ou n'y figurant pas mais relevant du même centre d'intérêt, suivi d'une brève définition ou d'un bref commentaire en anglais. La traduction de ces explications ne figure pas à l'Appendice mobile de traductions, mais les mots figurent avec leur prononciation et leur traduction au Glossaire Général.

Pronunciation : bref rappel phonétique permettant de sensibiliser l'étudiant sur la prononciation de certains termes (cf. **to 'advertise, an ad'vertisement ; e'conomy, an e'conomist, eco'nomic**). Certes on n'attend pas toujours d'un homme d'affaire la correction exigible d'un linguiste. Mais qu'il n'oublie pas qu'il existe un seuil d'intelligibilité qui dépend de la correction phonétique même :

— trop de mots mal prononcés peuvent rendre le message totalement incompréhensible à l'interlocuteur

— une oreille mal exercée peut ne rien comprendre à ce qu'elle reçoit

C'est pourquoi le Glossaire Général renseignera toujours sur la prononciation des termes, selon l'alphabet phonétique international, figurant page 16.

Les notes phonétiques de chaque Unit comportent :
— des indications sur la place de l'accent tonique ; ainsi :
  - 1 - : signifie que les mots de 2 syllabes ou plus qui suivent sont accentués sur la première syllabe
  - 2 : signifie que les mots de 2 syllabes ou plus qui suivent sont accentués sur la seconde syllabe
  - - 3 : signifie que les mots de 3 syllabes ou plus qui suivent sont accentués sur la troisième syllabe, etc.
— des indications sur la position de l'accent lorsqu'il est déterminé par la présence de certains suffixes (-ic-, -ion, etc.)
— des groupements de mots contenant le même son (le signe figure entre crochets en début de ligne, et les lettres ou syllabes concernées sont en italiques). Ex. [ʃ] *cash*, *sure*, **oper*a*tional, dimen*s*ion**
— une comparaison de mots de la même famille ou voisins par la graphie dans lesquels on peut rencontrer des différences de prononciation ou d'accentuation
— la prononciation figurée intégralement de certains mots difficiles.

2. SUMMARY :

C'est un résumé-présentation de l'épisode auquel on va assister dans la CONVERSATION.

PART II : CONVERSATION AND DOCUMENTS

1. CONVERSATION (**Recorded Text**) :

Longue conversation à plusieurs personnages qui donnera aux utilisateurs de THE LANGUAGE OF BUSINESS un exemple de la langue parlée par les hommes d'affaires, et leur fera voir comment le vocabulaire spécialisé de l'entreprise et des affaires s'intègre aux structures de la langue parlée contemporaine.

2. DOCUMENTS :

Lettres commerciales, circulaires, notes de service, rapports, procès-verbaux, etc...

L'enregistrement de la conversation est toujours suivi d'un exercice d'intonation (**practice sentences**) composé de phrases à répéter par l'auditeur.

PART III : NOTES AND PRACTICE

1. RAPPEL GRAMMATICAL :

Ce COURS s'adresse à des étudiants ayant une certaine expérience commerciale en français, et des bases en anglais général. Certes, l'anglais écrit du Summary comme l'anglais parlé de la Conversation restent simples. Mais il se peut néanmoins que certains étudiants désirent rafraîchir, préciser, confirmer, compléter leurs connaissances sur certains points.

On trouvera donc ici un bref rappel de petits points de grammaire. Il ne s'agit pas d'un cours de grammaire, mais d'observations pratiques permettant d'imiter les structures rencontrées après les avoir assimilées.

Ces notes succinctes renvoient à des phrases du Summary puis de la Conversation, et les rappels sont précédés de la numérotation des lignes.

2. EXERCISES :

L'étudiant pourra faire un contrôle oral rapide de ses acquisitions, tant en vocabulaire qu'en grammaire, grâce à une série d'exercices divers et nombreux, qui brasseront une dernière fois l'acquis.

CONSEILS AUX AUTODIDACTES UTILISANT CE COURS

Bien entendu, les conseils qui suivent ne s'adressent pas au Professeur qui voudrait bien utiliser THE LANGUAGE OF BUSINESS en classe : il saura choisir ses éléments, l'enchaînement du travail et les exercices les mieux appropriés à son public. Signalons néanmoins que les EXERCICES sont le plus souvent conçus pour être sans retouches majeures reportés sur bandes magnétiques pour faire des travaux oraux en laboratoire le cas échéant : ils sont nombreux, divers, longs, si bien que le Professeur pourra toujours faire enregistrer à son Assistant anglophone la mesure exacte de travail oral correspondant au temps dont il dispose et aux besoins très particuliers d'un groupe d'étudiants précis. Nous avons à son intention préféré ce système — toute Ecole possède son Assistant — à l'adjonction d'une collection coûteuse de bandes magnétiques inséparables du COURS. L'exploitation orale pourra donc être personnalisée.

Les remarques qui suivent s'adressent donc exclusivement à l'autodidacte.

Nous recommandons tout d'abord à l'étudiant de suivre les UNITS dans l'ordre où ils se présentent dans THE LANGUAGE OF BUSINESS. Chaque UNITE doit être parfaitement comprise et assimilée avant qu'on ne passe à la suivante. En d'autres termes, l'étudiant doit se refuser la tentation d'écouter les différentes conversations à la suite les unes des autres, afin de savoir ce qui se passe ; bien sûr, l'histoire d'une entreprise peut connaître son « suspense » et ceux qui la font ont souvent conscience de vivre une aventure passionnante : parce que HARPER & GRANT Ltd connaît les problèmes d'une authentique entreprise moderne en pleine expansion, l'auditeur pourra avoir envie de connaître le succès de la campagne publicitaire, d'apprendre si l'affaire projetée a finalement été enlevée, et si les nuages d'une prise de contrôle sur l'entreprise sont définitivement écartés ; mais les UNITS ont essentiellement une fonction linguistique : permettre à l'étudiant d'entendre, de répéter, de lire, de pratiquer le vocabulaire, la langue des affaires en situation, cela autant de fois qu'il sera nécessaire pour que comprendre et se faire comprendre lui deviennent dans chaque cas particulier une question de routine, de spontanéité totale. Lorsqu'il aura la certitude de bien dominer la matière de l'Unité, il pourra passer à l'Unité suivante.

Et que soit posé au départ le principe suivant : on peut toujours aller de la langue orale à la langue écrite. Aller de l'écrit à l'oral est par contre quasiment impossible. Le langage est affaire « de bouche à oreille ». Lorsque les yeux s'en mêlent, l'oreille n'entend plus. Ce que l'œil voit, c'est une ligne composée de lettres, groupées en syllabes, en mots isolés, avec des séparations, des points, des coupures rassurantes. Ce que l'oreille entend par contre, c'est souvent une chaîne sonore ininterrompue, avec des hauts et des bas, des accents forts et des syllabes atones, des sons dont l'écriture ne rend presque jamais compte.

Comment procéder à présent pour profiter au mieux de chaque UNIT ?

1re Étape :

Le travail commencera donc par une audition, à livre fermé, du texte enregistré.

Il est indispensable d'acquérir la compréhension de l'anglais oral à la vitesse normale. Suivre le dialogue avec les yeux serait plus facile. Mais lorsque l'homme d'affaires français rencontrera des hommes d'affaires anglais ou américains, il lui faudra comprendre immédiatement ce qu'ils disent. Il n'y aura aucun texte de support. Il ne pourra guère que leur demander, de loin en loin, de répéter ce qu'ils viennent de dire. Qu'il écoute donc le dialogue directement, de manière détendue, sans trop se préoccuper s'il ne comprend pas tout d'emblée. Une deuxième, une troisième audition du même dialogue le lui rendront à chaque fois plus clair, tandis que, chemin faisant, la prononciation des mots nouveaux se gravera de manière indélébile et juste dans l'esprit. Peu importe à ce stade si le sens de quelques mots reste indécis : ce qui compte est d'en assurer une audition juste. Entendre le mot en le voyant, nous ne le répèterons jamais assez, provoquerait une interférence, c'est-à-dire que la combinaison des lettres auxquelles on est habitué en français « interférerait », empêchant réellement d'entendre le son anglais véritable.

2e Étape :

A présent, on peut faire une nouvelle audition avec le texte sous les yeux. S'il est nécessaire, on pourra également ici contrôler le sens de certains mots en consultant le vocabulaire donné au début de l'Unité. En aucun cas, il n'est utile ni recommandé de lire toute la liste, qui n'est là, aussi complète que possible, que pour satisfaire à chaque leçon aux besoins particuliers du plus grand nombre d'étudiants. Ces listes pourront servir plus tard à revoir rapidement le vocabulaire de l'Unité, lorsqu'une autre sera en cours, et qu'on souhaitera faire de brefs retours en arrière.

3e Étape :

On pourra alors lire les brèves notations sur le vocabulaire (**other useful terms**) qui permettront d'étendre encore le lexique.

L'étudiant qui se méfierait de sa prononciation pourra consulter la *Prononciation*. Ces notes ont pour but tout d'abord d'attirer nettement l'attention sur la prononciation et l'accent de certains mots qui, malgré l'audition, auraient pu échapper à une oreille rebelle, ou déformée par trop de lecture antérieure, et ensuite aussi de confirmer que l'audition de détails, peut-être surprenante à la réflexion, était bien correcte. Dans tous les cas donc, ces rappels phonétiques seront utiles. On pourra répéter plusieurs fois les mots signalés, puis chercher la phrase du dialogue dans laquelle ils se trouvaient, et, ce dialogue encore « frais » dans l'oreille avec son intonation et son rythme propres, on répétera toute la phrase contenant le mot, une fois, deux fois, autant de fois qu'il sera nécessaire pour que la diction en soit claire, spontanée, aisée.

4e Étape :

Lire les rappels grammaticaux, qui remettront un certain nombre de petits détails en mémoire.

5e Étape :

Faire une nouvelle audition de la conversation, sans texte écrit sous les yeux. On pourra alors répéter les exercices d'intonation, en s'efforçant de bien mémoriser le *chant* de la phrase, sa *ligne mélodique* caractéristique.

6e Étape :

Faire les exercices, jamais par écrit, mais oralement, et si possible à haute voix. On en trouvera la correction à l'appendice mobile ; l'étudiant hésitant pourra y contrôler son travail à l'aide du corrigé, puis refaire l'exercice une seconde fois après ce contrôle, et revenir sur ces exercices à la fin d'une autre Unité pour les confirmer à nouveau.

Il sera bon du reste de faire le plus grand nombre de retours en arrière, soit de vocabulaire, soit de structures grammaticales. On écrira le minimum, seulement en cas d'hésitation trop grande. On pourra également consigner dans un carnet ce qui aura été d'une acquisition la plus rebelle au cours d'une Unité : ainsi chaque étudiant aura un aide-mémoire personnalisé de ses petits problèmes, qu'il pourra consulter rapidement à loisir.

Seul le thème pourra être fait par écrit (20 phrases comme à l'examen de la Chambre de Commerce Britannique).

7e Étape :

Lire les indications sur la correspondance commerciale, les notes, circulaires, etc... On en trouvera le vocabulaire dans la liste de vocabulaire en tête de l'Unité, et la traduction intégrale (très littérale à dessein) en Appendice. Il conviendra de chercher de temps à autre à retraduire en anglais, cette traduction des lettres, puis de confronter ce thème avec le texte original.

Summary :

On pourrait se dispenser d'étudier les textes écrits figurant dans la première partie de chaque Unit. Toutefois, ils ont été prévus à plusieurs fins :

— ils donnent des exemples de la langue sous son aspect écrit, donc des modèles de ce que seraient éventuellement des comptes rendus écrits des séances ou événements auxquels on assiste dans les conversations enregistrées.

— le Professeur pourra l'utiliser comme support de préparation à l'audition de la conversation enregistrée, ou comme sujet de petites dictées (Il y a une dictée à l'examen de la Chambre de Commerce Britannique).

— l'étudiant dont l'anglais est mal assuré pourra lire ce texte lentement avant une audition dont il craint qu'elle serait difficile, afin d'avoir un aperçu de ce qu'il va entendre, sans toutefois connaître exactement le texte qu'il va entendre : il l'entendra avec plus d'assurance, en respectant néanmoins les règles du jeu, c'est-à-dire, sans le texte sous les yeux. Qu'il veille bien à consulter les notes de prononciation avant de lire le Résumé.

— on pourra utiliser ces résumés pour faire de brefs retours en arrière sur les événements précédents.

— on pourra s'entraîner à faire une sorte de compte-rendu oral ou écrit de ce que l'on a entendu dans la conversation, comme si l'on avait à faire le rapport de la journée de travail dans l'entreprise, puis se contrôler en lisant ce texte afin de voir ce que l'on a oublié, ou ce que l'on aurait pu mieux dire.

— le texte du Résumé étant traduit intégralement dans l'Appendice, l'étudiant courageux pourra s'entraîner au thème de longue haleine en essayant de retrouver là encore l'anglais original : l'homme d'affaires a besoin aussi de savoir écrire la langue étrangère. Et que cet exercice lui soit une occasion de contrôler l'orthographe, qui chez des étudiants où l'on a pu constater que l'oral était souvent assez satisfaisant, est parfois entaché de petites erreurs fâcheuses (consonnes simples ou redoublées, certains suffixes, etc...).

— enfin ces textes contiennent certaines structures grammaticales intéressantes, qui sont brièvement commentées dans les Notes de la 3e partie, et renforcées par des exercices propres.

Cet exercice pourra intervenir plus tôt dans le travail, entre la 4e et la 5e Etape par exemple.

Ainsi, nous l'espérons, la variété des exercices permettra aux utilisateurs de manier avec aisance et justesse l'Anglais des Affaires.

Note : L'auteur de The Language of Business, Angela MACK, unit une connaissance des affaires et de la rédaction à une grande expérience de l'enseignement de l'anglais à l'étranger.

— Mr. Henry BEST, Directeur des Ventes d'une importante entreprise de constructions mécaniques qui a des ramifications dans le monde entier, a apporté de précieux conseils sur la pratique des affaires.

— Pierre VIREY, Agrégé d'Anglais, est Professeur en Classes Préparatoires aux l'ENS-Cloud-Fontenay, au Lycée Faidherbe de Lille, Professeur à l'Ecole Supérieure de Commerce et d'Administration des Entreprises de Lille et Chargé de Cours à l'UER de Philosophie de Lille-III.

SIGNES PHONÉTIQUES

VOYELLES

longues (*tense*)

[a:]   part, craft, partner, staff, market, clerk, draft, branch
[ɔ:]   four, law, course, all, draw, store, order, board, port
[u:]   two, rule, through, move, lose, proof, boom, crew
[i:]   be, see, sea, keep, meet, free, scheme, deeds, team .
[ə:]   turn, word, work, early, firm, world, certify, term, first

brèves (*lax*)

[æ]   man, bad, tank, bank, lack, value, cancel, finance
[e]   yes, ten, left, best, trend, cheque, expense, heavy
[i]   it, big, ship, since, fit, business, liquidity
[ɔ]   not, got, box, loss, what, model, stock, stop, bond, product
[u]   book, look, put, full, goods, wool, bull
[ʌ]   but, come, some, done, must, money, other, current, country
[ə]   allow, broker, again, debenture, customs, harbour, forward

diphtongues et triphtongues

[ai]   my, like, five, design, provide, divide, sign, flight
[ɔi]   coin, oil, join, Lloyds, spoil, alloy, employ, exploit
[ei]   eight, say, weight, made, waste, ratio, pay, raise, sale
[au]   out, now, house, how, down, bounties, amount, allow, endow
[ou]   no, gold, load, own, code, slow, broker, quota, cargo
[ɛə]   fair, share, bear, wear and tear, vary
[iə]   near, here, zero, career, cashier, clearance
[uə]   your, poor, assure, insure
[aiə]   fire, tyre, wire, hire, empire, higher, via
[auə]   our, hour, power, tower

CONSONNES

[d]	do, add	[g]	go, gear, get	[l] { (*clair*) long, leave
[t]	tap, top	[k]	car, dock, key	{ (*sombre*) well, all
[m, n, b, p, v]				
[ð]	the, this, that			[w] well, with
[θ]	thing, path, through			[h] high, hang
[j]	you, yard			[r] read, very, bridge
[z]	as, lose	[ʒ]	measure, decision	[ŋ] bring, thing
[s]	see, so	[ʃ]	ship, shop	[dʒ] just, adjust [tʃ] cheque, branch

Note : Dans les exemples du cours, le signe ′ au-dessus de la ligne indique un accent principal, et accessoirement le signe ˌ au-dessous de la ligne un accent secondaire. La syllabe concernée est la syllabe qui suit le signe.

GENERAL INTRODUCTION

THE HISTORY OF THE COMPANY

1. WORD STUDY

Vocabulary

achieve réaliser *something*
actual proprement dit *abstract*
advice conseils
afford pouvoir s'offrir
appoint nommer
assembly montage
  assembly shop atelier de montage
attend (*trans.*) assister (à)
aware (of) conscient, au courant
basket panier, corbeille
bin poubelle, corbeille
board conseil
bolt boulon, boulonner
business les affaires
  business management administration des entreprises, gestion
call (on) faire appel (à)
cane bambou, rotin
capture emporter, saisir, enlever (marché)
chairman président
changeover changement
company société, compagnie
competitive concurrentiel
consultant conseiller d'entreprise, organisateur-conseil, etc...
contract contrat

control contrôle
cupboard (*ici*) armoire de bureau
data données, information
  data processing traitement de l'information, informatique
department service, rayon
desk bureau
despatch expédition, expédier
drill forer, percer
efficiency rendement
enlarge agrandir, étendre, développer
equipment matériel
expert spécialiste
failure échec
file dossier, classer
  filing-cabinet classeur
  filing-tray casier, boîte de rangement
growth croissance, expansion
hire embaucher, engager
hole trou
increase accroître ; accroissement
irreplaceable irremplaçable
item article
join assembler
lack manque ; manquer
likelihood vraisemblance

machine shop   atelier d'ajustage, atelier des machines
management   gestion, direction
manage   gérer, diriger
Managing Director   administrateur délégué, présid[t] direct[r] génér[l]
manager   directeur, gérant
meeting   réunion, assemblée
nearly   presque
office   bureau
operational research   recherche opérationnelle
outpace   distancer, dépasser
over (ici)   au cours de
packing   emballage
paint shop   atelier de peinture
pending   pendant ; en attente
pressed steel   acier embouti
press shop   atelier d'emboutissage
Production Manager   directeur de la production, chef de l'ordonnancement
profitability   rentabilité
require   demander, exiger
retired   à la retraite
sale   vente
   Sales Manager   direct[r] des ventes

sheet   feuille, tôle
solve   résoudre
sophisticated   complexe, compliqué
spread   étendre, étaler ; se propager
staple   agrafe ; agrafer
   stapling machine   agrafeuse
staff   personnel
steady   régulier, constant
steel   acier
stores   réserves, stocks
straw   paille
supply   fournir, approvisionner
team   équipe
tool   outil
   tool room   salle des outils
tray   plateau, corbeille, bac, tiroir de rangement
treble   triple ; tripler
up-to-date   à jour, très moderne
warehouse   entrepôt, magasin
wastepaper basket ⎰ corbeille à
   wastepaper bin ⎱ papiers
weld   souder
works   usine
workshop   atelier

Abbreviations

O.R.   operational research
D.C.F.   discounted cash flow (cf. Unit 1, p. 29)
P.E.R.T.   Project Evaluation and Review Technique (méthode PERT)

Phrases

he is in his fifties	il a entre cinquante et soixante ans
he keeps an eye on the business	il ne perd pas l'affaire de vue
	il continue de s'occuper un peu de l'entreprise
he put the business on its feet	il a mis l'affaire sur pied

— 18 —

he landed his contract	il a décroché son contrat
the best way to run a business	la meilleure façon de gérer une affaire
they must get up-to-date	ils doivent se moderniser, se recycler
they can't afford to have all sorts of experts on the staff	ils ne peuvent se permettre d'avoir toutes sortes de spécialistes dans leur personnel

Explanations and Other Useful Terms

director   one of the stockholders who is elected to serve on the managerial board, called the *Board of Directors*, of the company.

Ltd. (Limited)   Harper & Grant Ltd. A *limited company* is one that has, legally, a limited liability or responsibility. The shareholders are not individually or personally responsible for its actions. The abbreviated form is the more common.

Operational Research   The application of mathematical techniques to the study of problems in a business.

P.E.R.T.   A system used in planning and controlling a project by making a diagram showing the actions and timing needed to complete the independant parts. Similar to **C.P.A.** (*critical path analysis*, cf. Unit 9).

Pronunciation

1 — 1 - (- -) business, capture, catalogue, company, contract, document, failure, government, limited, nephew, office, present, product, problem, regularly, warehouse

     - 2 (- -) appoint, assembly, attend, begin, coincidence, command, consider, continue, department, despatch, destroy, development, director, efficiency, enlarge, inevitable, machine(ry), particular, production, retired, supply, technique, together

     - - 3 - manufacture

2 — '-ion : ‚auto'mation, ‚conver'sation, e‚valu'ation, ins'pection, ‚organi'sation

     'ility : ‚profita'bility

3 — [ʌ]   *c*ompany, l*u*ck, *o*ther, r*u*n, s*o*n, b*u*dget

    [ɔ]   d*o*cument, m*o*dern, *o*ffice, s*o*lve

    [ɔ:]   b*oa*rd, c*au*ght, st*o*res

    [ou]   ag*o*, b*o*lt, fl*ow*, gr*ow*th, h*o*le

    [dʒ]   mana*g*e, mana*g*er, mana*g*ement ; *j*oin ; bu*dg*et

    [tʃ]   despa*tch*, cap*t*ure, manufa*ct*ure

4 — Compare : an 'increase [s], to in'crease [s]

    an 'export, to ex'port

    a 'product, to pro'duce

    com'petitive, ‚compe'tition

    board [bɔ:d], cupboard ['kʌbəd]

5 — Note : aware [ə'wɛə], budgetary ['bʌdʒitəri], bureaux ['bjuərouz], business ['biznis], corporate ['kɔ:pərit], government ['gʌvnmənt], item ['aitim], nephew ['nevju:], science [saiəns], securing [si'kjuəriŋ].

———————

II. THE HISTORY OF THE COMPANY

The company of Harper & Grant Ltd. was started forty-two years ago by Ambrose Harper and Wingate Grant. Wingate Grant died many years ago, and his son Hector, who is in his fifties (aged between fifty and sixty) is the present Managing Director. Ambrose Harper is the Chairman. He is now an old man, semi-retired, but he still comes in to the office 5 regularly to attend the board meetings and keep an eye on the business.

The company started by making steel wastepaper bins for offices. With the increase in smoking, these were considered much safer than the old type of basket made of cane or straw, because there was less likelihood of fire (but, strangely, we still continue to use the expression 'wastepaper 10 *basket*', as well as 'bin'). Old Mr. Grant, the present Managing Director's father, put the business on its feet when he captured a big contract to supply government offices with steel wastepaper bins. He always said that luck, or happy coincidence, turned a business into success or failure. He was rather like Napoleon, who always asked if an officer was lucky before 15 giving him a higher command. Mr. Grant Senior used to tell the story that, in the week before he landed his contract, a cane wastepaper basket had caught fire in a government department, the fire had spread rapidly and destroyed a number of irreplaceable documents.

From wastepaper bins, Harper & Grant began to manufacture other 20 items of office equipment: desks, chairs, cupboards, filing cabinets and smaller objects, such as filing trays, stapling machines and so on, until now when there are fifty-six different items listed in their catalogue. Today, nearly all the items produced by this company are made of pressed steel. The steel arrives in sheets from a steel works in South 25 Wales. It is then cut by machinery into the required pieces; these pieces are then pressed into shape and fixed together by *welding* (joining two metal parts by heating so that the metals flow together), or by drilling holes in the metal and securing the two pieces with a *bolt* or a rivet.

The factory consists of *workshops* where the actual making of a desk or 30 filing cabinet is done. These are divided into the *Tool Room, Works*

Stores, Press Shop, Machine Shops, Assembly Shop, Paint Shop, Inspection, Packing and Despatch Departments. There is also the *Warehouse* where finished articles are stored *pending*, waiting for, sale.

The firm has a history of slow, steady growth. Hector Grant firmly 35 believes that he knows the best way to run a business. However, his nephew Peter Wiles (son of Mr. Grant's sister), who joined the company six years ago and is Production Manager, and John Martin, appointed two years ago to be Sales Manager, are more adventurous. They want to treble Harper & Grant's business over the next few years and are certain that, 40 with modern business techniques and increased exports, they can achieve this.

Modernising a business to increase its profitability and competitiveness is a complicated affair. It requires a management team which is aware of such aids and tools of efficiency as electronic data processing, O.R. 45 (Operational Research), D.C.F. (Discounted Cash Flow), budgetary control, corporate planning, P.E.R.T. (Project Evaluation and Review Technique), automation, etc. We shall be dealing with some of these words and expressions as the series goes along. Business management is a rapidly developing science (some call it an art), and new techniques and 50 words, very often of American origin, are used more and more in everyday business conversation.

A small business cannot possibly afford to have on its staff experts in every modern management technique. It usually hires expert advice from outside consultants and bureaux. On the other hand, it is important that 55 members of a firm's management are aware of the more sophisticated techniques they might call on to solve particular problems. Inevitably while this changeover from the old way to the new is taking place, there are often difficulties and conflicts. But Harper & Grant Ltd., like their rivals, must get right up-to-date and enlarge their business, or they will be 60 outpaced by a firm whose business organisation is better than their own.

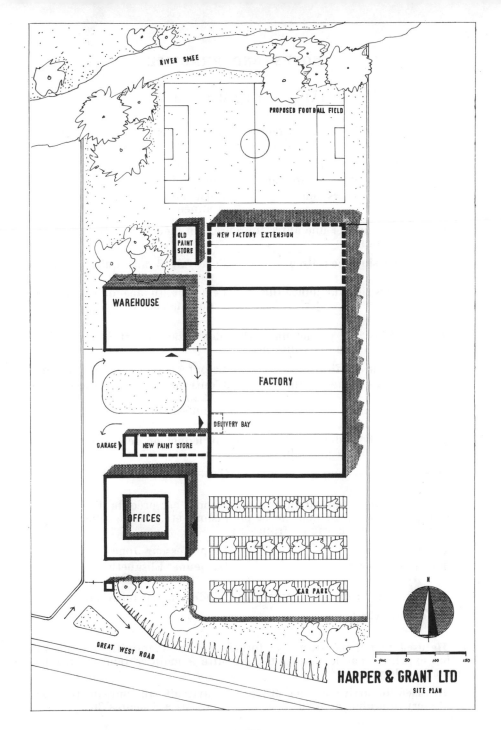

RIVER SMEE

PROPOSED FOOTBALL FIELD

OLD PAINT STORE

NEW FACTORY EXTENSION

WAREHOUSE

FACTORY

DELIVERY BAY

GARAGE   NEW PAINT STORE

OFFICES

CAR PARK

GREAT WEST ROAD

N

0 feet   50   100   150

HARPER & GRANT LTD
SITE PLAN

III. **NOTES AND PRACTICE**

1. RAPPEL GRAMMATICAL

1-3. **Ago** sert à indiquer le temps écoulé depuis la fin d'une action. Le temps de la phrase est le *prétérit (simple past)* :

He retired 6 years ago	Il a pris sa retraite il y a 6 ans
She was appointed 2 years ago	Elle a été nommée il y a 2 ans
He died many years ago	Il est mort il y a de nombreuses années

On peut rencontrer une autre tournure, qui met en vedette le complément de temps :

It's 3 years since he retired	Cela fait 3 ans qu'il a pris sa retraite
It's 10 years since he joined the company	Cela fait 10 ans qu'il est entré dans la société

3. **In his fifties** : le pluriel du chiffre des dizaines sert à désigner les années comprises entre deux dizaines :

The boss is in his fifties	Le patron a passé la cinquantaine
The firm was started in the twenties	L'entreprise a été lancée entre 1920 et 1930 (dans les années 20)

7 et 27. Le verbe indiquant le *moyen* par lequel on réalise un objectif est introduit par **by** + gérondif :

It is fixed by welding	C'est fixé par soudure

11. **Old Mr. Grant** : Lorsqu'un nom ou prénom est précédé d'un adjectif descriptif, d'un titre, du nom de la profession, etc., on ne rencontre pas l'article comme c'est le cas en français :

Professor Jones	Le professeur Jones
Young Elizabeth	La jeune Elisabeth

15. **He asked if...** : dans un style plus guindé, on rencontrerait :

He asked whether...

16. **He used to tell the story** : la forme **used to** + infinitif indique que l'action exprimée par le verbe s'est produite à maintes reprises, régulièrement dans le passé :

He used to arrive at the office every morning at 8.30	Il arrivait au bureau tous les matins à 8 heures 30

La forme **used to** n'a pas de présent correspondant. Au présent, c'est le présent forme simple qui rend compte de la répétition, de la fréquence, souvent avec un adverbe :

He usually arrives at 8.30   Habituellement, il arrive à 8 h 30

25. Notons que **works**, terminé par -s, est singulier :

A steel works, a gas works   Une aciérie, une usine à gaz

36. Au sens de *les affaires*, **business** est invariable et toujours singulier :

Business is business   Les affaires sont les affaires

Mais au sens de *une affaire, une entreprise*, le mot prend le pluriel :

He is at the head of 6 or 7 businesses   Il est à la tête de 6 ou 7 affaires de
of this kind in Western Europe   ce genre en Europe occidentale

39. **The Sales Manager** : dans la langue économique comme dans la langue scientifique, il n'est pas rare de rencontrer des noms composés dont le premier terme, contrairement à ce qui se passe en anglais général, a la forme du pluriel :

Customs duties, a savings-bank   Droits de douane, une caisse
                                        d'épargne

Notons du reste, en ce qui concerne ce mot utile, **customs**, que l'on dit :

customs agency (agence en douane), **customs charges** (frais de douane), **customs check** (vérification en douane), **customs clearance** (dédouanement), **customs-declaration** (déclaration-soumission), **customs-manifest** (manifeste de douane), **customs pass-book** (carnet de passage en douane), **customs tariff** (tarif douanier), **customs warehouse** (entrepôt en douane), **Customs Union** (Union Douanière), et : **Custom-House** douane, **Custom-House broker** (agent en douane), **Custom-House officer** (douanier), **Custom-House receipt** (acquit de douane).

55. Notons que la proposition de but **it's important (that)** est suivie du présent de l'indicatif ; on pourrait également rencontrer :

It's important that they should be aware of the new techniques

56. **The more sophisticated techniques** : pourquoi ce superlatif (les techniques les plus poussées) n'a-t-il pas la forme **the most** ? The most, et le suffixe -est pour les adjectifs courts, s'emploient lorsqu'on distingue un terme de plusieurs. Lorsque deux éléments seulement entrent en comparaison, le superlatif a la forme du comparatif :

Of the two machines, this one is   De ces deux machines, celle-ci est
undoubtedly the more efficient   sans aucun doute celle qui a le
                                        meilleur rendement

It's the easier solution   C'est la solution la plus facile
                                 (*des deux*)

2. EXERCISES

EXERCISE 1. — *Answer affirmatively as follows* :

Did you attend the meeting ? — **Of course I did.**

1. Is the new type safer ? 2. Will they make another model ? 3. Could they put the business on its feet again ? 4. Was the company started by your grandfather ? 5. Can they really achieve this within two years ? 6. Would they appoint a new Sales Manager ? 7. Have they solved all the problems ? 8. Would it catch fire easily ?

EXERCISE 2. — *Change the following sentences as follows* :

It was started two years ago → **It's two years since it was started**

1. The Manager died three weeks ago. 2. I attended the board meeting a fortnight ago. 3. It was destroyed by fire 5 months ago. 4. He was appointed a week ago. 5. She joined the company a long time ago. 6. He retired ten years ago.

EXERCISE 3. — *Turn into the past as follows* :

He comes to the office... → **He came to the office...**

1. He attends every meeting of the Board. 2. These items are much safer. 3. They make lots of different items. 4. They begin using modern techniques. 5. The firm has a history of steady growth. 6. He knows the best way to do it. 7. He says it's a piece of luck.

EXERCISE 4. — *Answer the following questions about the text* :

1. When was the company started ? 2. What did they make at the start ? 3. What else are they making now ? 4. What are these items made of ? 5. What are Peter Wiles and John Martin's ambitions ?

EXERCISE 5. — *Answer the following questions* :

1. What is a warehouse ? 2. What do the following abbreviations mean : O.R. ? D.C.F. ? 3. What aids and tools of modern efficiency could you mention ? 4. How can the Manager of a small firm get expert advice to modernise his business ?

EXERCISE 6. — *Translate into English* :

1. Il a enlevé un gros contrat. 2. Des documents irremplaçables ont été détruits. 3. La modernisation du service ne sera pas de la petite besogne. 4. Vraiment, nous ne pouvons pas nous offrir ce luxe. 5. Il faut nous remettre à jour. 6. Il n'a pas perdu le contact avec l'affaire. 7. C'est beaucoup plus sûr que le modèle qu'ils faisaient auparavant. 8. Ils ont fourni du matériel de bureau aux services gouvernementaux. 9. Il y a 67 articles différents au catalogue. 10. Ils veulent doubler la production au cours des deux prochaines années. 11. Nous n'avons pas de spécialiste de recherche opérationnelle dans notre personnel. 12. Un chef d'entreprise moderne doit être au courant des techniques de gestion les plus poussées. 13. Je ne sais pas quand Mr. Smith l'aîné prendra sa retraite. 14. Cela exigeait les techniques les plus complexes.

UNIT 1

NEW MARKETS ARE VITAL

PART 1 : INTRODUCTION

1. WORD STUDY

Vocabulary

act (for) représenter, agir pour le compte (de)

agent concessionnaire, agent commercial

back up soutenir, donner son appui

Board of Trade Ministère du Commerce

book réserver

channel canal (de distribution)

competitor concurrent

consider examiner, envisager

crazy fou

contact (*trans*.) entrer en rapport (avec)

desk research étude (théorique)

direct directement

drive campagne, effort

duties droits de douane

expanding en expansion

expense frais, dépenses

expensive coûteux

export market marché extérieur

fact-finding d'exploration

facilities installations ; facilités

fed up écœuré

field survey étude de marché

find out chercher à savoir

flight vol

forward-looking entreprenant, dynamique

goods marchandises

home market marché intérieur

import licence licence d'importation

income revenu

income per capita revenu par habitant

involve entraîner, impliquer

keep up (with) rester au courant

labour main-d'œuvre

labour trouble difficultés avec la main-d'œuvre

liable (to) susceptible (de) passible (de)

liable (for) responsable (de) soumis (à)

likely vraisemblable, possible

meet faire face à, honorer

newly récemment

office equipment matériel de bureau
oil pétrole
old fashioned vieux-jeu, démodé
outlook conception, point-de-vue
point question, problème
probe sonde, coup de sonde
Production Manager directeur de la production
profit bénéfice
red tape paperasse
resign démissionner
retailer détaillant
return ticket billet aller et retour
rise augmenter, s'accroître

sailing ligne, voie maritime
Sales Manager directeur des ventes
shipping expédition ou transport maritime
sort out trier ; obtenir, se procurer
supplier fournisseur
tariffs tarifs douaniers, taxes à l'importation
transship transborder
via par (*itinéraire*)
waste gaspillage, perte
wholesaler grossiste
wish souhaiter, désirer

Phrases

To open up a new market   créer un marché, trouver un débouché
To break into the market   s'implanter sur un marché, pénétrer dans
On balance   à tout prendre
All over the place   partout
To cool my temper a bit   pour me calmer les nerfs

Explanations and Other Useful Terms

agent   one who acts for a person or business. In this case it means a resident in a foreign country who acts for, or represents, several companies abroad. He works for a *commission*, that is, a payment of a percentage on the value of goods coming into a country.

automation   using machines to do work previously done mainly by people. It describes the automatic machining and transfer of parts from one operation to another including feedback, the ability of machines to notice mistakes, or change operations to meet predetermined requirements.

board meeting	a meeting of the Board of Directors, group of organisers in control of a business.
The Board of Trade	a British Government Department which deals with trade and commerce.
budgetary control	plans of future expenditure on labour, materials, etc., which are later compared with actual expenditure to evaluate and control policy.
Chairman	the top executive of a company (U.S.A. : president) concerned with policy and long-range aspects. He presides at, or chairs, board meetings ; hence his name.
channels of distribution	different ways of getting the goods to the buyers. This may be direct to government departments, to retailers, or through wholesalers.
corporate planning	integrating the three basic functions of a business (finance, production and distribution) in planning future company objectives.
D.C.F.	Discounted Cash Flow. A method of calculating the profitability of a new plant and machinery.
dock dues	fees paid for the use of a dock.
duty	a government tax levied (put) on goods entering a country (see tariff).
E.D.P.	Electronic Data Processing. The method of analysing and recording business information by means of a computer.
field survey (= market research)	an investigation during which information is collected in the field by means of interviews. A report is then prepared on : possible demand ; type of consumer (buyer) ; methods of selling ; number of rivals ; what sort of packaging is preferred, etc., in any country or area where a company wishes to begin trading. A desk survey would be done in the office by using all statistical information available.
income per capita	average income, money earned per head of the population.
import licence	permission given by government to bring goods into a country.
port rates	fees paid for the facilities of a port.
probe	here means a preliminary survey of a possible new market.

red tape	unnecessary formalities. So called from the tape used by lawyers to tie up legal documents.
tariff	an import tax charged or levied by the importing country.
telex	a message sent by teleprinter line.

Pronunciation

1 — 1 -(-) Africa, capital, catalogue, recent, yesterday

- 2 (- -) address, allow, assure, attempt, convince, discovery, disastrous, equipment, expense, expensive, facilities, involve, particular, preliminary, production, remember

- - 3 introduce, understand

2 — [s] inclusive, decision, episode

[z] lose, propose, disastrous

[ai] licence, vital, resign, buy, specialise

[ʌ] country, discovery, government, money, company, worried, some

[i] office, build, article, busy, business

[ɔ] boss, what, want, profit, product, quality

3 — Compare : decide [di'said],   decision [di'siʒən]
county ['kaunti],   country ['kʌntri]
compete [kəm'pi:t],   competitive [kəm'petitiv]
rise [raiz],   risen ['rizn] ;   were [wə:],   where [wɛe]
resign [ri'zain],   resignation [ˌrezig'neiʃən]
expand [iks'pænd],   demand [di'ma:nd]

4 — Note : allow [ə'lau],   cautious ['kɔ:ʃəs],   foreign ['fɔrin],   furniture ['fə:nitʃə],   government ['gʌvnmənt],   itinerary [ai'tinərəri], liable ['laiəbl],   per capita ['pə: 'kæpitə],   scheme [ski:m], via [vaiə].

2. SUMMARY

In this episode, the Managing Director, Hector Grant, has to make a decision about allowing his young Sales Manager, John Martin, to go on an expensive fact-finding tour of a country in Africa called Abraca.

First we hear John Martin discussing with Peter Wiles, the Production Manager, an article he has just read in *The Times* newspaper about the 5 recent discovery of oil in Abraca. He thinks that the firm should find out whether it would be possible to export to Abraca, and in particular to the capital city, Djemsa, where a lot of new government offices are shortly to be built. He wants to go there at once and try to open up a new market. Hector Grant (or H.G. as his staff generally call him, using his initials) 10 remembers a disastrous attempt a few months ago to export to a country in South America when the firm lost a lot of money. He is inclined to be cautious, a bit worried about the difficulties involved, and the expense. So we discover some of the points which have to be considered by a firm wishing to export. 15

PART 2 : CONVERSATION AND DOCUMENTS

1. CONVERSATION

(Recorded Text)

(In Peter Wiles's office)

JOHN MARTIN	**Hello, Peter! Have you seen the article in *The Times* this morning about Abraca? It says here that income *per capita* is rising fast.**
PETER WILES	**I can't keep up with all these newly independent countries. Is Abraca the country that's just found a lot of oil?** 5
JOHN	**That's the one. Apparently they're going to build a lot of new offices in the capital, Djemsa, and I think it might be a good market for our furniture and office equipment.**
PETER	**Ah, the export market. Well, you know what H.G.'s views are on that!** 10
JOHN	**But we must export more, Peter. You really must try and help me to convince Mr. Grant that we're crazy not to look for more foreign business. Will you back me up?**
PETER	**Yes, of course I will; but you know what the boss thinks about exports. He thinks it's all a big waste of time and** 15 **money for very little profit. Anyway, I'll do what I can.**

(In Hector Grant's office)

SECRETARY (ELIZABETH CORBY)	**Mr. Martin to see you, Mr. Grant.**
HECTOR GRANT	**Oh yes, ask him to come in, please, Elizabeth.**
JOHN	**Good morning, H.G.**
GRANT	**Ah, John, I've been thinking about this scheme of yours to** 20 **sell our products to Abraca.**
JOHN	**Oh, I'm glad.**
GRANT	**Yes, it's all very well to say we should export more, but is** **the expense worth it? Look what happened over our** **attempt to break into that South American market.** 25
JOHN	**That was because we had that labour trouble at the time** **and we weren't able to meet our delivery dates. But we** **can't let that one failure stop us from trying to break into** **a new market.**
GRANT	**You say Abracan imports are going to rise rapidly. Well,** 30 **let's have some figures. What are the difficulties? Who are** **our likely competitors? What about tariffs ?**
JOHN	**There are tariffs on certain products, but the Board of** **Trade assure me that our office equipment would not be** **liable for duty.** 35
GRANT	**What about shipping facilities? It seems there are few** **direct sailings, and a lot of goods have to be trans-** **shipped via Rotterdam. And then there's all this red** **tape involved in getting an import licence.**
JOHN	**Well, if I find an agent in Abraca to act for us we can get** 40 **him to sort out the import licence.**
GRANT	**Have you considered what channels of distribution are** **needed within the country?**
JOHN	**I'll have to find out, but we might be able to sell direct to** **government departments and oil companies. Maybe we** 45 **should have a field survey to find out exactly how the** **firms in Abraca prefer to buy their products.**
GRANT	**Field surveys are too expensive.**
JOHN	**Oh, I don't agree, Mr. Grant. As you see from my pre-** **liminary desk research, Abraca is a young, rich, expand-** 50 **ing country. I'm convinced that we can work up a big** **demand for our goods there.**
GRANT	**I'm sorry, John. On balance, I don't think it's quite the**

right time for this probe. I don't want the expense of sending you out there. You've got plenty to do in the home market. 55

JOHN But surely we ought to go ahead now. Why wait and let somebody else get there first? We can't live on our old markets for ever!

GRANT Let's say we have a different way of looking at things. 60

JOHN I'm sorry, Mr. Grant, but I do feel strongly about this. If this is really your policy, then I must think about leaving the firm.

GRANT You're being very foolish, John.

JOHN Perhaps I am. But as our opinions differ so much about 65 the future of the firm, perhaps I'd better go somewhere a little more forward-looking. I'm sorry, H.G.

JOHN: 'Perhaps I'd better go somewhere a little more forward-looking.'

(In John Martin's office)

PETER	Good morning, John. Where were you yesterday after-noon? I tried to contact you all over the place.
JOHN	I went out for a long drive to cool my temper a bit. 70
PETER	Oh? What happened?
JOHN	You know H.G. decided not to let me go to Abraca.
PETER	Oh no! I thought he'd be bound to agree. I'd have said that particular market was wide open.
JOHN	That's what I think. Anyway, I just suddenly got fed up 75 with H.G.'s old-fashioned outlook and I resigned.
PETER	Did he accept your resignation?
JOHN	I didn't give him much chance. I was so angry I just walked out of his office.
SECRETARY	Excuse me, Mr. Martin, this letter has just come for you 80 from Mr. Grant's office.
PETER	What is it, John?
JOHN	Good Lord! It's a reservation for a first-class return flight to Abraca!

PRACTICE SENTENCES

Say the practice sentences on the record :

  i Income per capita is rising fast.

  ii It might be a good market for our products.

  iii We must export more.

  iv Their imports are going to rise rapidly.

  v I'd like to go there and find a new agent to act for us.

  vi Our products would not be liable for duty.

  vii We can't let that one failure stop us from trying to break into a new market.

  viii I'm convinced that we can work up a big demand for our goods.

— 34 —

2. EXAMPLES OF LETTERS

The following letters are from Harper & Grant Ltd., with the name of the firm, address, telephone number, telex number and telegraphic address on the paper. If you are not using 'headed' paper, but writing as a private individual, put your address (address, *not* your name) on the top right-hand side of the paper. The name and address of the person or business you are writing to goes on the left-hand side.

Great West Road
London W25
Telephone 01-567 1112
Telex 80153
Telegrams Harp LDN

Directors:
Ambrose Harper *(Chairman)*
Hector Grant *(Managing)*
William Buckhurst FCA *(Secretary)*
Margaret Wiles

Harper and Grant Limited

The Commercial Attaché,
British Embassy,
Avenue 30th March,
Djemsa, ABRACA.

8th July, 197..

Dear Sir,

      Miss Crawshaw of the Export Services Branch, Board of Trade, asked me to write to you direct.

      My company specialises in making better quality office furniture and equipment. I propose to visit Djemsa for about ten days in early November to study on the spot ways of introducing our products to the Abracan market. I understand there is no import duty. A check with the customs has shown that little British equipment of this kind has ever been sold to Abraca and I understand French and Dutch firms have been the main suppliers.

      Six copies of our catalogue are enclosed. If you can help me in planning an itinerary and introduce me to possible buyers and agents during my visit I should be most grateful.

Yours faithfully,

J. Martin

John Martin
Sales Manager
HARPER & GRANT LTD.

Great West Road
London W25
Telephone 01-567 1112
Telex 80153
Telegrams Harp LDN

Directors:
Ambrose Harper *(Chairman)*
Hector Grant *(Managing)*
William Buckhurst FCA *(Secretary)*
Margaret Wiles

Harper and Grant Limited

The Manager,
Date Palm Hotel,
Djemsa, ABRACA.

15th July, 197..

Dear Sir,

      Our Sales Manager, Mr. John Martin, will be in Djemsa on business for ten days. We would like to reserve for him a single room, with bath, from 30th October to 9th November inclusive.

      We should be glad if you would confirm this booking as soon as possible.

                         Yours faithfully,

                         Sally Langley

                         Sally Langley
               Secretary to John Martin
                 HARPER & GRANT LTD.

PART 3 : NOTES AND PRACTICE

1. RAPPEL GRAMMATICAL

Summary :

1.14 : he has to make a decision ; points which have to be considered :

To have to n'est pas seulement l'équivalent de **must** aux autres temps que le présent. On le rencontre au présent où il a une autre valeur que **must** : **have to** indique alors une obligation habituelle ou prévue, connue d'avance, alors que **must** exprime une obligation soudaine, imprévue :

I have to go to the bank every Thursday	Je dois aller à la banque tous les jeudis
Excuse me, the bank have just phoned and I must go immediately to see Mr. Brewer	Excusez-moi, la banque vient de téléphoner et il faut que j'y aille tout de suite (*obligation imprévue*) voir M. Brewer

5. Le passé récent s'exprime avec **just** et le *present perfect* :

I've just read it in the paper	Je viens de le lire dans les journaux

Cf. conversation, ligne 5 :

It's just found a lot of oil	On vient de découvrir une quantité de pétrole

6. **Should** sert à exprimer l'idée de *ce qui devrait être fait*. Il peut comporter une nuance de *doute* quant à l'exécution des conseils que l'on donne :

You should carry out a field survey	Vous devriez faire une étude de marché
You should have let us know	Vous auriez dû nous informer

8. *Futur de convention* : cette construction, appelée futur de *convention* ou d'*intention*, composée de **to be** + infinitif, sert dans la langue économique beaucoup plus souvent que dans l'anglais ordinaire à exprimer une notion de futur :

They are shortly to be built	On doit prochainement les construire

L'auxiliaire **will** du futur garde toujours un peu sa valeur de *vouloir*, et des choses ou événements ne peuvent avoir de volonté. Dans un monde où l'avenir ne peut jamais être envisagé avec une certitude absolue, une autre structure sert aussi souvent à exprimer l'idée de futur (cf. Rappel Gr., Unit 24) :

You're likely to face very tough competitors	Vous rencontrerez des concurrents très durs (sans doute...)
Their currency is likely to be devalued	Leur monnaie risque d'être dévaluée

Conversation :

6. **That's the one.** Par rapport à **that's it**, **that's the one** marque une intention particulière de la part du locuteur. **One** est pronom de rappel (qui remplace un nom déjà employé), mais il est ici surtout un déterminatif : on considère le sens numérique de **one**, on isole l'élément rappelé, le mettant ainsi en relief.

6. **Futur proche** : la notion du futur proche s'exprime à l'aide de la construction **to be going to** + infinitif :

They're going to launch an advertising campaign	Ils vont lancer une campagne publicitaire

7. **Might** exprime l'éventualité. Comparons la construction portant sur le présent-futur, avec la construction portant sur le passé :

It might be a good bargain	Cela pourrait être une bonne affaire
They might have gone on strike	Ils auraient pu se mettre en grève

11. **Must** exprime la nécessité vitale ici :

We must export more	Il nous faut exporter davantage

La langue familière connait l'expression :

It's a must	C'est une chose obligatoire, cela s'impose

11. Les verbes **go**, **come** et **try**, lorsqu'ils sont suivis d'un verbe, sont généralement reliés à ce verbe par **and** lorsque leur forme est identique à celle de l'infinitif. Comparons :

Go and tell them we're ready	Allez leur dire que nous sommes prêts
He came to tell us they were ready	Il est venu nous dire qu'ils étaient prêts

14. N'oublions pas que la réponse affirmative ou négative reprend l'auxiliaire du verbe exprimé dans la question :

Did you see him ? — **Of course I did**	L'avez-vous vu ? — Bien sûr que oui
Will they charge you anything ? — **No, they won't**	Vous feront-ils payer quelque chose ? — Non

20. Pourquoi pas **your scheme** ? **This scheme of yours** a une valeur ironique, son emploi ici révèle de l'hostilité, de la méfiance de la part du patron à l'égard de John.

23. A la ligne 11, John considère les exportations comme une nécessité vitale pour l'entreprise. Il ne doute pas que Peter soit de son avis. Ici, c'est Hector Grant qui parle, et **should** exprime la nuance de doute de sa part.

27. Au passé, la possibilité matérielle s'exprime de deux manières :

We could meet our delivery dates = we were able to meet...	Nous avons pu respecter nos délais de livraison

L'impossibilité s'exprime de trois manières :

we could not = we were not able = we were unable

Notons que **were able** a une valeur de passé indicatif, tandis que **could** exprime d'autres nuances : *nous ne pourrions pas* ou *nous ne pouvions pas*.

28. **one = only.**

40. *Faire faire* quelque chose à quelqu'un peut s'exprimer de plusieurs manières :

I made her type the letter again	Je lui ai fait dactylographier la lettre à nouveau
They had him check his list	Ils lui ont fait vérifier sa liste
We could get Smith to see to it	Smith pourrait s'en occuper pour nous
You should get him to contact the customer once more	Vous devriez lui faire contacter le client une fois de plus

On le voit, la construction rencontrée dans la conversation et ces deux derniers exemples exprime une *idée de persuasion*.

44. Nous voyons ici combinées les notions d'éventualité (**may**) et de possibilité matérielle (**can**, par son équivalent **be able**) :

We might be able to sell direct to oil companies	Peut-être nous serait-il possible de vendre directement aux compagnies pétrolières

57. **Ought to** est pratiquement équivalent de **should** pour indiquer une ligne de conduite qu'il faudrait suivre. Il comporte parfois un peu plus une idée d'obligation morale.

61. **I do feel strongly about it** : forme emphatique :

He did convince the boss	Il a bel et bien convaincu le patron

64. La forme progressive a une valeur restrictive. Elle indique que Hector Grant ne considère pas généralement et constamment son collaborateur comme un sot, mais qu'à cet instant, John fait des sottises :

You may be very clever but now you're being wrong	Vous avez beau être très malin, en ce moment vous vous trompez

66. Les constructions **I had better** (*je ferais mieux*) et **I had rather** (*j'aimerais mieux*) se comportent comme des défectifs : elles n'existent qu'à un temps (prétérit à valeur modale, c'est-à-dire ce que nous appelons valeur conditionnelle, en fait un mode exprimant l'*hypothèse*, le *doute*, l'*irréel*). Comparons le présent-futur et le passé :

You'd better tell the Production Manager immediately	Vous feriez mieux d'en parler tout de suite au Directeur de la Production
She'd better have phoned our forwarding agent	Elle aurait mieux fait de téléphoner à notre transitaire

73. Les équivalents de **must** sont nombreux :

Will you have to repay all this large amount at once ?	Devrez-vous rembourser toute cette grosse somme tout de suite ?
We were obliged to replace the damaged articles	Nous avons dû remplacer les articles endommagés
You won't be compelled (forced) to do it	On ne vous forcera pas à le faire
It was bound to happen	Il fallait que cela arrive

2. EXERCISES

EXERCISE 1. — *Change as follows* :

They found a lot of oil → they've just found a lot of oil

1. They built a lot of offices. 2. He read the article in The Economist.
3. It was discovered in this country. 4. They broke into this new market.
5. We went out of the office. 6. They bought a new cutting machine.

EXERCISE 2. — *Change as follows* :

We couldn't meet our delivery dates → we were unable to meet our delivery-dates

1. We couldn't discuss the matter with the boss. 2. He couldn't keep up with all these modern techniques. 3. I couldn't convince the Production Manager. 4. They couldn't increase their productivity. 5. Our agent couldn't sort out the import licence.

EXERCISE 3. — *Change as follows* :

You can back me up → you might be able to back me up

1. We can export more to that country. 2. We can open up a new market.
3. We can increase the efficiency. 4. He can help me at the office. 5. We can break into the Australian market. 6. You can sell direct to government departments.

EXERCISE 4. — *Change as follows* :

**They're going to build new offices
→ new offices are shortly to be built**

1. They're going to solve this last difficulty. 2. They're going to despatch the goods. 3. They're going to carry out a market research. 4. He's going to sort out the licence. 5. They're going to allow him to go to Africa.

EXERCISE 5. — *Supply the missing words in the following* :

1. Before sending goods to a foreign country you have to apply for...
2. Goods entering a foreign country may be... 3. An agent working for a company abroad receives a... 4. If you have promised to supply goods by a certain date, you must do everything you can to... 5. When there is no direct sailing from the home port to the port of destination, goods must be...

EXERCISE 6. — What do you call . . . ?

1. A booklet containing information about a firm's products ? 2. The man who is responsible for running a company ? 3. Research carried out on a possible new trading area ? 4. A meeting of directors who run a company ?

EXERCISE 7. — Try and define . . . :

The Managing Director. The Sales Manager. The Production Manager. A retailer. A wholesaler.

EXERCISE 8. — Answer the following questions :

1. Why does John Martin want to go to Africa ? 2. Why does Abraca seem to be a favourable market ? 3. Why does John ask Peter to back him up ? 4. Why is Mr. Grant so cautious ? 5. What does H.G. worry about? 6. Why does John resign ?

EXERCISE 9. — Translate into English :

1. Le revenu par habitant augmente rapidement. 2. Cela pourrait être un bon débouché pour nos produits. 3. Il faut absolument que nous exportions davantage. 4. Leurs exportations vont s'accroître rapidement. 5. Je voudrais y aller pour trouver un nouveau concessionnaire qui nous représenterait. 6. Nos produits ne seraient pas soumis à des droits de douane. 7. Nous ne pouvons laisser cet unique échec nous empêcher d'essayer de pénétrer sur un nouveau marché. 8. Je suis convaincu que nous pouvons susciter une demande importante pour nos marchandises. 9. L'entreprise a perdu beaucoup d'argent. 10. Tu sais ce qu'il en pense. 11. C'est un gaspillage d'argent pour très peu de bénéfice. 12. Avez-vous réfléchi à mon projet ? 13. Votre projet ne me dit rien. 14. Et les tarifs d'importation ? Et les facilités de transport maritime ? 15. Nous n'avons pas la même façon de voir les choses. 16. Je pensais bien qu'il serait forcé d'être d'accord avec vous. 17. Il estime qu'on a encore beaucoup à faire sur le marché intérieur. 18. Ils avaient des difficultés de main-d'œuvre à cette époque-là. 19. Il se tracasse au sujet des difficultés que cela soulève. 20. Vous devriez faire une étude de marché.

UNIT 2

A VISIT TO THE FACTORY

PART 1 : INTRODUCTION

1. WORD STUDY

Vocabulary

account compte
acquaintance connaissance
agree être d'accord
appointment rendez-vous
block bâtiment
    office block bâtim^t administratif
boss patron
call appel ; appeler
charges frais
compare comparer
complete achever, terminer
conveyor belt courroie de transport
deadline limite ultime
delivery livraison
    delivery bank quai de livraison,
      de déchargement
    delivery bay hall de décharge-
      ment, de livraison
expect attendre ; *ici* : penser
formal officiel
forthcoming prochain, futur
fertilizer engrais
furnish meubler
grateful reconnaissant
install installer
limited liability company société à
    responsabilité limitée

lines produits
load charger
look forward attendre avec plaisir
luckily heureusement
market research étude de marché
opposite en face
output production
partnership association, société en
    nom collectif
quotation prix, cours
range gamme
reluctantly à contre-cœur
remind rappeler
requirement besoin
see over (a place) visiter
short-tempered vif, emporté
size taille, importance
solicitor avoué, chef du contentieux
suggest proposer
suit convenir
telephone call appel téléphonique,
    communication
unload décharger
waste gaspillage ; gaspiller
whenever toutes les fois que

specify : préciser

— 43 —

Phrases

She'll show him round the factory	elle lui fera visiter l'usine
As agreed	comme convenu
In the meantime	entre temps
She's on her way	elle arrive, elle est en route
It's completing construction	la construction s'achève

Explanations and Other Useful Terms

blanking cutting metal sheets to the required sizes.

deadline last possible moment when an event, e.g. delivery of goods, may take place.

delivery bank a raised platform, rather like a bar, on to which goods can be easily unloaded.

delivery bay side or back entrance of a factory where goods can be delivered.

drill a rotating tool which makes holes in metal or wood.

line product made by a firm. Often used to mean a series or type of goods. For example, a new design for an office desk would be referred to as *the new line*.

pressing bending or shaping pieces of metal into the form required.

stock goods ready for sale. *In stock* : the goods are available for despatch ; *out of stock* : there are no more goods for sale until the factory produces (or delivers) further supplies ; *stock items (lines)* : those made for stock ; *non-stock items* : those made against individual orders only.

Pronunciation

1 — 1 - (- -) attitude, customer, factory, telephone

    - 2 (- -) acquaintance, administrative, agree, apparently, appointment, arrange, compare, delivery, excuse, reluctantly, remember, result, whenever

    - - 3 interrupt, understand

2 — [s]   seat, house, warehouse, research
    [z]   as, visit, phase, houses, warehouses
    [ʌ]   some, London, company, result
    [ɔ]   lot, block, not, what, want, office
    [a:]   fast, market, charges, afterwards, rather
    [ɔ:]   order, course, bought, warn
    [ei]   stay, late, change, range, arrange, grateful
    [ju:]   mutual, few, new, interview

3 — conveyor-belt [kən'veiə-belt], favourably ['feivrəbli], fortune ['fɔ:tʃən], furniture ['fə:nitʃə], friend [frend], interview ['intəvju:], personnel [,pə:sə'nel], quotation [kwə'teiʃən], valuable ['væljuəbl].

2. SUMMARY

Today Mr. Grant's secretary, Elizabeth Corby, gets a telephone call from a man called George Duncan. He has an introduction to Harper & Grant from a mutual acquaintance, Jock Macpherson. Mr. Duncan is only staying in London for a few days and he telephones to fix an appointment to see Mr. Grant. Elizabeth tells him that Mr. Grant is very busy and   5 suggests a later date. But Mr. Duncan, who is rather short-tempered, expects that he can have an appointment whenever he wants one. He also asks if he can see over the factory itself to see how some of the office furniture is made. Elizabeth has a good secretary's sixth sense that this might be a valuable customer, so she finally fixes an appointment for him   10 at half-past three that afternoon. When Mr. Grant comes into the office she tells him about the appointment. As Mr. Grant is so busy, she suggests that she herself should show Mr. Duncan round the factory. Mr. Grant reluctantly agrees to see him. He also remembers that the mutual acquaintance, Jock Macpherson, is a great talker who in the past has   15 wasted a lot of time and then bought very little. He thinks that perhaps his friend, Mr. Duncan, will be the same, so he warns Elizabeth to interrupt the interview after a short time with the excuse that there is someone else waiting to see him.

Elizabeth shows the visitor round the works. He visits the different   20 departments of the factory, or *shops* as they are called. Then he goes to see Mr. Grant. As agreed, after a short time Elizabeth interrupts the interview. But in the meantime Mr. Duncan has indicated that he wishes to place a large order for office furniture for his new office block which is completing construction in Scotland. Mr. Grant is no longer so interested   25 in escaping from his visitor! Luckily Elizabeth knows her boss very well and is not at all surprised by his sudden change of attitude.

PART 2 : CONVERSATION AND DOCUMENTS

1. CONVERSATION

(Recorded Text)

(In Hector Grant's office)

ELIZABETH CORBY	Good morning, Mr. Grant.
HECTOR GRANT	Good morning.
ELIZABETH	I've just had a Mr. George Duncan from Glasgow on the phone. Apparently our customer Mr. Macpherson suggested he came to see you. 5
GRANT	Oh, he did, did he! Well, I can't think any friend of his will make the company's fortune.
ELIZABETH	He said he would like to see you this afternoon and visit the factory.
GRANT	Did he indeed? If he's like Macpherson he'll take up the 10 whole day and then order one chair.
ELIZABETH	Perhaps I could take Mr. Duncan round the factory for you.
GRANT	All right. You take him round first, and then I'll see him afterwards. But you'd better interrupt me after fifteen min- 15 utes and remind me that I've got another appointment.
ELIZABETH	Yes, I will, Mr. Grant.

(At the reception desk)

DUNCAN	Good afternoon. I want to see the Managing Director, please.
RECEPTION GIRL	Good afternoon. Have you an appointment? 20
DUNCAN	Of course. I wouldn't be here if I hadn't.
GIRL	What is your name, please?
DUNCAN	Duncan.
GIRL	Just a moment, please. Miss Corby? I have a Mr. Duncan here to see Mr. Grant. He says he has an appointment. 25 Yes ... Yes, I will. Mr. Duncan, would you take a seat, please. Mr. Grant's secretary will be down in a moment.
DUNCAN	Thank you. I hope she won't be long; I haven't much time.

— 46 —

GIRL	She's on her way now.	30
DUNCAN	Good.	
GIRL	Here she is.	
ELIZABETH	Good afternoon, Mr. Duncan, I'm Elizabeth Corby, Mr. Grant's secretary. Would you like to see round the factory first?	35
DUNCAN	Yes, I would ...	
ELIZABETH	Now this is our office block. We have all the administrative departments here: Sales, Accounts, Personnel, Market Research and so on.	
DUNCAN	What's that building opposite us?	40
ELIZABETH	That's the warehouse where the larger items of office equipment are stored. We try and keep a stock of the faster-moving items so that urgent orders can be met quickly from stock.	
DUNCAN	If I ordered a desk today, how long would it be before I got delivery in Scotland?	45
ELIZABETH	I think perhaps you'd better speak to our Works Manager, Mr. Fielding. You'll meet him when we go over to the factory. We'll go there now.	

(*In the workshop*)

MR. FIELDING	This is one of our three workshops. This is the delivery bay here.	50
DUNCAN	Oh, yes.	
FIELDING	The steel sheets and bars come in, as you see, in different sizes and are unloaded on to the delivery bank here. We buy them in from a steelworks in Wales. This machine here is a spot welder, and this is the new conveyor belt which we had installed last year. We doubled our output in this department as a result.	55
DUNCAN	Oh, really.	
FIELDING	I'll take you to the assembly shop	60

(*In Mr. Grant's office*)

GRANT	Now Mr. Duncan, what can I do for you? I understand that you're a friend of Jock Macpherson's.	
DUNCAN	Yes, Mr. Grant. He told me that you make the best, and cheapest, office furniture on the market.	
GRANT	I think we make the best.	65

DUNCAN	But is it the cheapest? That's what interests me.
GRANT	We have a wide range of prices, Mr. Duncan. Here's our catalogue. We think our prices compare favourably with anything on the market today.
DUNCAN	If I had an office I wanted you to furnish, how much 70 would it cost me?
GRANT	It would largely depend on the lines you chose.
DUNCAN	My trouble is that I'm very short of time. Can you supply me from stock?
GRANT	If you could give me some idea of your requirements, 75 Mr. Duncan, I might be able to help you. Unfortunately, I have someone coming to see me shortly and I ...
DUNCAN	I'll tell you what I want. This is my card. I'm the Managing Director of G. P. Duncan & Company. We make artificial fertilisers. I want our new office block 80 furnished. I'd like you to give me a quotation, including delivery charges, as soon as you can.
GRANT	How many offices are there?
DUNCAN	Twenty-eight.

ELIZABETH: 'Mr. Grant, Mr. Frame is waiting to see you.'

GRANT	Twenty-eight offices. Oh, I see. Well, how much time can you give us? 85
DUNCAN	Two months is my deadline.
GRANT	I'd like to send a man up to Glasgow to get details. I never like promising a date until I know we can honour it—however, I think . . . 90
ELIZABETH	Er . . Mr. Grant, Mr . . er . . Frame is waiting to see you.
GRANT	Well, never mind about that. . . . Tell him he'll just have to wait. You can see I'm busy with an important customer!

PRACTICE SENTENCES

Say the practice sentences on the record :

  i I want to see the Managing Director, please.

 ii I have an appointment.

iii We have a wide range of prices.

iv Here is our catalogue.

 v We think our prices compare favourably with anything on the market.

vi Can you supply me from stock ?

vii It would depend on the lines you chose.

———————

2. LETTERS

Here are two short letters. The first is an example of what is called a *letter of introduction*. Mr. Macpherson ought to have written to Mr. Grant to introduce his friend, George Duncan. If he had written this letter (but he did not) Mr. Grant, and Elizabeth, would have known all about him.

Mr. Duncan should also have written to ask for an appointment as he was only going to be in London for such a short time. Arriving, as he did, without much warning, he risked finding Mr. Grant away or too busy to see him.

47, Douglas Street,
GLASGOW.

17th July, 197..

Dear Mr. Grant,

    A good friend of mine, George Duncan, is shortly coming to London and would very much like to meet you and see over your factory.

    Mr. Duncan is the Managing Director of G.P. Duncan & Co. Ltd., manufacturers of artificial fertilisers.

    His company are building a new office block and he is interested in obtaining quotations for the cost of furnishing these new offices, so his visit may be of value to you.

    With best wishes to you and your wife,

Yours ever,

Jock Macpherson

Jock Macpherson.

Hector Grant, Esq.,
Managing Director,
*Harper & Grant Ltd.,
Great West Road,
London, W.25.

---

* Messrs. is sometimes used as a courtesy title before the name of firms which are not limited liability companies, or partnerships (*e.g.* a firm of solicitors).

G.P. DUNCAN & CO. LTD.

Telephone: GLASGOW CENTRAL 918721
Telex: GW 900
Telegrams: FERTGLAS

249 Cathaway Road
GLASGOW

Hector Grant, Esq.,
Managing Director,
Harper & Grant Ltd.,
Great West Road,
London. W.25.

17th July, 197..

Dear Mr. Grant,

      Mr. Jock Macpherson, whom we both know, has written to
tell you about my forthcoming visit to London.   I should very much
like to meet you and see over your factory if that could be arranged.
I hope to be in London on July 27th and 28th, and I should be
grateful if you could let me know the day and time which would suit
you best, as I can then go ahead and fit in my other appointments.

      Looking forward to the pleasure of meeting you,

Yours sincerely,

George Duncan

George Duncan
Managing Director
G.P. DUNCAN & CO LTD.

Notice that, in the first letter, Mr. Grant's name and address were on the bottom left-hand side of the paper. This is because Mr. Macpherson knows Mr. Grant. Mr. Duncan's letter to Mr. Grant, however, starts with the name and address, as it is the first time that he has written to him. Firms vary in this matter of position of the addresses, but the most commonly accepted method is to put the name and address first to give a more formal effect.

PART 3 : NOTES AND PRACTICE

1. RAPPEL GRAMMATICAL

Summary :

4. Il ne faut pas confondre **few** et **a few**. Tous deux ne se rencontrent que devant un nom au pluriel. Mais **a few** désigne une petite quantité tandis que **few** souligne toujours l'insuffisance de cette petite quantité :

They have few interesting lines	Ils ont peu d'articles intéressants
We've already got a few replies	Nous avons déjà reçu quelques réponses

Le singulier de **few** est **little**, celui de **a few** est **a little** :

Trade is just a little better	Le commerce va un tout petit peu mieux
We sold very little	Nous avons vendu très peu

6. **Rather**, *assez*, *plutôt*, s'emploie devant un adjectif ou un adverbe lorsque l'idée exprimée par ces derniers est désavantageuse au sujet. Si au contraire cette idée est avantageuse, positive, etc... on entendra **fairly** :

He works well, but rather slowly	Il travaille bien, mais assez lentement
The boss was fairly sympathetic	Le patron s'est montré assez compréhensif

7. **Short-tempered** : adjectif composé d'un adjectif et d'une imitation de participe sur un radical nom. Cette formation est fréquente avec des descriptions de traits physiques (**blue-eyed** : aux yeux bleus) ou moraux (**narrow-minded** : borné) notamment.

12. **She suggests that she should show Duncan round the factory** : **should** ici est une *valeur modale* qui rend compte de la déférence de la secrétaire à l'égard du patron ; **should** donne une idée *d'hypothèse*, elle se contente de suggérer une solution, c'est au Directeur de décider.

18. **Else** peut suivre tous les composés de **some, any** et **no** :

Could you phone someone else ?	Pourriez-vous téléphoner à quelqu'un d'autre ?
We must go somewhere else	Nous devons aller ailleurs

25. **No longer** = **not any... longer** :

They don't keep these items any longer	Ils ne font plus ces articles

Conversation :

5. Le prétérit des verbes a une valeur modale (cf. et cp. ci-dessus, ligne 13) :

He suggested Duncan came to see you	Il a suggéré que Duncan vienne vous voir

6. Une réponse ironique, amusée peut s'exprimer par la reprise à l'affirmative, puis à l'interrogative du sujet et de l'auxiliaire de la proposition de l'interlocuteur. Notez l'intonation de ce type de réplique dans le texte enregistré :

He would borrow the money from you — Oh he would, would he !	Il vous emprunterait l'argent — Voyez-vous cela !
He criticised your suggestions — Oh he did, did he !	Il a critiqué vos propositions — Ah oui, tiens !

7. Notons que le cas possessif s'emploie en anglais moderne avec des abstractions représentant des entités, ou tout mot désignant un inanimé qui a une certaine importance dans le contexte :

The company's turnover	Le chiffre d'affaire de la société
Our firm's policy	La ligne de conduite de notre entreprise
The mine's yield	Le débit de la mine

10. Ce **did he, indeed ?** exprime aussi un intérêt ironique.

15. Si le Directeur avait fait un reproche à la secrétaire pour ne pas l'avoir interrompu, il aurait bien sûr dit :

You'd better have interrupted me	Vous auriez mieux fait de m'interrompre

43. L'idée de *but* après **so that** (*pour que, afin que*) peut avoir pour auxiliaire **can** en anglais moderne. **So that** s'emploie dans la langue parlée, on trouverait plutôt **in order that** dans la langue écrite. Au passé, l'auxiliaire correspondant en anglais moderne serait **could**, la forme plus traditionnelle étant **should** :

He came personally so that there should be no misunderstanding	Il est venu personnellement afin qu'il n'y ait aucun malentendu
He explained it twice so that you could do it properly	Il l'a expliqué deux fois pour que vous le fassiez bien

48 et 81. Notons que **shall/will** et **should/would** ne se rencontrent pas dans la subordonnée temporelle (introduite par : **when, as soon as, etc...**).

Ne pas confondre cette règle avec la construction de l'interrogative (directe
ou indirecte) :

When will they meet ?	Quand se réuniront-ils ?
He asked when they would meet	Il a demandé quand ils se réuniraient

57. Nous avons vu l'expression de *faire faire* qqc à qqn (Unit 1, Rappel
Grammatical, p. 39). Lorsqu'on fait faire quelque chose, la construction
est : **have** + nom + participe passé du verbe :

We had an intercom installed	Nous avons fait poser un interphone
He ought to have the machine overhauled	Il devrait faire réviser la machine

70. Le verbe **want** est suivi de la proposition infinitive. Une nuance plus
polie s'exprime par le conditionnel **I'd like** (cf. plus bas) :

Mr. Grant wants you to show him round the shops	Mr. Grant veut que vous lui fassiez visiter les ateliers
I'd like you to make a photostat of these documents	Je voudrais que vous fassiez une photocopie de ces documents

2. EXERCISES

EXERCISE 1. — *Change as follows* :

He phoned every day   →   **he no longer phones**

1. He took an interest in that market.   2. He remained at the office late
at night.   3. We saw his representative every month.   4. They made
desks and chairs.   5. They bought all their furniture from us.   6. He
chose the most expensive lines.   7. They wanted you to furnish their
offices.   8. He thought you were too adventurous.

EXERCISE 2. — *Answer ironically, as follows* :

He suggested it to your secretary   — **Oh he did, did he !**

1. He said he would complain.   2. She said she was disappointed.   3. I
could show him round the factory.   4. I would replace the boss.   5. She
wants to speak to the Managing Director himself.   6. He will come from
Glasgow.   7. This new device could make your fortune.   8. It would
take me a whole week.

EXERCISE 3. — Change as follows :

They might (could) do it → they might (could) have done it

1. I could take him round the firm.   2. He might resign.   3. They might phone later.   4. You could easily make another appointment.   5. You could have a look at our catalogue.   6. He might tell you to do it yourself. 7. We could send a man up to Glasgow.   8. We might be able to help you. 9. It might cost a great deal.   10. You could explain it better than I could.

EXERCISE 4. — Change as suggested between brackets :

There was no intercom (install) → I had an intercom installed

1. The lock was broken (*repair*).   2. The delivery-van was dirty (*wash*). 3. There was no chief-clerk (*appoint*).   4. The goods were not wrapped (*pack*).   5. The letter was badly set out (*type again*).   6. These machines were obsolete (*replace*).   7. The office was dirty (*re-decorate*).   8. The agent's commission was too low (*raise*).   9. There was only one copy of the documents (*duplicate*).   10. The goods were not in Germany (*transfer*).

EXERCISE 5. — Answer the following questions :

1. What does welding consist in ?   2. What use are artificial fertilisers ? 3. What is a quotation ?   4. What are delivery charges ?   5. What use is a conveyor belt ?   6. Where are the component parts of an object put together (assembled) ?   7. What is the Personnel Department?

EXERCISE 6. — Answer the following questions :

1. What part of a factory are the goods stored in ? 2. If a factory or shop has run out of (finished its stock of) certain articles, what could the person responsible say ?   3. When an offer of goods is made, what is the stated price called ?   4. What is said of prices which are no higher, and perhaps even lower, than those quoted by rival firms ?   5. If you want to see someone on business what must you arrange ?

EXERCISE 7. — Answer the following questions :

1. When will Mr. Duncan come ? 2. Why does Mr. Grant beware of Mr. Duncan ?   3. What does Elizabeth suggest ?   4. Does Mr. Duncan look like McPherson ?   5. Does Mr. Duncan appreciate the visit ? 6. What does he want to know first and foremost ?   7. What is Mr. Duncan in fact ? 8. What did he come for ?   9. How many offices are to be furnished ? 10. What is Mr. Duncan's deadline as to delivery dates ?

EXERCISE 8. — *Translate into English* :

1. Je désirerais voir Monsieur le Président Directeur Général. 2. J'ai un rendez-vous. 3. Nous avons une gamme de prix étendue. 4. Voici notre catalogue. 5. Nous pensons que nos prix se comparent avantageusement avec tout ce qui se trouve sur le marché. 6. Pouvez-vous me fournir sur vos stocks ? 7. Cela dépendrait des articles que vous choisissez. 8. Je viens d'avoir un certain Mr. Mead au téléphone. 9. MacPherson a suggéré qu'il vienne vous voir. 10. Il y a un certain Mr. Duncan ici qui désire vous voir. 11. J'espère que la secrétaire ne tardera pas. 12. Nous l'avons fait installer l'an dernier. 13. Il m'a dit que vous faisiez le mobilier de bureau le meilleur et le moins cher. 14. Elizabeth a proposé de faire visiter l'atelier de montage à Mr. Duncan. 15. Nous ferions mieux de voir le Directeur de la Production à ce sujet. 16. Donnez-moi vos prix dès que vous le pourrez. 17. Combien de temps vous faudrait-il d'ici que nous soyons livrés ? 18. Heureusement, nous pouvons fournir ces commandes sur nos stocks. 19. Vous feriez bien de me rappeler que j'ai un autre rendez-vous. 20. Il voudrait que vous lui équipiez en mobilier tous ses locaux administratifs.

UNIT 3

AN EMERGENCY IN THE SALES OFFICE

PART 1 : INTRODUCTION

1. WORD STUDY

Vocabulary

acknowledgement accusé de réception
addressing machine machine à adresser
advertising publicité
agent concessionnaire, agent commercial
amount montant, somme
ash-tray cendrier
assessment estimation
bill of exchange lettre de change, traite
bill of lading connaissement
branch succursale
brief-case porte-documents
call back rappeler
chief clerk chef de bureau
clearance dédouanement
clear passer en douane, dédouaner
check up vérifier
cheer up reprendre courage
collect rassembler
commission commission

consign expédier
container container
cope with faire face à
crate caisse ou cadre à claire-voie, cageot
deal with s'occuper de, traiter
despatch expédier ; expédition
draft traite
due back qui doit rentrer
duplicate double ; faire un double
Dutch hollandais
efficient efficace
emergency urgence
expect penser
exporter exportateur
fail échouer, ne pas arriver à
fate destin
file dossier
flimsy papier pelure
flu grippe
fold plier
formal officiel, guindé
forwarding agent transitaire

frank affranchir
freight frêt
get on to mettre en communication
get through avoir la communication
hectic (*journée*) chargée, affolante
helpful utile
hint indication
hold-up empêchement, arrêt, retard
handle s'occuper
inform informer
intake arrivée
   order intake entrée des commandes
'in' tray bac, corbeille des arrivées
invoice facture ; facturer
irrevocable irrévocable
letterhead entête
letter of credit lettre de crédit ; accréditif
lend prêter
long-term à long terme
mail courrier
manage arriver à, faire en sorte que
memorandun, memo note de service
monthly mensuel
order commande
outer extérieur
outgoing sortant, partant
out-of-date démodé, dépassé
phrase expression
position situation
post courrier
printing impression, tirage

publicity publicité
rate estimer
release libérer, laisser sortir, laisser partir
report faire un rapport
see (that) veiller (*à ce que*)
send round envoyer, diffuser, faire circuler
set out (letter) présenter
seal cachet ; cacheter
shipping documents documents d'expédition, d'embarquement
shorthand sténographie
   shorthand typist sténo-dactylographe
sight draft traite à vue
sort trier
sound sain
  spare économiser ; *ici* : se passer de, disposer de
spell épeler
  spelling orthographe
staff personnel
stamp timbre ; affranchir
statement (of accounts) relevé
stationery papeterie, fournitures
subscriber abonné (*du téléphone*)
through par l'intermédiaire de
trip voyage
type dactylographier
  type dactylographe
twice deux fois
unpleasant désagréable
vessel vaisseau, bateau, bâtiment
weep pleurer
willing plein de bonne volonté
wonder s'étonner

Phrases

He is due back on the 23rd	il doit rentrer le 23
To open up a new market	créer, ouvrir un marché nouveau
She is at her wits' ends	elle ne sait plus que faire
What's up ?	qu'est-ce qui se passe ?
It shows whether she's taken any action	cela indique si elle a pris des dispositions, des mesures
By the way	au fait, en passant
It'll be fun to have a change	ce sera drôle de changer un peu
I did try to do my best	vraiment, j'ai essayé de faire de mon mieux
Do cheer up !	allons ! ne vous laissez pas abattre !
Along the line	quelque part dans le circuit
They rate him as sound	ils estiment qu'il est solide, sûr ; que sa situation est saine

Explanations and Other Useful Terms

bill of lading — form giving relevant information about *freight,* goods, being shipped. The plural form *bills of lading* is often used, as they are made out in sets of two or three. One copy is signed by the captain of, or agent for, a ship to acknowledge that the goods have been placed on board ship (see specimen bill of lading Unit 15).

brief-case — also sometimes called a despatch-case.

clearing agent — one who supervises and helps goods through customs, paying duties, etc.

container — large metal box in which goods are transported by road which are gradually replacing the wooden crates in which goods used to be shipped.

duplicating — making copies by means other than printing, i.e. by using office duplicating-machines, ink duplicators, spirit duplicators and photocopiers.

forwarding agent — sometimes called a **clearing agent** ; someone importing speaks of a clearing agent, and someone exporting uses the term forwarding agent.

frank — to put an official mark (instead of a stamp) on a letter, with a franking machine.

I. S. D.	International Subscriber Dialling.
irrevocable letter of credit	means that a buyer cannot change his mind if he decides that he does not want the goods (see also Unit 15).
letterhead	see Unit 4.
long term assessment	an experienced guess at what the sales or expenditure etc., will be in the future.
memo	short for memorandum, a note to help memory ; or a short note of instructions or information for internal office use.
outgoing	*opposite* : **incoming.**
to roll off	to make copies on a duplicating machine (the verb comes from the *roller*, or *drum*, to which the stencil is attached.
sight draft	a Bill of Exchange attached to shipping documents. The goods are only released to the buyers when he pays the amount of his bill. The exporter does not receive the money so quickly because it is paid in the buyer's country.
set out	here : to plan the position of the address, letter, etc. To make it look attractive.
stationery	paper, envelopes, files, etc... Be careful not to confuse with *stationary* = not moving.
stencil	special paper on which is typed the original of a letter, memo, etc. of which a number of copies are required. We say **to cut** a stencil because the typewriter *keys* cut the letters so that the duplicating ink can get through.
way bill	used for air freight goods, for which the documentation is slightly different from and, in general, easier to deal with, than the documentation necessary when goods are sent by ship (see Unit 15).

Pronunciation

1 — 1 - (- -) detail, general, manage, reasonable, shorthand

 - 2 (- -) account, address, ago, agree, arrange, assess, assessment, capacity, collect, consign, container, delivery, direct, discuss, employ, exact, expect, efficient, emergency, inform, mistake, percent, percentage, publicity, report, responsible, (to) transport

 - - 3 (-) ͵corres'pondence, ͵corres'pondent, ͵inexpe'rienced, ͵irre'vocable

2 — [r] ring, bring, trip, round, proof, through, promise, agree, arrive, surprise, very

[i] hint, flimsy, printing, promise, billing

[æ] bank, frank, handle, panic, thanks

[ju:] unit, due, few, use, usual, issue, new, duplicate

[ou] cope, no, also, fold, load, note, both, open, telephone, envelope, appropriate

[ʌ] month, money, other, some, done, discuss, just, cover, wonder, something, someone, country, reluctant

[u:] proof, prove, move, through, flu

[ɛə] there, where, spare

[iə] clear, nearly, experience

[aiə] hire, wire, fire, dial, buyer, client

3 — Compare : sign [sain], consign [kən'sain], signature ['signitʃə] agent ['eidʒənt], manage ['mænidʒ] ; nation ['neiʃən], national ['næʃnəl]

advertise ['ædvətaiz], advertisement [əd'və:tismənt], an ad [ən 'æd] chance [tʃa:ns], change [tʃeindʒ] ; bank [bæŋk], branch [bra:ntʃ] ; a use [ju:s], to use [ju:z], useful ['zju:sfəl], usual ['ju:ʒuəl]

execute ['eksikju:t], execution [ˌeksi'kju:ʃən], an executive [ig'zekjutiv]

4 — Note : acknowledgement [ək'nɔlidʒmənt], bill of lading ['bil əv 'leidiŋ], crisis ['kraisis], clerk [kla:k], drawer ['drɔ:ə], financial [fai'nænʃəl, fi'n-], forwarding-agent ['fɔ:wədiŋ 'eidʒənt], heavens ['hevənz], honestly ['ɔnistli], probably ['prɔbəbli], promise ['prɔmis], souk [su:k].

2. SUMMARY

John Martin is due back from his trip to Abraca today and there is a pile of work on his desk. Unfortunately, there is also an unpleasant surprise waiting for him. His very efficient secretary, Sally Langley, has just telephoned to say that she is ill and cannot come into the office today. Elizabeth Corby, Mr. Grant's secretary, copes with the emergency by going to see the Chief Clerk in the General Office and asking him if he will lend Mr. Martin one of his shorthand-typists while Sally is away.   5

The General Office is a very busy place. It handles, among other things, all the office printing and duplicating. It also deals with the mail : the staff open all the letters in the morning and send them round to the 10 appropriate offices. Twice daily they collect all the outgoing letters, frank them and post them. They also have an addressing machine, which prints addresses on envelopes, folds the letters and seals the envelopes very rapidly. This is used for advertising and publicity, as well as addressing all order acknowledgements, delivery notes and monthly statements of 15 account. The Chief Clerk, Mr. Baker, reluctantly agrees to lend Fenella, who is inexperienced but willing. Elizabeth tells her where to find the stationery, gives her a few helpful hints and then leaves her to her fate.

Mr. Martin has a much bigger emergency to cope with as soon as he arrives. Thirty desks have failed to arrive in Holland, and the agent there, Mr. 20 Van Eyck, rings Mr. Martin in a panic because he is responsible for seeing that they are delivered by a certain date to the Dutch customers. The firm use forwarding agents to clear the goods through customs, transport them and deliver them. But something has gone wrong somewhere along the line. Apart from this, and many other jobs which need his atten- 25 tion, John has also got to report to Mr. Grant on his trip to Abraca.

They discuss the chances of opening up a new market there, who they will use as an agent and how the money to pay for the goods will be transferred to Britain. Mr. Grant decides he wants an irrevocable letter of credit. A *letter of credit* is sent by a bank to an exporter informing him 30 that payment for goods is at the bank. When the exporter proves that the goods have left the country (by showing a copy of a bill of lading with the signature of the captain, or person responsible, proving that the goods have been loaded on to the ship) the money is then paid to the exporter. The buyer—say in Abraca—tells his own bank to send a letter of credit 35 to the exporter's bank in London. It is therefore a promise to pay as soon as the exporter has shown proof that he has sent the goods.

At the end of the day John has cleared up some of his work, but poor Fenella is nearly at her wits' end.

PART 2 : CONVERSATION AND DOCUMENTS

1. CONVERSATION

(Recorded Text)

(In the General Office)

ELIZABETH	Good morning, Mr. Baker, we've got a bit of a crisis on in Mr. Martin's office, and I was wondering if you could help us.
MR. BAKER	I certainly will if I can. What's up?
ELIZABETH	Mr. Martin is due back from Abraca this morning, and 5 his secretary has just telephoned to say that she's ill. She thinks she's got flu.
BAKER	I'm sorry to hear that.
ELIZABETH	Mr. Martin will need someone to help him. The other two girls in the Sales Office can't do shorthand, so could you 10 possibly spare a girl from your department?
BAKER	Oh dear! Well, I suppose I could let him have Fenella.
ELIZABETH	What's her shorthand like?
BAKER	Reasonable. She sets her letters out well, although I wouldn't say she was the world's fastest worker. 15
ELIZABETH	Oh, I expect she'll manage. Thanks for your help.

(In John Martin's office)

ELIZABETH	Here's today's post, Fenella.
FENELLA	Thank you.
ELIZABETH	It was sorted · and stamped with today's date, as you know, in the General Office. In this 'in' tray are all the 20 letters and memos which have come in while Mr. Martin has been away. You'll see that Sally has written a note with each one to show whether she has taken any action or not. By the way, Sally keeps all the stationery in this drawer here, letterheads, envelopes, flimsy and so on. 25 Mr. Martin will probably be in any minute now. If you need help you can come into my office down the corridor. Do you think you'll be able to manage?

FENELLA	Oh, I think it'll be fun to have a change.
ELIZABETH	Yes, well, you'll be very busy. The work here is rather 30 different from the work in the General Office, you know. I must leave you now.
FENELLA	Thank you, Elizabeth.

(Later that morning, Mr. Martin is dealing with a telephone call)

JOHN MARTIN	Hello. What? Desks? Oh, Mr. Van Eyck ... Yes ... But they were sent off days ago. Yes, of course they were 35 ... wait, I'll give you the exact date. Fenella, quick!
FENELLA	Yes, Mr. Martin.
JOHN	See if you can find the copies of the shipping documents for the thirty M-type desks sent to the Netherlands. They'll be in the outer office in the file under Bills of Lading. 40 Hello ... hold on ... we're trying to find it. I'm sorry about this, Mr. Van Eyck, I can't understand the hold-up.
FENELLA	Is this it, Mr. Martin?
JOHN	Yes, that's it. Here we are, Mr. Van Eyck, yes, consigned motor vessel *Kelpie*, date of clearance London Docks, 45 12th September. You should have them by now. I'll get on to our forwarding agents and call you back. O.K. Goodbye. Fenella! Get me the Globe Forwarding Company— Mr. Alan Smith. The number's on the list by the phone. Something has happened to our two containers for 50 Rotterdam. Our agent in Holland promised our clients would get the desks on Friday. When you've got him, ring through to Mr. Best, the Sales Clerk, and ask him to bring up the invoiced sales and order intake for the month. Be as quick as you can. 55

(An hour later)

JOHN	Hello, oh, Mr. Smith. Any luck? What! Oh, no. Left on the dock. Why weren't they cleared? Well, surely the agent's responsible. Look, I'll try and get the containers cleared. O.K. I'll ring you back. Fenella! Get me Mr. Van Eyck in Amsterdam. 60
FENELLA	Oh, Mr. Martin, how do I telephone to Holland?
JOHN	You can dial the number direct, it's on I.S.D.. Oh, heavens! It's eleven-thirty already. As soon as I've got through, I'll have to go and see Hector Grant. I shan't be long. 65

(In Mr. Grant's office)

HECTOR GRANT **Come in, John. Well, you seem to have covered a lot of ground in Abraca. What about an agent?**

JOHN **I think I've found a good one. I think he'll handle our business well.**

GRANT **What's his financial position?** 70

JOHN **When I was in Djemsa I checked up with the Abracan National Bank, who rate him as sound.** '

GRANT **Did you agree a commission if we decide to employ him?**

JOHN **Yes. The usual ten per cent.**

GRANT **How are we going to arrange payment from Abraca? I'm** 75 **against sight draft.** '

JOHN **Oh, I agree. It must be irrevocable letter of credit. Payment will be made through a London branch of the National Bank of Abraca when they receive our bills of lading and all the other documents.** 80

GRANT **Well, I'd like a more detailed report from you on paper, plus your long-term assessment.**

(Back in John Martin's office)

JOHN **Fenella, these letters are full of spelling mistakes.**

FENELLA **Oh, Mr. Martin, I did try to do my best. Honestly I did.**

JOHN: 'I bought this ash-tray in the souk in Djemsa. Would you like it?'

JOHN	Oh, Fenella! Don't weep all over my letters, they're so 85 nicely set out. You can easily correct the spelling mistakes. Do cheer up. I'm sorry. I expect I'm a bit tired too. It's been a hectic day for both of us.
FENELLA	Oh dear.
JOHN	Look, I really am sorry. I shouldn't have expected so 90 much from you. You've done splendidly. I know . . . pass me my brief-case. I bought this ash-tray in the souk in Djemsa. Would you like it?
FENELLA	Oh, yes, Mr. Martin. Thank you ever so much . . . and can I work for you tomorrow if Sally is still away? 95
JOHN	Yes, of course. I shouldn't be able to manage without you.

PRACTICE SENTENCES

Say the practice sentences on the record :

  i I'll give you the exact date of despatch.

  ii Please find the copy of the shipping documents.

  iii I can't understand the hold-up.

  iv Why weren't the goods cleared ?

  v The goods were consigned motor vessel Kelpie, date of clearance London docks, 12th September.

  vi You should have the goods by now.

  vii I'll get on to our forwarding agents.

  viii I'll call you back.

—————————

2. THE STYLE OF BUSINESS LETTERS

When writing a business letter in English, be careful not to use an old-fashioned commercial instruction book as a guide. The style of writing is changing rapidly. Every year it gets simpler and less formal. Instead of using an out-of-date phrase like 'we are in receipt of your favour', we now write 'thank you for your letter'. Except for a few firms who still live in the past, business correspondents prefer simple English to express what they want to say as effectively as possible. Time is more precious than ever to a busy executive and he does not want to have to read a lot of unnecessary words. But the writer of a business letter must create a good impression, especially if he is selling, so a few words to promote a feeling of friendship and goodwill are not wasted. However, compliments must not be exaggerated, as they may produce the opposite effect, and the reader may feel that the writer is being insincere.

We suggest the following points should be remembered when writing a business letter in English:

1 make a new paragraph for a new subject;
2 say what you want to say in the simplest, clearest way;
3 don't sell aggressively;
4 don't exaggerate compliments;
5 remember that real feelings will have more effect than pretended ones.

Here is a letter called an enquiry letter, that is, one asking for information about something, possibly a product which the writer of the letter may wish to buy. Of course, enquiry letters vary according to the type of product, the writer's own style and the information he or she requires, but this letter could be varied to fit most first-enquiry situations.

DOGBERRY & SONS

BARLOW AVENUE
YORK

The Sales Manager,
Harper & Grant Ltd.,
Great West Road,
London, W.25.

1st September, 197..

Dear Sir,

We are interested in the new filing cabinets advertised by you in the current number of the 'Office Equipment' magazine (issue No. 1056, page 24), and we should like some more information.

At present we are using the drawer type filing cabinets and we should like to know:

(1) if the new system is easier and quicker to operate

(2) how many files can be stored in each cabinet.

(3) what is the capacity of each file.

Our present office furniture is a light grey and we should like to match it as closely as possible.   Could you let us see samples of the colours available?

We should be grateful to receive a prompt reply as we are in the process of replanning our filing system throughout the firm.

Yours faithfully,

George Watkins

George Watkins
DOGBERRY & SONS

PART 3 : NOTES AND PRACTICE

1. RAPPEL GRAMMATICAL

Summary :

1. **There is a pile of work** : cette construction est bien connue au présent, mais la manie-t-on toujours avec aisance et spontanéité aux autres formes ?...

There might be a hold up	Il pourrait y avoir du retard
There ought to be a larger safe in this office	Il devrait y avoir un plus grand coffre-fort dans ce bureau
There would have been a lot of red tape	Il y aurait eu beaucoup de paperasserie

6. **By + -ing** indique le moyen par lequel on réalise un objectif. Ce n'est que l'un des équivalents de *en* + participe présent. Comparons notamment :

He rushed out of the shop, shouting ' Fire ! '	Il sortit précipitamment de l'atelier, criant : « Au feu ! »
I filed all these documents while waiting for the chief clerk	J'ai classé tous ces documents en attendant le chef de bureau

9. Notons la place de l'adverbe court de manière ou temps : entre le sujet et le verbe s'il y a une seule forme verbale, entre la première et la deuxième forme verbale s'il y en a deux ou plus de deux :

He never comes on Thursday	Il ne vient jamais le jeudi
He would never have come on a Saturday	Il ne serait jamais venu un samedi

Notons toutefois ce qui se passe avec le verbe **to be** :

He's always there at 8	Il est toujours là à huit heures
But his secretary never is	Mais sa secrétaire n'y est jamais

Dans cette dernière phrase, **is** a la forme accentuée, et la voix monte (*intonation ascendante*)

10. **Staff** est suivi de la forme du pluriel car il est de sens collectif : Cf. également plus bas, ligne 23 : **The firm use a forwarding agent.**

11. Notons : **once** = une fois, **twice** = deux fois, **three times** = trois fois, **four times, five times,** etc. En américain, on entendra : **two times** et non plus **twice.** Dire **once more** : une fois de plus.

— 69 —

14. Ne pas confondre :

This is used for ['ju:zd fə] **franking letters**	Cela sert à affranchir le courrier
They used to do it ['ju:stə] **in the most archaic manner**	Ils le faisaient auparavant de la manière la plus archaïque

19. Le rejet de la préposition doit être spontané :

Who were you talking with ?	Avec qui discutiez-vous ?
Is that all he has to complain about ?	Est-ce tout ce dont il a à se plaindre ?
What did he do that for ?	Pour quoi a-t-il fait cela ?

20. L'idée négative (insuccès d'une action, etc.) est souvent exprimée par le verbe **fail** dans des constructions de ce type :

The government has failed to tackle the question properly	Le gouvernement n'a pas su prendre cette question comme il fallait
The firm has failed to take advantage of this new market	L'entreprise n'a pas su profiter de ce nouveau marché

19. Le comparatif peut être modifié par **much** :

They'll have to pay much heavier duties	Ils devront payer des droits beaucoup plus élevés

28. Notons les constructions :

I paid for the goods	J'ai payé les marchandises
I paid the men	J'ai payé les ouvriers

Conversation :

9. Notons la construction de **other, next, last, first** avec les numéraux :

Where are the other three files ?	Où sont les trois autres dossiers ?
The next two items on the agenda will be difficult to solve	Les deux questions suivantes à l'ordre du jour ne seront pas faciles à résoudre

13. **Leave** est suivi d'un nom :

He's left her to her fate	Il l'a abandonné à son sort

Let suivi d'un nom a le sens de *louer* :

He let a flat in the suburbs	Il a loué un appartement en banlieue

Let + verbe = *laisser* (ou auxiliaire de l'impératif) :

Can you let me have your stapler ?	Puis-je avoir votre agrafeuse ?
Let's deal with this question first	Occupons-nous de cette question en premier

15. **I wouldn't say she was : was** ici est au passé parce que la proposition dépend d'une proposition principale d'opinion exprimée sous une forme modale (concordance des temps). Mais l'observation de Mr. Baker reste valable pour le présent.

17. **Today's post** : les appréciations de distance et de temps se construisent au cas possessif :

He took a fortnight's leave	Il a pris quinze jours de congé

23. La conjonction **whether** introduit une alternative :

Whether the manager is here or not, I want an immediate reply	Que le directeur soit là ou non, je veux une réponse tout de suite

On a vu qu'après **ask, enquire,** etc., dans la langue contemporaine, on entendait beaucoup plus souvent **if** que **whether** :

He asked if the circular had been printed	Il a demandé si la circulaire avait été tirée
See if you can find their invoice	Voyez si vous pouvez trouver leur facture

46. Outre la nuance de *conseil*, **should** s'emploie lorsqu'on estime que certaines conditions devraient être remplies :

He should have the documents by now	Il devrait être à présent en possession des documents
She should have cut out the stencils	Elle devrait avoir fini de faire les stencils

68. **One** sert de pronom de rappel, c'est-à-dire qu'il s'emploie pour remplacer un nom déjà exprimé et que l'on ne veut pas répéter une seconde fois :

It's in the large filing-cabinet over there ; sorry, it's in the other one	C'est dans le grand classeur là-bas; pardon, c'est dans l'autre

One prend la marque du pluriel :

Have you signed the other ones ?	Avez-vous signé les autres ?

84 et 87 : notons les formes emphatiques. Voyons encore :

Do sit down   Veuillez vous asseoir
I did cross the cheque !   Mais j'ai barré le chèque !

88. Notons : **both of them** = eux deux, **all of you** = vous tous, etc.

2. EXERCISES

EXERCISE 1. — *change as follows* :

Can you help us   →   **I was wondering if you could help us**

1. Will they reach Holland in time ?   2. Did you meet our forwarding agent ?   3. Will she be an efficient secretary ?   4. Can he cope with the emergency ?   5. Did he take out an insurance policy ?   6. Has he crossed the cheque ?

EXERCISE 2. — *Change as follows* :

With whom was he talking   →   **Who was he talking with ?**

1. About what did he complain ?   2. By whom was it signed ?   3. This is the problem with which we have to deal.   4. Is he the gentleman for whom you have been waiting ?   5. There might be a much bigger emergency with which to cope.

EXERCISE 3. — *Place the adverb between brackets correctly* :

1. It deals with the duplication of documents (*also*).   2. He may mention another plan of his (*also*).   3. He is busy (*often*).   4. He would spare one of his typists (*certainly*).   5. She opens my mail (*never*).   6. Have they sent the letters round the offices (*already*).   7. He is late (*always*)   8. But his secretary is not (*never*).

EXERCISE 4. — *Change as follows* :

a **There is a delay**   →   **There would have been a delay**
b **There may be a delay**   →   **There might have been a delay**
c **There must be a reform**   →   **There ought to have been a reform**

1. There is a pile of work on my desk.   2. There may be an unpleasant surprise waiting for you.   3. There must be another lock on that door. 4. There must be a man at the gate.   5. There are a lot of problems to cope with.   6. There may be something wrong with the spot welder. 7. There may be a chance of opening up a new market.   8. There is a memo on her desk.

EXERCISE 5. — *Change as follows* :

They didn't tackle the problem properly → **They failed to tackle the problem properly**

1. They didn't break into the market.   2. They didn't take advantage of this opportunity.   3. He hasn't used all his power of persuasion.   4. He didn't keep up with all these modern techniques.   5. They haven't covered all their expenses.   6. We didn't foresee that their currency would be devalued.

EXERCISE 6. — *Change as follows* :

You'll have to pay heavy duties → **You'll have to pay much heavier duties**

1. The cost price will be high.   2. German firms are competitive.   3. They obtain spectacular results.   4. The economic situation can't be bad. 5. Fenella is a fast working secretary.   6. The new night watchman is a reliable fellow.   7. The new process is fast.   8. Yes, but it is monotonous too.

EXERCISE 7. — *Answer the following questions about exporting* :

1. Who is responsible for seeing that goods pass through customs into the country of destination ?   2. What do you call the document a copy of which accompanies all goods sent by ship ?   3. What are goods packed in to protect them and keep them together on a long journey ?   4. What method of payment may an exporter arrange so that he is paid as soon as the goods are put on board a ship ?

EXERCISE 8. — *Answer the following questions on work in the office* :

1. What is flimsy used for ?   2. You want 150 copies of a letter ; what might you ask your secretary to do ?   3. Where would you go to buy envelopes ?   4. What is a shorthand typist ?

EXERCISE 9. — *Just two questions on business phraseology* :

1. What was John's aim in Abraca ?   2. How did he find out that the man who might act as their agent in Abraca was financially sound ?

EXERCISE 10. — *Translate into English* :

1. Je vous indiquerai la date exacte de l'expédition. 2. Veuillez trouver la copie des documents d'expédition maritime. 3. Je n'arrive pas à comprendre ce retard. 4. Pourquoi est-ce que les marchandises n'ont pas été dédouanées ? 5. Les marchandises ont été expédiées à bord du Kelpie, date de sortie du Port de Londres, 22 septembre. 6. Vous devriez désormais être en possession des marchandises. 7. Je vais contacter nos agents de transport. 8. Je vous rappellerai. 9. Il doit rentrer le 31. 10. J'ai lu les deux premiers rapports, mais pas les deux autres. 11. Venez dans mon bureau et discutons de cette question ensemble. 12. Leur facture n'était pas au courrier de ce matin. 13. Je l'ai trouvé en classant ces documents. 14. Cette machine sert à affranchir le courrier. 15. Elle m'a donné quelques indications précieuses. 16. Ils nous envoyaient régulièrement des relevés de comptes hebdomadaires. 17. L'entreprise grandira en exportant davantage. 18. Pourriez-vous m'accorder une minute ? 19. La journée a été affolante pour nous tous. 20. J'ai pris des renseignements auprès de la banque, ils l'estiment digne de confiance.

———

UNIT 4

TROUBLE WITH A SPECIAL ORDER

PART 1 : INTRODUCTION

1. WORD STUDY

Vocabulary

anneal recuire, détremper
against (*ici*) pour exécuter (travail)
borrow emprunter
break down tomber en panne
buyer acquéreur, client, acheteur
buying department service achats
cancel annuler
check vérifier
chemical chimique
claim réclamer
coat revêtement, couche ; revêtir
compensation indemnité, indemnisation
computer ordinateur
computerize passer à l'ordinateur
console console
control system système de contrôle
deal with avoir affaire à
delay retard
desk bureau, pupitre
dial cadran ; composer un numéro
dictating machine dictaphone

double time heures à double tarif
dreadful terrible
ex works (au) départ (de) l'usine
expedite activer, accélérer, pousser
extra cost frais supplémentaires
foreman contremaître, agent de maîtrise
form part faire partie
fully automatic entièrement automatisé
headed paper papier à entête
headmaster directeur d'établissement secondaire
heat chaleur
hurry up activer, presser
inconvenient désagréable, gênant
internal phone téléphone intérieur
involve entraîner, impliquer
left out omis
meet (*ici*) observer, respecter
mess pagaïe, gâchis
nuisance embarras, tuile
offset compenser

— 75 —

otherwise sinon, autrement
oven four
overdue en retard sur les délais
penalty sanction, pénalisation
  penalty clause clause pénale
phone back rappeler
plant usine
production line chaîne de production
public address système d'appel général (par hauts-parleurs)
receiver récepteur, combiné
report rapport
re-scheduling révision de la programmation
sales people les vendeurs

schedule horaire, programme, planning
share partager
spare (ici) accorder
steel sheet plaque, feuille d'acier
supplier fournisseur
tape recorder magnétophone
term trimestre scolaire
time limit délai
treatment traitement
trouble ennuis, difficultés
type dactylographier
wire télégramme ; télégraphier
Works Manager directeur de l'usine
worried soucieux

Phrases

On Thursday week jeudi en huit
We stand to lose 10 % Nous risquons de perdre 10 %
To meet delivery dates respecter les délais de livraison
You put us in a nice mess vous nous avez mis dans de beaux draps
The point is, ... la question, le problème, c'est que...
He is on the line il est au bout du fil
I can't help that je ne peux empêcher cela

Explanations and Other Useful Terms

double time employees are paid double their normal wage for working at certain times, e.g. on Sundays.

ex works ready to leave factory.

honour a contract do just what the contract specifies despite unforeseen difficulties.

overtime work which is in addition to the normal working hours.

penalty clause a paragraph in a contract allowing the buyer to deduct a percentage of the price as a penalty for late delivery.

plant	machinery, apparatus, fixtures, etc... used in an industrial process. Also used instead of factory or works in large industries (e.g. chemical plant, oil plant).
production line	the process through which the raw materials pass to make a finished product.
	To keep the production line clear : to keep the necessary machines free to be used for a particular series of operations.
Production Manager	the man in charge of production. He is responsible for co-ordinating all the factors such as the stock levels, deployment of labour and use of machinery so that the goods will be produced when required and at a minimum cost.
public address (system)	a series of loudspeakers installed in various places in the factory and office block to call staff who are temporarily out of their offices and so cannot be reached by telephone.

Pronunciation

1 — 1 - - borrow, a contract, limit, memo, offer, offset, penalty, reference, telegram, urgent

   - 2 (- -) accept, anneal, complain, computer, computerize, console, important, initial, involve, myself, prepared, receive, receiver, return, supply, convenient

2 — '-ic : automatic, hectic, plastic, public

3 — [ʃ]   sheet, sure, assure, special, initial, machine, schedule
    [l]   (*dark*) full, well, will, tell, steel, trouble, people, responsible
    [l]   (*clear*) fully, telling, delay, deliver, lose, telegram, telephone
    [ð]   this, that, these, those, there, whether, rather
    [θ]   thing, think, three, through, something
    [i:]   heat, anneal, each, reason, receive, machine
    [ʌ]   must, oven, luck, company, double, trouble, Monday, worry
    [ou]   no, coat, home, borrow, hello, memo, those, console
    [ei]   date, fail, dictate, delay, able, break, O.K.
    [ɔ:]   clause, course, recorder
    [ɔ]   gone, wrong, what, borrow, job

4 — Compare : to say, I say, you say, we say, they say [sei]
he says [sez], I *etc.* said [sed]
scheme [ski:m], schedule ['ʃedju:l]
a record ['rekɔ:d], to record [ri'kɔ:d]

5 — Note : enquiry [in'kwaiəri], failure ['feiljə], material [mə'tiərjəl],
nuisance ['nju:səns], nephew ['nevju:], overdue ['ouvə'dju:],
pretty ['priti], spare [spɛə], quiet [kwaiət], Wednesday ['wenzdi].

2. SUMMARY

Peter Wiles, Hector Grant's nephew, is the Production Manager. He is
going to have a very hectic day, but he thinks he will have a quiet morning
dictating into a dictating machine a long report which his secretary,
Jane, can type back later. John Martin comes into Peter's office very
worried. He has just received a memo from the Production Department 5
telling him that there will be a delay in delivery of some special plastic-
coated steel sheets. These sheets are wanted for an important order. They
will form part of a *console* for a computerised control system, the place
where one man can sit and be responsible for the production of a large,
fully-automatic chemical plant. To get the order, Harper & Grant had to 10
promise to deliver these desks before a certain date. If they fail to deliver
on time they will lose money, because there is a penalty clause in the
contract. To make these desks, the firm need steel sheets which are coated,
or covered, with plastic. The plastic coating is finished in a heat-treatment
oven called an annealing oven. But the steel company who supply these 15
sheets are not able to deliver on the date they promised: that is to say,
they cannot honour their contract with Harper & Grant. But Harper &
Grant did not have a penalty clause in their contract with the suppliers, so
they may lose money unless something can be done about it pretty quickly.

PART 2 : CONVERSATION AND DOCUMENTS

1. CONVERSATION

(Recorded Text)

(*Peter Wiles's office*)

PETER WILES   **Jane, will you go and see if you can borrow John Martin's
tape recorder for me? I've left my machine at home.**

JANE   **Here is Mr. Martin.**

— 78 —

PETER	Oh, hello, John. Are you using your dictating machine this morning? I've got a long report I must dictate. Could I borrow your machine?	5
JOHN	Of course. But can you spare me a second? This memo you sent me about the delivery delay on the console control desks. What's gone wrong?	
PETER	Everything, John. We have to get the steel sheets which we need for these desks from new suppliers. Well, the suppliers have got some trouble or other. They say they'll be a bit late with delivery.	10
JOHN	But they can't be! Those console control desks are a special order. They're wanted for one of the big computer companies. It's a very important contract.	15
PETER	When did we promise delivery?	
JOHN	On Thursday week. And there's a penalty clause. We stand to lose ten per cent of our price for each week of overdue delivery.	20

JOHN: 'But they can't be. . . . It's a very important contract.'

PETER	Oh, these penalty clauses! Why do you sales people accept them?
JOHN	We have to accept them, otherwise we don't get the contracts.
PETER	Well, let's get on to the Buying Department. I only heard about the delay yesterday because we kept the production line clear to handle these special sheets. It's a dreadful nuisance.
JOHN	It'll be more than a nuisance if we don't meet our delivery date ! It'll cost us a lot of money.
PETER	Keep calm, John. We can perhaps claim compensation from the steel suppliers for failure to deliver on time. That'll offset the penalty clause.
JOHN	Well, if you can . . .
PETER	(*He dials on internal phone*) Hello, Jones? Those plastic coated sheets—Mid Wales Steel Company are the suppliers, aren't they? Who do you deal with there? Mr. Morgan. Can you find out why there's this hold-up on delivery? Those sheets are urgent. Yes, they're wanted for a special order. What? You didn't know? Well, does that mean there was no time limit in the contract? Yes, phone me back, will you. If you like, I'll speak to Morgan myself.
JOHN	Does that mean we can't claim compensation if they fail to deliver on time?
PETER	It looks like it. Jones is checking our order now. He didn't know they were being ordered against a special job. He thought they were wanted for stock.
JOHN	Just our luck!
JANE	Mr. Jones for you on the phone, Mr. Wiles.
PETER	Hello. What did Morgan say? Oh, no! Well, if that's true, why did Mid Wales offer a delivery of thirty days? They must have known they couldn't honour it. Why did they accept our order at all? Yes. O.K. Morgan is ringing me, is he? Yes. I'd like to hear his excuses. Thanks, Jones. (*He puts the receiver down.*)
JOHN	What's the reason for the delay?
PETER	Deliveries are held up because one of their annealing ovens broke down. (*Telephone rings*) Ah, that may be Morgan now.
JANE	Mr. Morgan of the Mid Wales Steel Company on the line.

PETER	Hello. Good morning, Mr. Morgan. Yes, Mr. Jones has been telling me. Well, you've put us in a nice mess. Those sheets of yours are for a special order. We're due to deliver the finished console desks by next Thursday, and now you say there's a two-week delay . . . When did the oven break down? Yes. Well, the point is, what can you do to help us? It's too late to get the material for this job from another firm now. . . . What? Well, if you can, that will help. Yes, I think we'd be prepared to share the extra cost of sending the goods by road. Yes . . . Goodbye.
JOHN	What does he say?
PETER	He says he can have half the items ready ex works by noon on Monday. That'll give us a day and a half to assemble the desks . . . one day for packing and delivery. Yes, well, we'll have to make this a crisis operation. Jane! Come in here, will you.
JANE	Yes, Mr. Wiles.
PETER	Get the Works Manager on the phone for me as soon as you can.
JANE	Yes, Mr. Wiles.
JOHN	What about the other half?
PETER	Morgan thinks he can let us have them on Wednesday. By the time we get them assembled and delivered . . . let's see . . . they'll be about a week late, but maybe the customer will accept this. What do you think, John?
JOHN	I'll get on to them and find out.
PETER	Have you got the Works Manager yet, Jane?
JANE	I'm trying to get him; he's not answering his phone.
PETER	Well, try him on the public address. He's never in his office.
JANE	He's on the line now, Mr. Wiles.
PETER	Ah, Fielding. We have a crisis. How soon can we assemble those console-type desks? Yes, it'll involve re-scheduling the production line, but what I want to know is . . . if we get the sheets by Monday, can we have them assembled, packed and ready to leave by Wednesday afternoon? It'll be only half the order arriving on Monday. The rest of the sheets will be delivered on Wednesday, which will give us the weekend. . . . I can't help that. Paying double time will still be cheaper than the loss we shall make if the customer insists on the

Line numbers in right margin: 65, 70, 75, 80, 85, 90, 95, 100 penalty. Yes. You think you can? Good man. O.K. Thanks. Jane! Get the customer on the phone here for Mr. Martin, and then I must get down to that report.

PRACTICE SENTENCES

Say the practice sentences on the record :

  i The suppliers say they'll be late with delivery.
 ii It's a very important contract.
iii They're wanted for a special order.
 iv We promised delivery next week.
  v They offered a delivery of thirty days.
 vi There's a penalty clause.
vii Can you find out why there's this hold-up on delivery?
viii We're due to deliver the finished desks by next Thursday.
 ix What can you do to help us?

2. LETTERS OF COMPLAINT

If goods are not delivered on the day on which they were promised the buyer might send a letter, or a telegram (it depends how urgently he needs the goods), to complain and ask the manufacturers, or suppliers, to hurry up, *expedite*, the delivery. The following is a typical 'complaint' letter.

Brentwood School,
Hambledon,
Cumberland.

The Manager,
Sales Department,
Harper & Grant Ltd.,
Great West Road,
London, W.25

16th September, 197..

Dear Sirs,

With reference to our order of 30th July for twenty-five student-type desks, we shall be glad to know when we may expect delivery, as these are now urgently required.

When we made the initial enquiry, your department assured us that delivery would only take three weeks, and we placed the order on that understanding as we wished to have the desks before the beginning of the new term. Your failure to deliver by the promised date is very inconvenient.

Will you please inform us by return, by telegram or telephone, of the earliest possible date when you can deliver these goods. Should the delay be longer than two or three days, we shall regretfully have to cancel the order.

Yours faithfully,

Paul Wilson

Paul Wilson
HEADMASTER

If the buyer needed the goods very urgently indeed he might send a telegram or a telex if he could not get through by telephone. The English used in telegrams is naturally short, as every word costs money. Words such as 'the', 'a', 'an', etc., are usually left out, unless the meaning would not be clear without them. Most firms have a telegraphic address which can be used for telegrams, and a telex number, both of which are printed on the firm's *letterhead*, their headed paper for letters.

Here is a telegram which the irritated headmaster might have sent to hurry up delivery of his desks.

TO: HARPO LONDON

OUR ORDER 25 DESKS NOT RECEIVED STOP WIRE IMMEDIATELY WHEN WILL BE DELIVERED

FROM: WILSON—BRENTWOOD SCHOOL

PART 3 : NOTES AND PRACTICE

1. RAPPEL GRAMMATICAL

Summary :

10. **They had to promise** : autres temps que le présent, la notion d'obligation s'exprime à l'aide de **to have to** ou **to be obliged, compelled, forced, bound to** entre lesquels il existe des nuances tenant au sens évident des équivalents :

We had to replace these articles	Nous avons dû remplacer ces articles
They'll be bound to do it	Ils seront contraints de le faire

18. Notons que **to have**, lorsqu'il n'est pas auxiliaire d'un temps composé, se comporte comme un verbe ordinaire et a donc pour auxiliaire **do** :

We didn't have to replace them	Nous n'avons pas dû les remplacer
They didn't have such a clause in their contract	Ils n'avaient pas de clause semblable dans leur contrat

19. Il ne faut pas confondre **less, unless, lest, last** et **least** :

Last but not least	Le dernier, mais non le moindre
Ring him up again, lest he forgets his appointment	Rappelle-le, de peur qu'il n'oublie son rendez-vous
I'll be in the Paint Shop, unless Mr. Fielding needs me at the Assembly Shop	Je serai à l'atelier de peinture, à moins que M. Fielding n'ait besoin de moi à l'atelier de montage

19. **Pretty** est ici adverbe, et a le sens de *très, assez* :

Business is pretty slack at the moment	Les affaires sont assez au ralenti en ce moment

Conversation :

9. **What's gone wrong** : attention à la forme contracte **'s** qui est mise ici pour **has**, mais est également la contraction de **is** :

It's a telegram for you	C'est un télégramme pour vous

Notons également **'d** qui est la contraction de **had** et de **would** :

She'd done her best, though	Elle avait pourtant fait de son mieux
She'd do her best, I'm sure	Elle ferait de son mieux, j'en suis sûr

25. **'s** est également la contraction de **us** à l'impératif 1re personne du pluriel. Rappelons que l'impératif affirmatif est l'infinitif sans **to** à la 2e personne du singulier et du pluriel, et qu'aux 1res et 3es personnes il a pour auxiliaire **let** suivi du pronom à la forme complément :

Come in ! Sit down !	Entrez ! Asseyez-vous !
Let her come in !	Qu'elle entre !

A l'impératif négatif, ces formes sont précédées de **don't**, y compris lorsque le verbe est **to be** :

Don't be silly ! Don't do that !	Ne sois pas sot ! Ne fais pas cela !
Don't let us be outpaced by these new competitors	Ne nous laissons pas distancer par ces nouveaux concurrents

37. **(aren't they ?)** et **55.** **(is he ?)** : Rappelons l'importance de ces construction appelées **tag-questions** ou **colloquial queries** dans la langue parlée, et qui correspondent à la formule *n'est-ce pas ?* en français. Il s'agit d'une interrogative, qui est négative lorsque la principale est affirmative, et non-négative lorsque la principale est négative.

Rappelons certaines formes contractes négatives : **shan't** pour **shall not**, **won't** pour **will not**. Que l'on ne soit pas surpris d'entendre **aren't I ?** Par ailleurs, lorsque la principale contient l'expression **there is**, c'est **there** qui est repris dans le *tag-question* à la place du sujet.

37. Notons que si l'interrogation avait commencé par la préposition **with**, on aurait **whom**, comparons :

With whom were you yesterday ?	Avec qui étiez-vous hier ?
Who were you talking to ?	A qui parliez-vous ?

53. **Must**, outre l'idée d'obligation, de stricte nécessité, a le sens de nécessité logique imposée par la déduction :

He must be over 60, since he retired last year	Il doit avoir passé la soixantaine, puisqu'il a pris sa retraite l'an dernier

Aux formes du passé, il n'a pas d'équivalent. Son complément se met à l'infinitif passé :

You must have made a mistake	Vous avez dû vous tromper

Dans la subordonnée, au passé en français, on rencontre en anglais la forme **must** + infinitif présent :

He said you must be mad to do so much work	Il a dit que vous deviez être fou de travailler tant

Il ne s'agit pas en fait d'un vrai passé, puisque dans l'exemple ci-dessus par exemple, la personne concernée travaille certainement encore autant aujourd'hui.

65. **A two-week delay** : Pourquoi **week** ne porte-t-il pas la marque du pluriel ? En fait, il s'agit ici d'un nom composé, et en général, le premier terme est invariable et à la forme du singulier :

The new Managing Director is a thirty-two year old whiz-kid out of the American business schools	Le nouveau P.D.G. est un jeune loup de 32 ans tout frais émoulu des business schools américaines

82. **By** + date renseigne sur la date limite à laquelle aura lieu l'action :

It shall be done by Friday	Ce sera fait vendredi au plus tard sans faute

Si le complément de temps est une durée, la préposition est **within** :

It would be delivered within a week	Cela pourrait être livré sous huitaine

Letter :

Should the delay be... : forme littéraire, écrite équivalent à **if the delay was (were)**. Cette construction comporte une nuance de doute, voire, ici, de menace : si jamais... alors.

2. EXERCISES

EXERCISE 1. — *Complete by colloquial queries (tag-questions) as follows :*

He is the boss, ...   →   **He is the boss, isn't he ?**

1. It's been a hectic day, ...   2. You'll use my tape recorder, ...   3. You had to promise to deliver them by Thursday, ...   4. There's a penalty clause ...   5. They failed to deliver the goods, ...   6. They would supply from stock, ...   7. They heard about this new process, ...   8. It would take six weeks, ...   9. We always do our best, ...   10. They were due on Monday, ...   11. We need them by the end of the week, ...   12. Mr. Wadsworth works in the Accountancy department, ...

EXERCISE 2. — *Complete by colloquial queries as follows :*

He isn't the boss ...   →   **He isn't the boss, is he ?**

1. It isn't a long report, ...   2. They couldn't cope with the emergency, ...   3. They won't have a penalty clause, ...   4. You haven't sent them such a letter, ...   5. They didn't pay double time, ...   6. It doesn't involve re-scheduling the line, ...   7. He hasn't claimed compensation, ...   8. We shan't have to work overtime, ...   9. It wouldn't offset the penalty clause, ...   10. You were not there when it happened, ...

EXERCISE 3. — *Complete with colloquial queries :*

1. There will be a delay ...   2. It was a special order ...   3. They can't honour their contract ...   4. They kept the production line clear ...   5. They'd share the extra cost ...   6. They'd accepted the clause, ...   7. They didn't say anything ...   8. You could let us have them on Tuesday ...   9. The customer won't accept this ...   10. It doesn't help at all ...   11. You think so too, Peter, ...   12. The oven's broken down ...   13. You left your recorder at home, ...

EXERCISE 4. — *Change as follows :*

We're going to check this   →   **We've just checked this**

1. We're going to write a report about it.   2. He's going to tell the works manager about it.   3. We're going to computerize all the production lines.   4. They're going to lose a lot of money.   5. I'm going to do something about it.   6. He's going to find out about the break down.   7. She's going to speak to the Sales Manager about it.   8. They're going to buy new German machines.   9. I'm going to get on to the forwarding agent.   10. They're going to send them by road.   11. She's going to ring the Chief Accountant.

EXERCISE 5. — *Rewrite these sentences, putting one of the following phrases into the appropriate sentence, adapting it where necessary* :

to meet a delivery date ; penalty clause ; ex works ; to pay compensation ; double time.

Write the sentences out in full :

1. To make sure that the goods are delivered on time, we'd better have a ... in the contract. 2. Some employees like working on Sundays and national holidays because they get paid ... 3. The firm had a strike last month and it looks as if they won't be able ... 4. Part of a machine tool fell on the foreman's big toe and broke it. The firm are responsible so they will have to ... 5. Can you let us know when the goods will be ready ... so that we can collect them ?

EXERCISE 6. — *Rewrite the sentences inserting the correct preposition or preposition/adverb* :

1. The steel company agreed to deliver the steel sheets ... thirty days. 2. The hold-up was due to the breaking ... of one of the steel company's annealing ovens. 3. If you use a dictating machine you can dictate ... it at any time. 4. The Production Manager is responsible ... co-ordinating all the processes of manufacture. 5. If there's a penalty clause in the contract you can claim compensation ... failure to deliver on time.

EXERCISE 7. — *Answer the following questions* :

1. What is compensation ? 2. What does re-scheduling a production line entail ? 3. What is the Buying Department responsible for ? 4. How much do they stand to lose if Mid Wales Steel can't deliver on time ? 5. Why were deliveries held up ? 6. What will Mid Wales Steel do to help Harper and Grant ? 7. How long overdue will the desks finally be ? 8. Can Peter have a rest after he's dealt with the trouble ?

EXERCISE 8. — *Translate into English* :

1. Les fournisseurs disent qu'ils auront du retard dans leur livraison. 2. C'est un contrat très important. 3. Il nous les faut pour une commande spéciale. 4. Nous avons promis la livraison la semaine prochaine. 5. Ils ont proposé de livrer sous 30 jours. 6. Il y a une clause pénale. 7. Pouvez-vous savoir pourquoi il y a ce retard à la livraison ? 8. Nous devons livrer les pupitres finis d'ici jeudi prochain. 9. Que pouvez-vous faire pour nous aider ? 10. Il a dû se tromper dans sa facture. 11. Si jamais le retard était de plus d'une semaine nous serions au regret de devoir annuler la commande. 12. Peter est assez ennuyé, n'est-ce pas ? 13. Ils n'arriveront pas avant mardi, à moins que vous ne les expédiez par la route. 14. Rappelez M. Fielding, de peur qu'il n'oublie son rendez-vous. 15. Cette panne est très gênante. 16. Vous nous avez mis dans un beau pétrin. 17. Il faut que je me mette à ce rapport à présent. 18. Nous serions disposés à partager les frais supplémentaires. 19. Ils devaient savoir qu'ils ne pouvaient pas payer. 20. Peut-être pourriez-vous réclamer une indemnisation ?

UNIT 5

THE FACTORY EXTENSION MEETING

PART 1 : INTRODUCTION

1. WORD STUDY

Vocabulary

accountant comptable
additional supplémentaire
agenda ordre du jour
apply (for) solliciter, demander
approval accord, approbation
area terrain, surface
assent acquiescement
attend assister (à)
avoid éviter
bay hall, atelier
Board of Trade Ministère du Commerce
Board Room Salle du Conseil
Building Inspector Inspecteur de l'Urbanisme et de l'Equipement
bye-law arrêté émanant d'une autorité locale
call in faire appel à
circulate communiquer
contractor entrepreneur
cope (with) faire face (à)
drawing plan
estimate devis, estimation

expand être en expansion
extension agrandissement, extension
folder chemise
formal guindé, officiel
foundation fondation
go over examiner (sujet)
go up monter, augmenter
grant accorder ; subvention
grow croître, s'agrandir
halve diminuer de moitié
health santé
hold tenir
informal sans cérémonies
item point
knock in (a door) percer (une porte)
labour main-d'œuvre
lawyer homme de loi, spécialiste de droit
layout disposition, agencement
likely to qui a des chances de, qui va vraisemblablement...

minutes procès-verbal
minute porter au procès-verbal
once dès que, aussitôt que
owing to dû à ; en raison de
position emplacement
provided that à condition que
remind rappeler, faire penser
safety sécurité
save gagner, économiser (temps, argent)

saving économie, gain
skilled spécialisé
stick to s'en tenir à
storage emmagasinage, entreposage
store entrepôt, magasin
stuff marchandise, matériaux
unload décharger
unskilled non qualifié

Abbreviations and Phrases

I.D.C. = Industrial Development Certificate

Certificat d'Urbanisme (*délivré pour une construction industrielle*)

He's called a meeting

Il a convoqué une réunion

We went over all this

Nous avons discuté de tout cela en détail

There's no point in...

Il n'y a pas lieu de ...

To put a programme in hand

Mettre en route un programme

Explanations and Other Useful Terms

Building Inspector — In Britain, as in most countries, you have to get permission from the local government authority to construct new buildings. The building plans must be submitted and accepted. Later the Building Inspector will come to make sure you build exactly according to the plans.

bye-law — building bye-laws are rules and regulations drawn up by the government concerning building in the area.

contractors — an outside firm doing a special job under contract. Usually associated with building work.

machine layout — the way in which machines are placed inside a building ; the disposition of machines.

minutes — a written summary of what is said at a meeting. It is a legal requirement in Great Britain that minutes are kept of board meetings, and all those attending as directors must sign them.

— 90 —

taken as read   a phrase used when it is decide not to read the minutes of the last meeting aloud. According to rules governing official meetings the minutes must be read aloud if they have not previously been circulated.

Pronunciation

1 — 1 - (- -) different, difficulty, estimate, interview, present, progress, sensible

    - 2 (- -) agree, agreement, apply, assent, attend, authorities, avoid, become, begin, beginning, committee, consider, continue, contractor, decide, decision, develop, development, efficient, exasperating, expand, inspector, obey, obtain, inflammable, propose, protect

    - - 3 (-) personnel, employee

2 — '-ion : expansion, extension, foundation, permission, position, production, situation, solution
'-onal : additional, exceptional, national, regional

3 — *h mute* : hour, hourly, honour, honesty, honestly, dishonest, honourable

    h aspirate : Hector, handle, hold, hold up, high, highly, height

[e]	health, head, headed, spread, instead, extension, again, against, present
[i]	busy, business, given, build, building, minute
[u:]	two, lose, prove, rule, approve, approval, through
[ʌ]	stuff, once, front, month, money, number, result, production
[a:]	car, park, last, charge, can't, grant, halve, argue
[ju:]	presume, assume
[idʒ]	manage, storage, courage, damage, postage

4 — Compare : 'industry, in'dustrial, in‚dustriali'zation
em'ployer, emplo'yee ; 'envelope ['enviloup], de'velop [di'veləp]
'manage ['mænidʒ], 'garage ['gæra:dʒ, 'gæridʒ, 'gæra:ʒ]
'certify ['sə:tifai], cer'tificate [sə(:)tifikit]
to estimate ['estimeit], an estimate ['estimit]
a country ['kʌntri], a county ['kaunti]

5 — Note : architect ['ɑːkitekt], area ['ɛəriə], agenda [ə'dʒendə], argue ['ɑːgjuː], bye-law ['bai-lɔː], circulate ['sɜːkjuleit], fuel [fjuːəl], fireproof ['faiəpruːf], an I.D.C. [ən 'ai 'diː: 'siː], factory ['fœktəri], layout ['leiaut], owing ['ouiŋ].

2. SUMMARY

The Company is expanding, and the present factory is rapidly becoming too small to cope with the increase in production. Some months ago it was decided that the Company would have to build an extension to the present factory (see plan in front of book). An architect, Mr. Norman Phillipson, was called in, and given the job. He drew up the plans and the 5 firm applied for an *I.D.C.* (Industrial Development Certificate), which is granted, given, by the Board of Trade. This was granted provided that the Fuel and Paint Stores were put in a different position. The authorities are very strict in seeing that certain rules are obeyed. Possible dangers to health and safety are carefully considered. When Harper & Grant's new 10 extension is built on, added, to the existing area they will have three more *bays*, divisions of a factory floor, but the present Fuel and Paint Stores would be too near the new extension. As both these materials are highly inflammable, it was considered that a fire could spread to the new extension very easily. The proposed new Paint Store will be protected by the 15 fireproof wall of the main factory. The County Planning Authority will also have to approve the plans.

Mr. Grant has called a meeting of a committee who are dealing with the new extension, with the architect present, to discuss progress. Mr. Grant is the Chairman in charge of the meeting. Also attending are Peter Wiles, 20 Production Manager; John Martin, Sales Manager; and William Buckhurst, the Company Secretary. Also present is Ian Hampden, who is the Personnel Manager; he is in charge of all *personnel*, the employees, employed by the Company. The meeting is just about to begin.

PART 2 : CONVERSATION AND DOCUMENTS

1. CONVERSATION

(Recorded Text)

(*In Hector Grant's office*)

HECTOR GRANT **Is the Board Room ready for the meeting, Miss Corby?**
ELIZABETH
CORBY   **Yes, Mr. Grant.**

— 92 —

GRANT	Where's the agenda ?
ELIZABETH	It's in the folder. Also a copy of the minutes of the last meeting. 5
GRANT	I shall need the drawing of the new extension. Where's that?
ELIZABETH	It's in the folder, too.
GRANT	You haven't forgotten anything?
ELIZABETH	I don't think so, Mr. Grant. 10

(*The meeting has just started*)

GRANT	Well, gentlemen, I don't think we need to read the minutes of the last meeting, as copies of them have already been circulated to you. (*Murmurs of agreement.*) Right. The minutes of the last meeting are taken as read. Now, let's get on. Mr. Wiles, will you report, please, on the result of 15 your interview with the Building Inspector ?
PETER WILES	Yes. The delay in getting bye-law approval was largely owing to the fact that the architect had not supplied detailed plans of the foundations of the new building.
NORMAN PHILLIPSON	I've now given the Building Inspector the detailed plans. 20
PETER	May I go on, Mr. Grant?
GRANT	Yes, Peter.
PETER	As you know, at the speed we're growing, I have felt right from the beginning that we ought to have planned a much larger extension. 25
GRANT	No. We mustn't grow too quickly. Slow but sure is the way this business will grow. But we went over all this in our original discussion, so there's no point in going over it all again.
PETER	But what will happen, Mr. Grant, when we need to 30 expand again? If we have to build another extension in a year or two it will be exasperating to have to go through all this work again. It's taken a long time to get permission to build, and to reorganise the machine layout, not to mention the building costs, which go up every year. 35 Wouldn't we be saving time and money, if, even at this late date, we build six bays instead of only three?
JOHN	I'd like to have a regional sales office on the new site, too.
PETER	If there's any additional space, Martin, I need it for production or stores. 40

GRANT	May I remind you gentlemen that the space you are arguing about does not exist. We stick to our present plan. Now, time's getting on. The next item on the agenda is the report from the Personnel Manager about the additional labour that's going to be required. So far, Ian, we've 45 had no difficulty in obtaining skilled workers, but is this situation likely to continue or not?
IAN HAMPDEN	Well, the position is this: skilled labour is getting harder to find. There's plenty of unskilled labour, and I think we should start a training programme now. Then by the 50 time the new extension is ready we should have the right number of trained men.
GRANT	Let's see. Phillipson, how long will the factory take to build once we've got our permission?
PHILLIPSON	If the contractors are very efficient I'd say five months, 55 possibly less.
GRANT	Well, Ian, can you produce enough skilled workers in, say, six months from now?
IAN	Yes, I think so.
GRANT	Very well, I think we all agree that a training programme 60 should be started immediately. (*Murmurs of assent.*) Good. You will minute that, Mr. Buckhurst, won't you? Also that Mr. Hampden will make an estimate of the cost. Now we come to item number three on the agenda. Peter? 65
PETER	Our I.D.C. was granted provided the Fuel and Paint Stores were placed in a different position to avoid the danger of fire. Mr. Phillipson has now proposed that we rebuild the present Managers' garage as a Paint Store. This would be a great saving in time. It's on the other side 70 of the delivery bay, and would halve the time taken to unload and store the stuff.
IAN	Where shall we put our cars?
JOHN	Well, they can stand in the car park like everyone else's.
GRANT	Just a minute, gentlemen. What is all this going to cost? 75
PHILLIPSON	I propose to extend the present garage to meet the west wall of the delivery bay and knock in a door here. The present Paint Store can then be used for other storage.
PETER	Splendid. Just what we need.

GRANT **Very well—yes, this does seem a sensible solution. If we** 80
are all agreed...? (*Murmurs of 'yes'.*) **Right. I presume**
there is no other business? (*Chorus of 'no's', 'don't think*
so's'.) **Very well, the meeting is over. Thank you very**
much, gentlemen. . . .

PRACTICE SENTENCES

Say the practice sentences on the record :

  i **The minutes of the last meeting are taken as read.**
 ii **Will you report on the result of your interview?**
iii **The next item on the agenda is the report from the Personnel**
    Manager.
 iv **Skilled labour is getting harder to find.**
  v **There's plenty of unskilled labour.**
 vi **I think we should start a training programme now.**
vii **I think we all agree that a training programme should be**
    started immediately.

2. MINUTES OF MEETINGS

There are different kinds of meetings: committee meetings, staff meetings and so on; and some are more formal than others. The meeting which has just taken place was rather informal. We talk of holding a meeting, which means the same as having a meeting. During the meeting the Company Secretary (a position usually held, by the way, by a man highly qualified in accounts, often an accountant, like Mr. Buckhurst, or a lawyer, and not to be confused with an ordinary secretary) made a note of the business discussed, decisions taken and so on. Later that day he dictated these notes to his secretary, who then typed them. Everyone who was at the meeting, and others who may have to know about it, will get a copy of the *minutes*, as they are called.

MINUTES OF A MEETING TO DISCUSS FACTORY EXTENSION, 10th OCTOBER, 197..
3 p.m.

1 Minutes of last meeting held on 26th September, at 3 p.m., were approved.

2 (*a*) The Production Manager reported on his interview with the local Building Inspector, and said that detailed plans of the foundations were required.
(*b*) The architect reported that the plans had been drawn up and sent to the Building Inspector.

3 (*a*) The Personnel Manager reported on labour available for the new extension, and suggested a programme should be put in hand to train workers.
(*b*) It was agreed that a training programme should be started immediately, and that an estimate of the cost should be provided by the Personnel Manager.

4 (*a*) The Production Manager reported that the I.D.C. was granted, provided that the Fuel and Paint Stores were placed in a different position to avoid the danger of fire.
(*b*) The architect's proposal to rebuild the present Managers' garage as Fuel and Paint Stores was agreed.

PART 3 : NOTES AND PRACTICE

1. RAPPEL GRAMMATICAL

Summary :

3. Il importe de manier avec aisance les équivalents des défectifs à tous les temps et formes ; ainsi :

They would have had to build an extension	Il leur aurait fallu construire de nouveaux bâtiments
Will they have to meet again ?	Devront-ils se réunir à nouveau ?

5. Il en est de même des constructions passives, très fréquentes en anglais :

A meeting was held on November 3rd.	Une réunion a eu lieu le 3 novembre
Was he finally given the job ?	Lui a-t-on finalement confié le travail ?
Has an I.D.C. been applied for ?	A-t-on fait une demande de certificat d'urbanisme ?
It hasn't been granted yet	Il n'a pas encore été accordé

Conversation :

4. Comparons les formes du comparatif et du superlatif de **late** :

It will be despatched later	Ce sera expédié plus tard
Is this the latest issue ?	Est-ce le numéro le plus récent ?
He came last week	Il est venu la semaine dernière

10. So sert à reprendre toute une phrase après un verbe d'opinion :

The firm will continue to grow, at least I hope so	L'entreprise continuera de croître, du moins je l'espère

24. **Ought to** aux premières personnes ne comporte pas toujours une nuance morale comme c'est plus souvent le cas aux 2es et 3es personnes. Il exprime l'idée de ce qu'il serait, ou aurait été, plus judicieux de faire, comme **should** aux 2es et 3es personnes. Il se peut qu'il soit préféré à **should** dans ce sens aux 1res personnes car **should** est plus ambigu, étant aussi l'auxiliaire du simple conditionnel, cela bien que la prononciation soit différente : au conditionnel **should** est inaccentué, alors qu'il est accentué lorsqu'il exprime le conseil, etc. Là encore, il importe de bien jongler avec les formes :

We ought to build it now	Nous devrions le construire à présent
They ought to have packed them yesterday afternoon	Ils auraient dû les emballer hier après-midi

41. La construction **the space about which you are arguing** est plus lourde.

47. Un futur plus ou moins prévisible s'exprime souvent dans la langue des affaires, de la politique, etc... à l'aide de la construction **to be likely to** (cf. ex. Unit 24) :

They aren't likely to change their minds about the project	Il y a peu de change qu'ils changent d'avis concernant le projet
If so, our competitors are most likely to sweep the board	Dans ce cas, nos concurrents ont toutes les chances d'emporter un succès sur toute la ligne
The workers are likely to claim a wage rise	Les ouvriers vont sans doute demander une augmentation de salaire
Are they likely to call a strike ?	Risquent-ils de lancer un ordre de grève ?

48. (**harder to find**) et 52. (**how long will it take to build**) : Notons ces emplois passifs de l'infinitif actif : en fait, c'est la main d'œuvre qui est trouvée, et l'usine qui est construite. Sous-jacentes sont les structures :

We find it hard to find skilled labour	Nous avons du mal à trouver de la main-d'œuvre qualifiée
How long will it take us to build the factory ?	Combien de temps nous faudra-t-il pour construire l'usine ?

50. **By the time...** au moment où (et au plus tard à ce moment là) est suivi de l'indicatif présent, comme toute conjonction introduisant une subordonnée temporelle (cf. plus bas, ligne 54, **once we've got our permission**) :

As soon as John arrives, tell him to come and see me	Dès que John arrivera, dites lui de venir me voir
Once the permission is given, it may take 5 or 6 months	Dès que le permis sera accordé, il faudra 5 ou 6 mois

57. **Enough,** *assez,* doit se placer obligatoirement après un adjectif ou adverbe ; mais il peut se placer devant le nom :

We haven't got enough time	Nous n'avons pas assez de temps
Are they working fast enough ?	Travaillent-ils assez vite ?

74. Le composé de **somebody** avec **else** peut prendre le cas possessif :

I thought it was my brief-case ; but it must be somebody else's	Je croyais que c'était mon porte-documents ; mais ce doit être à quelqu'un d'autre

2. EXERCISES

EXERCISE 1. — *Change as follows* :

The space about which you're arguing doesn't exist →
the space you're arguing about doesn't exist

1. The man to whom I was talking was their Sales Manager. 2. The commission on which they agreed is much too high. 3. With whom did you deal there ? 4. The problem with which we have to cope is particularly difficult. 5. The fellow of whom you heard is their new Marketing Manager. 6. The delay about which you complained was really due to an act of God.

EXERCISE 2. — *Change as follows* :

We ought to plan a much larger extension →
We ought to have planned a much larger extension

1. We ought to start a training programme. 2. You ought to claim compensation. 3. She ought to correct all her spelling mistakes. 4. You ought to set out your letters properly. 5. We ought to place the machines in a different position. 6. We ought to hold another meeting. 7. He ought to stick to the present plan. 8. We ought to find more skilled workmen.

EXERCISE 3. — *Change as follows* :

The firm called in an architect → **An architect was called in**

1. They will build an extension. 2. He drew up the plans. 3. They built it 2 years ago. 4. He's called a meeting. 5. She may have lost the invoice. 6. We can't avoid the danger. 7. They will discuss the other point, too. 8. They've given him the job. 9. She would have typed the report. 10. They'll have to approve our project. 11. They've planned a new extension. 12. We must re-schedule the production line.

EXERCISE 4. — *Change as follows* :

They complained → **They're likely to complain**

1. They went on strike. 2. He rang late in the evening. 3. He took a decision by himself. 4. They came every day. 5. Did he change his mind ? 6. He drew up a long report. 7. He didn't alter his plans. 8. They didn't wire. 9. They sent the goods by goods train. 10. Production was held up. 11. Skilled labour got harder to find. 12. It took over a year.

EXERCISE 5. — Try and improvise a comment on the following terms :

1. An extension.   2. The Board Room.   3. The agenda.   4. A folder.
5. Skilled workers.   6. A training programme.   7. An estimate.

*EXERCISE 6. — Can you answer the following questions about business
meetings ? Please answer with complete sentences.*

1. Where do directors of a firm usually have their meetings ?   2. How do
meetings usually begin ?   3. What do we call the prepared list of the
matters to be discussed ?   4. How would the Chairman of the meeting
refer to the next subject to be discussed ?

EXERCISE 7. — Some questions about building :

1. What is the first part of a building to be constructed ?   2. Who would
make sure you built according to the plans which you have submitted ?
3. Who would do the actual construction ?

*EXERCISE 8. — Finally, two questions to make sure you understood
the text :*

1. What three reasons did Peter Wiles give for wanting a larger extension
than the one planned ?   2. What labour problems did Ian Hampden see in
connection with building the extension ? How did he propose to solve
the problem ?

EXERCISE 9. — Translate into English :

1. Nous considérons comme lu et approuvé le procès-verbal de la dernière
assemblée.   2. Voulez-vous faire un compte-rendu de votre entrevue ?
3. La question qui est ensuite à l'ordre du jour est le rapport du
Directeur du Personnel.   4. Il est de plus en plus difficile de trouver
de la main-d'œuvre qualifiée.   5. Il y à beaucoup de main-d'œuvre
non qualifiée.   6. Je crois que nous devrions commencer un programme de formation professionnelle dès maintenant.   7. Je crois
que nous sommes tous d'accord pour que l'on commence immédiatement un programme de formation professionnelle.   8. Il n'y a
pas lieu de reprendre à nouveau tous ces arguments.   9. C'est votre
voiture ? — Non, c'est celle de quelqu'un d'autre.   10. Combien de
temps faudra-t-il pour obtenir le certificat ?   11. Il pensait que nous
n'aurions pas assez de temps.   12. Il va sans doute vous rappeler (*au téléphone*).   13. La réunion se tiendra le vendredi 2 juin à 15 heures.   14. Lui
a-t-on finalement confié la tâche ?   15. Sa situation financière est-elle
saine ? — Je le pense.   16. Le Secrétaire Général dit qu'il n'a pas eu copie
de votre rapport.   17. Ceci me parait vraiment être une solution raison-
nable.   18. Il a oublié quelque chose dans son devis.   19. Ceci pourrait
réduire le coût de la construction de moitié.   20. La séance est levée,
merci de votre attention, Messieurs.

UNIT 6

APPOINTING THE NEW ADVERTISING MANAGER

PART 1 : INTRODUCTION

1. WORD STUDY

Vocabulary

ache faire mal
account compte, budget, dossier
(*chez un agent publicitaire*)
account executive chef de publicité
'ad man' homme de publicité
advertise faire de la publicité
advertisement réclame ; annonce
advertiser annonceur
Advertising Manager directeur de la publicité
apply (for) solliciter, poser sa candidature
applicant candidat
assistant (executive) sous-(directeur)
board planche, panneau
display board panneau d'affichage
box boîte postale
branch service annexe
brief mettre au courant
brochure brochure, plaquette

campaign campagne
carry away emporter
check vérifier, contrôler
copywriter rédacteur
(*des textes publicitaires*)
design concevoir ; conception
designer graphiste
display étaler, afficher, exposer
editor rédacteur en chef
entail entraîner, impliquer
exhausted épuisé, éreinté
field domaine
go through examiner, étudier
handle s'occuper de
hoarding panneau publicitaire
involve impliquer, entraîner
join suivre (cours)
lately récemment
layout présentation, mise en page
leaflet imprimé, prospectus
liaise assurer la liaison
make sure s'assurer

medium (*pl.* **media**) support
publicitaire
old-fashioned démodé
plan envisager
proof épreuve
public relations relations publiques
relieve soulager
run organiser, diriger (*cours*, etc.)
salary traitement
shame honte

space espace
suit convenir
suitable qui convient
supervise superviser
trade press presse professionnelle
training scheme stage de formation
undertake entreprendre, s'occuper
de
vacant situations offres d'emploi
visualiser concepteur publicitaire

Phrases

The public at large le grand public

On behalf of au nom de, pour le compte de

An honours degree diplôme supérieur

The firm is looking up l'entreprise s'améliore, prend bonne
tournure

Explanations and Other Useful Terms

account executive
an account executive is an advertising term; it
means a person in an advertising agency who looks
after the affairs of one particular firm or client
(called an **account**).

brochures and leaflets
a leaflet is a single sheet of paper, or a few sheets
loosely bound together, usually advertising something or giving information. A brochure is more
elaborate than a leaflet, it is a printed booklet
giving information.

layout
in the last unit we had the *layout of machines* in a
factory. As used here it means the arrangement of
material in an advertisement, i.e. where the photograph, or drawing, is put relation to the words or
copy.

salary and wages
wages are paid for the labour or service of a workman
or a servant. A salary is a payment made as compensation for non-manual or non-mechanical work.

short list	when offering a new job most firms select from the total number of applicants a small number who they think have the best qualifications on paper. Their names are put on a short list and they are subsequently interviewed.
typographer	as applied to advertising it means a person who chooses the letters or type to make the printing in an advertisement look attractive.
visualiser	someone whose job it is to invent or visualise an idea for a good advertisement.

Pronunciation

1 — 1 - (- -) artist, certain, a contact, copy, copywriter, editor, go-ahead, interest, leaflet, newspaper, several, supervise, television, ultimate, vacant

- 2 (-) account, appoint, appropriate, assistant, behalf, belong, campaign, convince, correct, design, display, entail, exactly, executive, experience, explain, however, imagine, involve, mistake, persuade, professional, responsible, select, support, tomorrow, typographer

- - 3 (- -) opportunity

2 — [æ]   ad, fact, plan, handle, salary
    [ə:]   firm, girl, word, work, world, certain, insert, prefer
    [i:]   magazine, media, relieve, detail, brief
    [a:]   car, staff, far, branch, behalf, example, department
    [ɔ:]   board, support, hoarding, exhausted, enormous
    [ai]   kind, right, find, decide, design, invite, advertise, supervise
    [ei]   sale, place, space, able, liaise, agency, display, campaign, explain, entail, detail, vacant

3 — Compare : an 'ad, an 'ad-man, to 'advertise, an ad'vertisement
to 'train, 'training, a trai'nee
to ap'ply, an 'applicant
to plan [plæn], a plant [pla:nt]
to write [rait], written ['ritn]
a product ['prɔdʌkt], produce ['prɔdju:s], to produce [prə'dju:s]

— 103 —

4 — Note : ache [eik], aching ['eikiŋ], brochure ['broʃjuə], client [klaiənt], catalogue ['kætəlɔg], column ['kɔləm], coordinate [kou-'ɔ:dineit], expert ['ekspə:t], liaise [li'eiz], magazine [mægə'zi:n], qualification [‚kwɔlifi'keiʃən], scheme [ski:m], suit [sju:t], suitable ['sju:təbl]

2. SUMMARY

As we saw in the Factory Extension Meeting, Harper & Grant is a growing company. A growing firm needs to advertise . Up till now, the Sales Manager, John Martin, has dealt with the advertising. He employs an *Advertising Agency* to design the advertisements and place, or put, them in certain newspapers or magazines. An Advertising Agency is an 5 organisation which undertakes to handle advertising on behalf of the advertiser. It employs artists, copywriters, etc., who are specialists in the field. Its staff are also specialists in buying space in newspapers, or time on radio and television. They are usually able, therefore, to do a far more professional job than the advertising manager who belongs to a firm and 10 who therefore has a limited experience. However, many firms now employ an advertising manager as well to liaise with the agency.

At Harper & Grant, John Martin is now too busy on the sales side to be able to handle the work involved. He needs an expert to supervise an advertising campaign, check proofs, make sure that the agency use the *media* 15 which best suit the company's interests. The media (singular: *medium*) are the various means by which one may advertise, for example in newspapers, magazines, on television, and on *hoardings*, large display boards, etc.

John Martin also cannot cope with the increasing public relations work. This side of the business involves contacts with the public at large through 20 newspapers, magazines and television, giving editors correct information about the company and its products when such information is needed.

Mr. Grant has agreed that they should appoint a new advertising manager, who will relieve John Martin of this work but still be ultimately responsible to him for advertising. In fact, the new department will be a 25 branch of his Sales Department. However, Mr. Grant is very interested in public relations and insists that the new 'ad man' will be responsible to him for this side of the job.

An advertisement has been inserted, put in, in the 'situations vacant' column of several appropriate newspapers, giving details of the new 30 appointment and inviting applications for the job.

John Martin has the work of going through the written applications and deciding which of the applicants have the right qualifications for the post. He will then interview the selected applicants from his short list and send his candidate, or candidates, to Mr. Grant for the final interview. 35

PART 2 : CONVERSATION AND DOCUMENTS

1. CONVERSATION

(Recorded Text)

(In John Martin's office)

JOHN MARTIN	**O.K. Sally. I'm ready to see the applicants for the new job. Let's have the first one in. Who is it?**	
SALLY	**It's a Mr. Windsmore.**	
JOHN	**Ask him to come in, will you?**	
SALLY	**Mr. Windsmore.**	5
JOHN	**Ah, how do you do, Mr. Windsmore.**	
WINDSMORE	**How do you do.**	
JOHN	**Do sit down.**	
WINDSMORE	**Thank you.**	
JOHN	**Now, let me explain the job. We plan to increase our advertising quite considerably. At the present moment a firm of advertising agents handles our account, but we haven't been too pleased with results lately and we may give our account to another agency.**	10
WINDSMORE	**What would my work entail?**	15
JOHN	**You'd be responsible to me for all advertising and to Mr. Grant for public relations. You would brief the agency, whoever it is, on the kind of advertising campaign we want. You would also be responsible for getting our leaflets, brochures and catalogues designed.**	20
WINDSMORE	**I presume you advertise in the national Press as well as the trade Press?**	
JOHN	**Yes, we do.**	

WINDSMORE	Have you thought about advertising on television?
JOHN	We don't think it's a suitable medium for us. And it's 25 much too expensive.
WINDSMORE	I can just imagine a scene with a typist sitting on an old-fashioned typing chair, her back aching, exhausted . . . then we show her in one of your chairs, her back properly supported, feeling full of energy, typing twice as 30 quickly. . . .
JOHN	Before you get carried away with your little scene, Mr. Windsmore, I regret to have to tell you again that we are not planning to go into television.

WINDSMORE: 'I can just imagine a scene with a typist sitting on an old-fashioned typing chair, her back aching, exhausted . . .'

WINDSMORE	That's a shame! I've been doing a lot of television work 35 lately and it interests me enormously.
JOHN	Then I really don't think that this is quite the right job for you here, Mr. Windsmore. . . .

(*Mr. Windsmore has gone*)

JOHN	Sally, who's next?

SALLY	There are two more. The rest are coming tomorrow. Er— one is a woman.	40
JOHN	What! Really? There weren't any women applicants.	
SALLY	Yes. It's J. P. Harvey. The 'J' is for Joanna.	
JOHN	Miss or Mrs.?	
SALLY	Miss.	45
JOHN	Where's her letter of application? I can't find it. Has she had any experience? I wonder why I picked her out for an interview?	
SALLY	Here's her letter.	
JOHN	Thanks. Yes, she signs the letter J. P. Harvey. H'm, let's see. Did I make a mistake? I can't think a woman would be likely to have the right qualifications....	50
SALLY	Why not, Mr. Martin? The letter says that she's been an account executive for a year....	
JOHN	Oh, yes. Well, well! What's she like, Sally?	55
SALLY	I'll show her in, Mr. Martin, and then you can decide.	

(*The interview has started*)

JOHN	How did you begin in advertising, Miss Harvey?	
JOANNA HARVEY	I joined a training scheme run by the Palmer & Vincent Agency and stayed with them for a year.	60
JOHN	That was before you moved to your present agency?	
JOANNA	That's right. And I've worked with them for the past three years. Last year I became an account executive.	
JOHN	What exactly is your work at the moment?	
JOANNA	Well, I handle quite a number of accounts. I plan the advertising campaign, co-ordinate the work of the visualiser, the copywriter, artists and typographers. I discuss the layout with the clients, check proofs and, sometimes, have to do the work of the specialists when there's a crisis, as there usually is!	65 70
JOHN	You seem to have had the right kind of experience. I think you'd do the work well, but ... well, all the executives are men and—er—	
JOANNA	And I always thought industry was so go-ahead and modern!	75
JOHN	I don't mind telling you you're quite high on my list, but ...	

JOANNA	But you'd prefer a man?
JOHN	No. I was going to say . . . If only I can convince our Managing Director. I'll do my best.

80

(Later)

PETER WILES	I don't believe it, John! You mean the old man's really appointed the girl? Fantastic! How did you manage to persuade him?
JOHN	I didn't, Peter. She persuaded him herself. He saw the two best candidates, and the girl got the job.

85

PETER	Splendid! I can't wait to meet her. I say, this firm is looking up!

PRACTICE SENTENCES

Say the practice sentences on the record :

i I'm ready to see the applicants.

ii Let's have the first one in.

iii Ask him to come in, will you.

iv Do sit down.

v Let me explain the job.

vi We plan to increase our advertising.

vii What would my work entail ?

viii I've worked with my present firm for three years.

iiix Last year I became an account executive.

x What exactly is your work at the moment ?

2. ADVERTISEMENTS

Here is the advertisement which John Martin inserted in several newspapers:

ADVERTISING AND PUBLIC RELATIONS MANAGER required by expanding company manufacturing office furniture and equipment. Applicants should have agency experience and be able to co-ordinate all aspects of publicity, from design to production. Write giving details of previous experience, salary, etc., to Box No. 9081.

Joanna Harvey read the advertisement and wrote a letter applying for the job. This is her letter of application.

```
                                    16 Oakleaf Avenue,
                                    London, N.W.22.


                                    2nd October, 197..

Dear Sirs,
        I should like to apply for the position of Advertising and
Public Relations Manager which you advertised this morning.   I am
27 years old and I graduated from Leeds University with an honours
degree in English.   Before going to University, I spent a year in
Spain studying Spanish.   I taught for six months at a language
school in Madrid.

        I spent one year as a trainee in advertising with the
Palmer & Vincent Agency.

        For the past three years I have been with the agency
Thrust, William & Knox.   I was an assistant account executive for
the first two years and have been an account executive for the
past year.   My present salary is £2,000 a year.

        I should very much like the opportunity to work in industry
and I hope you will feel able to give me an interview.

                                    Yours faithfully,

                                    J. P. Harvey

                                    J. P. HARVEY.
```

PART 3 : NOTES AND PRACTICE

1. RAPPEL GRAMMATICAL

Summary :

8. **Staff,** nom singulier de sens collectif est suivi d'un verbe au pluriel.

9. Variante possible : **much more professional.**

16. Ne pas confondre le superlatif de **good,** qui est **the best,** avec le superlatif de **well,** qui est **best** :

Our furniture is the best on the market	Notre mobilier est le meilleur qui soit sur le marché
Which of these three copies do you like best ?	Lequel de ces trois textes préférez-vous ?

22. **Information** est singulier de forme et d'accord, mais collectif de sens.

Un renseignement se dit : **a piece of information.** De même, notons :

advice, *des conseils,* **a piece of advice,** *un conseil*
news, *des nouvelles,* **a piece of news,** *une nouvelle*

News, terminé par -s, s'accorde au singulier :

What's the news ?	Quelles sont les nouvelles ?

Notons au passage que **means** s'emploie au singulier et au pluriel ; **wages** est pluriel au sens propre en anglais :

His wages are very low	Son salaire est très bas

23. **Should** combine ici la nuance de devoir (ce qui s'impose) et l'idée de futur.

36. L'interrogatif which est mis pour une personne lorsqu'il y a choix :

Which of the two brothers is the Chairman of the Board ?	Lequel des deux frères est président du conseil d'administration ?

Conversation :

2. Comparons les interrogatifs. Ci-dessus, **which** interroge sur un *choix.* **Who** ici interroge sur l'*identité* (c'est M. Windsmore). Lorsqu'on emploie **what** pour les personnes, c'est que l'on cherche à se renseigner sur la fonction, la profession :

What is that Mr. Windsmore ?	Qu'est-ce que fait ce M. Windsmore ?
I think he is an advertising agent	Je crois qu'il est agent de publicité

18. Le suffixe **-ever** peut s'ajouter à certains relatifs et interrogatifs pour leur donner une certaine valeur indéfinie :

> **Whatever happens while I am away, let me know**
>
> Quoi qu'il arrive en mon absence, avisez m'en

19. Attention à l'orthographe de **responsible**, et à la préposition qu'il régit : **for**

19. Get + nom + participe passif = have + nom + participe passif :

> **You must get (have) these folders printed by Monday**
>
> Il faut que vous fassiez tirer ces dépliants d'ici lundi

23. La réponse affirmative ou négative n'est jamais un ' **yes** ' ou ' **no** ' isolés ; on ne répète pas le titre de la personne, sauf dans certains cas précis (**yes, Sir** = oui, mon colonel), mais il faut reprendre le pronom sujet suivi de l'auxiliaire (ou défectif) de la proposition précédente :

> **Elizabeth, can you type this now**
>
> Elizabeth, pouvez-vous taper ceci maintenant ?
>
> **-Yes, I can**
>
> -Oui, Monsieur le Directeur
>
> **Would they refund you ?**
>
> Vous rembourseraient-ils ?
>
> **-No, they wouldn't**
>
> -Non.

30. Attention à la conjonction :

> **It's twice as fast**
>
> C'est deux fois *plus* rapide
>
> **It would be three times as expensive**
>
> Ce serait trois fois *plus* cher

42. (**any women**) et 47 (**any experience**) : Notons qu'on ne rencontre **some** en interrogative que lorsqu'on est sûr que la réponse sera affirmative. Sinon, de même qu'en négative, on rencontre **any** :

> **They haven't had any rise for ages**
>
> Ils n'ont pas eu d'augmentation depuis des siècles
>
> **Are there any welders on the list ?**
>
> Y a-t-il des soudeurs sur la liste ?
>
> **We haven't seen anyone**
>
> Nous n'avons vu personne

53. (**she's been... for a year**) et 62 (**I've worked... for three years**) :

L'action commencée dans le passé et qui dure dans le présent s'exprime au *present perfect*. Si le complément de temps exprime une durée (depuis le début de l'action), il est introduit par **for** ; s'il exprime le point de départ de l'action, il est introduit par **since** :

> **He's been working in the firm since 1969**
>
> Il travaille dans la maison depuis 1969

I've seen him working at his report for a whole week	Je le vois travailler à son rapport depuis une bonne semaine
He's been doing a lot of television work lately	Il fait beaucoup de télévision depuis quelque temps

On rencontrera d'autres manières d'introduire le complément de temps :

They've doubled their output over the last two years	Ils ont doublé leur production au cours des deux dernières années
They've been losing their markets abroad for the last ten years	Ils perdent leurs marchés à l'étranger depuis une dizaine d'années

Nous aurons l'occasion de pratiquer ces constructions dans les exercices des prochaines unités.

70. Notons la place de **usually** avec le verbe **be** dans la phrase elliptique et comparons :

There is usually a peak before the summer holidays	Il y a généralement une période de pointe avant les grandes vacances

2. EXERCISES

EXERCISE 1. — Answer negatively as follows :

Is his financial position sound ? — No, I'm afraid it isn't.

1. Have you received a reply from the insurance company ?   2. Would he be a reliable cashier ?   3. Can they claim compensation ?   4. Did they make any profit ?   5. Does the Managing Director know about it ?   6. Had the advertisement been correctly worded ?   7. Have you read the proofs ?   8. Would the article suit you ?   9. Does the Board meet regularly ? 10. Will training be efficient ?

EXERCISE 2. — Turn into the interrogative :

1. Some of the goods have arrived this morning.   2. There's some flimsy in the bottom drawer.   3. There was some packing canvas in the paint store.   4. They have some skilled welders.   5. He raised some objections to my proposal.   6. He has seen some of his clients.   7. He will interview some of the applicants.   8. The production manager took some rest after that.

EXERCISE 3. — *Use* **for** *or* **since** *with the complement between brackets* :

1. He has worked with them (1968).   2. The Board has been sitting (3 hours).   2. We have been doing business with them (ten years).   4. The post has been vacant (January).   5. The company has made losses (2 years).   6. They've been exporting on a large scale (ten years).   7. Profits have doubled (the last two years).   8. He's been in the Manager's office (2 p.m.).   9. John has been in Abraca (September 19th).   10. We've placed advertisements in the trade Press (a month).   11. He's been the Chairman of the Board (his brother retired).   12. She's been his secretary (29 years).

EXERCISE 4. — *Can you answer these questions about advertising* ?

1. Who usually looks after advertising in a firm ?   2. What organisation would he (or she) deal with if the firm did a lot of advertising ?   3. In this organisation, what is the name of the person he would deal with ?   4. Also in this organisation, who looks after : (a) writing the words of an advertisement ?   (b) the choice of lettering or type ?   5. What will a printer ask you to check before he starts to print the material in large numbers ?

EXERCISE 5. — *Here are questions about interviews* :

1. What is someone called who applies for a job ?   2. An employer may select a small group of people from the total number who want the job he is offering. What is this group of names called ?   3. If you answer an advertisement for a job, what sort of letter do you write ?

EXERCISE 6. — *Translate into English* :

1. Je suis prêt à rencontrer les candidats.   2. Faisons entrer le premier. 3. Voulez-vous lui demandez d'entrer.   4. Veuillez vous asseoir.   5. Permettez-moi de vous expliquer le travail.   6. Nous envisageons d'augmenter notre publicité.   7. Qu'est-ce qu'impliquerait mon travail ?   8. Je travaille dans mon entreprise actuelle depuis trois ans.   9. L'an dernier, je suis devenu chef de publicité.   10. Quel est exactement votre travail à l'heure actuelle ?   11. Il faut que vous fassiez reproduire ces documents d'ici 17 heures.   12. Il est responsable des relations publiques.   13. Lequel d'entre vous est Mr. Fielding ?   14. Ecrire en indiquant le curriculum vitae. 15. J'ai l'honneur de poser ma candidature pour le poste de directeur des ventes.   16. Il ne semble pas avoir l'expérience requise.   17. Il ne croit pas qu'une femme aurait les qualifications requises.   18. Nous envisageons de passer une annonce dans les offres d'emploi.   19. Vous dépendriez de moi pour la publicité.   20. Le Directeur insiste pour que le nouveau chef de publicité dépende de lui.

UNIT 7

COMPLAINT FROM AN ANGRY CUSTOMER

PART 1 : INTRODUCTION

1. WORD STUDY

Vocabulary

angry en colère, mécontent
apologise s'excuser
appreciate comprendre
assuming en supposant que
bet parier
bang about cogner
call back rappeler (*téléphone*)
cardboard carton
carelessly sans soin
components éléments, pièces
complaint plainte, réclamation
condition état
crate caisse à claire-voie, emballer dans une caisse...
cupboard armoire de bureau
damaged endommagé
deal with s'occuper de
disappointed déçu
drag tirer
faulty défectueux
fit apte, conforme, bon
fit into loger, se loger

Goods Inwards arrivée des marchandises
handle manier
handling manutention
head chef
head office siège social
hint laisser entendre
imply sous-entendre
knock about se cogner
knocked down démonté, à monter
leave partir, quitter
legible lisible
maintain maintenir, garder
mind trouver à redire, objecter
mishandling faute de manutention
overseas à l'étranger
place (an order with) passer commande (à)

printed imprimé
record archive
representative représentant

respray faire une nouvelle pulvérisation de peinture
right away sur le champ, immédiatement
salesman représentant
scratch égratignure, éraflure ; érafler
sheet bordereau
sound (*ici*) sembler
solve résoudre
spray pulvériser (*peinture*) ; peindre au pistolet

standard niveau, degré
straight away immédiatement
supervisor surveillant, inspecteur
tear déchirer
tightly de manière serrée
trust faire, avoir confiance
waste gaspillage, perte
warning notice, avis, avertissement
wrap emballer, envelopper
wrapping emballage

Phrases

Use No Hooks	ne pas utiliser de crochets
Handle With Care	fragile
This Side Up	haut - bas
They're in the wrong	ils sont en tort
We'll put the matter right	nous arrangerons cela
For your sake	dans votre intérêt
All the same	tout de même
At our expense	à nos frais

Explanations and Other Useful Terms

be on the road
a rep., or salesman, is on the road when he is out on the job of selling, i.e. travelling in order to sell.

built up
description of goods which are sent assembled.

container
in this case, a large framework or structure which completely encloses the goods to be transported. It can be loaded on an articulated lorry, a railway truck or on board ship.

hook
here, a steel hook with a wooden handle which dock-workers, etc... often use in handling heavy packages.

knocked down (K.D.) description of goods which are sent unassembled and packed flat for assembly on site following delivery.

to load	to put goods into a container, or into a vehicle for transfer from one place to another. **to unload** : to take them out. **Loaders** and **unloaders** are the men who do the putting in and taking out.
order number	each order is given a number to make it easy to identify.
respray	to spray is to disperse liquid in small drops. Here it refers to paint applied by means of a spraying machine. To respray means to paint again.
the stuff	a slang term used a great deal and meaning the ' things ', the ' material ', ' the goods ', etc.

Pronunciation

1 — 1 - (- -) angry, cabinet, customer, decency, legible, mystery, offer, personally, regular, satisfied

   - 2 (- -) according, apparently, appreciate, apologise, assembly, assuming, complete, component, consider, delivery, imagine, immediately, insist, importance, regret, report, suggest, suppose

   - - 3 (- -) manufacture, manufacturer, manufacturing, manufactory ; incomplete ; represent, representative

2 — [-iz]   *he* places, despatches, catches, fetches, damages
         plural : places, scratches, boxes, taxes

3 — [ŋ]   bang, ring, bring, wrong, being, angry, packing
   [æ]   pack, wrap, thanks, scratch, matter, happen, handle, standard, cabinet
   [e]   less, bet, sent, check, head, says, said, legible, regular, special
   [u]   goods, look, hook [u:] you, prove, group
   [ou]   go, load, home, though, road, phone, most, *o*verseas, comp*o*nents
   [ei]   sake, rail, crate, str*ai*ght, aw*ay*, complaint, m*ai*ntain
   [ɛə]   their, care, careful, where, rare, there, *a*rea
   [iə]   hear, here, near, clear, easier, appear, mat*e*rial, sinc*e*rely
   [aiə]   fire, wire, buyer, hire, require, society

4 — Compare : a rep [rep], a representative [ˌrepriˈzentətiv]
   a record [ˌrekɔ:d], to record [riˈkɔ:d]
   a cupboard [ˈkʌbəd], cardboard [ˈka:dbɔ:d]

5 — Note : comparison [kəm'pærisən], discover [dis'kʌvə], faulty ['fɔːlti],
future ['fjuːtʃə], mishandling [ˌmis'hændliŋ], properly ['prɔpəli],
quality ['kwɔliti], respray ['riː'sprei], subsequently ['sʌbsikwəntli],
supervisor ['sjuːpəvaizə], transit ['trænzit].

2. SUMMARY

John Martin, head of the Sales Department, has an angry customer to deal
with. The head office of a large group of companies ordered twelve desks,
and, according to their buyer, Mr. Brown, most of them arrived in a
damaged condition. Mr. Brown knows John Martin and insists on speaking to him personally. He says that most of the desks have got deep 5
scratches on the sides. He implies that they were not inspected properly
before being despatched. He hints that future orders will be placed with
another manufacturer. John immediately gets on the internal phone to the
Works Manager to ask him to check the inspection records.

All goods leaving the factory are *inspected*, that is, examined carefully 10
to make sure that the right standard of quality is maintained, and that no
faulty, damaged or incomplete items go out of the factory. Most firms
keep inspection records of their products. The inspector signs an inspection sheet with the details of the goods he has seen and passed as being fit
for sale. The goods then go to the packing and despatch department. 15
Here the components, or parts, of desks, filing cabinets and cupboards
are packed. They are then either packed in crates or loaded into containers. Home deliveries or deliveries sent by container normally require
much less packing than goods which have to be sent overseas. The goods
are then despatched to the buyer. Boxes and crates carrying goods usually 20
show printed warnings such as: USE NO HOOKS, HANDLE WITH CARE or
THIS SIDE UP. Sometimes the firm's salesman for the area where the buyer
is situated calls when the goods are delivered to supervise assembly;
in other words, see that the components are put together correctly.

When John Martin has checked that the goods left the factory properly 25
inspected and correctly packed he asks Mr. Shuttleworth, his sales
representative in the area, to pay Mr. Brown a visit and see if he can
solve the mystery of the scratched desks. Mr. Shuttleworth subsequently
discovers that the goods have been handled badly by the men who
unloaded the goods from the containers. Even though the parts were 30

wrapped in strong cardboard, it was not strong enough to protect them, as hooks were used for unloading.

In the end, even though Harper & Grant are not in the wrong, they agree to respray the desks. They consider that the time and money involved is small in comparison with the importance of keeping a customer satisfied.

PART 2 : CONVERSATION AND DOCUMENTS

1. CONVERSATION

(Recorded Text)

(John Martin is in the middle of a telephone call from Bruddersfield)

JOHN MARTIN	... **I'm very sorry to hear this, Mr. Brown. ... Yes, of course. ... Yes, if it's our fault we'll certainly put the matter right. Goodbye. Sally! Get me the order number for twelve desks sent on Monday to the Bruddersfield Building Society, will you, while I get through to Ted Fielding. We've got trouble.** 5
TED FIELDING	**Hello.**
JOHN	**Hello, Ted. John here.**
SALLY	**Here are the details, Mr. Martin.**
JOHN	**Thank you, Sally. Ted, can you check the inspection re-** 10 **cords for an order for twelve desks which were sent to Bruddersfield—er—the order number was D67/8–9053.**
TED	**Yes.**
JOHN	**Find out if they were properly checked before despatch, assuming the signature on the inspection sheet is legible.** 15 **You might see if anyone knows how they were packed. The customer's just made a strong complaint. He says the sides of nearly every desk are badly scratched.**
TED	**I can't understand how that could have happened. Was our rep. called in to supervise the assembly ?** 20
JOHN	**Apparently not. I'm just going to get through to him now. Anyway, let me know fast, Ted, will you?**
TED	**I'll call you back.**
JOHN	**Sally, Bruddersfield's in Area 4, I think. Get me Shuttleworth!** 25

SALLY	**Mr. Shuttleworth, the rep? But it's 9.45. Surely he'll be on the road by now.**
JOHN	**Not if I know Shuttleworth. I'll bet he's still at home writing reports.** (*The telephone rings.*) **All right, Sally, it's the internal phone. I'll take it. Hello. Ah, Ted.** 30
TED	**John, I've got the inspection record here. The twelve desks were checked by Robinson and I've just had a word with him. He remembers the order and he says they left here in perfect condition.**
JOHN	**What about the packing?** 35
TED	**They went off by container, so we didn't crate them. You know, we have standard boxes now. All our regular parts fit into them exactly. The packers assure me they were packed tightly into the container—one of these special containers for transport by rail—so they wouldn't get 40 banged about. It sounds to me like mishandling during unloading.**

SHUTTLEWORTH: 'I was just leaving for York, Mr. Martin.'

JOHN	Well, thanks, Ted. It doesn't sound like our fault. I'll get Shuttleworth to see if he can find out what happened when the goods arrived. Sally, have you got through to Shuttleworth yet?	45
SALLY	The number's ringing now. Hello. Oh, good morning, Mr. Shuttleworth. Mr. Martin would like to speak to you.	
JOHN	Hello. Ah, I suppose I'm lucky to find you in at this time.	
SHUTTLEWORTH	Er—yes—I was just leaving for York, Mr. Martin.	50
JOHN	I've got something I'd like you to deal with right away if you can. . . .	

(*Later: Mr. Shuttleworth meets the angry customer*)

MR. BROWN	Here you are, Mr. Shuttleworth. Look at this desk, and this one. I think nine desks out of the twelve are scratched like this. I'm very disappointed in your firm.	55
SHUTTLEWORTH	I'm sorry you feel like that, Mr. Brown. Complaints of this sort are very rare indeed.	
BROWN	I should hope so, for your sake. I trust you will get these desks replaced by new ones straight away. Look at this deep scratch here.	60
SHUTTLEWORTH	Oh yes. Yes, they have been knocked about. Do you mind if I check with your Goods Inwards? They might still have the packing material. It's worth having a look at, don't you think?	
BROWN	I suppose you can if you want to, but you'll find it's a waste of time. I'm quite convinced that the goods were not properly inspected at your factory, or else they were carelessly packed.	65
SHUTTLEWORTH	All the same, I'd like to have a look if you don't mind.	
BROWN	Very well. My secretary will take you to the building supervisor.	70
SHUTTLEWORTH	Thank you very much, Mr. Brown.	

(*Later that day, Mr. Shuttleworth telephones John Martin*)

SHUTTLEWORTH	Hello, Mr. Martin. Shuttleworth here. I've discovered what happened to those desks when they arrived.	
JOHN	Good.	75
SHUTTLEWORTH	I had a look at the packing, and the top pieces of cardboard of several of the components were badly torn. I spoke to the men who unloaded the container. They used hooks to drag each package out on to the loading bank.	

Just imagine. They said they never saw the USE NO HOOKS 80
sign. But it was on the wrappings, because I saw that
too.

JOHN   What did their boss say?

SHUTTLEWORTH He told me that his men like using hooks because it
makes unloading much easier. They don't have to lift the 85
stuff by hand. It's their fault all right. I proved it!

JOHN   Well done. I hope that man Brown had the decency to
apologise.

SHUTTLEWORTH Yes, he did.

JOHN	Well, now we've proved it wasn't our mistake we'd better 90
	offer to respray the desks.
SHUTTLEWORTH	I was just going to suggest that, Mr. Martin. He's a good
	customer of ours and ... I rather think, there may be
	quite a big order on the way. ...

PRACTICE SENTENCES

Say the practice sentences on the record :

   i I'm very sorry to hear this.

  ii If it's our fault, we'll certainly put the matter right.

 iii The customer's just made a strong complaint.

 iv Find out if they were properly checked before despatch.

   v I can't understand how that could have happened.

 vi The twelve desks were checked by Robinson.

 vii They left here in perfect condition.

viii They went off by container, so we didn't crate them.

---

2. REPLYING TO A COMPLAINT

Here is John Martin's letter replying to Mr. Brown's complaint about the damaged desks.

Great West Road
London W25
Telephone 01-567 1112
Telex 80153
Telegrams Harp LDN

Directors:
Ambrose Harper *(Chairman)*
Hector Grant *(Managing)*
William Buckhurst FCA *(Secretary)*
Margaret Wiles

Harper and Grant Limited

16th November, 197..

Dear Mr. Brown,

We regret to hear that the twelve desks you ordered from us have been badly scratched.

We have checked our records here and find that the components left our factory in good condition and were, as usual, carefully packed. We then asked our representative to try and find out whether the desks had been damaged in transit or on arrival. He subsequently discovered that the goods had been unloaded by using hooks, although the packages were clearly marked with a warning against using hooks. We therefore do not feel in any way responsible for the damage.

We appreciate, however, that you do not want to use these damaged desks as they are. If you will return them to us we will have them resprayed at our expense. We can assure you that the scratches will not show and that the desks will, in fact, appear just as good as new.

Yours sincerely,

J. Martin

John Martin
Sales Manager
HARPER & GRANT LTD.

George Brown, Esq.,
The Bruddersfield Building Society,
117 Bunyan Avenue,
Bruddersfield, Yorks.

PART 3 : NOTES AND PRACTICE

1. RAPPEL GRAMMATICAL

Summary :

4. **He insists on speaking** : notons que le sujet de **speak** et celui de **insist** est la même personne. Sinon, on aurait eu la construction suivante :

He insisted on our replacing the damaged articles	Il a insisté pour que nous remplacions les articles endommagés

5. **Most** se construit différemment selon que le nom qui le suit est défini ou non. Comparons :

Most of our employees have been in the firm for years	La plupart de nos employés sont dans la maison depuis des années
Most people disagree about what cash flow represents	La plupart des gens sont en désaccord sur ce qu'est le cash flow

cf. également l. 12 : **most firms**, la plupart des entreprises.

19. Le comparatif d'infériorité marqué par **less** est, comme le comparatif de supériorité, modifié par **much** ou **far** :

The other applicant was far less qualified for the job	L'autre candidat convenait beaucoup moins bien pour l'emploi

Conversation :

16. **Anyone** est employé ici à l'affirmative car en fait John doute fort qu'on retrouve un témoin de l'emballage.

51. Le désir, la volonté s'expriment avec **want** + proposition infinitive à l'indicatif, et **I'd like** + proposition infinitive au conditionnel :

He wants you to come immediately	Il veut que vous veniez tout de suite
I'd like you to do this for me	Je voudrais que vous me fassiez cela
He would have liked us to share the cost of transport	Il aurait voulu que nous partagions les frais de transport

61. **Do you mind if I check** : une autre construction est possible, ainsi :

Would you mind my using your dictating machine ?	Cela vous dérangerait-il que j'utilise votre dictaphone ?
He doesn't mind John's taking a leave in early March	Cela ne le dérange pas que John prenne un congé au début de mars

63. **It's worth having a look at.** N'oublions pas que **to be worth,** *valoir la peine d'être...* est suivi d'un gérondif actif :

Their stand at the Trade Fair is really worth seeing	Leur stand à la foire commerciale vaut la peine d'être vu
This desk isn't really worth repairing, it's much too damaged	Ce bureau ne vaut pas la peine d'être réparé, il est beaucoup trop abîmé

65. La préposition **to** après certains verbes exprimant le désir, l'intention, le goût, etc... est en fait une véritable pro-phrase qui reprend une phrase déjà exprimée :

Would you like to see our new lines ? — I'd love to	Voudriez-vous voir nos nouvelles réalisations ? — Oh oui, bien sûr
Will they build an extension ? — At least they intended to	Vont-ils construire une extension ? — C'était du moins leur intention

Correspondance :

Try and find out whether the desks have been damaged in transit, notons que dans une lettre, **whether** s'emploiera plus volontiers que **if** dans une alternative.

Dans la langue parlée, John aurait dit à Mr. Shuttleworth :

Try and find out if they have been damaged in transit or on arrival

2. EXERCISES

EXERCISE 1. — Change as follows :

a. **it is much less important**	→	**it is much more important**
b. **it is much less easy**	→	**it is much easier**

1. It would be much less expensive.   2. It could be much less fast.   3. They were much less heavy.   4. Isn't it much less convenient ?   5. The desks were much less comfortable.   6. He was much less fit for the job.   7. This one is much less damaged.   8. It would be much less costly.   9. Brown was much less polite.   10. This process is much less accurate.

EXERCISE 2. — Change as follows :

Mr. Robinson checked the packing →
the packing was checked by Mr. Robinson

1. A building society in Yorkshire has ordered fourteen desks.   2. One Mr. Brown wrote a bitter letter of complaint.   3. Jim and Bob unloaded all the crates.   4. Mr. Robinson had marked all the packages himself.

5. Another workman will have to respray the desks.   6. Ted would have checked the records.   7. Your employees may have mishandled the boxes. 8. The men didn't use any hooks.   9. Did your men lift the stuff by hand ? 10. The new secretary has typed all the mail.

EXERCISE 3. — Change as follow :

Do you mind if he (John) uses your tape recorder   →
Do you mind his (John's) using your tape recorder ?

Do you mind if : 1. We park our car in front of the shop.   2. Sally goes to the bank.   3. I check with your Sales Department.   4. They leave the goods in the yard.   5. The men use hooks for unloading.   6. I have a look at your records.   7. My secretary uses one of your typewriters. 8. I have a word with your unloaders.   9. She puts these folders away in the old cupboard.

EXERCISE 4. — Write in full, when possible :

1. She's just phoned.   2. We'd certainly find it difficult.   3. They'd already complained a lot before.   4. He's still in John's office.   5. The firm's salesman was called in.   6. I'd seen their rep before.   7. The number's ringing now.   8. I'd like you to deal with it right away.   9. He'd liked our new lines very much.

EXERCISE 5. — Change as follows :

I must change this £ 10 note   →   **I'll have to change this £ 10 note**

1. I must refund the money.   2. You must ring up our forwarding agent. 3. She must type the invoice in triplicate.   4. He must share the commission with me.   5. This must be taken into account.   6. I think the Chairman must resign.   7. We must promise delivery by April 10th.   8. Heavy vehicles must use the by-pass.   9. She must lay out the brochure more attractively.

EXERCISE 6. — Can you answer the following questions about buying and selling :

1. When a customer wants to buy something from a firm, what does he place ?   2. What is the person called who is responsible for sales in a certain fixed territory ?

EXERCISE 7. — These questions are about the transportation of goods :

1. In what department of a factory are goods prepared for sending to the customer ?   2. What does a firm do to ensure the satisfactory condition of its goods before they leave the factory ?   3. What is the material called which is much thicker than paper, and is used for packing goods ?

EXERCISE 8. — *Here are a few general comprehension questions on the text* :

1. What complaint did the Bruddersfield Building Society make about the desks ? 2. What had caused the damage ? 3. What did John Martin offer to do for his customer ?

EXERCISE 9. — *Translate into English* :

1. Je regrette d'apprendre cela. 2. Si c'est de notre faute, nous arrangerons sûrement cela. 3. Le client vient de faire une vive réclamation. 4. Essayez de savoir s'ils ont été correctement vérifiés avant expédition. 5. Je n'arrive pas à comprendre comment cela aurait pu arriver. 6. Les douze bureaux ont été vérifiés par Robinson. 7. Ils sont partis d'ici en parfait état. 8. Ils sont partis par container si bien que nous ne les avons pas mis dans des caisses à claire-voie. 9. Il a laissé entendre qu'il passerait ses commandes ailleurs désormais. 10. Nous devons nous assurer qu'il ne sort de l'usine aucun article défectueux ou abîmé. 11. Qui a signé le bordereau d'inspection ? 12. S'il prouve que nous sommes en défaut, nous devrons supporter tous les frais. 12. Vous pourriez voir si quelqu'un sait qui a signé ce bordereau. 13. Voudriez-vous visiter l'atelier de montage ? — Cela me plairait énormément. 14. Je parierais qu'il est encore avec ce représentant. 15. Je voudrais bien que vous m'expliquiez comment c'est arrivé. 16. Cela ne vaut pas la peine d'en parler. 17. Les éléments n'ont pas été emballés assez serré. 18. Cela m'a l'air d'être une erreur de manutention. 19. En tous cas, cela n'a pas l'air d'être de notre faute. 20. Tout de même, j'espère qu'il a eu l'élégance de s'excuser.

UNIT 8

AN ACCIDENT IN THE FACTORY

PART 1 : INTRODUCTION

1. WORD STUDY

Vocabulary

action   action en justice, procès
adequate   suffisant, adéquat
allege   alléguer, prétendre
anxious (to)   très désireux (de)
apologetic   qui s'excuse
appoint   nommer, désigner
break (regulations)   enfreindre
carry out   exécuter
chap   type, individu, gars
civil court   tribunal civil
claim   exiger, réclamer
clothing   vêtements
compensation   indemnité, dédommagement, réparation civile
damages   préjudice ; dommages-intérêts
disagree   être en désaccord
drive   campagne
employer   employeur, patron
enforce   mettre en vigueur, appliquer
entitled to   qui a droit à

factory inspector   inspecteur du travail
file   limer
filings   limaille
fit   ajuster
fitter   ajusteur
fitters'shop   atelier d'ajustage
first aid   premiers secours
first aid room   infirmerie
foresee   prévoir
free   gratuit
full pay   salaire complet
full time   à plein-temps
gather (*ici*) comprendre
goggles   lunettes de protection
grind   rectifier
grinding machine   meule à rectifier
grinder   rectifieuse
inadequate   insuffisant, inadéquat
incidentally   par ailleurs, en passant
injured   blessé, accidenté

— 128 —

improve améliorer
industrial accident accident du travail
institute (proceedings) intenter *(procès)* engager *(poursuites)*
lathe tour
legal department contentieux
main principal
maintenance entretien
make up compenser, compléter
milling machine fraiseuse
nasty laid, vilain, sérieux
National Health Service Sécurité Sociale
notice avis
nurse infirmière
obviously évidemment
occur arriver, se produire
plane rabot
prevent empêcher
proceedings poursuite, procès
provisions dispositions, précautions
rate taux, tarif

regarding concernant, au sujet de
repair réparer
safety sécurité
safeguard protection, garantie
send (for) envoyer chercher
shop steward délégué syndical d'entreprise
sick-pay scheme système d'allocation de maladie
statutory prévu par la loi
sue poursuivre en justice
supply fournir
swarf limaille, copeaux, boue de meule
throughout partout
tighten up resserrer, renforcer
tough dur, insensible
trade union syndicat
trained entraîné, préparé, formé
tricky délicat
unfortunate malheureux
warn avertir

Phrases

We're up to our eyes in work nous avons du travail jusqu'au cou
Don't rush things ne précipitez pas les choses
For goodness'sake pour l'amour de Dieu
It's best to keep out of the way mieux vaut ne pas s'en mêler
By the sound of it à ce qu'il semble
He'll make the most of this il exploitera cela à fond
Make out a case justifier une plainte, constituer un dossier

Explanations and Other Useful Terms

chargehand a worker in charge of work in a factory who is responsible to the foreman.

full-time here, one who works permanently at this job only. You can either work full-time, that is, a full working day, or part-time, part of the day only.

machine tool	apart from presses, there are three basic types of machine tool : a lathe, where the piece of metal to be machined revolves and is cut by a single point tool. The tool itself does not revolve. The metal machined away in a lathe is called swarf. A grinding machine or grinder ; in this machine the tool itself revolves. The metal removed is in the form of dust. A milling machine ; this works rather on the principle of a carpenter's plane. Material is removed by a stroking operation. The cutting tool can be fixed or rotating.
steel filings	small particles of steel.
supervisor	in a large department, there may be several foremen under a supervisor, each with a special responsibility.
sue	to bring a legal action against someone, to bring them to court and make an accusation against them.

The Workers' Compensation Act   *la loi sur les accidents du travail.*

Pronunciation

1 — 1 - (- -) accident, always, ambulance, anyway, civil, criminal, injured, injury, interest, national, negligence, organise, politics, service

  - 2 (- -) activity, affair, allege, apart, capacity, department, eliminate, encourage, entirely, event, encourage, experience, inadequate, inevitable, particular, prevent, proceedings, protective, regard, repair, routine, unfortunate

  - - 3 (- -) incidental, incidentally ; engineer, engineering

  - - - 4 (- -) responsibility

2 — ed → [t] asked, checked, hoped, looked, noticed, reduced, worked, packed

     → [dʃ] called, carried, caused, claimed, concerned, happened, killed, organised, phoned, realised, received, repaired, ruled, seemed, stayed, suffered, supposed, supplied, sued, trained, used, warned, wondered, worried

     → [id] added, admitted, expected, estimated, fitted, granted, instructed, inspected, interested, invited, insisted, instituted, prevented, protected, reacted, suggested, visited, waited, wanted

3 — [dʒ]   allege, courage, damages, injured, manage, management
    [ɔ]   not, lot, shop, goggle, obvious, hospital, possible, proper
    [ʌ]   rush, tough, trouble, worry, wonder, government, encourage
    [ɔ:]   court, form, thought, cause, awful, foreman, foresee, fault, warn, precaution
    [ai]   grind, find, mind, remind, eyes, filings
    [ei]   fatal, today, safe, safety, claim, pay, train, aid
    [ju:] sue, use, unit, reduce, human, steward, union
    [u:]   soon, tool, group, prove, rule, routine

4 — Compare : sometimes ['sʌmtaimz] *or* [səm'taimz]
    maintain [mein'tein], maintenance ['meintənəns]
    pro'vide [prə'vaid], pro'vision [prə'viʒən]
    able [eibl], capable ['keipəbl], capacity [kə'pæsiti]
    ne'glect, ne'glectful ; 'negligence, 'negligible

5 — Note : adequate ['ædikwit], basic ['beisik], 'fitters'shop ['fitəz 'ʃɔp], human ['hju:mən], idea [ai'diə], injured ['indʒəd], legal ['li:gəl], measure ['meʒə], routine [ru:'ti:n], safeguard ['seifga:d], serious ['siərjəs], various ['vɛərjəs].

2. SUMMARY

In the best-organised businesses accidents sometimes happen. Today's accident happened to a worker who had been using a grinding machine in the fitters' shop. Harper & Grant Ltd., like most engineering companies, have a fitters' shop where routine maintenance repairs and modifications are done on machine tools. Obviously it is in the management's interest to 5 . do everything they can to prevent accidents, but it is not always possible to foresee people's actions, in other words 'the human factor'. Two people react to the accident in a particular way. The first is Peter Wiles, who hopes that the accident is not *fatal* (a fatal accident is when someone is killed). But he is very concerned in case his company are sued for 10. *negligence*.

    Negligence is lack of proper care, in this case, in the provision of *safety measures*, or safeguards, for the men working the machines. There are various forms of negligence for which a person or firm can be sued for compensation in a civil court action. In the event of an accident, the 15 injured person could sue for damages which he alleges are caused by th negligence of his employer. If it is also found that statutory regulations, *i.e.* the laws regarding health and safety, have been broken the local factory inspector (a government employee) might institute criminal proceedings against the company.   20

If the company can be proved to have been negligent, Reg Arnold, the man who was injured, may be able to claim a lot of money in compensation. *Compensation*, in this case, means money paid to an employee who has had a serious accident which has reduced, or may reduce, his working capacity.   25

The other interested person in the accident is the shop steward, Mr. Jack Green. He thinks the safety precautions are inadequate. A company can be held negligent even if it supplies goggles and other protective clothing and encourages their use. A court could rule that the management should see that its own instructions, or those of the factory inspec- 30 tor, are actually carried out. If Arnold were to make a claim against the company he would almost certainly do it through his trade union. This is the main activity of a union's legal department. Incidentally, he will get money from the State while he is not able to work, and all the care he receives in hospital will be free under the National Health Service.   35

PART 2 : CONVERSATION AND DOCUMENTS

1. CONVERSATION

(Recorded Text)

(*In John Martin's office*)

PETER WILES   **Hello, John. A lot of work going on here, I see.**
JOHN MARTIN   **Yes, we're up to our eyes. We've had a record sales week.**
PETER   **Splendid.**

(*Telephone rings*)

JOHN   **Hello? John Martin here. Yes, Mr. Wiles is here, Ted. What! Oh, no. How frightful! Is the man all right? Yes,   5 come on up.... That was Ted Fielding. He's been phoning for you all over the building. There's been an accident in the fitters' shop.**

— 132 —

PETER	Oh Lord! Why didn't he go straight to the Personnel Manager? That's his business.	10
JOHN	Ian Hampden's away.	
PETER	Oh, I'd forgotten he was going away this week. Then I suppose it is my responsibility. Is it serious?	
JOHN	Ted didn't say. He seemed anxious to come up and see you right away. Ah, here he is . . . come in, Ted.	15
PETER	Good heavens, man, you look awful. It's not a fatal accident, is it?	
TED	No, but it's very nasty.	
JOHN	Sit down, Ted. What happened?	
TED	It's Reg Arnold in the fitters' shop. He didn't put on goggles when he was using the grinding machine and a lot of steel filings flew up. . . . Oh, he looks terrible; one eye's very bad. . . . The foreman called me, and I sent for Robinson, who's trained in first aid. I called you as soon as I could.	20

25 |
PETER	Where is Reg now?	
TED	They've taken him to the first aid room, until the ambulance arrives.	
TED	Ah, there's the ambulance now.	
JOHN	Let's go down.	30
PETER	Not so fast, John.	
JOHN	What do you mean?	
PETER	Don't rush things.	
JOHN	For goodness sake! Surely we can see the poor chap into the ambulance.	35
PETER	I think we'll all stay here. An industrial accident can be a tricky affair. It's best to keep out of the way.	
JOHN	Surely not. It was the man's own fault by the sound of it.	
PETER	My experience is that when there's an accident it's never the man's fault; anyway, in the opinion of our own particular shop steward. You'll see, Jack Green will make the most of this. He'll suggest that the supervisor should have noticed that he wasn't wearing goggles and insisted that he put them on. It could cost the firm a lot of money.	40

(*An hour later, in Peter Wiles's office*)

| JANE | Oh, Mr. Wiles, Jack Green, the shop steward, is waiting to see you. | 45 |

PETER	Ah, the inevitable! All right. Ask him to come in.
JANE	Yes.
PETER	Ah, Jack, I've been expecting you.

(Later that day, John comes into Peter's office)

JOHN	Hello, Peter. You've had a visit from Green, I gather. 50
PETER	Yes. He says the safety precautions are inadequate.
JOHN	Surely they can't be. After all, there's a notice hanging over every machine warning the men to wear goggles.
PETER	Yes, but Green wants a full-time safety manager. I wonder what H.G. will say to that! 55
JOHN	Well, you haven't got to worry about Reg Arnold sueing the company. H.G. asked me to go down to the hospital to see him. I did, and he admitted it was entirely his fault.
PETER	What did he say?
JOHN	He was almost apologetic. As if we were the ones who 60 were suffering! He said he was sorry he'd caused so much trouble.
PETER	H'm. Did anyone else hear him say that, apart from you?
JOHN	Yes. Ted Fielding, who came with me, and two nurses. 65
PETER	Good. Arnold won't be able to make out a case of negligence against us, when Green gets hold of him.
JOHN	I never realised how tough you could be. You haven't given a thought to the poor unfortunate man. All you care about is the politics of the affair. You're as bad as Jack 70 Green.
PETER	Well, someone's got to be tough if you want to stay in business.
JOHN	I couldn't disagree with you more. Where are you going? Golf, I suppose. 75
PETER	Not a bad idea on a lovely afternoon like this. No, as a matter of fact I thought I'd call at the hospital on my way home to see Reg Arnold. But I'll get the Personnel Department to check up first how many weeks at full pay he's entitled to under the company sick-pay scheme. You 80 know, it makes up the difference between National Insurance payments and his normal basic rate. That should cheer him up!

'. . . I thought I'd call at the hospital on my way home to see Reg Arnold.'

PRACTICE SENTENCES

Say the practice sentences on the record :

  i **There's been an accident in the fitters' shop.**

 ii **Is it serious ?**

iii **What happened ?**

 iv **Is the man in the first aid room ?**

  v **There's the ambulance now.**

 vi **It could cost the firm a lot of money.**

vii **He admitted it was entirely his fault.**

viii **He won't be able to make out a case of negligence against us.**

 ix **The safety precautions are inadequate.**

  x **He's entitled to some weeks at full pay under the company sick-pay scheme.**

2. A MEMO ABOUT SAFETY PRECAUTIONS

As a result of today's accident, Mr. Hector Grant, the Managing Director, feels that the safety precautions should be re-examined and, if necessary, tightened up, enforced more strictly. He does not think it necessary to appoint a full-time Safety Manager, but he wants the opinion of his Personnel Manager as to how the safety regulations can be improved.

He also wants all the staff members to be made more aware of possible dangers. Here is Mr. Grant's memo:

```
From:    The Managing Director

                                    date:  23rd September,197.

Subject:   SAFETY PRECAUTIONS

To:      The Personnel Manager


          As a result of the accident which occurred in the fitters'
shop, we are going to have a drive to improve our safety precautions
throughout the Works.   We want, first of all, to eliminate the
sources of accidents:  in other words, we want to see where the
possible danger points are and remove them.   Secondly, we want to
make all employees more aware of danger to themselves if they do not
follow instructions.

    1.    Would you please prepare a report for me on what you
          consider the danger points to be and how our safety
          rules can be improved.   Any suggestions from members
          of staff will be most helpful and will be very
          carefully considered.

    2.    Would you inform all employees, in the strongest terms,
          of the risks they run if they do not follow the safety
          regulations.
```

(Hector Grant)

PART 3 : NOTES AND PRACTICE

1. RAPPEL GRAMMATICAL

Summary :

1. **Best-organised** : n'oublions pas que le comparatif et le superlatif d'adjectifs ou adverbes composés peut se former sur le premier terme du composé :

She isn't the fastest-working of our secretaries	Elle n'est pas la plus vive de nos secrétaires
Jim is a harder-working fellow than Bob	Jim est plus travailleur que Bob

2. Pourquoi avons-nous le *pluperfect* progressif ? Le progressif parce qu'il s'agit d'une action concrète décrite dans son déroulement, et le *pluperfect* parce que l'action durait depuis un certain temps lorsque l'accident s'est produit :

He'd been working with us for over ten years when he resigned	Il travaillait avec nous depuis plus de dix ans quand il a démissionné
How long had he been the Chairman when he retired ?	Depuis combien de temps était-il président lorsqu'il a pris sa retraite ?

10. **In case** est ici suivi de l'indicatif, ce qui est peut-être un peu plus moderne et moins " écrit " que le subjonctif avec **should**, mais aussi parce que Peter est un réaliste qui envisage les poursuites comme une menace réelle. Comparons encore :

Phone him in case he forgets his appointment	Téléphonez-lui de peur qu'il n'oublie son rendez-vous
Warn him again, in case he shouldn't see the notice	Prévenez-le encore, pour le cas où il ne verrait pas la notice

16. Notons cette structure assez fréquente et particulière à l'anglais :

Those are the desks which they claim have been damaged owing to your negligence	Voici les bureaux dont il prétend qu'ils ont été endommagés par suite de votre négligence
This is the tool which he says was found near the lathe	C'est l'outil que, dit-il, on a trouvé près du tour

21. Notons cet infinitif après **prove** :

He was proved to be wrong	On a prouvé son erreur
He was proved to have used a hook when unloading the goods	On a prouvé qu'il avait utilisé un crochet en déchargeant le matériel

29-30. Le verbe **rule** est suivi ici du subjonctif composé (auxiliaire **should**) qui rend compte du but. Notons que l'on a l'indicatif après **see that** ici. Au contraire, à la ligne 31, l'hypothèse d'une éventuelle plainte déposée par l'ouvrier accidenté est évoquée à l'aide du subjonctif de **be** :

If he were to sue them	Si jamais il devait leur intenter un procès

Should permet ainsi d'exprimer un certain nombre de nuances :

— l'*hypothèse* assez peu vraisemblable :

Suppose he shouldn't see the notice	Et si jamais il ne voyait pas l'avis
Should an accident occur... (*dans un rapport écrit*)	Pour le cas où quelqu'accident se produirait

— la crainte : après **for fear that, lest** = de peur que, et **in case** (cf. ci-dessus)

On vient de voir que l'indicatif est fréquent après **in case**. On rencontre toujours le subjonctif après **lest** et **for fear** par contre.

— la *suggestion*, une *proposition*, l'*intention*, un *ordre* :

He insisted that you should always wear your goggles	Il a demandé que vous portiez toujours vos lunettes
He suggested that you should see the applicant yourself	Il a proposé que vous voyiez le candidat vous-même
He was very anxious that you should come personally	Il tenait beaucoup à ce que vous veniez personnellement

— la *surprise*, l'*étonnement*, l'*invraisemblance*, etc... (après un certain nombre de locutions et expressions exprimant ces idées) :

I'm surprised he shouldn't have put on his goggles	Je suis surpris qu'il n'ait pas mis ses lunettes
I don't see why you should complain after all	Je ne vois pas pourquoi vous vous plaignez, après tout
It's incredible that you should be so negligent	C'est incroyable que vous soyez si négligent

Conversation :

31. Le comparatif d'égalité à l'affirmative et à la négative s'exprime à l'aide de **as... as** :

Is it as serious as he said ?	Est-ce aussi grave qu'il a dit ?

La négative s'exprime le plus souvent avec **not so... as** (**not as** est possible toutefois) :

Not so fast, John	Pas si vite, John

34. **For goodness'sake** : le cas possessif est possible avec certains termes abstraits devant **sake**. Lorsque le premier terme se termine par le son [*s*] (quelle que soit son orthographe), et bien que le mot soit singulier, le cas possessif n'est marqué à l'écrit que par l'apostrophe :

For God's sake, for pity's sake, for Peter's sake

42. **The supervisor should have noticed** : ici, **should** rend compte de ce qui aurait dû se passer.

56. **You haven't got to worry** = **you don't have to worry.**

60. Celui qui = **the one who (which)** (attention : jamais **this**). Ceux qui = **those who, the ones who (which)** : (jamais **these**) :

Is this the one you bought ?	Est-ce celui que tu as acheté ?

68. L'exclamative à l'ordre affirmatif ne doit pas être confondue avec l'interrogative :

How old he is !	Qu'il est vieux !
How old is he ?	Quel âge a-t-il ?

69. All you care about : ce que = **what**, tout ce que = **all that** :

I'll tell you what I saw	Je vais vous dire ce que j'ai vu
Repeat all that he said in front of the other witnesses	Répétez tout ce qu'il a dit devant les autres témoins

Documents :

It sert à introduire un adjectif (ou un nom) attribut d'un infinitif ou de toute une proposition ; le pronom **it** sert à annoncer cet infinitif ou cette proposition après des verbes tels que **find, think,** etc. :

I thought it very improbable	Je l'ai jugé très improbable
I found it difficult to explain this to the boss	J'ai eu du mal à expliquer cela au patron
I find it surprising that you can't remember who was there	Je trouve dommage que vous ne puissiez vous rappeler qui était présent

2. EXERCISES

EXERCISE 1. — *Change as follows :*

He is negligent → **He can't be proved to have been negligent**

1. They packed the desks badly. 2. The men used hooks to unload the goods. 3. You paid them the whole amount. 4. He stole the money on my desk. 5. She is responsible for the accident. 6. He forgot to post the letter. 7. He broke the regulations. 8. It is the man's own fault. 9. Smith came into the manager's office. 10. He reported it to the customer.

EXERCISE 2. — *Change as follows* :

He insisted that we should follow the instructions →
He insisted on our following the instructions

He insisted that : 1. I should inform the Personnel Manager. 2. They should improve safety regulations. 3. You should enforce them more strictly. 4. She should repeat what she had heard. 5. I should apologise to the Company Secretary. 6. You should see the nurse about it. 7. We should take the injured man to the first aid room. 8. I should check up with the Chief Accountant. 9. We should do it in the fitters' shop.

EXERCISE 3. — *Change as follows* :

Put on your goggles! → **I suggested that he put on his goggles**

1. Do everything you can. 2. Find out the cause of the breakdown. 3. Go straight to the tool room. 4. Sweep the floor around the lathe. 5. Send for the shop steward. 6. See the foreman about it. 7. Take him to the first aid room. 8. Keep out of the way. 9. Wear protective clothing. 10. Hang notices over the machines.

EXERCISE 4. — *Change as follows* :

Sally types as fast as Elizabeth →
Sally doesn't type so fast as Elizabeth

1. I wrote as many reports as you. 2. That solution is as good as mine. 3. In this firm, marketing is as important as engineering. 4. Import prices rose as rapidly as export prices. 5. I sold as many desks as you did. 6. We made as high profits as they did. 7. They pay their reps as well as we do. 8. They employ as much labour as we do. 9. Our labour force is as adaptable as the American one. 10. French managers are as enterprising as American ones.

EXERCISE 5. — *Turn into the pluperfect* :

1. They don't meet the customer's requirements. 2. Do they seek new outlets? 3. They retain and re-invest their earnings. 4. Did they distribute higher dividends? 5. Do they take this into consideration? 6. Labour relations are very poor. 7. Improved efficiency brings higher benefits to all. 8. He re-sells them at a profit. 9. There are lots of difficulties to overcome. 10. Did he go to the bank?

EXERCISE 6. — *Make questions to which the sentences could be the answers. To help you, we will underline the subject of the question.*

Example : *A grinding machine* is used for cutting or grinding metal.

Question : What is a grinding machine used for?

1. *A plane* is used for smoothing the surface of wood. 2. *The person who represents the interests of a group of workers in a trade union* is called a

shop steward. 3. *A foreman* is in charge of a particular department in a factory. 4. *Accidents in a factory* can be avoided by taking safety precautions. 5. *Tools and machinery* are made and repaired in the Machine Tool Shop. 6. *To sue* means to bring a legal action against someone.

EXERCISE 7. — *Can you answer these vocabulary questions about accidents* :

(*Please answer with complete sentences*)

1. What do we call an accident in which someone is killed ? 2. What is the vehicle called in which the injured person is taken to hospital ? 3. In the case of an industrial accident, what might the employers be accused of by a union, or by an individual ? 4. What do employers do to try to prevent accidents ? 5. If an employee is injured, and it is proved that the firm employing him were to blame, what would he receive ?

EXERCISE 8. — *Improvise a quick oral comment on the following words* :

1. The shop steward. 2. The fitters' shop. 3. Goggles. 4. A record sales week. 5. The foreman. 6. The tool room.

EXERCISE 9. — *Translate into English* :

1. Il y a eu un accident à l'atelier d'ajustage. 2. C'est sérieux ? Que s'est-il passé ? 3. Est-ce que l'ouvrier est à l'infirmerie ? 4. Voici l'ambulance. 5. Cela pourrait coûter cher à l'entreprise. 6. Il a reconnu que c'était entièrement de sa faute. 7. Il ne pourra pas constituer un dossier de négligence contre nous. 8. Les mesures de sécurité sont insuffisantes. 9. Il a drcit à quelques semaines de salaire plein aux termes du système d'allocation maladies. 10. C'est l'homme qu'il dit avoir vu dans le magasin des carburants juste avant que l'incendie n'éclate. 11. Il va de l'intérêt de la direction d'éviter les accidents. 12. La société pourrait être poursuivie en dommages-intérêts devant le tribunal civil. 13. L'inspecteur du travail estime que l'on a enfreint les règles de sécurité prévues par la loi. 14. La direction doit veiller à ce que ses propres instructions soient appliquées avec rigueur. 15. Il mettra l'affaire entre les mains du contentieux de son syndicat. 16. Nous avons du travail par dessus la tête. 17. Je crois que vous feriez mieux de ne pas vous en mêler. 18. Je ne m'étais jamais rendu compte de ce que tu pouvais être insensible ! 19. Je n'ai pas jugé utile de nommer un directeur de la sécurité à plein-temps. 20. Nous allons faire une campagne pour améliorer la sécurité dans tous les points de l'entreprise.

UNIT 9

PRODUCTIVITY – A WORK STUDY SURVEY

PART 1 : INTRODUCTION

1. WORD STUDY

Vocabulary

apply s'appliquer
advise conseiller
amazed stupéfait
area secteur
benefits avantages
bonus prime
check vérifier, examiner
consultant organisateur-conseil, ingénieur-conseil
corporate planning *planification concertée* (cf. note p. 144)
critical path analysis (*recherche opérationnelle*) méthode du chemin critique
data données, informations
decrease diminuer, réduire
delay retard ; retarder
diary agenda
dislike détester, ne pas aimer
efficient ⎫
effective ⎬ efficace
efficiency rendement

engage faire appel à
engagement rendez-vous
executive cadre
expenditure frais
face affronter, envisager
fair honnête
file dossier
final souverain, sans appel
fee honoraires
group rates rémunération d'équipes de travail avec prime
hardly à peine, difficilement
implication portée
intend avoir l'intention
investigator chercheur, enquêteur
invoice facture
involve entraîner, impliquer
look forward to se faire un plaisir de
maximise améliorer au maximum, maximiser
operational research recherche opérationnelle

operator ouvrier
O & M (**Organisation and Methods**)
   O.S.T. (Organisation Scientifique du Travail)
paperwork écritures
piece rates paiement à la tâche
present offrir
previous antérieur, préalable
prize prix, récompense
put forward proposer, présenter
rate cadence, vitesse ; taux
refer (to) se référer
sample échantillon
   a sample study étude témoin

set about se mettre à, commencer
share partager
sort trier
spur éperon, stimulant
step up accélérer, augmenter
streamline rénover, remanier
survey étude d'ensemble
therefore donc, par conséquent
time chronométrer
vital essentiel, primordial
with a view to en vue de
work study étude de postes
wasteful en pure perte
works usine

Phrases

What on earth has happened ?   mais que s'est-il donc passé ?
She's had a hand in it   elle y est pour quelque chose
It was not to hand   il n'était pas à portée de la main
I hadn't bargained for that   je ne m'attendais pas à cela

Explanations and Other Useful Terms

bonus scheme — a plan for giving extra money to workers in certain circumstances. In this case, they will receive a bonus if their productivity rises.

consultants — professionnal business experts who, for a fee, advise clients on aspects of their business. In this case the firm are specialists in Organisation and Methods.

critical path analysis — method of planning the undertaking of a complex project in a logical way, by analysing the project into its component parts, and recording them on a diagram which is then used for planning and controlling the inter-connected activities which carry the project to completion.

incentive payments scheme — a bonus plan. An incentive is offered to encourage employees to work harder, and more efficiently.

Management by Objectives (MbO) and Corporate Planning	In **Management by Objectives**, each manager has an objective, spelt out and agreed with his boss. After a certain period, say three months, he and his boss will get together and review his performance, identify obstacles, etc... and set a new objective. Objectives must be in quantitative terms wherever possible.
	MbO works from the bottom up. **Corporate Planning** starts from the other end, i.e. from the objectives of the firm itself, and from there works down to the jobs of individuals.
operator	here, another word for a worker, particularly someone who operates a machine.
pay piece rates	to pay a workman according to the work done, not by the time taken to do it.
rationalisation	simplification ; the organisation of a business on logical lines, avoiding unnecessary work, actions or expenditure.
sample study	a sample is a specimen, a part of something which shows what the whole is like.
standardise	bring to a uniform size, shape or quality, according to fixed standards.
streamline	colloquial term meaning cut out, or get rid of, unnecessary action.
work study	the detailed study of manual, or semi-manual, work cycles. Through analysis, non-essential work can be eliminated and operations carried out with maximum efficiency. Sometimes called **time and motion study**.
	time study : the detailed study of the time taken to complete a specific work cycle. Data obtained is analysed to determine the time required to do the job at a standard level of work performance.

Pronunciation

1 — 1 - (- -) bargain, benefit, corporate, demonstrate, gentlemen, listen, manual, operator, output, specialist, study, suddenly

- 2 (- -) allow, amazed, attempt, become, begin, competitive, consultant, delay, efficiency, engage, executive, improve, incentive, include, intend, investigate, involve, objective, observe, particular, refer, selected, suggest, technique

- - 3 (-) introduce, satisfactory, conversation

2 — '-ic(ally) : economic, technically, systematically
-'ivity, -'ility : activity, productivity, responsibility

3 — [ʃ]   efficient, special, sure   [ʒ] decision, measure, usual
  [s]   research, advice, price   [z] result, observe, advise, prize
  [ə:] work, firm, earth, spur, earth, first, world, person, survey, service
  [i]   office, study, efficiency, incentive, engage, productivity
  [i:] keen, piece, need, scheme, field, routine, technique, machine, previous
  [ai] type, find, private, decide, outside, analyse
  [a:] sample, answer, aren't, last, path, example
  [ɔi] boy, point, join, invoice

4 — Compare : tech'nique, 'technical ; 'system, ˌsyste'matically
  at 'present, to pre'sent, ˌrepre'sent
  'study ['stʌdi], a student ['stju:dənt]
  to analyse ['ænəlaiz], an analysis [ə'nælisis]

5 — Note : bonus ['bounəs], co-operate ['kou-'ɔpəreit], diary ['daiəri], major ['meidʒə], manual ['mænjuəl], method ['meθəd], O & M ['ouən'em], soluble ['sɔljubl], view [vju:].

2. SUMMARY

Hector Grant, Managing Director, is worried about productivity. He has decided to engage consultants, who are specialists in work study techniques, to see how Harper & Grant can improve efficiency and output. Any good management is keen to improve efficiency, but nowadays this has become a largely specialised field, and outside consultants who are   5
experienced in particular techniques can be called in to study work systematically and suggest improvements and ways of stepping up, increasing, productivity. When this applies to manual work it is usually called work study, and the idea is to find out the most efficient way of doing something before the formulation of piece rates or incentive bonus schemes. The 10
study of office systems and paperwork is usually called O. & M. (Organisation and Methods). Work study could, of course, be applied to routine office jobs, such as invoice typing.

Mr. Grant has decided to call in a firm called Smith-Weston Consultants Ltd. Their representative, Mr. Scott, is present at a meeting 15 called by Mr. Grant to explain the service to his executives. Mr. Grant thinks that production methods on the factory floor could be improved, but he has never considered that a check on efficiency might run from the top to the bottom of the firm.

PART 2 : CONVERSATION AND DOCUMENTS

1. CONVERSATION

(Recorded Text)

(In Hector Grant's office)

HECTOR GRANT **Ah, good morning everyone. Are we all here? Peter? John? Ian? Good. Let's sit down. Now, to work, gentlemen. Let me first introduce Mr. Scott, from Smith-Weston Consultants. As you know, I have been thinking for some time that we ought to have an O. & M. and work study** 5 **review. Mr. Scott has come along to tell us what his firm could do for us if we decided to have a productivity study made in the company. Mr. Scott ...**

MR. SCOTT **Good morning, gentlemen. I am sure I don't need to tell you what improved productivity involves. It means, for a** 10 **start, analysing jobs throughout a firm with a view to re-organising them in order to decrease time and expenditure and increase efficiency and production. We would propose starting work study in the factory in conjunction with a scheme under which the employees could share** 15 **some of the benefits of improvement.**

PETER WILES **May I ask a question?**

SCOTT **Yes, do, by all means.**

PETER **We all agree, of course, in maximising productivity, but when you study and time a job isn't it normal to find an** 20 **operator going as slow as he can so that you'll allow him more time for the job?**

SCOTT **Yes, that, of course, can happen. But our investigators are experienced. We'd first do a sample study in a selected area of the works, and this would demonstrate** 25 **how we think productivity could be increased as a result of our proposed activities.**

'I understand you were looking round the works yesterday.'

PETER   **Well, that seems a fair answer. But I have another question. Don't you find workers dislike your investigators telling them they aren't doing the job in the most efficient way?** 30

SCOTT   **That is, of course, a big problem. But soluble, I think, if our survey is conducted in conjunction with an incentive payments scheme. If operators know they will be paid more as a result of increased productivity they will want to co-operate. We would suggest, for example, putting everyone on group rates as a spur to productivity.** 35

GRANT   **Good. Well now, Mr. Scott, I think you have covered some of the main points. Perhaps I could now ask you to tell us in detail how you would set about your investigation? I understand you were looking round the works yesterday, and don't you already...** 40

(After the meeting, John and Peter get together)

JOHN   **Well, I'm amazed! I really am. What on earth has happened to the old man? You'd have thought he would be the last person to consider a thing like work study or group bonus schemes. I gather there was a major battle years ago to get him to agree to piece rates even in the few areas where they operate now.** 45

PETER	Yes, he's suddenly decided to change with the times. I think our new advertising manager may have had a hand 50 in it! Joanna is always talking about things like corporate planning, operational research, critical path analysis and so on.
JOHN	That's just what this firm needs.
PETER	Yes, but you know, the story's not finished yet. I don't 55 think H.G. has quite realised the full implication of all this.
JOHN	What do you mean?
PETER	You wait and see. Some of these consultants never know where to stop. . . . 60
JOHN	Well, we shall see . . .

(*Later Mr. Scott reports to Hector Grant*)

GRANT	So, Mr. Scott, this seems very satisfactory. I'm very interested in this sample survey. I think we should like you to go ahead and do the full review.
SCOTT	Er—there is one other point we've not yet mentioned.
GRANT	Oh, what's that? 65
SCOTT	We haven't yet done anything on the management side.
GRANT	Management! Surely that's not necessary?
SCOTT	In our experience it's as vital as it is in any other department. Perhaps more vital. Just as a matter of interest, would you mind if I gave you the results of some research 70 I did myself, while waiting for you this morning.
GRANT	Well?

(*Mr. Scott reads from his notebook*)

SCOTT	'10 a.m. Managing Director arrives at office. Finds mail has not been correctly sorted. Two letters are for other people to deal with. To answer the next letter, it was 75 necessary to refer to a previous letter which could not be found in the file. Diary was not to hand. This caused delay and confusion over making an engagement by phone while the secretary was out of the room looking for the missing letter.' 80
GRANT	Well, really! Do your methods usually include listening to private conversations through open doors?
SCOTT	No. But this time I could hardly help it. Our job, Mr. Grant, is to observe and report objectively.

GRANT	I see. Well, thank you very much, Mr. Scott, for your re-	85
	port, and I look forward to studying it carefully. But as to ...	
SCOTT	... As to including a survey on the organisation of your management ...?	
GRANT	I hadn't bargained for that, you know. I shall have to think about it. Hm, yes, I don't quite like the idea of being	90
	told how to run my own business, but ... well, I'll let you know, Mr. Scott. Good morning.	

GRANT: 'Well, really! . . . I hadn't bargained for that, you know.'

PRACTICE SENTENCES

Say the practice sentences on the record :

i Let me first introduce Mr. Scott.

ii Mr. Scott has come along to tell us what his firm could do for us. Mr. Scott...

iii Good morning, gentlemen.

iv May I ask a question?

v We would propose starting work study in the factory.

vi We'd first do a sample study in a selected area of the works.

vii This would demonstrate how we think productivity could be increased.

2. INTER-OFFICE MEMO

Mr. Grant finally decided to have the productivity review in the factory only. He could not face having his own work methods investigated! However, the results of the work study and time study in the factory were very encouraging. So much so, that Mr. Grant thought he might try to improve the methods of work in the offices. Before calling in the firm of consultants again, however, he has decided to hold a competition among the office staff. He has just sent out the following memo:

From: The Managing Director

date: 7th December, 197..

To: All Office Staff

        As a result of the productivity review carried out in the works, faster and more effective ways of operating are now being applied.   In some sections of the works, productivity has been increased by over 50 per cent.   The management intends to apply these study methods to office staff, in the near future, in an attempt to reduce costs and improve work techniques.   We live in a competitive world.   Our objective is to find ways of eliminating wasteful and unnecessary actions by all staff.

        The management therefore proposes to present a prize of £50 to any member of the staff who, in the management's estimation, has put forward the most practical suggestion to streamline a particular office routine.   All suggestions should reach the Managing Director's office before the end of this month.   The management's decision is final.

(Hector Grant)

PART 3 : NOTES AND PRACTICE

1. RAPPEL GRAMMATICAL

Summary :

6. N'oublions pas que le passif, construction plus fréquente en anglais qu'en français, s'emploie aussi avec les verbes intransitifs comme les verbes composés :

The meeting was presided over by Mr. Grant	La réunion fut présidée par M. Grant
The investment programme hasn't yet been worked out	Le programme d'investissement n'a pas encore été élaboré

9. Rappelons que le superlatif des adjectifs courts se forme avec le suffixe -est, et celui des adjectifs longs avec **the most**. Le problème de la " longueur " des adjectifs est complexe. Il faut s'en tenir à quelques indications générales :

— sont courts les adjectifs d'une syllabe (rares exceptions)

— les adjectifs de deux syllabes en -y (**happy**), -er (**clever**), -ow (**narrow**), -le (**gentle**) sont courts ; ceux en -ful, -al, -less, -ous, -ish, -ive, -ile sont longs ; les autres ont les deux constructions

— les adjectifs de plus de deux syllabes sont longs, sauf les contraires des disyllabes courts formés avec le préfixe **un-**.

Rappelons : **good, better, the best ; bad, worse, the worst**

Conversation :

4. **I've been thinking for some time :** think, verbe désignant une activité abstraite, est rarement au progressif. Ici, le progressif souligne l'intensité de la réflexion et sa continuité. Dans quel cas aurions-nous **since...** ?

I've been thinking about it since I met Mr. Scott	J'y réfléchis depuis que j'ai fait la connaissance de M. Scott

8. On n'a pas oublié *faire faire* :

They had a market research carried out	Ils ont fait effectuer une étude de marché.

Comparons avec une phrase de John, ligne 47 :

There was a battle to get him to agree to piece rates	Il y a eu une bataille pour lui faire consentir à un salaire aux pièces

To get + infinitive active donne une idée de persuasion.

9. **I don't need to tell you.** Variante possible : **I needn't tell you.** Lorsque **need** a pour complément un verbe, il peut se comporter comme un défectif (sans auxiliaire **do** à la négative ou à l'interrogative, non suivi de **to**, pas d'-s à la 3e personne du singulier). Lorsque son complément est un nom, il se comporte comme un verbe ordinaire :

I don't need my dictating machine, you can have it	Je n'ai pas besoin de mon dictaphone tu peux le prendre

Need s'emploie pour exprimer la négative de **must.** Distinguons **must not,** qui exprime l'interdiction, de **needn't** qui marque l'absence de nécessité :

He mustn't come	Il ne faut pas qu'il vienne
He needn't come	Il n'a pas besoin de venir

Dans ce sens, **needn't** a la valeur d'un passé dans une subordonnée :

He said you needn't come	Il a dit que tu n'avais pas besoin de venir

Si une action a eu lieu alors qu'elle n'était pas nécessaire, on fera suivre **need** de l'infinitif passé :

She needn't have duplicated these documents	Elle n'avait pas besoin de reproduire ces documents (*mais elle l'a fait*)

Comparons cette dernière phrase avec la suivante :

She didn't need to duplicate the documents	Elle n'a pas eu besoin de reproduire les documents (*et elle ne l'a pas fait*)

11. Notons que de nombreuses locutions prépositives contenant **to,** et **to** elle-même après certains adjectifs, verbes, etc..., sont suivies de la forme en **-ing** ; **to** est suivi de l'infinitif seulement lorsqu'il marque le but :

I'm looking forward to reading your report	Je me fais d'avance un plaisir de lire votre rapport
This was decided with a view to streamlining the work on the shop floor	Ce fut décidé dans l'intention de remanier le travail à l'usine

66. **We haven't yet done anything** = **we have done nothing yet.**

74. **Two letters are for other people to deal with. For** sert à introduire des propositions infinitives :

That isn't for me to say	Ce n'est pas à moi de le dire
It's too long for you to finish by 5 p.m.	C'est trop long pour que vous le finissiez d'ici 17 heures

It's high time for them to re-organise the Sales Department	Il est grand temps qu'ils réorganisent le service des ventes
It will be difficult for the Manager to accept	Il sera difficile au Directeur d'accepter
It's very unusual for Mr. Grant to be so enthusiastic	Il est très rare que M. Grant soit aussi enthousiaste

83. **I can't help** est suivi de -ing :

| She couldn't help listening to your conversation | Elle n'a pas pu s'empêcher d'écouter votre conversation |

2. EXERCISES

EXERCISE 1. — Change as follows :

a. **I must borrow a large sum** → **I needn't borrow a large sum**
b. **I must listen to conversations** → **I must not listen to conversations**

1. You must finish your report by Monday. 2. We must order the goods in large quantities. 3. You must repeat what you heard. 4. She must wait till he goes out of his office. 5. You must stick posters on this wall. 6. We must examine the question once more. 7. You must go into the boss's office while he's away. 8. You must pay the whole sum now.

EXERCISE 2. — Change as follows :

We'll pay them more → **They'll be paid more**

1. They will increase productivity. 2. They made a productivity study. 3. Can you improve our methods ? 4. They must reorganise jobs. 5. This would certainly decrease time. 6. It might have reduced the costs. 7. This might increase efficiency. 8. They'd studied and timed every job. 9. They always do a sample study to begin with. 10. They haven't yet given the results. 11. She couldn't find the letter.

EXERCISE 3. — Use the superlative as follows :

It is a large firm → **It's one of the largest firms**

1. Sweden is a rich country. 2. This technique is advanced. 3. This has been a satisfactory improvement. 4. Jim is a hard-working fellow. 5. This has been a good reform. 6. It's a large producer of sulphur. 7. It's a light alloy. 8. It is a new brand of detergent. 9. This is a sound and useful decision. 10. Abraca is a promising export market. 11. This is our fundamental objective. 12. Harper & Grant are a successful company. 13. Antwerp is a fast growing industrial centre.

EXERCISE 4. — *Change as follows* :

They will decide upon the restrictions at a later meeting →
The restrictions will be decided upon at a later meeting

1. They have worked out the investment programme. 2. This compensated for the decline in cereal exports. 3. You should provide for all sorts of expenses in your estimate. 4. They should aim at higher efficiency on the shop-floor. 5. Can we rely on the new cashier ? 6. They won't comply with the necessary formalities. 7. They might call in another firm of consultants. 8. We would have immediately attended to your order.

EXERCISE 5. — *Use* **for** *or* **ago** *with the complement between brackets and put the verb in the correct tense as follows* :

  a. **The battle over piece rates is fought (years)** →
     The battle over piece rates was fought years ago
  b. **He is worrying about it (months)** →
     He's been worrying about it for months

1. I think about it (months). 2. He calls in a firm of consultants (a year). 3. They hold a competition among the staff (six months). 4. H.G. sends a memo about productivity (three weeks). 5. They now apply these techniques (several months). 6. Mr. Robinson wins the prize (a fortnight). 7. He is writing his report (a whole week). 8. She answers the letter (two days). 9. They are studying work on the shop floor (several days). 10. I hear him say so (a couple of days). 11. He takes a decision (a few days). 12. He works in the firm (13 years).

EXERCISE 6. — (*Perhaps this is going to be a difficult exercise*) *Try and use the correct form* (*infinitive or gerund*) *in the following sentences* :

1. They want (to maintain the profitability of the enterprise). 2. There is a strong objection (to have this job done on the management side too). 3. He began (to realise the consultants had planned an across-the-board survey). 4. I've begun (to study your report, Peter). 5. John was reduced (to type his report by himself). 6. Any country wants (to achieve full employment without inflation). 7. H.G. objects (to see outsiders in his office). 8. When do you intend (to set about that investigation of yours). 9. We're looking forward (to meet your representative). 10. We're looking forward (to hear from you). 11. They'd like (to preserve management's freedom to manage). 12. He invited Mr. Brown with a view (to show him all our new lines). 13. He devoted his whole life (to make his firm one of the most efficient in the country). 14. We are not used (to have all these investigators on our backs all the time).

EXERCISE 7. — *What action verbs do you associate with the following nouns, frequently used in business (use either* **make** *or* **do** *- in some cases both may be possible)* :

1. ... a suggestion. 2. ... a test. 3. ... a study. 4. ... a job. 5. ... an investigation. 6. ... an appointment to meet someone.

EXERCISE 8. — *Fill in the missing words (refer to the episode if necessary)*.

1. I've been thinking ... some time that we ought to have an investigation into productivity. 2. Our survey is conducted ... conjunction ... an incentive payments scheme. 3. If operatives know they will be paid more ... increased production, they will co-operate. 4. What on earth has happened ... the old man ? 5. The letters were for other people to deal ... . 6. Mr. Grant understood that Mr. Scott had been looking ... the works.

EXERCISE 9. — *Please answer the following questions (with complete sentences)*.

1. If you were the manager of a firm, what service might you call in if you were anxious to improve productivity ? 2. Who would this firm send you if you decided to have a survey carried out ? 3. What might this visiting firm suggest if they saw you were not convinced that their services would be useful ? 4. Again, as manager of your firm, what scheme would you suggest to overcome possible opposition to the survey from your own employees ?

EXERCISE 10. — *Translate into English* :

1. Permettez-moi tout d'abord de vous présenter M. Scott. 2. M. Scott est venu nous dire ce que sa maison pourrait faire pour nous. 3. Puis-je vous poser une question ? 4. Nous envisagerions de commencer l'étude des postes dans l'usine. 5. Nous ferions d'abord une étude témoin dans un secteur choisi de l'usine. 6. Ceci donnerait un exemple de la manière dont nous pensons que l'on pourrait accroître la productivité. 7. Il est très désireux d'améliorer le rendement. 8. Bonjour Messieurs. Je crois que je n'ai pas besoin de vous présenter M. Wiles. 9. Je crois comprendre qu'il s'est livré une bataille importante sur la question des primes de productivité. 10. Le nouveau chef de publicité n'arrête pas de parler de gestion prévisionnelle, de ratios, de recherche opérationnelle et d'informatique ! 11. Il est grand temps qu'ils réorganisent leur chaîne de production. 12. Il n'a pas pu s'empêcher de signaler qu'il avait passé deux ans à Harvard. 13. Nous attendons votre nouveau catalogue avec impatience. 14. Le programme d'investissement n'a pas encore été élaboré. 15. J'avais prévu une marge bien plus étroite. 16. Le patron n'a pas pu supporter l'idée qu'on enquête sur ses propres méthodes. 17. Notre objectif est de trouver des moyens d'éliminer des actions dispendieuses et inutiles de la part du personnel. 18. Cela vous dérangerait-il que je vous communique les résultats de recherches que j'ai faites personnellement ? 19. Cela a été très difficile de lui faire accepter le paiement à la pièce. 20. Le patron s'est finalement décidé à vivre avec son temps.

UNIT 10

THE PENSION FUND MEETING

PART 1 : INTRODUCTION

1. WORD STUDY

Vocabulary

alter   modifier
amount   montant, somme
appoint   nommer
articles   statuts
aware   conscient
bound to   obligé de
carpenter   menuisier
carve   sculpter
close down   fermer
compensate   indemniser
complete   terminer
contribute   cotiser
contribution   cotisation
copy   exemplaire
craftsman   artisan
cunning   rusé
deed   acte, contrat
determined   décidé
dismiss   renvoyer, congédier
elaborate   complexe, fignolé
elderly   âgé
evil   mal
fire   saquer, renvoyer

fund   caisse (*de retraite*, etc.)
funds   fonds
get rid (of)   se débarrasser
govern   régir
guess   deviner
hardly ever   presque jamais
ingenuity   ingéniosité
look up   consulter (*documents*, etc.)
make up   compléter
nowadays   aujourd'hui, à l'heure
    actuelle
operate   gérer, exploiter
own   posséder
ownership   propriété
pay (into)   verser (cotisation à)
pension-fund   caisse de retraites
point out   faire remarquer, souligner
preposterous   absurde, ridicule
qualify (for)   faire valoir ses
    droits (à)
reach   atteindre
redundant   qui fait double emploi
redundancy   chômage technologique

relative parent
retire prendre sa retraite
retirement retraite
sack renvoyer, mettre à la porte
set-up organisation
share action
shareholder actionnaire
shortly très prochainement
shrewd finaud, avisé
slight peu conséquent, petit
speak up parler en faveur de quelqu'un

state état
straightforward simple
streamline rénover
take over succéder ; prendre le contrôle
trust groupe, administration
trustee administrateur (d'une caisse)
tribute hommage
vested dévolu, assigné

Phrases

There's no call for such work now plus personne ne demande du travail semblable

For the sake of the record pour les archives

You'll see to that, won't you ? vous vous en occuperez, n'est-ce pas ?

As things stand at present dans l'état actuel des choses

At a rough guess approximativement

He won't change his mind il ne changera pas d'avis

He's determined on it il y tient

Explanations and Other Useful Terms

articles (in this case of the Pension Fund Trust) the legally registered rules of the Trust, the most important of which will deal with the qualifications for membership and how long an employee must work to be entitled to a full pension, and with all the possible variations that could arise, including how the amount of the pension is calculated.

be compensated receive some asset, usually money, to balance some loss. A redundant worker may be compensated with a lump sum of money, a sum of money paid at one time (see Unit 4).

deed a legal document.

qualify for a pension	become entitled to a pension, to have fulfilled the necessary conditions, and to have the right to receive a pension.
redundant	when an employee's job becomes unnecessary to a company, he becomes redundant. Redundancy, therefore, leads to dismissal, premature retirement or transfer to another department.
sacked (also **fired**)	a slang word for dismissed, told that one's services are no longer required.
shares	in a public company, the shares can be bought and sold through the Stock Exchange by anyone who wants, or can afford, to buy them. A person who invests in such a company receives a share of the profits, if any, according to the number of shares he holds. Harper & Grant are a private company and they sell shares to selected individuals.
pension scheme	most states have national pension schemes or plans. There are also private pension schemes, like Harper & Grant's. The money is paid by the company and by the employee into a fund during the latter's working life, so that the employee can receive a continuing income from the fund, after he has retired from the company.
take over	to assume some work or responsibility.
a take over	a much used word in modern business, in which there is an increasing tendency for larger firms to take over smaller ones by buying a controlling number of shares, each share entitling them to one vote.
a trust	a legally formed body in which legal ownership can be vested and which is managed for the benefit of others. In this case the trust is formed to provide retirement pensions for those of Harper & Grant employees who join the pension scheme and contribute to its funds.

Pronunciation

1 — 1 - (- -) article, Britain, difference, equally, invalid (*noun*), pension, period, relative, separate, streamline

- 2 (- -) absorb, account, amount, assent, attend, aware, complete, compulsory, effect, elaborate, employer, example, examine, however, impeccable, initiative, persuade, preposterous, redundant, retire

- - 3 interrupt, independent

— 158 —

2 — -s → [s] amounts, invests, operates, looks, results
       -► [iz] advertises, decreases, dismisses, increases, places, reaches, realises
       →   [z] gives, leaves, pays, qualifies, remembers, retires, rules

3 — [ʃ] share, shortly, machine, pension, initiative
    [æ] bad, sack, hand, value
    [a:] half, craft, carve, start, heart, hardly, article, carpenter
    [e] get, says, guess, many, pension, however, impeccable, percentage, death
    [ə] Britain, worker, amount, craftsman, alter
    [ʌ] fund, tough, rough, trust, enough, cunning, number, redundant compulsory
    [i] effect, money, Thursday, retire, carpenter, separate (adjective), examine
    [au] out, announce, amount, undoubted, allow, however
    [ou] so, own, only, note, know, whole, episode, progress (noun)

4 — (adv., adj.) close [klous], (verb) close [klouz]
    employer [im'plɔiə], employee [,emplɔi'i:]
    (adj.) : separate ['seprit] ; (v.) : to separate ['sepəreit]
    (adj.) : precedent [pri'si:dənt] ; (noun) : precedent ['presidənt]

5 — Note : absorb [əb'sɔ:b], case [keis], evil [i:vl], fixed [fikst], ingenuity ['indʒin'juiti], real [riəl], shrewd [ʃru:d], straightforward [streit'fɔ:wəd], trustee [trʌs'ti:], tribute ['tribju:t].

2. SUMMARY

A pension is money paid to an employee when he *retires*, leaves on reaching a certain age. In Britain there is a compulsory scheme in which the employee pays a fixed amount every week and the employer a larger amount. Then on retirement, the worker gets his state pension. Nowadays, however, an increasing number of companies operate their own pension 5 schemes to give their employees more money to retire on. These schemes are usually governed, or ruled, by a trust deed. The trust is separate from the company. Trustees are appointed and they hold meetings regularly to approve money for pensions, examine the fund accounts and so on. Every employee working for Harper & Grant, for example, pays a certain amount 10 of his wages into the fund. This money is invested to increase its value, and after a certain period of employment the employee qualifies for a pension.

As a result of the productivity drive, Mr. Grant wants to close down unprofitable departments. Nearly all the redundant workers have been absorbed into other departments, but there is one, Bob Hardiman, who, 15 Mr. Grant says, will have to go. He is a craftsman in the old style, that is, he is a carpenter able to do fine hand carving, which is now hardly ever required. Ian Hampden, the Personnel Manager, thinks that Mr. Grant is wrong to get rid of someone who has been with the firm so many years. He tries to make Mr. Grant change his mind. Mr. Grant, however, is 20 determined on his new plans to streamline the company, and make it more profitable and competitive. Ian goes to see Peter to find out if he can suggest a way of persuading Mr. Grant to see reason.

PETER: 'He's been with the firm since it started, and he's the only real craftsman we've got.'

The pension fund meeting is due to be held shortly, and Bob Hardiman's pension will have to be approved. Peter remembers that a few years ago Bob Hardiman had to leave the company to look after his father, who had become an invalid. When his father died, Bob Hardiman rejoined the company. Peter realises at once that according to the articles 5 of the trust, if an employee leaves the firm for a time he must then work a certain number of years in order to qualify for the full pension. Bob Hardiman has not yet completed this time. He has, in fact, three more years to go. If he is sacked, or fired, now and not given his full pension it would have an extremely bad effect on everybody, since he has been with 10 the firm so long. Peter, at the meeting, cunningly suggests that the company makes up the difference. In other words, the company pays Bob Hardiman the money to make up his pension from the fund to the full amount that it would have been if he had not interrupted his employment. Peter is shrewd enough to know that Mr. Grant will not want to do this 15 and may perhaps decide that the lesser of the two evils is to let the man stay until his proper retirement age.

In this episode we hear that the chairman, Ambrose Harper, who is an elderly man, is very ill. Peter is worried because he knows that Ambrose Harper owns half the shares in the company. If these are bought by a 20 rival firm, or a larger company that wants to take them over, the present set-up, organisation, could change completely.

PART 2 : CONVERSATION AND DOCUMENTS

1. CONVERSATION

(Recorded Text)

(*In Peter Wiles's office*)

PETER WILES **Ian, what's this about Bob Hardiman being sacked? He's been with the firm since it started, and he's the only real craftsman we've got.**

IAN HAMPDEN **Yes, but H.G. rightly points out that there's no call for elaborate hand-carving on desks nowadays; we don't need** 5 **desks like this one you've got here, for example. He says Hardiman is now redundant.**

PETER	It'll break the old boy's heart. Wait. I've got an idea.
IAN	What?
PETER	The Pension Fund Trustees' Meeting. It's this Thursday. 10 His name's bound to come up if he's being dismissed; his pension'll have to be approved.
IAN	How will that help him? It won't save him from redundancy.
PETER	No, but that's when we can speak up. There's you and me 15 on one side and H.G. and our dear company secretary on the other. Which leaves our Chairman, Ambrose Harper. And you know what a soft heart he has. The pension scheme itself was his idea. He'll be bound to agree with us.
IAN	But Ambrose Harper's ill. He's not coming to the Pension 20 Fund Meeting.
PETER	Oh Lord! We've got to think of something. . . . Look, I've got another idea. Hardiman left the firm for a while, didn't he?
IAN	Yes, about five years ago. He came back to us two years 25 ago.
PETER	Why did he leave?
IAN	He went to live in Scotland to look after his father. When his father died, he came back to us.
PETER	I see. And what happened to all the contributions he had 30 paid into the pension fund before he went to Scotland?
IAN	He left them in the fund.
PETER	So he still qualifies for a pension ?
IAN	Yes. H.G. will say he'll get his pension, so what is there to worry about? 35
PETER	But the thing is, Ian, is Hardiman entitled to the full pension if he broke his employment with us? Let's look up the articles of the pension fund. Have you got a copy?
IAN	I'll have a look.

(Thursday: the Pension Fund Meeting is in progress)

HECTOR GRANT	Well, gentlemen, this isn't going to take us very long. 40 You've seen Mr. Buckhurst's pension fund accounts. They're impeccable as usual. So it's only a question of approving them for the sake of the record. Right. Do you all agree the accounts? (*Murmurs of assent.*) Good. Well, that's all. I presume there's no other business? 45
IAN	Well, there is one thing more, H.G. The question of redundancy, the case of Bob Hardiman. . . .

GRANT	That's a straightforward case. He gets his pension, less three years, or whatever it is. You'll see to that, won't you?
IAN	I don't think it's quite as simple as that. 50
GRANT	Why on earth not?
IAN	Peter will explain.
PETER	There seems to be some slight difficulty, H.G. You see, Hardiman left us for three years, as you know.
GRANT	I know very well he did. I've just said so. 55
PETER	Quite so. But I felt I should look up the articles of the fund. Ian, of course, is already aware of this. It seems that if a period of employment is interrupted for more than six months a further period of five years has to be worked before the employee is entitled to a full pension. If 60 Hardiman continues with us until he's due to retire, that is, in three years' time, there is, of course, no problem. He will be fully entitled. But as things stand at present he would get, at a rough guess, only about three-quarters of his pension. And we could hardly allow that situation 65 with such an old employee. It would do the company no good at all. He will, naturally, have to be compensated out of the company's funds to make his pension up to the proper amount.
GRANT	But that's preposterous! 70
PETER	But it does seem to be the only thing to do.
GRANT	We'll just have to alter the articles.
PETER	That would require the Chairman's vote, of course.
GRANT	Oh dear!
PETER	You don't think we could pay the remaining pension out 75 of the company's profits?
GRANT	No, that would be a very dangerous precedent. No, no. I won't consider that. Ian, this is your scheme, I'm sure.
IAN	Mine, H.G.?
GRANT	Well, you win. We keep Hardiman on for three more 80 years. But, Peter, I shall expect you to use your undoubted ingenuity in making full use of him.
PETER	Of course, sir.

(*Peter and Ian get together afterwards*)

IAN	Well done, Peter.
PETER	Not bad. Well, we saved old Hardiman his job. But 85 something else is worrying me.

IAN	**What's that?**
PETER	**Have you heard the latest? Old Ambrose Harper is seriously ill. If anything happens to him this company will be in a serious position.** 90
IAN	**Wouldn't Grant take over as Chairman?**
PETER	**I wasn't thinking about who will be the next Chairman. I was thinking of Ambrose Harper's shares in the company.**
IAN	**What percentage does he hold?**
PETER	**About fifty per cent, I think. Grant's father held the other** 95 **fifty, but when he died they were divided equally among his three children.**
IAN	**What'll happen to Ambrose Harper's shares?**
PETER	**They'll be left to his sister, I should think. She's his only surviving relative.** 100
IAN	**She wouldn't be able to sell them, would she?**
PETER	**I imagine they'd have to be offered, through the company, to the other shareholders first. But can the firm manage to buy them? If not, and if they get into the hands of a firm looking for a takeover, well, we'll be in trouble.** 105

PRACTICE SENTENCES

Say these practice sentences on the record :

   i He's been with the firm almost since it started.

  ii He left his contributions in the fund.

 iii He still qualifies for a pension.

 iv Do you all agree the accounts ?

  v A further period has to be worked before the employee is entitled to a full pension.

 vi He'll have to be compensated out of the company's funds.

vii He holds fifty per cent of the shares.

2. MEMO TO ALL DEPARTMENTS

A short time after the Pension Fund Meeting, the Chairman, Ambrose Harper, died. The Managing Director, Hector Grant, had a memo typed and copies sent round to all the departments in the firm announcing the Chairman's death. This is the memo he sent:

From: The Managing Director

date: 20th December, 197..

To: All Personnel

       It is with very deep regret that I have to announce the death of our Chairman, Ambrose Harper. As many of you will know, he had been ill for a very short time, following an operation. He died peacefully in his sleep at four o'clock this afternoon. Only this morning he had been reading the minutes of the last Pension Fund Meeting which, owing to his illness, he had been unable to attend for the first time in forty years. The Pension Fund, which he himself had started, was one of the first independent schemes in the country.

       Work will stop for one minute at noon tomorrow so that the whole company may pay silent tribute to one whose initiative helped found this great business and whose selfless energy guided its destiny over a lifespan. All who knew him regarded him as a true colleague and friend.

H G

(Hector Grant)

PART 3 : NOTES AND PRACTICE

1. RAPPEL GRAMMATICAL

Summary :

1-2. **On + -ing** : rend compte de l'action immédiatement antérieure à celle exprimée par la principale :

On seeing your letter, I guessed you wouldn't come	En voyant votre lettre, j'ai deviné que vous ne viendriez pas

5. Notons la place de **however**, qui vient après le premier mot ou groupe de mot le plus généralement.

9. The fund accounts, 13, the productivity drive, etc... Notons que dans la langue contemporaine, notamment celle de l'économie, de la politique, etc... le tiret ne s'écrit que très rarement dans les noms composés.

19. Comparons encore ces formes, dont cette leçon contient plusieurs exemples :

He has been in the firm for so many years	Cela fait tant d'années qu'il est dans l'entreprise
He has been in the firm since it started	Il est dans la maison depuis les origines
He had been in the firm for ten years when he left us to go to Scotland	Il était dans la maison depuis dix ans lorsqu'il nous a quittés pour aller en Ecosse
He joined us three years ago	Il est revenu chez nous il y a trois ans

25. It will have to be approved notons la notion de devoir combinée au futur avec le passif. Il faut manier avec aisance ces formes complexes :

It would have had to be approved	Il aurait fallu qu'on l'approuve

39. The lesser : **lesser** est un adjectif de forme comparative (comparatif de l'adjectif **little**, petit) mais de sens superlatif qui s'emploie lorsque deux éléments sont opposés par le superlatif :

Of the two partners he is the lesser scoundrel	Des deux associés il est le moins scélérat
One must choose the lesser evil	Il faut choisir le moindre mal

La comparaison, sinon explicite, est toujours implicite :

Peter gave him an idea of his lesser talents	Peter lui a donné un aperçu de ses menus talents

Conversation :

11. If he's being dismissed : la forme progressive exprime ici une notion de futur assez imminent que l'on se représente d'avance :

I'm seeing their manager tomorrow	Je vois leur directeur demain

Cf. plus bas, ligne 20 : **he's not coming to the meeting.**

23. He left us for a while, didn't he ? Ces tag-questions sont un réflexe difficile à acquérir pour un francophone, et pourtant, elles sont à haute fréquence dans la langue parlée. A la difficulté du montage, s'ajoute une importante question d'intonation.

En effet, si le locuteur (la personne qui parle) pose la question uniquement pour obtenir confirmation de ce qu'il a dit — mais il est persuadé que ce qu'il a dit est vrai —, la voix descend à la fin du *colloquial query* :

It's a nice day, isn't it ? ↘   Il fait beau, n'est-ce pas ?
(*falling tune*)

Mais si au contraire le locuteur est véritablement en train de poser une question dont il ignore cette fois la réponse, la voix monte à la fin du **tag** :

You can come, can't you ? ↗   Vous pouvez venir, dites ?
(*rising tune*)

Il existe également un problème d'intonation dans les questions commençant par un interrogatif (**who, what, why,** etc.). Dans ce type de question (question ouverte, elle débouche sur un complément d'information) la voix descend généralement à la fin de la question :

Why did he come ? ↘   Pourquoi est-il venu ?

Mais si la réponse à la question est seulement **yes** ou **no** (question fermée, la réponse n'amène aucun élément non contenu déjà dans la question), la voix monte en général :

Do you like it ? ↗   Cela vous plaît ?

Il ne faut pas oublier par ailleurs qu'il peut y avoir des variations d'intonation sur le même contenu. Ces variations ont une valeur émotionnelle. Ainsi :

Where do you come from ? ↘   D'où venez-vous ?
— Timbuctoo   — De Tombouctou
Where do you come from ? ↗   D'où venez-vous ?

Dans la seconde question, l'intonation ascendante exprime l'extrême surprise devant une telle réponse.

59. Le comparatif de **far** est **farther** ou **further**, et le superlatif **farthest** ou **furthest**. **Farther** et **farthest** on un sens concret (idée de distance), **further** et **furthest** ont un sens figuré, mais on les rencontre aussi souvent au sens de distance :

Will Shuttleworth go farther away from home ?	Shuttleworth ira-t-il plus loin de chez lui ?
Carlisle is the farthest place in his area	Carlisle est l'endroit le plus éloigné de son secteur
The boss didn't give any further details	Le patron n'a pas donné plus de détails
Could he give any further information ?	Pourrait-il fournir d'autres renseignements ?

71. **It does seem to be the only thing to do** = forme emphatique.

81. Comme les verbes de volonté (**to want, to require**), les verbes d'attente sont suivis de la proposition infinitive (**expect, wait**) :

I don't expect them to refund us   Je ne compte pas qu'ils nous remboursent

Wait est peut-être suivi d'une proposition à l'indicatif. Comparons :

I'll wait for him to phone }
I'll wait till he phones }   J'attendrai qu'il téléphone

88. **The last** désigne le dernier d'une série achevée (**the last chapter, the last days of Ambrose Harper's life**), ou dans des expressions de temps comme : **last Friday, last month, last year. Latest** désigne le plus récent :

**This is the latest catalogue of   C'est le dernier catalogue de
Harper & Grant   Harper & Grant**

Latest désigne le dernier en date, mais il y en aura d'autres.

95. Notons une fois encore la place de **other** (cf. : **the other three, the last two, the first four, the next three**).

2. EXERCISES

EXERCISE 1. — *Complete with tag questions* :

1. He died in December.   2. You sent a memo round to all the departments. 3. She will type it.   4. He didn't mention it.   5. He hadn't been able to attend the meeting.   6. He had been ill for a long time.   7. You have read the articles.   8. He hasn't read the minutes.   9. He would look up the articles.   10. The firm can't manage to buy the shares.   11. Weston & Mead seem to be looking for a take-over.   12. She wouldn't be able to see them.   13. We shan't keep him for another three years.   14. You'll make full use of his talents.   15. We saved him his job.   16. They used to send their catalogues.   17. The Chairman wasn't there.   18. His father held the other shares.

EXERCISE 2. — *When you have decided how you would say the following sentences note whether the voice goes* up *or* down *at the end. Then go back and listen to them on the record again, and try to repeat the intonation exactly* :

1. What's this about Bob Hardiman being sacked ?   2. How will that help him ?   3. Hardiman left the firm for a while, didn't he ?   4. Why did he leave ?   5. Have you got a copy ?   6. Wouldn't Grant take over as Chairman ?   7. What percentage does he hold ?   8. What'll happen to Ambrose Harper's shares ?   9. She wouldn't be able to sell them, would she ?

EXERCISE 3. — *Use the infinitive or the gerund in the following sentences :*

1. He isn't willing (to recruit foreign labour).   2. These policies are designed (to bring about mergers).   3. We are not used (to have those investigators behind our backs).   4. They used (to send their catalogue a little before Christmas).   5. He understands how (to re-organise the whole works).
6. The Chief Accountant will have to submit (to have his books examined).
7. Coalminers don't easily take (to retrain).   8. Advertising does not seek (to be informative), it seeks (to persuade).   9. Anyway, this was a start (to tackle the problem of productivity).   10. Great energy has been devoted (to rationalise the plant).   11. I'm looking forward (to join your staff).   12. We now prefer (to recruit our own advertising people).   13. The firm got exclusive rights (to make and sell toys to Abraca).   14. I think the senior executive will refuse (to collaborate with Scott).

EXERCISE 4. — *Make sentences with the words between brackets, using the appropriate tense :*

1. Ambrose Harper, (to die) (two years).   2. Ambrose Harper, (to be dead) (two years).   3. Hector Grant, (to announce old Mr. Harper's death) (a few hours).   4. Hardiman, (to be with us) (the firm was founded).
5. Ambrose Harper, (to found the Pension Trust) (forty-five years).   6. They, (to hold a meeting) (a week).   7. They, (to be discussing the problem) (hours).   8. The advertising manager, (to place an advertisement in the trade Press) (a week).   9. Joanna, (to be working in the firm) (October).
10. He, (to be Chairman of the Board) (his father died).   11. The old boy, (to be in the firm) (so many years).   12. I, (to hear the news) (a couple of hours).   13. He, (to retire) (1 few months).   14. Arnold, (to be in hospital) (November 12 th.).

EXERCISE 5. — *Change as follows :*

They'll have to approve it   →   It will have to be approved

1. You may have to do it.   2. She might have to type it again.   3. Will you have to repair the grinder ?   4. You would have to take out another insurance policy.   5. Would they have to recruit foreign labour ?   6. We shouldn't have to replace all the desks.

EXERCISE 6. — *Supply the missing words or phrases. Please answer with a complete sentence :*

1. Mr. Grant is determined to ... the old carpenter, Bob Hardiman.
2. An employee who has worked for a firm for a certain number of years ... for a pension.   3. Bob Hardiman is a real ... of the old days.   4. A meeting which is going on at the moment can also be said to be ...   5. In a private company, shares for sale have to be ... first to the other shareholders.

EXERCISE 7. — *Improvise quickly a brief oral comment on the following terms* :

1. a pension. 2. a deed. 3. a fund. 4. a craftsman. 5. a contribution.
6. a precedent.

EXERCISE 8. — *Translate into English* :

1. La réunion doit avoir lieu sous peu, ce jeudi-ci, je crois. 2. Il a laissé ses cotisations à la caisse. 3. Il peut toujours prétendre à une retraite. 4. Approuvez-vous tous le rapport financier ? 5. Il faut effectuer une autre période de travail avant que l'employé puisse avoir droit à la retraite complète. 6. On devra le dédommager sur les fonds de la société. 7. Il détient 50 % des actions. 8. Ils fermeront sûrement certains services peu rentables. 9. Vous avez tort de vouloir vous débarrasser d'un homme qui est dans la maison depuis si longtemps. 10. Essayez de lui faire changer d'avis, si vous pouvez. 11. Il tient à rendre la maison plus rentable et plus concurrentielle. 12. Je crois cette fois qu'il lui faudra choisir le moindre des deux maux. 13. Il n'a pas pu me donner d'autres renseignements. 14. Une importante société américaine veut les absorber. 15. Il faut qu'on trouve quelque chose pour lui garder son travail. 16. Vous devriez consulter le procès-verbal de la dernière assemblée. 17. Cette réunion ne va pas nous prendre longtemps. 18. Il semble bel et bien qu'il y ait une petite difficulté. 19. Dans l'état actuel des choses, il ne touchera que les trois quarts de sa retraite. 20. Mais c'est absurde ! Nous ne pouvons pas acheter toutes ces actions !

UNIT 11

THE CASE OF THE MISSING FILE

PART 1 : INTRODUCTION

1. WORD STUDY

Vocabulary

accounts department   service de la comptabilité
assistant   adjoint, sous-, employé de magasin
break down   flancher
cancel   annuler
cash   liquide, espèces ; comptant ; trésorerie
carefree   insouciant
character   personnage
cheerful   joyeux, gai
clerk   employé de bureau
crossed   (chèque) barré
design   conception, projet
Design Department   bureau des études
drawer   tireur *ou* tiroir
drawing   dessin, plan
eventually   finalement
exhibition   exposition
ex-policeman   ancien policier
file   dossier

frantic   hors de soi
go astray   s'égarer
guilty   coupable
handle   avoir en main
investigate   faire une enquête
launch   lancer, sortir
lock   fermer à clef
manufacture   fabrication
measurement   mesure, dimension
night watchman   veilleur de nuit
old   étrange, bizarre
payee   bénéficiaire, tiré
prosecute   poursuivre en justice
put back   retarder
range   gamme, série
receipt   décharge, reçu
rush   se précipiter
safe   coffre-fort
Sales Assistant   vendeur
sandwich course   cours avec stage intégré, cours mi-théorique, mi-pratique

security officier responsable de la sûreté	**subsidiary** filiale
security-minded conscient des problèmes de sécurité	**trace** trouver la trace
	trainee stagiaire
specifications caractéristiques	**unauthorised** non autorisée
spy espionner	**unlike** différent
steal voler	**van** camionnette
	watch veiller

Phrases

He bought £ 200 worth of...	il a acheté pour ·200 livres de...
He paid for it in cash	il a payé en liquide, en espèces
I haven't got £ 20, let alone £ 200	je n'ai pas 20 livres, alors encore moins 200

Explanations and Other Useful Terms

design department	where new products are developed, or old ones redesigned and modified. In this case, the designs are for a desk made of a new material which cannot be scratched or damaged and which looks like a high quality wood.
management trainee	someone who is considered to have the right qualifications to be trained for a management job. The training includes working, for a time, in various departments before being given a specific job with responsibility.
range	a group or series of the same kind, in this case a series of desks of one design, only differing in colour or size.
sales figures	calculations relating to total goods sold for any given period, or as here, an assessment of possible future sales.
sandwich course	colloquial term for a course consisting partly of study at a college and partly of practical work in a firm (see unit 20).
subsidiary factory	a second factory owned by a company but run by different personnel. In this case, the subsidiary factory makes office chairs.

Pronunciation

1 — i - (- -) character, limited, officer, practical, prosecute, reference, secretary, stupid

     - 2 (- -) assistant, because, behave, believe, confess, contain, design, dismiss, enjoy, eventually, important, industrial, investigate, inspector, material, policeman, propose, receipt, remember, replace, sarcastic, security, subsidiary, suspect (*verb*), suspicious, unscrupulous

     - - 3 (-) university, confidential, opportunity, international

2 — '-ion : precaution, circulation, information, confirmation, exhibition, prosecution, specification, investigation

3 — [s]   sign, case, miss, absorb, disappear, disappointed, *s*ub*s*idiary
     [z]   lose, observe, design, po*ss*ess
     [tʃ]   furniture, signature, expenditure, manufacture
     o → [ʌ]   does, done, Monday, other, worry, wonder, company
        → [u:]   do, lose, appr*o*ve, prove
        → [ou]   know, won't, only, hold, old, broke, st*o*len
        → [ə]   pens*io*n, c*o*mpulsory, reas*o*n, cust*o*mer
        → [ɔ]   got, not, gone, *o*ffice, wrong, soft, c*o*py, boss, lock
        → [ɔ:]   more, port, rep*o*rt, m*o*rning, imp*o*rtant
     [ai]   sign, file des*i*gn, find, Fr*i*day, r*i*val
     [ei]   main, change, range, cont*ai*n, rem*ai*n, d*a*nger

4 — Compare : confidence ['kɔnfidəns], confidential [ˌkɔnfi'denʃəl]
    a comment ['kɔment], to comment ['kɔment] *rarely* [kə'ment]

5 — Note : absolutely ['æbsəlu:tli], clerk [klaːk], false [fɔːls], figure ['figə], good gracious [ˌgud 'greiʃəs], guilty ['gilti], key [kiː], launch [lɔːntʃ], receipt [ri'siːt], spying ['spaiiŋ], unauthorised ['ʌn'ɔːθəraizd], espionage [ˌespjə'naːʒ], 'espjənidʒ *or* is'paiənidʒ].

2. SUMMARY

It is Monday morning in the Sales Office. John Martin's secretary, Sally, is very worried because her boss wants to see a file containing the designs for a new range of desks. She cannot find it anywhere. The file was marked 'Confidential —Limited Circulation', meaning that only a few people, in this case only heads of departments, were allowed to look at 5 it. This is because the design and material used for the desks is very new and the contents of the file are, therefore, secret. If it were stolen and got into the hands of an unscrupulous rival firm the designs could easily be copied. The file contains all the details of cost of manufacture, specifications, measurements, drawings, details of materials and planned 10 sales.

Sally has checked with the Design Department, who say they sent the file to John Martin on Friday. What is more, they have a signature for the receipt of the file, and that signature is Sally's. She is frantic as she remembers signing for some files but not that one. She rushes into the 15 main Sales Office and asks Sid (short for Sidney) Harris, the Sales Assistant, if he has seen it. She has already asked him once before. He, however, has his own troubles, as a customer came in early that morning, bought £200 worth of office furniture, paid for it in cash, and drove it away in a van. Sid left the money on his desk for five minutes, and when 20 he got back with the key to the safe to lock the money away it had all disappeared.

The Security Officer is called in to investigate the loss. To stop people stealing from a factory or office block, there is usually a Security Officer, often an ex-policeman. Nowadays, industrial espionage, spying, is unfor- 25 tunately on the increase, and because of this fact, the Security Officer has to try to make the staff aware of the possible dangers and to take stricter precautions. The system of signing for files, for example, proves which person or office handled them last. The Security Officer is responsible, too, for appointing night watchmen to go round the building at night, to 30 see that doors are locked and that no unauthorised person, one without permission, has remained behind after working hours.

When the loss of money is reported to him the Security Officer interviews all those people who might have had the opportunity to go into the Sales Office. He later calls in the police. One of the clerks, who has only 35 been with the firm two months, behaves in a suspicious way. When they check his references it is found that this clerk, Frank Wallis, has given false information. He eventually breaks down and confesses.

There is another character we have not met before: Christopher Thorn. He is a management trainee, that is, he is training to be a manager by 40 learning the work of all the different departments. He is at a university, on a sandwich course, and this is his year of practical training. He is a cheerful, carefree person, who has a lot to learn about office routine.

1. CONVERSATION

(Recorded Text)

(Sally is talking to Sidney Harris, the Sales Assistant)

SALLY	Sid, are you sure you haven't seen the missing file? I could have brought it into this office with some other files. Please have a good look everywhere. It's marked 'Confidential' and it has a limited circulation.
SIDNEY HARRIS	Oh, Sally! Do go away. I've got much worse troubles than 5 a lost file.
SALLY	But it's serious. The file's got all the details of the new desk range. Mr. Martin says if anyone copied our designs it could put the work on the new desks back at least a year! And we're supposed to be launching them at the 10 International Office Equipment Exhibition.
HARRIS	Sally, please, something much worse has just happened.
SALLY	Why, what's the matter?
HARRIS	I've got the Security Officer coming up in a minute. It's just a matter of a loss of £200 in cash. 15
SALLY	Oh, no! When did that happen, and how?
HARRIS	Somebody came in this morning, bought two hundred pounds worth of office furniture and paid in cash.
SALLY	How odd. Don't most people pay by cheque ?
HARRIS	Yes, usually. Well, there was no one in the Accounts 20 Department, so I went to get the key of the safe. When I got back ... the money had gone!
SALLY	How terrible, Sid. Is it your responsibility? Will they expect you to replace the money?
HARRIS	Well, I haven't got £20, let alone £200. Oh, here's the 25 Security Officer now. Good morning, Mr. Johnson.
MR. JOHNSON	Good morning. Good morning, Miss Langley. This is a very unfortunate affair. Now, Sid, I'll have to ask you some questions about the money that's missing.
SALLY	Oh, Mr. Johnson, before you start, I'm afraid I have to 30 report the loss of an important file. It's a very serious matter.

(Later Mr. Johnson goes to see John Martin)

JOHN   Yes, do come in, Johnson. I've just had the police inspector here. I would never have believed that the new clerk would have been so stupid as to steal the money. We'll 35 have to dismiss him, I suppose, but, as I told the inspector, I don't want to prosecute. But what I want to know now is whether you've any news for me about that missing file?

JOHNSON   I'm very sorry, Mr. Martin, I can't trace it at all. Your 40 secretary signed for it on Friday, there's no doubt about that.

JOHN   It's very unlike Sally. She's usually so careful.

JOHNSON   Surely she should have locked it up on Friday night before she left? 45

JOHN   She usually does lock everything away before she leaves the office, but in this case she doesn't even remember seeing the file.

JOHNSON   Mr. Martin, how long has she been working for you?

JOHNSON: 'Mr. Martin, how long has she been working for you?'

JOHN   Oh, good gracious, I trust Sally absolutely. She's worked 50 for me now ... let's see ... for just over two years ... ever since I joined the firm myself.

JOHNSON   You trust people very easily, Mr. Martin.

JOHN   Of course I do. How can you work with people if you suspect them all the time? 55

JOHNSON	Well, in my job . . .
SALLY	Oh, excuse me, Mr. Martin, Mr. Thorn is here. He's been over to visit the subsidiary factory in Essex today. He wants to know if he can have a word with you.
JOHN	Ask him to come in, Sally. 60
SALLY	Right.
JOHN	Johnson, you know Christopher Thorn, don't you?
JOHNSON	He's the management trainee, isn't he?
JOHN	Yes, that's right. Hello, Christopher. Come in.
CHRISTOPHER	I just wondered what you wanted me to do tomorrow, Mr. 65 Martin.
JOHN	Well, first of all, did you read all those papers I gave you on Friday?
CHRISTOPHER	Yes, I've got them here in my brief-case. Here you are. And . . . er . . . here's another file. I took this home as well 70 and had a look through it over the weekend. I enjoyed reading Mr. Grant's sarcastic comments about the proposed sales figures !
JOHNSON	Mr. Martin! Isn't this the missing file?
JOHN	What? Yes, it is. Thank goodness. Sally! 75
SALLY	Yes, Mr. Martin?
JOHN	We've found the missing file. Christopher, here, is guilty! He had it all the time.
CHRISTOPHER	Oh, I'm sorry. I'd no idea you'd been looking for it.
JOHNSON	Something will have to be done to make everyone in this 80 company more security-minded.

PRACTICE SENTENCES

Say the practice sentences on the record :

  i I'm afraid I have to report the loss of an important file.

 ii The file's marked Confidential.

iii Your secretary signed for the file on Friday.

 iv The Security Officer is coming.

  v I've got the papers in my brief-case.

 vi He's the management trainee.

vii He's been to visit the subsidiary factory

2. PAYMENT BY CHEQUE

There is not much to be done about stolen cash, unless the thief can be caught, but if a cheque is stolen or lost you can stop payment of it, cancel it. It is discovered in the Accounts Department of Harper & Grant that The Maple Addressing Machine Co., from whom they have bought a new addressing machine, have never received the crossed cheque sent in payment (for *crossed* see Unit 13). The Chief Accountant is afraid it may have been stolen or have gone astray in the post. He sends the following telegram to the firm's bank:

TO: WINBANC LONDON

PLEASE CANCEL CROSSED CHEQUE B 394068 DRAWER HARPER & GRANT PAYEE MAPLE ADDRESSING MACHINE COMPANY AMOUNT £250 CONFIRMATION FOLLOWS

FROM: HARPO LONDON

Here is the letter of confirmation mentioned in the telegram:

Great West Road
London W25   *Directors:*
Telephone 01-567 1112 Ambrose Harper *(Chairman)*
Telex 80153   Hector Grant *(Managing)*
Telegrams Harp LDN William Buckhurst FCA *(Secretary)* **Harper and Grant Limited**
                    Margaret Wiles

The Manager,
Windermere Bank,
68 Cambridge Street,
London, W.27.   2nd January, 197..

Dear Sir,

    This is to confirm our telegram sent to you earlier today.   Will you please stop payment of crossed cheque No. B. 394068.   The payee was The Maple Addressing Machine Co. Ltd., and the amount was £250.

    Please acknowledge that this cheque will not now be honoured so that we may issue a duplicate cheque in payment of our account.

    With thanks,

                Yours faithfully,

                Ferguson

                Chief Accountant
                HARPER & GRANT LTD.

PART 3 : NOTES AND PRACTICE

1. RAPPEL GRAMMATICAL

Summary :

3. Rappelons encore que **some** désigne une quantité limitée mais certaine. Il s'emploie donc en affirmative (la quantité existe) et en interro-négative (on défie l'interlocuteur de nier qu'elle existe). **Any** désigne toute valeur de zéro à l'infini. En affirmative, il a la valeur indéfinie de n'importe lequel ; il sert de déterminant au nom : en négative (quantité niée = zéro) et en interrogative (toute quantité possible de zéro à l'infini) :

Were any of the crates damaged ?	Certaines caisses ont-elles été endommagées ?
Weren't some of these boxes to be despatched to day ?	Certaines de ces caisses ne devaient-elles pas être expédiées aujourd'hui ?
She can't find it anywhere	Elle ne peut le trouver nulle part

4. Notons que devant un singulier indénombrable on rencontre plutôt **some** :

There's some carbon paper in the cupboard	Il y a du papier carbone dans l'armoire

Mais avec le pluriel d'un nom dénombrable, on trouve le plus souvent **a few** :

Only a few people had seen the designs	Quelques personnes seulement avaient vu les nouveaux projets

Few dénote une insuffisance :

Few people could carve wood as finely as Hardiman	Rares sont ceux qui pourraient sculpter le bois aussi bien que Hardiman

7. **If it were stolen** : le subjonctif **were** exprime ici l'idée que l'hypothèse n'apparaît pas encore comme vraisemblable.

12. **Department** est suivi d'un relatif **who** et d'un pluriel bien que neutre et singulier, parce qu'il désigne ici le groupe de personnes travaillant dans ce service.

15. Comparons les deux constructions de **remember** :

She remembered to post the mail	Elle pensa à poster le courrier
She remembered posting the letter just after going out of the shop	Elle se rappela qu'elle avait posté le courrier après être sortie du magasin

20. **For** peut amener un complément de temps à un verbe au prétérit, au parfait, ou au pluperfect. Comparons :

He's been away for a month	Il est absent depuis un mois
He was away for a month	Il a été absent pendant un mois (*il est revenu*)
He'd been away for a month when we got his report at last	Il était absent depuis un mois quand nous avons enfin eu son rapport

28. **Which** s'emploie ici parce qu'il y a choix.

34. **May, might** expriment l'éventualité. **Might** exprime une plus grande incertitude :

She may be in John's office	Elle est peut-être dans le bureau de John
You might have an accident	Vous pourriez avoir un accident

Comparons :

She may have lost the file	Peut-être a-t-elle perdu le dossier
He might have had to replace the money	Il aurait pû devoir remplacer l'argent

Conversation :

2. Il n'est pas rare en anglais moderne que **can** « encaisse » certaines des valeurs qu'une grammaire plus traditionnelle assigne exclusivement à **may**. Ainsi, l'idée de permission est souvent exprimée par **can** :

Can I have your stapler just a moment ?	Puis-je avoir votre agrafeuse un petit instant ?

ci-dessus, ligne 34) :

Notons du reste que **may** n'a la nuance de permission qu'à l'interrogative, et ses corollaires (réponse à cette interrogative et discours indirect, où **might** a le sens passé, et non la valeur modale comme dans l'exemple

May I smoke in this shop ?	Puis-je fumer dans cet atelier ?
Christopher asked if he might smoke in the fuel store	Christopher a demandé s'il pouvait fumer dans le magasin aux carburants

Dans l'exemple présent, ' **I could have brought it** ', Sally n'envisage pas le fait comme une chose matériellement impossible (nuance de **can** = pouvoir physique, matériel) et le prétérit, qui a une valeur modale ici et non une valeur de passé, exprime l'hypothèse, l'éventualité.

10. We're supposed + infinitive. Notons certaines constructions semblables

He is known to have stolen a large sum of money	On sait qu'il a volé une importante somme
He is said to have made a large fortune	On dit qu'il a amassé une importante fortune
He is expected to come early	On s'attend à ce qu'il arrive tôt

A remarquer que la négative de **to be supposed** et **to be expected** exprime une interdiction polie :

You are not expected to take those files home	Vous ne pouvez pas emporter ces dossiers chez vous
You are not supposed to mention it to the boss	Ce n'est pas à vous d'en parler au patron

34. Would à la première personne souligne l'idée que John n'aurait jamais accepté de croire une telle chose possible.

49. L'interrogation correspondant aux compléments de temps introduits par **for** s'exprime à l'aide de **how long** :

How long has he been away?	Depuis combien de temps est-il absent ?
How long was he in Abraca?	Combien de temps est-il resté en Abraca ?

Pour interroger sur le temps écoulé depuis la fin d'une action, l'interrogation commencera par **how long ago**, ou simplement par **when** :

How long ago was that?	Il y a combien de temps que cela a eu lieu ?
When did you meet him? **— A week ago**	Quand l'avez-vous rencontré ? — Il y a huit jours

La réponse de John (ll. 50-52) est un bel exemple de toutes ces constructions.

2. EXERCISES

EXERCISE 1. — *Change as follows* :

She can find some → **She can't find any**

1. We sent some catalogues.   2. There is some money in the safe.   3. They will show you some of their designs.   4. You'll be able to find it somewhere. 5. She met somebody at the Sales Office.   6. They can find it somewhere else.   7. We have to replace some of the articles.

EXERCISE 2. — Change as follows :

    She can find some →   Can she find any ?

1. They've shown you some new designs. 2. She ordered some flimsy for the office. 3. They found it somewhere. 4. You want something to pack these goods in. 5. She said it to someone else. 6. We can do something for you. 7. He left some money on the desk. 8. He has some news about the missing file.

EXERCISE 3. — Ask questions about the following statements :

1. He's been here *for a month.* 2. He came *a week ago.* 3. *It's three weeks* since he wrote. 4. He worked with Harper & Grant *for twenty years.* 5. She's been discussing it with him *for two hours.* 6. He phoned *an hour ago.* 7. He stayed in Abraca *for a week.* 8. He went there *a year ago.* 9. She brought this file for you *yesterday.*

EXERCISE 4. — Change as follows :

    Somebody stole it →   John is afraid it may have been stolen

1. Somebody lost it. 2. Somebody took it away. 3. Somebody sent the cheque. 4. Somebody mishandled the crates. 5. Somebody copied the new designs. 6. Somebody revealed the figures. 7. Somebody sent another telegram. 8. Somebody burnt these papers.

EXERCISE 5. — Change as follows :

    He stole the money, he was stupid→ I would never have believed that
    He would have been so stupid as to steal the money

1. Johnson stopped the thief, he was clever. 2. Sally finished before 6, she worked fast. 3. He did it by himself, he is courageous. 4. He repaired the tape recorder, he was clever. 5. She locked them away, she was cautions. 6. He wrote a report, he was intelligent.

EXERCISE 6. — Please say, in a short sentence, what you would do in the following circumstances : (Begin your answer ' I would', 'I might'. The answers in the Key will be a guide to what your answers should be) :

1. You are lucky enough to have a lot of money in your pocket. You want to buy a typewriter. What might you do ? (Use the word *cash*). 2. However, before you hand over the money, you discover that it has been stolen. What would you do ? 3. You are the Sales Manager and want to engage a new clerk. What would you do to find out if what he says about his last job is true ? 4. You are the Managing Director and have just given the O.K. to some designs for a new type of chair. At this stage, you only want a certain number of people in the firm to see the designs. How would you mark the file before it goes round ? 5. Where would you keep money and valuable documents to protect them from fire or theft ?

EXERCISE 7. — *The following are some expressions in everyday office use. Please give a commonly-used colloquial version of them.*

Example : Please *telephone* Mr. Brown.
Please *ring* Mr. Brown.

1. I want to *speak to* you. 2. 12 th. February is the *last possible date* (for production to start, delivery of goods to be made, etc.). 3. Please *get in touch with* him at once. 4. We should like you to *take immediate action*.

EXERCISE 8. — *Improvise a brief comment on the following terms* :

1. to launch a product. 2. limited circulation. 3. confidential. 4. to pay in cash. 5. a safe. 6. the Security Officer.

EXERCISE 9. — *Translate into English* :

1. Je crains d'avoir à signaler la perte d'un important dossier. 2. Le dossier porte la mention « Confidentiel ». 3. Votre secrétaire a signé une décharge pour le dossier vendredi. 4. Le responsable de la sûreté arrive 5. J'ai les papiers dans mon porte-documents. 6. C'est le stagiaire d'administration. 7. Il a été visiter la filiale. 8. Quelques employés connaissaient Wallis. 9. Il y a peu d'employés qui soient préoccupés par la sécurité. 10. J'espère qu'elle n'oubliera pas de poster le courrier. 11. Je ne me souviens pas d'avoir vu ce Monsieur auparavant. 12. Depuis combien de temps attendiez-vous quand le patron est arrivé ? 13. Vous ne pouvez pas fumer dans le dépôt des carburants. 14. Est-ce que la plupart des clients ne paient pas par chèque ? 15. Il est censé être allé chercher la clef du coffre au Bureau de la Comptabilité. 16. Il aurait pu avoir l'occasion de visiter l'exposition internationale de l'équipement de bureau. 17. Le stagiaire a beaucoup de choses à apprendre sur le travail courant du bureau. 18. Il vient d'arriver quelque chose de bien pire. 19. Je n'en ai pas parlé au sous-directeur, alors encore moins au directeur. 20. Je me demandais ce que vous vouliez que je fasse demain.

UNIT 12

A LABOUR DISPUTE

PART 1 : INTRODUCTION

1. WORD STUDY

Vocabulary

agitate faire de l'agitation
aid secours, assistance
aim but, objectif
amount (to) revenir (à)
argue discuter
behaviour conduite, comportement
besides en outre ; en plus de
break enfreindre, violer
bring up soulever (*question*)
cheat tricher
claim revendication
clerical de bureau
clock in pointer
comparatively relativement
cut réduction
day-to-day de routine
disown désavouer
District Organiser délégué syndical de district
dock rogner, réduire
drop laisser tomber
dues cotisation
elect élire

engineer monter, manigancer
fitter ajusteur
foreman contremaître, agent de maîtrise
grievance grief
ill feeling malaise
increase augmentation
insurance assurance
issue problème
level niveau
look after s'occuper de
machiner (machinist) mécanicien
medical scheme programme d'assistance médicale, mutuelle
meeting réunion, assemblée
operative ouvrier
overtime heures supplémentaires
premises lieux ; locaux
press room atelier d'emboutissage
pressure pression
profit sharing intéressement, participation aux bénéfices
punch perforer

— 184 —

relationship relations
reliable sûr, digne de confiance
reluctant peu enclin, peu disposé
rules règlement
share partager
shop steward délégué syndical
straightforward simple
strike grève
  strike pay allocation de grève
subscription cotisation
subtract soustraire

swear jurer
time card carte (*pour pointer*)
time clock horloge pointeuse
trade union syndicat
underpaid mal rétribué
unofficial spontanée (*grève*)
walk-out débrayage, grève
warn avertir
welfare bien-être, prévoyance
  sociale
wild cat strike grève sauvage

Phrases

They serve as a channel of communications both ways	ils servent de trait d'union dans les deux sens
What it amounts to is...	cela revient en fait à...
It will be a case of dismissal	ce sera un motif de licenciement

Explanations and Other Useful Terms

to bring up a question	to introduce a question as a subject for discussion
clocking in	on arrival an employee takes his card out of the rack and puts it in the time clock which registers the correct time on it. On leaving he takes his card out of the rack and again puts it in the time clock.
docked	to get one's pay docked is to lose some of one's wages : a portion of the wages normally payable is deducted and is not paid.
engineered by	organised by
District Organiser	a paid employee of a union who looks after the interests of members in a certain area.
overtime	extra hours over and above the ordinary working day : working late at night, on Saturdays and Sundays, etc.
press	a machine which shapes or forms metal by exerting pressure. By changing tools, one press can be made to produce a variety of components. The bodies of cars, refrigerators, washing machines and office equipment are usually made from pressed steel.

to press	here, to insist on.
profit sharing scheme	a system of allowing employees to share in profits by arranging for them to buy shares in the company, or by issuing a bonus scheme, etc.
shop floor	the shop floor is another way of referring to a particular shop, or department, of the factory or, in a general way, it refers to the whole working area of the factory.
time and a half	the usual pay for working overtime is the ordinary pay per hour, plus half as much again. For certain extra hours the pay can be time and a quarter, or double time.
union rules	the rules which a member of a union promises to follow when he joins.
wage claim	in industry a demand for higher wages. (**Wages** : money paid to workers, usually weekly ; a **salary** is usually paid monthly).
walk-out	a slang term for the actual leaving by employees of their place of work in protest. Usually the start of a strike.
wild cat strike	a slang expression used for an unofficial strike, which takes place without union approval, i.e. it is organised by the employees themselves.
work rules	the rules and regulations of a particular firm. These are normally agreed with the unions concerned.

Pronunciation

1 — 1 - (- -) agitate, consequence, district, general, grievance, incident, interesting, labour, medical, member, metal, operative, personal, premises, recognised, sponsor, system

   - 2 (- -) absurd, affair, agree, assembly, belong, between, collect, dispute, elected, engage, exact, machine, machinist, majority, obtain, offence, percent, reliable, ridiculous, reluctant, suppose, subtract

   - - 3 represent, correspond, understand, engineered

2 — '-ic (al) clerical, electrical, medical, technical, enthusiastic

3 — [ʃ]   shop, insure, insurance, permission, pressure, condition, ambitious, official

[ju:] new, dues, issue, union, dispute, steward

[ɔ]   clock, block, dock, solve, problem, belong, office, correspond

[e]   level, percent, member, assembly, recognise

[ei]   aid, aim, paid, trade, claim, wage, break, labour, vacant, day-to-day

[ai]   wild, strike, arrive, decide, serious-minded

[ɛə]   share, swear, welfare, affair, prepared, compared, profit-sharing

4 — Compare : clerk [klɑ:k],   clerical ['klerikəl]
subscribe [səb'skraib],   subscription [səb'skripʃən]
represent [ˌrepri'zent],   representation [ˌreprizen'teiʃən]
communicate [kə'mjunikeit],   communication [kəˌmjuni'keiʃən]
personal ['pə:sənl],   personnel [pə:sə'nəl]
compare [kəm'pɛə],   comparable ['kɔmpərəbl],   comparatively [kəm'pærətivli]
major ['meidʒə],   majority [mə'dʒɔriti]

5 — Note : behaviour [bi'heivjə], create [kri'eit], disown [dis'oun], premises ['premisiz], reliable [ri'laiəbl], negotiate [ni'gouʃieit], surely ['ʃuəli], a walk-out ['wɔ:k-aut], welfare ['welfɛə].

2. SUMMARY

Harper & Grant have not got a *closed shop*, that is, they do not make it a condition of employment that a worker must belong to a certain trade union. But ninety per cent of the workers are members of one or other of the unions. All the toolmakers, skilled machiners (machinists), sheet-metal workers, assembly-shop workers and fitters belong to one union, 5
the electricians to another and the office staff to a clerical union. Every member has to pay a subscription, that is, a sum of money paid regularly to the particular union (often referred to as *union dues*). Each union's affairs are looked after by a *shop steward*, who is elected by the workers on the shop floor. The shop steward is at the day-to-day level of repre- 10
sentation between a company and a union. He represents the workers in a particular shop, or department, in a factory. The shop stewards are recognised by the management, and they serve as a channel of communication both ways. They are allowed to collect union dues on the premises, but they can hold meetings in the factory or office block only 15
with the permission of the management.

Besides obtaining the best possible working conditions for their members, unions in Britain, as in many other countries, also organise medical schemes, insurance and legal aid for their members. And they use part of their funds, the money collected from the members, to pay a weekly sum 20 of money to their members if they are out on official strike. An official strike is one recognised by the union. Strike pay is small compared with the workers' normal wages. They do not draw it if it is an unofficial strike or a 'wild cat' strike.

In most firms the relationship between management and unions is good, 25 but sometimes a shop steward is ambitious to get more personal power. In this episode a certain shop steward uses a worker who has a grievance, something making him angry or annoyed, to create trouble in the works. His aim is to help put pressure on the management in connection with a claim for a general wage increase. Many employees, of course, think they 30 are underpaid, and some managements are reluctant to increase wages until forced to do so. Some firms have introduced profit-sharing schemes, so that employees can share directly in the results of harder work or better organisation. However, the difficulty here is that the majority are not prepared to take a cut in wages if the firm has a bad year. Good 35 employee–management relations often present difficulties and problems. Some firms solve these problems better than others. Usually Harper & Grant have good relations with their employees, as they are a comparatively small 'family' firm.

The episode starts with clocking in. When an employee arrives at a 40 factory to start work the first thing he does is to clock in. A time clock punches a mark on the worker's time card to correspond with the exact time of arrival. Trying to cheat this system is a very serious offence. The Works Manager, Ted Fielding, comes to consult the *Personnel Manager*, Ian Hampden, about an operative who seems to have decided to ignore 45 the rules. The chief responsibilities of a Personnel Manager are employing and dismissing staff and looking after and improving the employees' welfare and conditions of work.

PART 2 : CONVERSATION AND DOCUMENTS

1. CONVERSATION

(Recorded Text)

(*In Ian Hampden's office*)

TED FIELDING **Mr. Hampden, we've got trouble in the press room this morning.**

IAN HAMPDEN	Oh dear, what's it all about, Ted?
TED	One of the press operatives arrived an hour and a half late.
IAN	But that's a straightforward affair. He simply gets his pay 5 docked. That's why we have a clocking-in system.
TED	But the point is the man was clocked in at eight o'clock. Symes, who stands by the time clock, swears he saw nothing irregular.
IAN	Is Symes reliable? 10
TED	Yes, he is. That's why we chose him for the job.
IAN	Have you spoken to the man who was late?
TED	Not yet. I thought I'd have a word with you first. He's a dif- ficult man. And I think there's some trouble on the shop floor. I've got a feeling that one of the shop stewards 15 is behind this. The foreman told me that Jack Green's been very active around the shop the last few days.
IAN	Well, what do you want me to do?
TED	I was wondering if you'd see Smith, the man who was late, because you're so much better at handling things like 20 this than I am.
IAN	Oh, all right, I'll see him. I must say I agree with you about there being bad feeling in the works. I've had the idea for some time that Jack Green's been busy agitating in connection with the latest wage claim . He's not like 25 the other stewards. He's always trying to make trouble. Well, I'll get the foreman to send Smith up here.

(*Later*)

IAN	Ah, Smith. Come in, will you. Please sit down. I under- stand your card was punched for eight o'clock this morn- ing and that you arrived at nine thirty. 30
SMITH	That's right.
IAN	You mean you knew your card was punched by someone else at eight o'clock?
SMITH	Yes.
IAN	I suppose you know we can dismiss you for this? What it 35 amounts to is that you are asking to be paid for services you never gave.
SMITH	No, I'm not asking that.

IAN	Then I don't understand.
SMITH	I cleaned Mr. Wiles' car last night out of works' time. 40
IAN	Well, that doesn't affect the issue.
SMITH	I should be paid for it, shouldn't I?
IAN	But you are paid surely ...
SMITH	Overtime ? If I work overtime I want overtime pay—time and a half, that's the rule, isn't it? 45
IAN	But this is a private arrangement. It has nothing to do with the works. Have you discussed this with Mr. Wiles?
SMITH	There's nothing to discuss. If I work an hour on his car I take an hour and a half from my day's work. 50
IAN	Well, I'm not going to argue about something so absurd. As I see it, you've broken the rules. Naturally an hour and a half will be subtracted from your pay this week. And I must warn you that if this happens again it will be a case of dismissal. 55
SMITH	Just you try dismissing me. You'll have a walk-out on your hands.
IAN	I'm sorry, but those are the rules. If you break them you must take the consequences; you know that perfectly well. ... 60

(*In Peter Wiles's office*)

PETER WILES	But, Ian, that's ridiculous! Smith never complained to me about it. If he had I'd have paid him a bit more, or taken the car to the garage. They do a much better job there, anyway.
IAN	It's possible the whole thing has been engineered by Jack 65 Green. I've heard that he's going to get the District Organiser of the National Workers' Union to negotiate a wage claim.
PETER	Oh, not again!
IAN	Personally I feel there should be some system here of profit sharing. If not, we shall go on having little incidents 70 like this one. They're a direct result of ill-feeling in the works.
PETER	I can't see H.G. being enthusiastic about profit sharing! Why don't you bring it up at the Management Committee Meeting this afternoon. 75

IAN	Yes, I think I will. And then I'm going to send for Jack Green. I've just had a talk with Symes and found out something very interesting. Now listen to this. . . .

(In Ian Hampden's office)

JACK GREEN	I really don't see much point in this meeting, Mr. Hampden. As I said to you this morning, we're going to ask the 80 Union to press a wage claim. And unless you have some concrete proposals to make about a wage increase, I don't think we have anything to say to each other.
IAN	I'm sorry, I don't agree. First of all, I think I've got some information that may interest you. We discussed profit 85 sharing at the Management Committee Meeting today. What do you feel your colleagues will think about that?
GREEN	They'll think the same as I do. We don't want talk, we want figures.
IAN	I think they'll be very interested. I think they'll want to go 90 into details with us when the proposals have been worked out. I think they'll want to co-operate.
GREEN	Are you suggesting . . .?
IAN	I'm suggesting that you're using Smith to make unnecessary trouble. 95
GREEN	I don't like that accusation, Mr. Hampden.
IAN	I don't care whether you like it or not. Smith is not a co-operative man, but he wasn't capable of thinking this out for himself. He told me that if I dismissed him there'd be a walk-out. Who gave him that idea? Did you talk to him? 100
GREEN	I did. He told me about this car business.
IAN	And the clocking-in incident?
GREEN	I don't follow you.
IAN	I suppose you had nothing to do with arranging that Smith's card was punched by someone else? That's an 105 action which is against the works rules, which have been approved by all the trades unions represented on this site.
GREEN	Of course not.
IAN	Then why were you talking to Symes precisely at eight o'clock this morning? How was it that you got him to 110 turn his back long enough for Smith's ticket to be punched?
GREEN	I . . . er . . .

IAN   Look, Jack, I think you'd better drop this one fast. I know you're trying to make a name for yourself, but your own 115 union would disown you for this sort of behaviour. This isn't the way to do things. See Smith, will you, and explain what has happened.

JACK   I think ... er ... your ... er ... profit-sharing proposals do perhaps alter the situation. Yes, I'll ... er ... speak to 120 Smith.

IAN   Good. Well, we've no more to discuss for the moment, have we? Goodnight.

IAN: 'How was it that you got him to turn his back long enough for Smith's ticket to be punched?'

PRACTICE SENTENCES

Say the practice sentences on the record :

   i He arrived an hour and a half late.
  ii The man was clocked in at 8 o'clock.
 iii An hour and a half will be subtracted from his pay.
 iv If this happens again it will be a case of dismissal.
   v There should be some system of profit sharing.
  vi I'll bring it up at the Management Committee Meeting.
 vii The Union is going to negotiate a wage claim.

2. PERSONNEL MANAGEMENT AND REFERENCES

One of the main functions of a Personnel Manager is the engagement and dismissal of employees in the works. He ensures that conditions of work are good, because people who enjoy their jobs work better than those who do not. A measure of a Personnel Manager's efficiency is his *labour turnover*, the percentage of employees who leave in a year and have to be replaced. Labour turnover is expensive, because it costs a lot to advertise for, engage and train new staff. A good Personnel Manager is good at *selection*, at picking the right man for the right job, and will probably have been trained in modern selection techniques. Personnel management also includes safety and welfare, and the organisation of such social activities (dances, outings and sports) as the company wishes to sponsor. A Personnel Manager should always be available to give advice on personal matters to any employee.

THE FABMOD FURNISHING COMPANY LIMITED
Birmingham

The Personnel Manager,
Harper & Grant Ltd.,
Great West Road,
London, W.25.   9th January, 197..
                          CONFIDENTIAL

Dear Sir,

     We have received an application for the post of assistant director of our Research and Development Department from Mr. James Glover who, we understand, left your firm two months' ago. He has given us your name as a reference and we should be grateful if you would give us some information about him.

     We should like to know how long Mr. Glover worked for you; whether you were satisfied with his work; the reasons for the termination of his employment with you, and, above all, whether he is trustworthy. We have had some trouble in the past with some of our research secrets being sold to rival firms so the latter, is naturally, of the utmost importance to us.

     Any other information you can give us about Mr. Glover would be very gratefully received.

     With thanks,

                                     Yours faithfully,

                                     G. Hassock

                                     George Hassock
                                     Personnel Manager.

The following is a letter sent to Ian Hampden, asking for a reference. When a firm takes on a new employee it is usual to ask for a *reference*, that is, the name of someone or some firm who will be ready to answer questions about his character and work. The reference is for James Glover, who used to work in the Research and Development Department. He left the firm because he wanted to work in Birmingham for family reasons. The second letter is Mr. Hampden's reply.

Great West Road	*Directors:*
London W25	Ambrose Harper *(Chairman)*
Telephone 01-567 1112	Hector Grant *(Managing)*
Telex 80153	William Buckhurst FCA *(Secretary)*
Telegrams Harp LDN	Margaret Wiles

Harper and Grant Limited

G. Hassock, Esq.,
Personnel Manager,
Fabmod Furnishing Co. Ltd.,
Birmingham.   11th January, 197..
                    CONFIDENTIAL

Dear Mr. Hassock,

             In reply to your letter of 9th January, Mr. James Glover worked for us for two and a half years in our Research Department and proved a very valuable, inventive and co-operative member of the firm.   It was with considerable regret that we learnt of his wish to leave us and go to Birmingham, a decision which, we understand, was forced on him for family reasons.

             I would like to add that before we knew his reasons for leaving, we offered him the post of deputy head of our own Research Department which will be vacant this year.

             We were entirely satisfied with Mr. Glover during the period that he worked here.   Speaking personally, I consider him to be honest, serious-minded and enthusiastic.   He was popular with his colleagues and should prove very capable in a position of authority.

             To sum up, we were very sorry indeed to lose him.

                              Yours faithfully,

                              Ian Hampden
                              Personnel Manager
                              HARPER & GRANT LTD.

PART 3 : NOTES AND PRACTICE

1. RAPPEL GRAMMATICAL

Summary

1. Au sens de *posséder*, on emploie moins souvent **to have** que **to have got**. Il en est de même assez souvent au sens de *devoir* :

Have they got a computer ?	Ont-ils un ordinateur ?
I've got to see the boss	Je dois voir le patron

1. Notons encore au passage quelques exemples de l'emploi de **it** pour annoncer un infinitif ou une subordonnée :

When will it suit you for our representative to call ?	Quand cela vous conviendra-t-il que notre représentant passe ?
You'll find it so much easier to use our device	Vous trouverez tellement plus facile d'employer notre système
I consider it absurd to discuss any longer	J'estime absurde de discuter plus longtemps
Don't you think it unwise to send for the shop steward ?	Ne pensez-vous pas qu'il soit peu sage d'appeler le délégué syndical ?

14. **Both** est adjectif devant articles, possessifs et démonstratifs :

You'll find it in both these catalogues	Vous le trouverez dans ces deux catalogues

Il est pronom, employé seul ou avec **of** + pronom personnel :

We met them both	Nous les avons rencontrés tous deux
Ian Hampden warned both of them	Ian Hampden les a mis en garde tous deux

Il peut être adverbe avec le sens de *à la fois* :

She's got degrees both in modern languages and business management	Elle est en même temps diplômée de langues et d'administration des entreprises

29. **Help** est suivi soit de l'infinitif complet avec **to**, soit de l'infinitif sans **to** :

Would you help me to unload these crates ?	Voudriez-vous m'aider à décharger ces caisses ?
Shall I help you sort these papers ?	Voulez-vous que je vous aide à trier ces papiers ?

Help + infinitif sans **to** est plus fréquent en américain. Son usage se répand en anglais.

32. **To do so** : l'expression remplace ' **to increase wages** ' qui vient d'être exprimé.

33. De plus en plus en anglais moderne **so that**, conjonction de but, est suivi de **can** au lieu du plus traditionnel **may**. **Should** introduit plutôt une notion de contrainte. On peut également entendre une infinitive :

They introduced the scheme so that employees may share in the firm's profits	Ils ont adopté ce système pour que les employés profitent des bénéfices de l'entreprise
They put a notice on the containers so that the men shouldn't use their hooks	Ils ont mis une notice sur les containers pour que les ouvriers n'emploient pas leurs crochets
I left it on your desk for you to have a look (so that you can) may (have a look)	Je l'ai laissé sur votre bureau pour que vous y jetiez un coup d'œil

Conversation

4. Notons : **half an hour** = une demi-heure

a quarter of an hour = un quart d'heure

18. La construction infinitive après **want** est simple, pourtant les Français y sont très réfractaires. Voyons quelques exemples de verbes entraînant la proposition infinitive :

Do you wish me to demonstrate ?	Désirez-vous que je fasse une démonstration ?
You can't allow Green to do that	Vous ne pouvez pas permettre à Green de faire cela
I like the men to comply strictly with the rules	J'aime que les hommes observent rigoureusement le règlement
Green didn't want anyone to know what he'd done	Green ne voulait pas qu'on sache ce qu'il avait fait
Didn't I ask you to sign a receipt each time ?	Est-ce que je ne vous ai pas demandé de signer une décharge à chaque fois ?
I warned him not to be late	Je l'ai averti de ne pas être en retard
Why didn't you advise him to accept the post ?	Pourquoi ne lui avez-vous pas conseillé d'accepter la place ?
I should prefer you to talk to the shop steward	Je préfèrerais que vous parliez au délégué syndical

Il en est d'autres ; mais on voit que les plus difficiles pour un français sont ceux dont les équivalents en français sont suivis d'un subjonctif.

22-23. I agree about there being bad feeling in the works : la préposition est suivie de -ing. Si le verbe a un sujet dans la proposition personnelle correspondante, et même lorsque ce sujet, comme ici, est un sujet apparent (**there is bad feeling in the works, I agree with you about it**) on retrouve ce sujet devant le nom verbal :

I am surprised at the ship being late	Je m'étonne que le bateau soit en retard
You shouldn't wonder at there being a delay	Il ne faut pas vous étonner qu'il y ait un retard

63. Just you try. A l'impératif, deuxième personne, on peut entendre le pronom personnel devant la forme de l'impératif. Il ne faut pas confondre cette construction avec un présent de l'indicatif. Cet emploi a une valeur de menace, de défi, ou plus simplement sert à insister :

You stay where you are !	Vous, ne bougez pas de là !
You dare, Jack !	Osez un peu pour voir, Jack !

56. Try dismissing : **try** est suivi de l'infinitif dans le sens de *tenter, s'efforcer* de faire quelque chose. L'infinitif traduit l'intention :

I tried to see him but he wasn't there	J'ai essayé de le voir, mais il n'était pas là

Try+-ing s'emploie lorsqu'il s'agit de tenter une expérience :

He had tried applying other methods	Il avait essayé d'employer d'autres méthodes

On voit donc la nuance ici : faites donc l'expérience de me renvoyer !

87. What do you feel they will think : essayons de démonter cette phrase. Elle se décompose comme suit :

What will they think about it ?	Qu'en penseront-ils ?
What do you feel about it ?	Qu'en pensez-vous ?

114. You'd better drop : rappelons que **I'd better, I'd rather** se comportent comme des défectifs. Lorsqu'ils portent sur le passé, on construit comme suit :

I'd better have phoned Peter Wiles immediately	J'aurais mieux fait de téléphoner à Peter Wiles immédiatement
I'd rather have kept out of the way	J'aurais préféré ne pas m'en mêler

2. EXERCISES

EXERCISE 1. — *Change as follows* :

he saw nothing irregular → **he didn't see anything irregular**

1. I saw nothing new. 2. He chose nothing interesting. 3. There's no trouble in the office block. 4. He's broken no rules. 5. They dismissed no skilled workers. 6. I met nobody else. 7. There's nothing to discuss. 8. There was no medical scheme.

EXERCISE 2. — *Change as follows* :

If this happens again, it will be a case for dismissal →

if this had happened again, it would have been a case for dismissal

1. If you see him, this will not happen. 2. If he complains, I'll pay him 3. If he is late, he'll get his pay docked. 4. If you fire him, there may be a walk-out. 5. If Jack does that, his union will disown him. 6. If you explain this, the men will co-operate.

EXERCISE 3. — *Change as follows* :

What will they say about that ? → **what do you think they will say about that ?**

1. What does Hector Grant feel about a profit sharing scheme ? 2. What did Jack Green say to Smith ? 3. What could we do about it ? 4. What will they have to do ? 5. What did he use the money for ? 6. What shall I get if I do it ? 7. What were his responsibilities ? 8. What did he choose ? 9. What did he want me to do ? 10. What did she understand ?

EXERCISE 4. — *Change as follows* :

He couldn't work it out for himself → **he wasn't capable of working it out for himself**

1. He couldn't use the grinder. 2. She couldn't explain it. 3. He couldn't unload the crates by himself. 4. You couldn't do it better than I could. 5. We couldn't honour the delivery dates. 6. He couldn't convince the boss.

EXERCISE 5. — *Change as follows* :

The shop steward looks after the affairs of the union → **the affairs of the union are looked after by the shop steward**

1. Mr. Grant presided over the meeting. 2. Harper & Grant will call in a firm of consultants. 3. The board must agree upon the rate of interest. 4. Our Sales Manager would have attended to your order.

EXERCISE 6. — *Can you say what an employee does in the following situations ? Your answer need not necessarily follow the exact form given in the Key to Exercises, as long as the information is correct.*

e.g. : When an employee arrives at the factory, what is the first thing he must do ?

Answer : The first thing he must do is to clock in.

Please answer with complete sentences.

1. What does an employee do with his time card when he arrives or leaves his place of work ?   2. What would an employee expect to happen to his pay if he arrived late at work ?   3. If a worker belongs to a union, to whom does he pay his subscription (or union dues) ?   4. If an employee works late, what extra money would he claim ?

EXERCISE 7. — *Please answer the following as fully as possible. Later compare the number of points you have remembered with the details in the Key to the Exercises.*

1. What are the chief responsibilities of a Personnel Manager ?   2. What are the main functions of a trade union ?

EXERCISE 8. — *Improvise a brief comment on the following terms :*

1. a strike.   2. a foreman.

EXERCISE 9. — *Translate into English :*

1. Il est arrivé avec une heure et demie de retard.   2. L'homme a pointé à 8 heures.   3. On soustraira une heure et demie de sa paie.   4. Si cela se reproduit, ce sera un motif de renvoi.   5. Il devrait y avoir un système d'intéressement aux bénéfices.   6. J'évoquerai la question à la réunion du comité de gestion.   7. Le syndicat va négocier une revendication de salaires.   8. J'estime ridicule de changer nos techniques de production. 9. L'horloge a été installée pour que les ouvriers soient pointés à l'entrée de l'usine.   10. Désirez-vous que Ian en parle au délégué syndical ? 11. Que croyez-vous que le directeur pensera de mon projet ?   12. Vous auriez mieux fait de ne pas vous en mêler.   13. Il a été forcé de nous quitter pour des raisons familiales.   14. Nous aimerions savoir si vous étiez satisfait de son travail.   15. Les propositions de la direction apportent un élément nouveau.   16. Je ne saisis pas bien la raison d'être de cette rencontre.   17. Toute l'affaire a été manigancée par le délégué syndical. 18. L'ouvrier était peu empressé pour faire des heures supplémentaires. 19. Si nous faisons cela, nous aurons un débrayage sur les bras. 20.   Vous vous y entendez bien mieux que moi pour traiter de ce genre d'affaires.

UNIT 13

RISK OF A TAKEOVER

PART 1 : INTRODUCTION

1. WORD STUDY

Vocabulary

assets actif
authorised capital capital nominal
bank charges frais de banque
bank rate taux d'escompte de la
Banque d'Angleterre
bank statement relevé de compte
borrow emprunter
bounce être sans provision
branch succursale, agence
building society société de crédit
immobilier
carry a vote donner une voix
charge faire payer ; frais
Clearing House chambre de
compensation
close an account fermer un compte
commercial bank banque d'affaires
controlling interest intérêt prédomin^t
crossed cheque chèque barré
counterfoil souche, talon
current account compte courant
deeds titre de propriété
debit balance solde débiteur

deposit account compte de dépôt
dishonoured ne pas honorer,
laisser protester
draw tirer
drawee tiré, payeur
drawer tireur
endorse endosser
foresight prévoyance, flair
formerly précédemment, autrefois
further to comme suite à
fuss chichis, histoires
holder possesseur, détenteur
holding participation
late (*ici*) décédé, feu
lend prêter
liability responsabilité
limited company société anonyme
loan prêt, emprunt, crédit ; prêter
mattress sommier
membership qualité de membre
Memorandum of Association statuts, charte constitutive, acte
de société

mortgage hypothèque
night safe coffre de nuit
open market marché libre
overdraft découvert
outvote mettre en minorité
own posséder
payee bénéficiaire
paying-in slip bordereau de versement
private company société privée ; S.A.R.L.
property biens, propriété
provide fournir
public company société anonyme
raise a loan émettre un emprunt
rate taux
registered address siège social
registrar directeur de l'enregistrement des sociétés
relevant à propos, utile
remainder reste, solde
repayment remboursement
security garantie, nantissement

share-capital capital-actions
shareholder actionnaire
solicitor notaire
state indiquer
Stock Exchange Bourse
strike a balance faire le bilan
straight (loan)
subscriber souscripteur
summon convoquer
subsidiary filiale
takeover prise de contrôle
tip tuyau
trust fidéicommis, trust
unsecured sans garantie, à découvert
upset bouleverser, renverser
vital essentiel, prépondérant
wealthy riche
wily rusé
will testament
withdraw retirer
work out établir, calculer

Phrases

I'm in the red   j'ai un découvert

At such short notice   dans un aussi bref délai

To play a part   jouer un rôle

Explanations and Other Useful Terms

Account Payee Only (*or* : **not negotiable**) either expression written between the lines crossing a cheque means that is must be paid into the payee's account. It cannot be cashed over the counter or made payable, (endorsed), to someone else.

Articles of Association regulations which govern the running of a company (amount of capital, number of shares, names of directors, their powers and duties, etc.) divided into numbered paragraphs or articles. These are signed by the subscribers (people who first subscribe money, later to be called shareholders) and by the Registrar in the Office of the Registrar of Companies, or Companies Registration Office, which is a department of the Board of Trade.

bank charges interest on an overdraft, or for handling a client's affairs while abroad, buying stocks and shares, etc. To sum up, small commissions charged by the bank for the use of its different facilities.

bank rate in Britain there is a central bank, the Bank of England, from which the commercial banks may from time to time borrow funds. The bank rate is the rate of interest charged by the Bank of England for these loans. The bank rate has an influence on all other lending rates.

bank statement a record of the withdrawals and payments of a client's account, including charges made by the bank (*see above*) sent at the end of each month, or more often if required.

bankers' draft or bankers' order a document in which a bank undertakes to pay a sum of money for a client. Often used to pay regular accounts, such as insurance, etc.

building society a society or organisation of contributors who save money, invest it in the society, in return for interest, so that capital can be loaned to those wishing to buy a house.

Clearing House banks who use the Bankers' Clearing House send their cheques every day for clearing. A balance is struck and payment made. This usually takes three days.

crossed cheque a cheque can be crossed, that is, two vertical lines are drawn across it and the words & Co., or **Account Payee only**, or **not negotiable** written between the lines. **An uncrossed cheque** could be cashed over the counter in a bank by an unauthorised person. A crossed cheque is therefore safer.

current account money lodged with a bank which can be withdrawn on demand by means of cheques. No interest is paid by a bank on current accounts.

deposit account used for saving money. Notice has to be given some time in advance before money can be withdrawn. A small rate of interest is paid by the bank on **money on deposit,** as it is called.

dishonoured	if a cheque is rejected by the drawer's bank it is said to have been dishonoured. Sometimes the slang term ' **to bounce** ' is used : a cheque which is dishonoured is said to have ' **bounced** '.
drawer	the man who writes the cheque ; the bank in which he has his account is called the **drawee**. A cheque is **drawn** on a bank and made **payable** to a **payee**.
endorsement	the person to whom the cheque is made out, made payable, signs his name on the back of the cheque. *Note* : some British banks do not now require the payee to endorse a cheque. In the U.S.A. however, the drawer must sign in exactly the form in which the cheque is written out, e.g. if it is addressed to Mr. Harvey Z. Opalmeyer, he must sign like this and not his usual signature which may be Zebedee Opalmeyer.
limited company	in the case of failure, the liability of the members of the company is limited to the net value of its assets. (see Note p. 205).
Memorandum of Association	the charter or document stating the name of the company ; if it is limited or not ; the registered address ; the amount of share capital and how this is divided into shares.
mortgage	conveyance of property by debtor to creditor as security for debt, with proviso that it shall be reconveyed on payment of the debt within a certain period.
night safe	this provides a useful means of putting cash or cheques into safety after banking hours by opening a small steel door or letter-box in the outer wall of a bank.
overdraft	money lent by a bank, who normally charge interest, to enable a client to draw cheques from his current account up to an agreed amount. If a client has no money left in his account, the balance shown on his bank statement will be written in red, indicating that he owes the amount to the bank ; hence the expression **to be in the red**. (However this no longer applies when a bank has its accounting done by computer).
paying-in slips	these are pieces of printed paper supplied by the bank in duplicate (sometimes supplied in book form called a **counterfoil book**) for the purpose of recording the exact amount of cash and cheques paid into a customer's account. The bank stamps one slip (which acts as a receipt) and the customer keeps the other for his record of money paid into the bank.

private company	a company which limits its members (minimum two, maximum fifty) and restricts the right to transfer shares. Its shares cannot be bought by the public.
	company : two or more people who decide to start a commercial or industrial concern (see note below).
public company	a company whose membership is open to the public and who can raise more capital by selling shares in the open market, that is, on the Stock Exchange (see note below).
rate of interest	the agreed percentage to be paid on a loan. Mr. Grant will have to pay £ 9 for every £ 100 lent by the bank per year (9 %).
reference, *or* **referee**	a person willing to testify to your good character, ability, financial standing, etc.
security	something of value, e.g. the deeds, or legal documents, of a house, share certificates, etc. held by the bank to secure, make sure of, the repayment of a loan.
short term loan	money lent on the condition that it will be paid back before, or by a certain date in the near future.
& Co.	if the cheque is crossed **& Co**, it cannot be cashed over the counter in a bank, but must be paid into an account or endorsed to someone else.

A NOTE ON FRENCH AND BRITISH COMPANIES

The English word **private company** is here often translated as *Société à Responsabilité Limitée,* as both types of company to some extent have the same functions, whereas **public company** is translated as *Société Anonyme* yet these are only approximate terms, as a **Limited Company** is a creation of English law, and a *Société Anonyme* a creation of French law. Hence both words are only equivalent in general terms.

Limited Liability refers to the restriction on the liability of a shareholder to the nominal value of the shares he holds, if the company is put into liquidation because it is unable to pay its debts (cf. Unit 24, liquidation).

In the XXth century, the limited liability company is the predominant form of business organization : there are over 330,000 companies in the U.K. (approximately 315,000 private companies, and 16,000 public companies). The **Companies Act** of 1948 replaced all previous legislation and set out the law relating to compagnies in general and limited liability companies in particular.

These are two types of **limited liability** company :

— the **public company**, which must have at least 7 shareholders, and whose shares are bought and sold on the Stock Exchange.

— the **private company**, which need only have two shareholders but may not have more than fifty. It must not invite the public to subscribe capital and must restrict the right to transfer shares. It does not have to file a copy of its accounts with its annual return to the Registrar of Companies.

On the other hand, the French term *anonyme* mainly implies that a *Société Anonyme* is not necessarily in the name (or names) of the principal interested parties. The French *Société à Responsabilité Limitée* is more in the nature of a partnership with limited liability : the capital of the company must be at least Fr. 25,000 ; the shares are called *parts* that can only be transferred according to civil law, and are not dealable on the Stock Exchange. The minimum number of shares is 2, there is no maximum ; no public issue can be made.

An *S.A.R.L.* is not however assimilated to an *S.A.* as an English private company is to a public company, but is the subject of separate and distinct legislation.

The private company has enabled the convenience of limited liability to be shared by small one-man businesses that have formed companies with relatives, etc. as the shareholders. The **sole trader** (someone who owns a business alone) and the **partnership** have given way to the **private company**. In many private companies the controlling shareholders must often give personal guarantees for a bank overdraft or a lease of business premises ; to this extent their liability is not limited.

Pronunciation

1 — 1 - (- -) adequate, borrow, capital, credit, family, follow, formerly, generous, history, interest, limit, mattress, offer, overdraft, perfectly, private, summon

- 2 (- -) agreed, advance, belong, control, december, deposit, depend, inherit, originally, proportion, remainder, solicitor, successful, suppose, surprise, together, upset

- - 3 (-) memorandum, opportunity, inconsistency

2 — [ou] own, vote, loan, sold, grown, total, control
[ɔ] lot, want, probably, property
[ɔ:] ought, form, short, bought, cause, formerly, foresight, authorised

[ʌ]	plus, such, sum, enough, above, mother, hundred
[u:]	two, lose, approve, approval
[e]	lend, any, many, death, friend, threat, wealthy, jealous
[æ]	have, action, carry, mattress
[au]	out, house, sound, founded, thousand, pound, about
[aiə]	lion, society, require, client
[auə]	our, hour, power
[s]	case, house, closely, crisis, basis, precisely, subsidiary

3 — Compare : industry ['indəstri], industrial [in'dʌstriəl]
heir, heiress [ɛə,'ɛəris], to inherit [in'herit], inheritance [in'heritəns]
distribute [dis'tribju:t], to attribute [ə'tribju:t], to contribute
[kən'tribju:t]

4 — Note : concern [kən'sə:n], association [ə,sousi'eiʃən], guarantee
[,gærən'ti:], mortgage]'mɔ:gidʒ], per annum [pə'rænəm], percent
[pə'sent], second ['sekənd], security [si'kjuəriti], society [sə'saiəti],
take over ['teik'ouvə], value ['vælju:].

2. SUMMARY

Ambrose Harper, one of the two men who founded the company of
Harper & Grant Ltd., died at the end of December. His death causes a
crisis in the firm. Harper & Grant is a private company. It was started
originally by Hector Grant's father and the late Ambrose Harper together. A private company can be formed by two or more people. They   5
sign a Memorandum of Association, stating the number of shares they
agree to take, and their signature is followed by the signatures of anyone else, often members of the family, who will also take shares in the
company.

In a private company there cannot be more than fifty members, or   10
shareholders. The authorised capital of this company was originally
£5,000, but the company has grown, and each £1 share is now worth
about £100.* Each share carries a vote at a shareholders' meeting.

---

* The figures throughout the episodes apply as closely as possible to a real firm of this
size. A few inconsistencies have been allowed in order to include the widest possible
business vocabulary. We hope any financial experts among the students will excuse them.

Wentworths, a large and successful firm who manufacture mattresses for beds, own ten per cent of Harper & Grant shares. Mr. Wentworth 15 senior was a personal friend of Ambrose Harper. His firm now has an opportunity of buying some of the shares formerly belonging to Harper. Hector Grant wants to stop Wentworth getting as many shares as he owns himself for fear of upsetting the voting power at shareholders' meetings. If Wentworths owned fifty-one per cent of the shares they would have a 20 controlling interest, and would be in a very good position to take over Harper & Grant completely in time, making it a fully owned subsidiary.

Hector Grant is personally jealous of Alfred Wentworth and does not want him to own too many of the shares. He raises a *loan*, that is, he arranges with the bank to lend him money to buy enough of the shares to 25 outvote Wentworth's. It is a personal loan. It is also a short-term loan. He does not only have to pay back the money he borrowed, he also has to pay interest on it: in this case nine per cent, this is the rate of interest. The bank manager asked for security. He wanted to hold the deeds of Grant's house. But a building society lent him money long ago to buy the 30 property, and every year he repays a proportion of the loan to them, plus interest. By now, a lot of this loan has been paid back to the building society. Probably for this reason the bank agreed to a second mortgage. If Grant could not pay back the loan within the time limit his house would have to be sold and the first mortgage paid up. Then the remainder would 35 go to the holder of the second mortgage, in this case, the bank. Very few banks will give an unsecured loan, one without any security or guarantee they will get their money back.

Hector Grant has been to hear the reading of Ambrose Harper's will. As soon as he arrives at the office on Monday morning, he summons his 40 nephew Peter, the Production Manager, to talk things over.

PART 2 : CONVERSATION AND DOCUMENTS

1. CONVERSATION

(Recorded Text)

HECTOR GRANT **Ah, Peter. We've got the biggest crisis in the history of the firm facing us.**

PETER WILES **Good Lord! That sounds pretty fearful.**

GRANT	It is, I'm afraid.
PETER	Something to do with Ambrose Harper's death, I suppose. 5
GRANT	Precisely. Now you know how the shares of this company are distributed. Your mother and I own twenty per cent of the capital each. Ambrose Harper, of course, had the lion's share with fifty per cent, and the remaining ten per cent is in the hands of our friends the mattress-makers 10 over the road, Wentworth and Company. Well, Ambrose has left two thousand of his two thousand five hundred shares to form a trust. The remaining five hundred he's left to his sister, Caroline.
PETER	But she's a very wealthy woman. Surely she won't sell the 15 five hundred shares?
GRANT	My dear Peter, that's just the trouble. I spoke to her after the solicitor had finished reading Ambrose's will, and she told me she'd had a very generous offer for the shares.
PETER	But who from? Who knew she'd inherit them? 20
GRANT	That wily old bird Wentworth. He's wanted to get in here for a long time. He knew she was Ambrose's only remaining relative.
PETER	Well, that's easily prevented, isn't it? We're a private company. Caroline can't sell her shares without offering 25 them first to the other shareholders. We must make an offer, too. We can't allow Wentworth to own so many shares. If any of us had to sell at any time he could easily get a further interest in the company.
GRANT	Exactly! But who in our family has got the money to buy 30 them?
PETER	I certainly can't. I'm in the red as it is!
GRANT	The way you live that doesn't surprise me!
PETER	Somehow we'll have to raise a loan and buy enough of the shares ourselves to keep the controlling interest. 35
GRANT	Well, let's see, the total share capital must have a market value now of about five hundred thousand pounds. If we bought two hundred and fifty that would be ... er ... about twenty-five thousand pounds.
PETER	The bank ought to be able to lend you that amount. 40
GRANT	That's what I think. I'd better see the bank manager today.

GRANT: 'Good morning, Mr. Brewer. Good of you to see me at such short notice.'

(In the bank manager's office)

GRANT	Good morning, Mr. Brewer. Good of you to see me at such short notice.
BREWER	Oh, never too busy to see an important client like your- 45 self, Mr. Grant. Well, now, what can I do for you?
GRANT	I want a loan ... or an overdraft ... right away. Twenty-five thousand.
BREWER	Oh, I see. Twenty-five thousand? Well, now, that is quite a large sum. 50
GRANT	Not for me. You know how well the firm is doing.
BREWER	Yes, but of course the firm can't provide security, since the loan is, I understand, required by your good-self.
GRANT	Really, Mr. Brewer, this is rather unnecessary, isn't it? You have our record, my record of business as your 55 guarantee. You know me well enough to advance me an unsecured loan, surely.
BREWER	As you know, I shall have to apply to our Head Office, but they will go very much by my recommendation, and I don't think I would be prepared to do so without some 60 form of security.
GRANT	Oh! Well, what are you going to do about it? I can tell you one thing. If there's any question of not getting a loan, I'll consider taking my account, and that of the company, elsewhere. 65

BREWER	That could be an action you might have to consider, Mr. Grant. But if I may say so, I think you would find any bank manager would take the same view. Now, perhaps it might be more relevant to consider what forms of security you might be able to offer. You have a large house. Is it mortgaged? 70
GRANT	It is.
BREWER	That's a pity. The deeds of your house would have been perfectly adequate security. The house is worth, what, twenty thousand? 75
GRANT	Thirty. The mortgage is with the Albion Building Society.
BREWER	Well, now, it may be possible to raise a second mortgage on your property. Though I can tell you frankly that my Head Office doesn't like second mortgages. . . . However, I might be prepared to make a recommendation on this basis. 80
GRANT	How would you arrange the credit?
BREWER	Well, if my Head Office agreed, you could have a straight loan and pay two per cent above the bank rate, so the rate of interest would be about nine per cent. It'd be a short-term loan of, say, three years. 85
GRANT	Well, you work all that out. I accept your advice. All I want is the money, and I want it quickly.

(*A week later in Hector Grant's Office*)

GRANT	What did I tell you, Peter! After all that fuss about security I've got the loan. The Bank Manager wasn't going to risk losing our account. Well, we're saved. Wentworth can't get a holding equal to mine or your mother's. Aren't you pleased? 90

PETER	Of course I'm pleased ... but, you know, the other day Mr. Brewer was not at all in favour of the loan.	95
GRANT	How do you know?	
PETER	I went to see him about my overdraft. He told me he was very upset by what he called 'your threats'.	
GRANT	What did you say?	
PETER	Oh, I talked a bit about the vital part banks play in helping industry to expand. How a firm like ours depended a great deal on their foresight and business sense—you know the sort of thing.	100
GRANT	I don't see what difference that would make.	
PETER	One of these days I'll give you a few tips on how to deal with bank managers. It was one of the first things I learnt after I left school.	105

PRACTICE SENTENCES

Say the practice sentences on the record :

i You know how the shares of this company are distributed.

ii Your mother and I own twenty per cent of the capital each.

iii He's left two thousand shares to form a trust.

iv The remaining three hundred shares he's left to his sister.

v The total share capital must have a market value now of about five hundred thousand pounds.

vi I'll see the bank manager today.

vii I want a loan or an overdraft for twenty-five thousand pounds.

———————

2. A LETTER

When Mr. Brewer, the Bank Manager, received notification from his Head Office that he could lend £25,000 to Mr. Grant he immediately telephoned him, as he knew that Mr. Grant was anxious to have the news. Later that day he dictated a letter confirming his telephone conversation, so that the details of the loan would be on record. Here is his letter to Mr. Grant.

Haleys Bank Ltd.

Linden Branch
Great West Road
LONDON W.25.

Hector Grant, Esq.,
Managing Director,
Harper & Grant Ltd.,
Great West Road,
London, W.25.

10th February, 197..

PRIVATE AND CONFIDENTIAL

Dear Sir,

Further to our telephone conversation, I am glad to be able to inform you that my Head Office have agreed to make you a personal loan of up to £25,000, this loan to be repaid over a period of three years at an interest rate of nine per cent.

As arranged, we will now be taking a second charge on your property. We have already received the approval of the Building Society to this charge, and we shall be obliged if you would call at this office to complete formalities.

Yours faithfully,

Arthur Brewer,
Manager.

PART 3 : NOTES AND PRACTICE

1. RAPPEL GRAMMATICAL

Summary :

10. Ne pas oublier que **there** entre dans des constructions plus complexes que le simple **there is/are** ou **there was/were** :

There ought to have been a tighter control	Il aurait dû y avoir un contrôle plus strict
Couldn't there have been a notice on these crates ?	N'aurait-il pas pu y avoir une notice sur ces caisses ?

14. Notons ici que **firm** est suivi de **who** et d'un pluriel.

19. **For fear,** suivi d'une proposition, entraîne le subjonctif composé avec **should** :

He bought the shares for fear Wentworth should take over the company	Il a acheté les actions de peur que Wentworth ne prenne le contrôle de la société

Conversation :

1. Le complément de lieu du superlatif est introduit par **in,** par **of** ou **in** dans les autres cas :

It's the second largest bank in the country	C'est la deuxième grande banque du pays
Ambrose was the oldest of the shareholders	Ambrose était le doyen des actionnaires

12. Les numéraux, étant des adjectifs, sont invariables (lorsqu'on indique des chiffres précis) :

He left two hundred and forty shares to his sister	Il a laissé deux cent quarante-six actions à sa sœur

Mais si l'indication est imprécise, le numéral est alors un nom :

He left hundreds and hundreds of shares to his sister	Il a laissé des centaines et des centaines d'actions à sa sœur

20. Nous avons **who from,** mais si l'interrogation commençait par la préposition on aurait **from whom.** Comparons encore :

Who did you send it to?	A qui l'avez-vous envoyé ?
To whom did you send it ?	

22. Ce n'est que lorsque l'on a un pluriel régulier en -s que le cas possessif est marqué par la seule apostrophe. Dans tous les autres cas — pluriels irréguliers, et tous les singuliers, y compris les noms propres — le cas possessif est en 's. Lorsque donc le singulier ou le nom propre se termine par les sons [s, z, ʒ, ʃ] le cas possessif se prononce [iz]. Notons que pour les noms propres étrangers, le cas possessif se forme en ' seulement, et que l'usage hésite aujourd'hui entre 's et ' seulement pour les noms propres anglais. Ainsi, dans Unit 12, Smith a parlé de **Mr. Wiles' car** et non **Mr. Wiles's car.**

25. Signalons que **without** est toujours préposition et jamais conjonction. Lorsqu'il est suivi d'un verbe, ce verbe est donc à la forme en **-ing.** Si ce verbe a lui-même un sujet, on aura donc la construction suivante :

She sold her shares without Went- **worth. knowing**	Elle a vendu ses actions sans que Wentworth ne le sache

36. La déduction logique, la quasi-certitude s'expriment à l'aide de **must** qui a deux formes :

He must be bust, the way he lives	Il doit être fauché, au train où il vit
He must have seen our agent by **now**	Il a dû rencontrer notre agent commercial à l'heure qu'il est (*déduction*)

Que le français ne se laisse pas entraîner, par suite d'une regrettable habitude de continuer à penser en français, à exprimer la nécessité logique de la manière dont on exprime l'obligation au passé :

He had to see the agent about it	Il a dû voir l'agent commercial à ce sujet (*obligation*)

52. **Since** a également la valeur logique de puisque :

Since you have no guarantee, we **can't lend you the money**	Puisque vous n'avez pas de garantie, nous ne pouvons vous prêter l'argent

54. **Rather** + adjectif a une valeur un peu dépréciative. Si la valeur est laudative, on emploie **fairly** :

He is rather slow	Il est plutôt lent
She is fairly wealthy	Elle est assez fortunée

63. A la négative de l'infinitif ou de la forme en **-ing, not** précède toujours la forme verbale.

86-87. **All I want : all that I want.**

92. **A holding equal to mine or your mother's** : un mot déjà employé peut ne pas être répété et le cas possessif s'employer alors seul :

> **This isn't my car, this is Mr. Grant's**   Ce n'est pas ma voiture, c'est celle de M. Grant

On pourrait également dire : **it is that** (ou : **the one) of Mr. Grant.**

Lettre :

La forme **to be paid** a une valeur de futur :

> **It is to be paid within three years**   Il doit être payé sous trois ans

2. EXERCISES

EXERCISE 1. — Use the correct tense with the verb between brackets :

1. They (*to become*) partners 8 years ago.   2. They now (*to be*) established in the motor industry for 60 years.   3. James Glover (*to work*) with us for since December last.   4. Mr. Harper (*to be*) dead for 2 months.   5. Mr. Glover (*to live*) in Birmingham for a few months only.   6. The shareholders' meeting (*to take place*) a fortnight ago.   7. He (*to be*) the Chairman for 20 years when he died.   8. They (*to lend*) us the money long ago.   9. Mr. Hardiman (*to work*) with us since 1947.

EXERCISE 2. — Fill the blanks with the right preposition :

1. We depend ... your foresight.   2. He'll have to pay a high interest ... the loan.   3. He arrived ... the office at 10.30.   4. He'd been ... the bank.   5. The bank manager will ask ... security.   6. It's something to do ... the Chairman's resignation.   7. She had a generous offer ... the shares.   8. I'm afraid I am ... the red.   9. Thank you for seeing me ... such short notice.   10. Well, you have our record of business ... a guarantee !   11. They'll probably go ... my recommendation.   12. You'll have to pay 2 % ... the bank rate.

EXERCISE 3. — Use the verb between brackets as follows :

> **There are more than 1,000 shares (can't) →**
> **There can't have been more than 1,000 shares**

1. There is a crisis in the firm (*might*).   2. There is a second mortgage on the house (*couldn't*).   3. There is a notice on each crate (*ought*).   4. There is a meeting in June (*should*).   5. There is a fire in the paint store (*might*). 6. There is a delay because of the bad weather (*may*).

EXERCISE 4. — *Answer affirmatively as follows* :

Will he go to the bank ?   **— Yes, I think he will**

1. Will it cause a crisis ?   2. Can a private company be formed by two persons ?   3. Did she sell her shares ?   4. Would they have a controlling interest ?   5. Could we outvote Wentworths ?   6. Can you get your money back ?   7. Does he own over 51 % of the shares ?   8. Would you have to apply to the Head Office ? 9. Need you summon your representative ?

EXERCISE 5. — *Change as follows* :

It made a difference (what) →
I don't see what difference it would make

1. You found it (*where*).   2. They met him (*when*).   3. He suggested a solution (*what*).   4. She sold shares (*how many*).   5. He had power (*what*). 6. He provided a security (*what kind*).   7. They built an extension (*where*). 8. He made an appointment (*when*).   9. Peter gave him a tip (*what sort of*). 10. He bought shares (*how many*).

EXERCISE 6. — *Use the superlative as follows* (*be careful about the preposition*) :

It's an expensive device (all) →   **It's the most expensive device of all**

1. Our sales reached a high level (November).   2. It's a highly competitive market (Europe).   3. This is a big chain of women's wear shops (France). 4. They're going to make drastic cuts (their advertising programme). 5. It's a cheap portable TV set (the market).   6. The new supermarket will be large (the town).   7. They'll use up-to-date processes (the industry). 8. Mrs. Harper is a wealthy shareholder (all).   9. We are driving through a busy district (the town).

EXERCISE 7. — *Please answer these questions with complete sentences. Don't worry if your construction is different. If you can write the answers and get a native English speaker to correct you, so much the better.*

1. Could the Bank Manager decide on his own authority to lend £ 25,000 to Mr. Grant ?   2. What did Mr. Grant have to pay for the loan ?   3. Peter Wiles wants to continue to draw money from the bank, though he has no more money in his account until his next salary cheque is paid in. What does he try to arrange with the Bank Manager ?   4. Is Harper & Grant Ltd. a public or a private company ?   5. Can the Harper & Grant shareholders sell their shares to anyone who wishes to buy them ? 6. What do you think about Mr. Grant's manner when he was dealing with his Bank Manager ?

EXERCISE 8. — *And now here are some general questions about banking. Please answer each question with a complete sentence* :

1. If someone wants to put money into a bank, what must he do ?   2. Which is safer : to write a crossed or an uncrossed cheque ? Why ?   3. What do we mean when we say that a cheque ' bounced ' ?   4. In what circumstances can money left in a bank earn interest ?   5. What is a short term loan ?

EXERCISE 9. — *Improvise a brief comment on the following words* :

1. a cheque.   2. a bank account.   3. a branch.   4. a shareholder.   5. the interest.

EXERCISE 10. — *Translate into English* :

1. Vous savez comment sont réparties les actions de cette société.   2. Ta mère et moi possédons chacun 20 % du capital.   3. Il a légué 2 000 actions pour former un fidéicommis.   4. Quant aux 300 actions restantes, il les a laissées à sa sœur.   5. Le montant total du capital-actions doit avoir une valeur marchande de 500 000 livres.   6. Je verrai le directeur de la banque aujourd'hui.   7. Je veux une avance ou un découvert de 25 000 livres.   8. Ce n'est pas mon magnétophone, c'est celui de John Martin.   9. Nous devons nous procurer des capitaux sans que ce vieux renard de Wentworth le sache.   10. Il a dû lui proposer d'acheter ses actions, j'en suis sûr !   11. Tout ce que je veux, c'est une avance pendant quelques mois seulement.   12. Suite à notre conversation téléphonique, je suis heureux de vous informer que le prêt a été accordé.   13. La banque n'allait pas risquer de perdre notre clientèle.   14. Peut-être serait-il plus à propos que nous abordions le point suivant de l'ordre du jour.   15. Je pourrais être disposé à faire une proposition dans cet esprit.   16. On peut facilement empêcher cela, n'est-ce pas ?   17. On ne peut pas permettre à Wentworth de posséder autant d'actions, n'est-ce pas ?   18. Vous allez avoir la part du lion, maintenant.   19. Nous ne voulons pas qu'il possède trop d'actions, non ?   20. Une bonne partie de cette avance a été remboursée à la Société de Crédit Immobilier.

UNIT 14

THE ADVERTISING MANAGER AT WORK

PART 1 : INTRODUCTION

1. WORD STUDY

Vocabulary

account group équipe publicitaire
actually en fait, vraiment
attractive séduisant
bit petit morceau
  a bit un peu
blotter sous-main
book réserver, louer
brand marque
cloth toile, drap
coat veston
contractor entrepreneur
cord cordon
dawn aurore, aube
design réaliser, concevoir
display exposer, mettre en vue
  on display exposé
draped drapé, recouvert
eager avide, impatient
entail entraîner, impliquer
erect monter, dresser
exhibition exposition
faith foi, confiance

fit ajuster
forward-looking prospectif
  tourné vers l'avenir
furnishings fournitures,
  accessoires
get hold of mettre la main sur
hammer marteau ; marteler
household de la maison
  household expression expression
  consacrée
hold-up retard
lampshade abat-jour
launch lancer
layout disposition, arrangement,
  présentation
leather cuir
madhouse maison de fous
mess gâchis, pagaïe
nail clou
old-fashioned ⎱ démodé
out-of-date ⎰ dépassé
overall global, d'ensemble

party réception
potential en puissance, possible
put up monter, installer
puzzle énigme
range gamme, série
release communiqué, mise en circulation, une première
reliability sûreté, fiabilité, honnêteté
rent louer
requirement besoin
schedule programme, horaire prévu
screen écran
shot coup
  direct mail shot publicité directe par correspondance

settle down s'installer
site emplacement
skill habileté, compétence technique
steady régulier, traditionnel, constant
  the steadies les valeurs sûres du passé
stunt tour, coup d'épate, affaire sensationnelle
teaser publicité qui suscite la curiosité
trust confiance ; faire confiance à
well-tried bien rôdé
write-up battage, publicité ronflante
  to write up faire mousser

Phrases

They're all for keeping it   ils sont partisans de le conserver
There's a good chap   vous serez un chic type
I'll take a chance on it   je vais courir le risque
Could you give me a hand ?   pourriez-vous me donner un coup de main ?

They're behind schedule   ils ont du retard sur le programme

Explanations and Other Useful Terms

account group   a team of experts in an advertising agency who work together to create an advertising campaign for the account, which here means the client.

block   the reproduction of a design or photograph on metal, plastic, or rubber, which is mounted and fixed into the *forme* or unit of blocks and type to be printed.

blotter   a flat holder, usually with corners of leather, for blotting paper, used for drying ink.

brand	a particular product (e.g. a kind of marmalade, tinned food, or clothing) ; a type of consumer goods (things like food or clothing which directly satisfy human wants and needs). Note that one says a **make** of cars.
Brand Manager	some large companies appoint a Brand Manager to take charge of all marketing aspects of a particular brand of product.
classified ad.	ad., short for advertisement, is used informally, and in the advertising and newspaper business. Classified ad. : a small advertisement offering goods for sale, jobs vacant, etc.
controller	one who controls the process of an advertising campaign in an agency, following its progress from first ideas until the finished advertisement goes to press. He or she works very closely with the account executive.
consumer survey	an attempt to discover, by means of market research and statistics, what a certain type of person, living in a certain area, wants to buy, and why he, or she, wants to buy it.
direct mail shot	refers to all the advertisments sent on one occasion to a list of addressees. **Direct mail advertising** : leaflets, letters, brochures, and advertising material generally, sent to a selected number of people through the post.
a dry stand	one that does not provide drinks for special customers and visitors to the stand. Harper & Grant's stand at the Exhibition will however have a cupboard full of whisky and gin as well as a refrigerator with beer and soft drinks.
exhibition contractor	sometimes called a ' display contractor ', a firm who specialise in constructing stands for display purposes. They also design illuminated moving display units, supply a window-dressing service for shops, etc.
inter-communication system	a means of speaking to several offices linked to each other by means of a microphone and loudspeaker in each office. To call an office, you press a lever and speak into a box-like instrument about the size of a small radio. The person you are calling can answer. It is much quicker than an inter-office telephone system.
marketing budget	money allocated for advertising and sales promotion of a certain product. Also referred to as appropriation.

Marketing Manager	head of all the combined functions to do with selling a production. In many firms now the Sales Department, Advertising Department, Public Relations, and so on are combined into one department called Marketing.
schedule	a schedule is a table, or list of details. It can mean a time table or programme of events. If work is early, on time or late it can be said to be **ahead of, on,** or **behind** schedule. Sometimes people say that an event is scheduled to occur at such and such a time and place.
teaser-campaign	a series of advertisements which catch the eye but ' tease ' the reader into wondering exactly what they are advertising. When the problem is solved, the whole puzzle is likely to leave a greater impression than a straightforward advertisement.
write-up	an article drawing attention to a product written by a journalist and appearing in a newspaper or magazine.

Pronunciation

1 — 1 - (- -) actually, article, authorised, budget, carpet, ceremony, cinema, consequence, curtain, elegance, furnishings, hammer, instance, journalist, justify, magazine, mystery, number, photograph, programme, regular, slogan, special, television

- 2(- -) along, apparently, attractive, available, campaign, complete, contractor, design, direct, discuss, display, disastrous, entail, equipment, erect, exactly, example, excess, expenditure, ideal, including, magnificent, potential, project *(verb)*, promote, publicity, remarkably, tomorrow

2 — [ʃ] fashion, expression, efficient, special, official, sure, attention, exhibition, ambitious, national, potential, sure, surely

[dʒ] job, John, agent, agency, agenda, justify, manage, journalist, budget, range, change, image, suggest

-**sks** asks, tasks, desks, discs, risks

[ð] the, this, that, then, these, those, though, their, there, other, therefore, clothes

[θ] thing, think, thought, thanks, faith, through, wealth, wealthy, cloth, authorize, authority

[r] rent, range, right, write, try, wrong, screen, bring, print, praise, grant, through, create, programme, product, very, every, area, arrive, ceremony, pre-erected, secretary

[r *not pronounced*] Harper, Harvey, Martin, firm, worth, nearly, party, carpet, furnish, hardly, advertise, advertisement, journalist

[ə:]   work, word, world, firm, early, furnish, earning, first, advertisement

[ɔ:]   all, hall, dawn, drawing, launch, quarter, organise, *au*thorise, therefore

[e]   send, sell, well, settle, desk, proj*e*ct, st*ea*dy, r*ea*dy, l*ea*ther, alr*ea*dy

[ei]   place, change, range, mail, faith, praise, display, entail, campaign, unveil

[iə]   year, here, Windermere, exp*e*rience, mat*e*rial, id*ea*l, nearly, ar*ea*, earl*ie*r

[aiə]   hire, higher, buyer, reliable, reliability, require

3 — Compare : an exhibit, to exhibit [igʹzibit], exhibition [ˌeksiʹbiʃən] public [ʹpʌblik], publicity [pʌbʹlisiti], publicize [ʹpʌblisaiz] *n.* ʹprogress, *v.* to proʹgress — (a, to) ʹprogramme a project [ʹprɔdʒekt], to project [prəʹdʒekt] reliable [riʹlaiəbl], reliability [rilaiəʹbiliti] ʹperfect — perʹfection scheme [ski:m] ; schedule GB [ʹʃedju:l], US [ʹskedju:l]

4 — Note : consequence [ʹkɔnsikwəns], eager [ʹi:gə], ideal [aiʹdiəl], minute [ʹminit], old-fashioned [ʹould-ʹfæʃənd], slogan [ʹslougən], suit [sju:t].

2. SUMMARY

Joanna Harvey, who got the job as Advertising Manager, has had plenty of time now to settle down. How is she handling her new job? Does she justify the faith placed in her by the management? In this episode she goes along to John Martin's office to have a word with him about the firm's publicity programme (including the stand at an office equipment exhibi- 5 tion), and also to discuss the new advertising campaign. Publicity is all about getting a company and its products known and talked about by the public. For example, Joanna's scheme to have a big launching party to unveil the new executive-type desk is a publicity stunt, that is, a way to get attention. She plans to invite a number of journalists to the launching 10 ceremony of the new desk range. She hopes they will print photographs and give the desks a good write-up, write articles in their papers or magazines praising the goods. Harper & Grant are also going to rent a

special area in an exhibition hall to display the new desk range, and some 15
of their well-tried and well-known products as well. Joanna has already
booked a site for this display stand through the exhibition organisers. She
then has to find an exhibition contractor to build the stand. These are
special firms who design and manufacture stands to suit their client's
requirements. Sometimes these stands are pre-erected, that is, put up at
the place of manufacture to show the client exactly how they will look in 20
the exhibition hall. This entails getting the work done earlier, erecting the
stand and assembling and fitting all the furnishings required, such as
lights, carpets, curtains, etc., and the cost is therefore higher. Joanna has
authorised expenditure for the quarter in excess of her budget, so she
decides not to have the stand pre-erected, with nearly disastrous conse- 25
quences. The contractors are working on a number of stands which they
have to put up as soon as the exhibition hall is available. There are very
often last-minute hold-ups and difficulties, with the result that quite often
an exhibition opens with the paint hardly dry on some of the stands and a
lot of hammering still going on as the doors are opened to the public. 30

For her advertising programme, Joanna has an overall plan for the
coming year showing exactly where she plans to spend the advertising
budget, or money set aside for buying space in newspapers, magazines, or
(for larger firms) buying time on television or on the cinema screen. In
connection with launching the new desk range, Joanna has an idea for a 35
teaser campaign to promote the product. This is a form of advertising in
which a mystery is first created in the minds of the public, with the
explanation, or complete advertisement, following later. Joanna planned
to show a beautiful secretary in an ideal office, including everything
except the desk, the desk she was actually selling. 40

PART 2 : CONVERSATION AND DOCUMENTS

1. CONVERSATION

(Recorded Text)

(*In John Martin's office*)

JOHN MARTIN	**Oh, hello, Joanna. Can you find somewhere to sit?**
JOANNA	**Thanks. Now there are two things I'd like to tell you. Could we take the regular advertising programme first?**

JOHN	O.K.
JOANNA	Well, I'm changing the style of our advertisements. I think the old slogan 'H. & G. is your guarantee' is a bit out of date now.
JOHN	I agree it's old-fashioned, but it's been part of our publicity for so long now that it's almost a household expression.
JOANNA	I think we should change it. We need to project a forward-looking image. You know, modern efficiency plus elegance and old-time product reliability.
JOHN	I certainly think that applies to the new desk range, but I'm not so sure about... well, the old 'steadies' like the 'Windermere' range, for instance. That's run for years, and its still selling well. That style of desk is still far from the end of its product life cycle.
JOANNA	If you think that, I won't change the slogan for that range. The advertising agency are all for keeping it, too.
JOHN	And we've got a lot of older customers who trust our reputation, so let's keep the new campaign for the new lines.
JOANNA	Right. Now we come to the new desk range, the 'Standfirm'. I'm very excited about this. It's a most attractive range.
JOHN	I think so too. We've got great hopes for it.
JOANNA	I've planned a teaser campaign. We'll run it for two months before the official launching, and that, as you know, is to be at the International Office Equipment Exhibition. Here are the suggested layouts. What do you think of this one?
JOHN	The girl is marvellous. But where are the desks?
JOANNA	That's the idea! Here's the perfect secretary, the ideal office: all the boss needs now is one of our magnificent 'Standfirm' desks to complete the picture. Details will be given later.
JOHN	Splendid! Now what about the direct mail shot ?
JOANNA	We'll despatch that to two thousand potential customers. I think it should go out a few weeks before the exhibition.
JOHN	How's the exhibition stand coming along?
JOANNA	It's the first time we've taken a stand at this particular exhibition. I got hold of an exhibition contractor to design and build it for us. I've been down to the stand designers

The line numbers shown in the right margin are: 5, 10, 15, 20, 25, 30, 35, 40.

	to see how they're getting on. From the drawings it's 45
	going to look very nice indeed.
JOHN	Are we going to see it before the exhibition? I think we should see it assembled first, before it's delivered in pieces to the exhibition site. So many things can go wrong.
JOANNA	Well, I've already authorised expenditure for this quarter 50 in excess of my budget, and the contractors charge an extra fee, so I'll take a chance on it.
JOHN	Right.
JOANNA	Now the next thing is ... er ... I think it's very important that we should have a launching ceremony here at the 55 factory. I suggest we invite all the representatives of the trade press, as well as a number of other journalists, anyone, in fact, who might give us a write-up in their paper.
JOHN	Why not ask H.G. to make a speech? 60
JOANNA	Good idea! We'll have the blue executive-type 'Standfirm' desk draped in purple cloth at one end of the Board Room. All H.G. will have to do is pull a cord ...
JOHN	... Exposing our beautiful new desk to an eager world!
JOANNA	Yes, that's it. And another desk like it will be on display 65 on our stand at the exhibition, complete with leather blotter, telephone, inter-office communication system, the lot. Everything the ambitious executive dreams of sitting in front of.
JOHN	Just the job. Don't forget the real live pretty secretary 70 standing by to answer questions on prices, and so on.
JOANNA	Oh, I won't forget that. I'll be interviewing some girls with exhibition experience tomorrow.

(*On the site of the exhibition*)

PETER WILES	John! Are you there? Oh, hello, how's the stand going? I thought I'd come along to see if I could give you a hand. 75 I heard from Sally that the contractors were behind schedule. Good Lord, what a mess!
JOHN	Isn't it frightful! Joanna telephoned me from this mad-house earlier this afternoon, and I came here at once. Apparently the stand contractors have got two carpenters 80 away ill.
PETER	But it'll never be ready on time. The show opens tomorrow morning.

JOANNA: 'I'll be interviewing some girls with exhibition experience to-morrow.'

JOHN	It's got to be ready somehow.	
PETER	Where are the men who're supposed to be assembling the stand?	85
JOHN	Well, we've got Fred somewhere—ah, here he is. You've been working here since dawn, haven't you, Fred?	
FRED	What? Oh, it's always like this with these exhibitions. I've been doing them all my life. There's always a last-minute panic.	90
PETER	Look, give me a hammer. Just let me take my coat off first. I can knock those nails in, Fred, while you do something that requires skill. Only don't go on strike because I'm not a union man, there's a good chap!	95
FRED	Well, don't let the representative see you then.	
PETER	Where's Joanna?	
JOHN	She's gone to try and get some new lampshades for the wall lights. The ones she ordered haven't arrived. Oh, here she is.	100

JOANNA	**Hello. I got my foot in the door just as the shop was closing and bought these. I think they'll do. How's it all going?**
JOHN	**Slowly. Do you realise that in a remarkably few hours' time you and I, Joanna, will be back on this stand getting our big smiles ready for the opening crowd?**
JOANNA	**Oh, don't remind me! At this moment I never want to hear the word exhibition ever again.**

105

PRACTICE SENTENCES

Say the practice sentences on the record :

   i I'm changing the style of our advertisements.

  ii We need to project a forward-looking image.

 iii Let's keep the new campaign for the new lines.

 iv Here are the suggested layouts.

   v It's the first time we've taken a stand at this exhibition.

 vi I think we should see it assembled first.

 vii The contractors are behind schedule.

viii It'll never be ready on time.

2. A PRESS RELEASE

Just before the exhibition opened, Joanna Harvey sent out a press release, that is, advance information to newspapers and magazines.

Great West Road
London W25
Telephone 01-567 1112
Telex 80153
Telegrams Harp LDN

Directors:
Ambrose Harper *(Chairman)*
Hector Grant *(Managing)*
William Buckhurst FCA *(Secretary)*
Margaret Wiles

Harper and Grant Limited

NEW DESK DEVELOPMENT

Harper & Grant Ltd. are delighted to be able to introduce a revolutionary family of office desks, THE 'STANDFIRM' DESK RANGE. Each desk has been most carefully designed to suit every user from the Managing Director to the office boy. All the desk units can be grouped together if required for office work stations.

Designed in our own workshops, these attractive and imposing-looking desks are made of an entirely new material which is stain-resistant and absolutely scratch-proof. Prices start modestly, rising to the elegant and luxurious executive-type desk complete with filing drawer and tape recorder. These desks will be on display at the International Office Equipment Exhibition opening at Olympia next week. Come and visit the stand and see the desks for yourself.

For further information, please contact Joanna Harvey, Advertising Manager.

PART 3 : NOTES AND PRACTICE

1. RAPPEL GRAMMATICAL

Summary

1.   **As** et **like** : des confusions fréquentes sont faites par les francophones à propos de **as** et de **like**.

Like est préposition, c'est-à-dire qu'il ne se rencontre que devant un complément. Ce complément indique la manière, la comparaison :

He did exactly like me	Il a fait exactement comme moi

Like ne peut introduire de proposition, c'est-à-dire que le ' **like I did** ' que l'on peut entendre est une incorrection.

As par contre est tantôt préposition, tantôt conjonction, c'est-à-dire qu'il introduit tantôt un nom complément, tantôt une proposition subordonnée. Préposition, il marque l'identité :

As an Advertising Manager, she's certainly far better than Mr. Windsmore would have been	Comme chef du service publicité, elle est certainement meilleure que ne l'aurait été Mr. Windsmore

Comparons encore :

Like the Chairman, I think...	Comme (à la manière du) président du conseil d'administration, je crois...
As Chairman of the Board...	En qualité, en tant que Président...

Conjonction, **as** introduit une subordonnée de comparaison :

Do as I do myself and we'll convince the boss	Faites comme je fais moi-même, et nous convaincrons le patron.

On pourrait dire **do like me.**

As se rencontre devant une préposition, car on a en fait une subordonnée elliptique. **Like** ne peut précéder d'autre préposition, et **like in England, like in France** sont de grosses incorrections :

In Japan, they drive on the left, as in England	Au Japon, on conduit à gauche, comme en Angleterre

On connaît par ailleurs les autres valeurs de la conjonction **as** :

— le sens de *vu que, étant donné que* (expression de la *cause*)

As the stand wasn't ready, they had to work overtime	Comme le stand n'était pas prêt, ils ont dû faire des heures supplémentaires

— 229 —

— le sens de *comme, au moment où, à mesure que* :

As he grew older, H. G. became more and more interested in advanced techniques	En vieillissant, H. G. s'intéressa de plus en plus aux techniques de pointe
As he entered my office, I noticed he was frightfully worried	Au moment où il est entré dans mon bureau, je remarquai qu'il était terriblement contrarié

As if = as though a le sens de *comme si* :

She speaks of those desks as if they were her own children	Elle parle de ces bureaux comme s'il s'agissait de ses propres enfants
It sounds as if there were going to be a crisis in the firm	On dirait qu'il va y avoir une crise dans l'entreprise

On connait en outre ces emplois de **as** rappelés ici pour mémoire :

This one is as fast as the other	Celui-ci est aussi rapide que l'autre
Yes, but it's twice as big	Oui, mais il est deux fois plus gros
Rich as she is, she had to sell some of her shares	Si riche qu'elle soit, elle a dû vendre une partie de ses actions
Countries of the Common Market such as France, Belgium, Italy...	Des pays du Marché Commun, comme la France, la Belgique, l'Italie...

2. **Plenty of** : notons que **much** et **many** ne s'emploient pas en proposition affirmative, où l'on trouve **a great deal of, plenty of, a lot of** ou **lots of**.

She spent a lot of money on that stand	Elle a dépensé beaucoup d'argent sur ce stand
We didn't have much luck with all these men on sick leave	Nous n'avons pas eu beaucoup de chance avec tous ces ouvriers en congé de maladie

7. **Getting ... known and talked about** : **get** donne une idée de *persuasion* plus forte que **have**. Notons le passif de transitif suivi du passif d'intransitif. A l'actif de même, un complément peut être commun à deux verbes de construction différente. Ainsi, avec l'exemple présent, on pourrait dire :

The public know, and talk about, our products	Le public connaît nos produits et il en parle

Conversation :

1. **Somewhere** est employé dans l'interrogative et non pas **anywhere** bien sûr car John fait allusion à un endroit bien certain où Joanna s'assiéra.

15. **The steadies** : il existe un petit nombre d'adjectifs, vraiment très réduit qui prennent la marque du pluriel lorsqu'ils sont substantivés (employés seuls comme noms). Ce type de pluriel se rencontre toutefois de plus en plus dans la langue moderne :

The overforties find it difficult to get interesting jobs	Les plus de quarante ans ont du mal à trouver des emplois intéressants
Woollies ; the glossies	Des lainages ; les magazines illustrés (*sur papier glacé*)
Our elders ; our betters	Nos aînés ; nos supérieurs ·

17. **It's selling well** : la forme active de **to sell** s'emploie fréquemment avec une valeur passive.

25-26. **A most attractive range** : précédé de l'article indéfini, **most** a le sens de very. Ne pas confondre cet emploi avec le superlatif (relatif) formé de **the + most**, le plus. **Most** seul a ce sens de **very** également devant adverbe cf. texte publicitaire p. 228 : **most carefully designed**.

42. Remarquons que l'expression **it's the first time** est suivie du *présent perfect* alors que l'expression correspondante en français est suivie du présent :

It's the first time I've travelled by plane	C'est la première fois que je voyage en avion

54-55. Comparons ' **It's very important that we should have a launching ceremony** ' et ' **I suggest we invite all the representatives** '.

Should s'emploie souvent après des expressions, verbes, noms, adjectifs traduisant une idée *d'ordre*, *d'opportunité* (**require, desire, insist, etc. — the rule, desirability ... recommendation, determination that — desirable, important, necessary**).

Après **suggest**, on aurait également pu rencontrer : **I suggest that we should invite**, mais on constate que dans la langue moderne, pour des raisons de simplicité peut-être, le présent de l'indicatif s'emploie après **suggest** et d'autres verbes ou expressions entraînant également la forme avec **should**. On peut éventuellement y voir une influence de l'américain, qui a gardé le subjonctif à forme simple et a fait ré-entendre donc ces formes simples en anglais. La langue contemporaine a ré-introduit cette forme simple, mais ne s'est pas rendu compte qu'il s'agissait d'un subjonctif, puisque la seule différence apparaît à la 3e personne du singulier (*indicatif* : **he invites**, *subjonctif* : **he invite**) et a employé le présent de l'indicatif avec une valeur modale (notion de *but, finalité*) :

I suggest that he makes a speech	Je propose qu'il fasse un discours.

On trouverait le subjonctif forme simple dans des textes juridiques par exemple.

96-107. Rappelons que l'impératif négatif a les formes de l'impératif affirmatif précédées de **don't** :

> **Don't go ! Don't let them come in !**   Ne partez pas ! Qu'ils n'entrent pas !

La forme **let me not, let him not,** etc. est moins fréquente, plus littéraire et guindée.

2. EXERCISES

EXERCISE 1. — Turn into the interrogative :

1. They wanted to buy something else.   2. She ordered some carbon paper for the office.   3. Some of the representatives had reported about it.   4. He obtained some valuable information about this new process.   5. Somebody else had applied for the job.   6. Some of us will join the training course

EXERCISE 2. — Use **as** *or* **like** :

1. He got a job ... a clerk in an insurance company.   2. Do ... you are told.   3. Their new lines are very much ... ours.   4. ... he wasn't there, I left a note to his secretary.   5. The marketing budget is sometimes referred to ... the appropriation.   6. I'd like to have a car ... Mr. Grant's.   7. Their stand isn't at all ... yours.   8. H.G. isn't as wealthy ... Caroline Harper.   9. Joanna speaks Spanish ... a native, she'll act ... an interpreter.   10. Why don't you do ... me ?   11. Why don't you place an advertisement in the trade press, ... we do ?   12. It would be twice ... efficient.

EXERCISE 3. — Place the adverb correctly :

1. H.G. rings his wife at lunch-time (always).   2. He called at the bank (yesterday afternoon).   3. He called at the bank in the morning (often).   4. He has been disturbed this week (very often).   5. Elizabeth complains (never).   6. Elizabeth is late (never).   7. Shuttleworth may get a large order (soon).   8. His secretary wrote down my address (carefully), but I don't think they'll write (ever).   8. They meet in the afternoon (sometimes.   9. You must play that trick again (never).

EXERCISE 4. — Complete by **much, many, little, few** :

1. There were so ... letters to type that she had to work overtime.   2. We sent lots of folders, so I can't understand why we got so ... replies.   3. He's been with us for a week, so he knows very ... about the job.   4. Were there ... complaints about the new stapler ?   5. I'm up to my ears in work, you can't have as ... to do as I have !   6. He couldn't give us ... information, he said it was top secret.   7. The press didn't give the product a good write-up, so there were very ... inquiries.   8. There isn't

... Hardiman could do about those desks, they are much too demaged.
9. We have very ... time to do it, there isn't a minute to spare.   10. They
complained that too ... of our new articles had been sent without a notice.

*EXERCISE 5. — Compound nouns are very frequent in business and
economic language. Re-write the following sentences replacing the
phrases in bold type by compound nouns :*

1. He attended the **meeting of the committee** last week.   2. This is the work
of the **section for market research**.   3. Joanna thinks that **advertisement
by strip cartoons** will attract the readers.   4. The computer will give an
accurate answer to all our **problems of forecasting**.   5. It was **an agreement
for sale on credit**.   6. Their **imports of frozen food** have increased by 27 %
in 3 years.   7. I went to **an International Exhibition of Equipment for
Offices**.   8. She handed me **a note for ten pounds**. 9.   The consultants
recommended **schemes for reorganisation** at three **levels of investment of
capital**.   10. They made **an analysis sector by sector**.   11. They've claimed
an increase of their wages.   12. She consulted John about **the programme of
publicity** of the firm.   13. It's **a system for communication between the
offices**.

EXERCISE 6. — Please answer the following with complete sentences :

1. Who would Joanna get in touch with if she wanted a stand built to show
her firm's products at an industrial or business exhibition ?   2. If a journalist writes a flattering article about the new desk range, how will Joanna
refer to this ?   3. To draw an editor's attention to a new product, what
would an Advertising Manager do ?   4. Why did Joanna want a girl on
their stand with exhibition experience ? · 5. Can you invent a better
slogan for Harper & Grant ? If so, what is it ?

*EXERCISE 7. — Please choose the correct word or expression in the
following, and complete the sentence :*

1. The plan of a proposed advertisement is called a ... *visualiser ; copy ;
layout ; write-up*.   2. A small advertisement of a few lines only offering jobs
vacant, positions wanted, items for sale, etc. is called a ... *classified ad. ;
personal ad. ; column ad.*   3. Newspapers and magazines which deal with
specialized subjects are known as... *the glossies ; the press-trade ; the trade-
press.*

EXERCISE 8. — Improvise a brief comment on the following terms :

1. a stand.   2. a slogan.

1. Je vais changer le style de nos réclames. 2. Nous avons besoin de créer une image prospective. 3. Gardons la nouvelle campagne pour les nouvelles créations. 4. Voici les projets de maquettes. 5. C'est la première fois que nous prenons un stand à l'exposition. 6. Je crois que nous devrions le voir monté à l'avance. 7. Les entrepreneurs ont du retard sur le programme. 8. Cela ne sera jamais prêt à temps. 9. C'est une série des plus attrayantes. 10. Il est nécessaire que le Directeur des Ventes fasse un discours. 11. Elle a proposé que nous invitions seulement les représentants de la presse professionnelle. 12. Ils envisagent d'avoir des agents commerciaux dans les pays comme la Belgique, l'Italie et l'Espagne. 13. Joanna est très efficace comme chef de la publicité. 14. Nos éléments (units) sont en un matériau nouveau intachable et résistant aux griffes. 15. Pour plus ample informé, veuillez vous adresser au directeur du marketing. 16. Vous y trouverez tout ce qu'un cadre ambitieux rêve de trouver lorsqu'il est assis sur son fauteuil. 17. Quelle pagaïe ! Est-ce que je peux vous donner un coup de main ? 18. Nous devrions inviter toute personne susceptible de faire mousser nos produits dans la presse. 19. Nous mènerons la campagne deux mois avant le lancement officiel du produit. 20. L'agence publicitaire est partisan de garder l'ancien slogan, n'est-ce pas ?

UNIT 15

DEALING WITH AN IMPORTANT NEW MARKET

PART 1 : INTRODUCTION

1. WORD STUDY

Vocabulary

against en face de, vis-à-vis
accommodation logement, hôtel
additional en plus, supplémentaire
all-in global
below en-dessous
bill of lading connaissement
breakdown rapport détaillé, ventilation
budget inscrire, prévoir au budget
built-in incorporé
bulk volume, masse
c.i.f. c.a.f.
cocktail cabinet bar
confirm confirmer
cost évaluer le prix de revient
currency monnaie
demurrage surestaries
detail donner le détail
entertainment amusement, représentation
exchange change

expenses frais, dépenses
fluctuate fluctuer, varier
foreign exchange devises étrangères
fruitless stérile, vain
fulfil accomplir, remplir
go by passer
indent ordre d'achat
invoice facture
irrevocable irrévocable
letter of credit lettre de crédit, accréditif
mahogany acajou
marginal cost frais marginaux
Ministry ministère
merchandise marchandises
negotiate négocier
overheads frais généraux
prevail prévaloir, être en vigueur
package deal compromis
pro forma (facture) simulée
Public Works Travaux Publics

— 235 —

quarterly trimestriel
quote donner un prix, coter
quotation prix
rate of exchange taux du change
recovery récupération
refund rembourser
revoke révoquer, annuler
suitably comme il faut
summon convoquer
top dessus

transferable négociable, transmissible
turnover chiffre d'affaires
view voir, examiner
warehouse entrepôt
bonded warehouse entrepôt en douanes, magasins généraux
wharfage droits de quai
waybill lettre de voiture, feuille de route

Phrases

We're up against big competition nous avons affaire à forte concurrence

Explanations and Other Useful Terms

banker's transfer an order from a buyer to his bank to transfer a sum of money.

bill of lading (B/L) see illustration, and also Unit 3.

bonded warehouse where goods are stored under the control of the customs authorities until the duty on them is paid or the importer is ready to take delivery.

breakdown colloquial term for an analysis of statistics or figures (see also Unit 17 to break down).

a bulk order a large order. To order **in bulk** : to order in large quantities. It can also mean that the goods are loose, not packaged.

cash against documents the money for the goods will be paid on presentation of documents which prove shipment or delivery of the goods.

c.i.f. (cost, insurance, freight) the price of the goods includes all the charges (shipping, insurance, forwarding) until the goods reach the home port.

to clinch a deal to make a business transaction firm, definite.

costed **to cost** means to estimate the price to be charged for an article, based on the expense of producing it. Note that in this sense the verb is regular : John *has costed it.* Cp. : *it has cost us a great deal.*

BILL OF LADING - PARTICULARS

B/L no.

Shipper

Exporter's ref.

F/Agent's ref.

Consignee (if 'Order' state Notify Party)

GEEST LINE

CONTINENT—U.K.—CONTINENT

Notify Party (only if not stated above: otherwise leave blank)

WALING VAN GEEST & ZONEN N.V.

Monsterseweg 119,	Burgemeester de Jonghkade 33
's-Gravenzande	Maassluis
Telex 31103	Telex 23466
Telefoon 01748-2941	Telefoon 01899-3516

Vessel	Port of loading		
Port of discharge	Date of sailing	Freight payable at	Number of original Bs/L

Leading marks and numbers: (Declared by shippers without any responsibility for the carrier)	Number and type of packages (container)	Description of goods (Declaration of shippers, the carrier not taking any responsibility for the weight, measure, contents, quality, quantity, condition, value).	Gross weight
			MAXIMUM WEIGHT OF 4 TONS of 1016 Kos. PER CONTAINER

COPY

Shipped in apparent good order and condition at the aforesaid Port of loading (see Particulars) by SHIPPER (see Particulars) on board the good vessel (see Particulars) for carriage to Port Discharge (see Particulars) or so near thereto as the Vessel may safely get, subject to the terms and exceptions and with the liberties to call and/or discharge at any other port or ports as mentioned hereinafter the GOODS (see Particulars) which are to be delivered in the like good order and condition at the aforesaid Port unto CONSIGNEE (see Particulars) or to his or their Assigns, Shippers or Consignees (see Particulars) to pay freight plus other charges incurred in accordance with the provisions contained in this Bill of Lading.
Weight, measure, marks, number, quality, quantity, condition, contents and value unknown.
It is mutually agreed that in accepting this Bill of Lading the Shipper and/or Owner of the goods expressly accepts and agrees to all its stipulations, exceptions, terms and conditions on both pages, whether written, printed, stamped or incorporated, as fully as if they were all signed by such Shipper and/or Owner of the goods. In Witness whereof the Master or Agent of the ship has signed the number of original Bills of Lading stated below all of this tenor and date, one of which being accomplished, the others to stand void.

Disbursement
incl. shipper's charges forward
(if any)
£

Coll. fee £

Total £

Number of Packages (in words)

Place and date of issue

Signed for the Master

as agents

Port Agents	Booking Agents
GEEST INDUSTRIES LTD.	W. E. ANDERSON & CO. LTD.	GEEST INDUSTRIES LTD.
No. 3 TRANSIT SHED	THE DOCK	WHITE HOUSE CHAMBERS
CLIFF QUAY	BOSTON	SHIPPING DEPARTMENT
IPSWICH	LINCS.	SPALDING
TELEX: 98173	TELEX: 37633	TELEX: 32235
TELEPH: 55032/3	TELEPH: BOSTON 2261	TELEPH: 3901

credit gap	the gap between order, delivery and payment.
demurrage	charges made by railway, customs and port authorities if goods are not cleared and taken away by a certain time. It is usually a rate per day related to either the value or the volume of the goods involved.
duty paid	refers to the import duty or tax, levied (imposed) by the importing country.
entertainment expenses	money which a business spends on entertaining people. These could be customers, people who could help with publicity or even suppliers. When it comes to calculating the company's profits for tax assessment, such expenditure can only be regarded as a business expense if the people being entertained are overseas customers. All business entertainment in Great Britain used to be regarded as legitimate business expense when assessing profits for taxation purposes but this is not at present allowed.
ex warehouse	the cost of the goods includes all charges up to receiving them from the warehouse. The buyer has to provide, or pay for, transport from the warehouse.
a firm order	one that will not be cancelled. The seller can go ahead on production knowing that the buyer is committed to buying on the terms agreed.
franco dom	usually understood to mean that the price covers all costs and charges until the goods are delivered to the buyer. (see *c.i.f.*)
f.o.b. = free on board	the cost of the goods includes all charges up to the time when the goods are put on board the ship. After that, the charges must be met by the buyer.
f.o.r. = free on rail	price quoted includes all costs until the goods arrive at a specified railway station.
foreign bills of exchange	used for payment in foreign trade. The seller (the **drawer** or **creditor**) draws up the bill ; the purchaser (the **drawee** or **debtor**) accepts the bill. A bill of exchange becomes legally binding when it has been accepted or signed.
goods landed	the price quoted includes all the charges which may be incurred in landing the goods at the port of destination.

indent	instructions to a buying agency. The agency then places an order on a manufacturer. If it includes complete instructions as to brands of goods, manufacturers from whom they are to be bought, etc. it is called a specific indent. If certain details are left to the discretion of the firm, or agent, it is called an open indent.
irrevocable	see **letter of credit.**
letter of credit	is issued by the buyer's bank : a foreign buyer transfers money to a bank in the exporter's country. This bank then informs the beneficiary, the person to whom the money is owed, that a sum of money is available when certain documents (*e.g.* a bill of lading proving that the goods sold have been loaded on board a ship) are presented. Letters of credit are only valid for a certain time, after which they are said to have expired.
	irrevocable letter of credit : the agreement to pay a certain sum of money cannot be changed or revoked (to revoke is to refuse to fulfil an obligation).
	transferable letter of credit : the amount agreed to be paid can be transferred to another person.
overheads	overhead expenses incurred in running a business.
official confirmation	a letter, or document, received from someone placing an order which confirms a verbal or tentative order. On receipt of this ratification, the order is said to be firm.
package deal	this refers to a contract for the bulk sale or buying of a large variety of goods at a special all-in price, where any particular condition is contingent on all the others being accepted. A typical example or this would be a firm grouping together items of high profit margin with items of low profit margin and letting one subsidise the sale of the other.
profit margin	the difference between what it costs to make something and its net price, real price, off which discount is not allowed.
pro forma invoice	an invoice is a list of goods supplied, with prices and charges. A pro forma invoice is a sample invoice sent to a potential buyer so that he can see clearly what his total costs will be ; also sent in advance to a new client, or one whose references are not satisfactory, informing him that goods will be delivered only on receipt of payment.

quotation	the price of goods given to a potential buyer. (see also Unit 2).
shipping charges	charges made for loading goods into a ship.
ship's manifest	list of the cargo carried by the ship, giving all relevant details such as name of sender (**consignor**), name of the receiver (**consignee**), weight, contents, etc.
terms of payment	arrangements concerning the way in which the goods will be paid for : limit, place, currency, discounts, penalties if conditions are not fulfilled, etc.
waybill	a form or documentation giving details of freight sent by place (compare : bill of lading in shipping).

Pronunciation

1 — 1 - - (-) budget, cabinet, contract, noun, curious, currency, definite, envy, February, fruitless, furniture, invoice, marginal, mention, method, minister, ministry, overheads, quarterly, quantity, reference, sterling, suitably, visit

 - 2 (- -) against, amount, astonished, capacity, committed, conditional, confirm, delighted, department, devalue, disposal, equipment, entire, exchange, expense, immense, incur, magnificent, mahogany, negotiate, obliged, October, persuade, prevail, provide, quotation, reduction, ridiculous, supply

 - - 3 (- -) entertainment, irrevocable

2 — specialisaticn [ˌspəʃəlaiˈzeiʃən], rationalisation [ˌræʃənəlaiˈzeiʃən]

3 — *dark* 1 : well, sell, deal, build, building, single, level, hotel, fulfil, prevail, irrevocable, steel

 clear 1 : seller, selling, dealing, travelling, place, sleep, London, supply, sterling, delighted, splendid, planning, fluctuating

[ai]	try, by, buy, high, supply, either, provide
[ou]	open, local, below, hotel, propose, october, turnover, disposal, negotiate
[ɔ]	gone, cost, want, profit, policy, quantity, foreign, astonish
[ɔ:]	sort, all, draw, drawer, normal, because, quarterly, airport
[ʌ]	month, country, budget, London, summon, currency, discover, production, discovery, recovery
[u]	put, look, book [u:] true, route, fruitless
[ju:]	unit, produce, view, use

4 — Compare : a detail ['di:teil] *or* [di:'teil]
  a hotel ['houtel] *or* [hou'tel]

5 — Note : fluctuate ['flʌktjueit], itinerary [əi'tinərəri], merchandise ['mə:tʃəndaiz], method ['meθəd], pro forma ['prou 'fɔ:mə], quay [ki:], quiet [kwaiət], via [vaiə].

2. SUMMARY

In the first episode, John Martin, the Sales Manager, persuaded Hector Grant to let him try and open up a new export market in Abraca. Some months have gone by and there have not been any orders from Abraca. Hector Grant is having a look at the quarterly breakdown of overheads detailing actual expenditure against budget. He finds that the amount 5
spent by the Sales Manager on travelling and entertainment is rather high.

However, John Martin has had an enquiry from the Abracan government. He has been asked to give a quotation to supply office furniture for two new government buildings. If the order is placed with them, it will be one of the largest orders the firm has ever received. John Martin has been 10
keeping quiet about it because he wanted to wait until the order was definite, but he has checked with Peter to ensure they have the production capacity to meet the quoted delivery dates. A buyer from the Abracan Ministry of Public Works proposes to visit England to see the factory and negotiate the order. John Martin considers he will have to be suitably 15
entertained: his hotel booked for him, a car put at his disposal, etc. In the letter from the Abracan Ministry there is a curious reference to some 'special requirements'. Hector Grant is astonished to discover what they are.

PART 2 : CONVERSATION AND DOCUMENTS

1. CONVERSATION
(Recorded Text)

(John Martin is summoned to Hector Grant's office)
JOHN MARTIN **You wanted to see me, H.G.?**
HECTOR GRANT **Yes, I did, John. I've just been going through the expenses you incurred on the Abraca trip. We haven't had a single order out of your visit to Abraca.**

JOHN	It's a bit early to say, but I don't think the Abracan visit will be fruitless.	5
GRANT	You went there in October and it's now February and we haven't heard a thing from them. What's our agent doing out there? Sleeping?	
JOHN	As a matter of fact, I think there may be something moving out there. We've been asked for a quotation for a very large order—office furniture and equipment for two entire government departments.	10
GRANT	What are the chances of getting this large order? It's only an enquiry, isn't it?	15
JOHN	No, it's more than that. We've already sent *pro forma* invoices so that the Ministry of Works can apply to the National Bank for foreign exchange. They want a reduction on our unit price per desk for a larger quantity than we originally quoted for, the price to be *c.i.f.* Djemsa.	20
GRANT	*c.i.f.* Djemsa. Two government departments, you said? Well, this sounds more like it.	
JOHN	It would be the largest single order in the history of the firm. It's a package deal. We've costed it in detail. It's true we'd be below normal price levels, but we're up against big competition. We have the capacity to produce the order and it'd be in addition to the budgeted turnover for the year, so all recovery on marginal cost would be profit. I'm certain it'll lead to other orders in the country. Here's the letter.	25 / 30
GRANT	'A representative of our Ministry of Works will be coming to London ... obliged if you would book him accommodation ... glad to visit your factory and view the merchandise ... special requirements ...' Here what's this about 'special requirements'? What do they mean by that?	35
JOHN	I don't know, H.G. That's the one mystery. They mentioned it in their original letter of enquiry.	
GRANT	I don't much like the sound of that. What do they mean by 'special requirements'? I suppose we'll soon find out. What's the method of payment?	40
JOHN	We require an irrevocable letter of credit, confirmed on a London bank. We've quoted in local currency, and this, of course, is conditional. It's conditional on the rate of	45

	exchange which prevails on the date of our quotation not fluctuating more than three per cent either way. So we'd be protected if the Abracan currency, for instance, was devalued in relation to sterling.	
GRANT	Hmm! Is Peter happy about delivery dates?	50
JOHN	Yes, we can meet them. It's meant an immense amount of work in the production planning section.	
GRANT	Well, you'll arrange some sort of meeting for us all then? Have you booked their representative into a hotel?	
JOHN	Yes, I have, and I think we should provide a car and show him a bit of this country.	55
GRANT	All right. But you'd better find out more about the special requirements. It may be some condition we can't fulfil, and I don't think . . .	

(*Mr. Mahawi, the government representative, arrives and is entertained royally. His 'special requirements' cause some difficulty. John goes to see Hector Grant.*)

GRANT	A mahogany desk with built-in cocktail cabinet, secret drawer and radio! Leather top? Oh, really, John, what kind of firm does he think we are? Our business is mass-produced steel office furniture!	60
JOHN	I said we'd make it. It's for the Minister's personal use. They are prepared to pay. It would be additional to the main contract.	65
GRANT	Don't be ridiculous. We've dropped this sort of line from our range. That was part of our rationalisation policy.	
JOHN	Couldn't Bob Hardiman make it?	
GRANT	That old chap?	70
JOHN	Yes. He's a master craftsman of the old school. Look at this beautiful desk he made for you. You said at the time we introduced work study, during the productivity drive, that he was redundant. Well, here's a job he can be really useful on, and he'd be delighted to do it. He'd produce a magnificent piece of furniture, it'd be the envy of all the Minister's visitors and a splendid advertisement for us.	75
GRANT	Well, you have committed us to it, so we must go ahead, I suppose.	

061-**6863 682**

AIRPORT OF DEPARTURE	EXECUTION DATE DAY/MTH/YR	TC	CHGS CODE	CUR'CY CODE						

061-**6863 682**

AIRPORT OF DEPARTURE (ADDRESS OF FIRST CARRIER) AND REQUESTED ROUTING

AIRPORT OF DESTINATION

ROUTING AND DESTINATION

	TO	BY FIRST CARRIER	TO	BY	TO	BY	TO	BY

1/

NOT NEGOTIABLE
CONSIGNMENT NOTE/AIR WAYBILL
ISSUED BY

BOAC

2/ CONSIGNEE'S ACCOUNT NUMBER   CONSIGNEE'S NAME AND ADDRESS

BRITISH OVERSEAS AIRWAYS CORPORATION

LONDON   MEMBER OF INTERNATIONAL AIR TRANSPORT ASSOCIATION

If the carriage involves an ultimate destination or stop in a country other than the country of departure, the Warsaw Convention may be applicable and the Convention governs and in most cases limits the liability of carriers in respect of loss of or damage to cargo. Agreed stopping places are those places (other than the places of departure and destination) shown under requested routing and/or those places shown in carriers' timetables as scheduled stopping places for the route. Address of first carrier is the airport of departure. SEE CONDITIONS ON REVERSE HEREOF.

The shipper certifies that the particulars on the face hereof are correct and agrees to the CONDITIONS ON REVERSE HEREOF.

SIGNATURE OF SHIPPER

3/ SHIPPER'S ACCOUNT NUMBER   SHIPPER'S NAME AND ADDRESS

BY BROKER/AGENT

Carrier certifies goods described below were received for carriage subject to the CONDITIONS ON REVERSE HEREOF, the goods then being in apparent good order and condition except as noted hereon.

PHONE

4/ ISSUING CARRIER'S AGENT, ACCOUNT No.   ISSUING CARRIER'S AGENT, NAME AND CITY

EXECUTED ON_____AT_____
    (Date)   (Place)

AGENT'S IATA CODE

SIGNATURE OF ISSUING CARRIER OR ITS AGENT

Copies 1, 2 and 3 of this Air Waybill are originals and have the same validity.

5/

CHARGES PREPAID COLLECT	CURRENCY	DECLARED VALUE FOR CARRIAGE		COD AMOUNT	SPECIAL ACCOUNTING INFORMATION

6/

NO. OF PACKAGES --- --- NCP	ACTUAL GROSS WEIGHT	Kg./ lb.	RATE CLASS	COMMODITY ITEM No.	CHARGEABLE WEIGHT	RATE	NATURE AND QUANTITY OF GOODS (INCL. DIMENSIONS OR VOLUME)

7/ SPECIAL HANDLING INFORMATION

	VALUE FOR CUSTOMS	MARKS & NUMBERS	METHOD OF PACKING

P R E P A I D

8/

WEIGHT CHARGE	VALUATION CHARGE	TOTAL OF AIRLINE CHARGES BELOW	AWB FEE	CODE	TOTAL OF NON-AIRLINE CHARGES BELOW		COLLECT CHARGES IN DESTINATION CURRENCY
	V	C	F		ORIGIN 0	DESTINATION D	

Y

CLEARANCE & HANDLING	CARTAGE	INSURANCE	TRANSIT	WEIGHT CHARGE

TOTAL PREPAID	AIRLINE AND NON-AIRLINE CHARGES, OTHER THAN WEIGHT CHARGE, VALUATION CHARGE AND AWB FEE	VALUATION CHARGE
P	Z	

C O L L E C T

9/

WEIGHT CHARGE	VALUATION CHARGE	TOTAL OF AIRLINE CHARGES BELOW	AGENT'S DISBURSEMENTS	TOTAL OF NON-AIRLINE CHARGES BELOW		OTHER CHARGES INCL. COD FEE
	V	A		ORIGIN 0	DESTINATION D	

Y

AIRLINE AND NON-AIRLINE CHARGES, OTHER THAN WEIGHT CHARGE VALUATION CHARGE AND AGENT'S DISBURSEMENTS	COD

COD AMOUNT	COD FEE	DISBURSEMENT FEE	AIRLINE AND NON-AIRLINE CHARGES, CONTINUED	TOTAL COLLECT
M	Z			

L

FOR CARRIER'S USE ONLY AT DESTINATION

Form No. A.1877F.   Printed in U.K.

II. SPARE COPY (NO VALUE)   **M**

PRACTICE SENTENCES

Say the practice sentences on the record :

  i We've been asked for a quotation for a very large order.
 ii We've already sent pro forma invoices.
iii They want a reduction on our unit price per desk for a larger quantity.
 iv It would be in addition to the budgeted turnover for the year.
  v It'll lead to other orders in the country.
 vi What's the method of payment?
vii We require an irrevocable letter of credit, confirmed on a London bank.

2. ITINERARY FOR AN OVERSEAS BUYER

For Mr. Mahawi's visit, the Sales Manager of Harper & Grant has planned a sightseeing programme. When he arrives at London Airport a car is sent to meet him and he is given the *itinerary*, or planned route, for his visit.

Special Sightseeing Programme

Wednesday, 12th March	*11.00 a.m.:* Arrive London Airport. Car will meet and drive visitor to Granchester Hotel. Lunch with Sales Manager, Mr. John Martin. *Afternoon:* London sightseeing—visit the Houses of Parliament; Westminster Abbey; Buckingham Palace; St. Paul's; Stock Exchange; Tower of London.
Thursday, 13th March	*Morning:* Visit Harper & Grant factory. Car will arrive at hotel to drive Mr. Mahawi to the Works at 9.30 a.m. Lunch at factory with Managing Director, Mr. Hector Grant. *Afternoon:* At leisure. Information, car and shopping advice if required. *Evening:* Theatre visit. Car will be at hotel at 7.15 p.m. to drive Mr. Mahawi to New Theatre.

Friday, 14th March	*8.00 a.m.:* Car will be outside hotel to drive Mr. Mahawi to Shakespeare's birthplace, Stratford-on-Avon. Return via Woodstock and Oxford.
Saturday, 15th March	*10.00 a.m.:* Depart from hotel for London Airport. Take-off time: 12.10 p.m.

PART 3 : NOTES AND PRACTICE

1. RAPPEL GRAMMATICAL

Summary :

12-13. Notons ces termes composés : **production capacity, delivery dates** et plus loin : **rationalisation policy, productivity drive.**

Conversation :

19. Phrase de construction très dense de : **a larger quantity than we quoted for** : que celle pour laquelle nous avons indiqué des prix. **The one which** est sous-entendu.

25. Ne pas confondre **to cost, cost, cost,** verbe fort, *coûter* :

It cost me ten pounds   Cela m'a coûté dix livres

avec **to cost, costed, costed,** verbe faible : *évaluer le coût* :

He has costed the expenses   Il a évalué les frais

38. **The one mystery. One** a ici le sens de l'adjectif **only,** *unique, seul.*

47. **Either way. Either** est ici indéfini au sens de *l'un ou l'autre.*

Un bref rappel de points déjà connus, occasion pour faire davantage d'exercices pratiques :

2. EXERCISES

EXERCISE 1. — Replace **not any** (-) *by* **no** (-) :

1. This does not prove anything.   2. We did not see any other customer in the afternoon.   3. This method won't bring any results.   4. She didn't understand anything.   5. I haven't mentioned it to anyone.   6. There weren't any more stamps.   7. He didn't buy any ink for the office. 8. There wasn't anything the matter with the new staplers.   9. I haven't seen Jack anywhere in the Works.   10. You can't do anything to help them.   11. I hadn't any more questions to ask them.   12. There weren't any women applicants.

EXERCISE 2. — *Retort ironically as follows* :

Bob Hardiman can do that → **Oh he can, can he ?**

1. They want a desk with a secret drawer. 2. The foreman complained about you, Jack. 3. They have increased their sales in Scotland. 4. Abraca offers a very good maiket. 5. She said she sent the invoice on Friday. 6. I could give you valuable help. 7. It's the only cause of our delay. 8. All orders are dealt with very rapidly. 9. We'll place the case in the hands of our legal department. 10. The procedure of the meeting was quite regular. 11. She is a very efficient typist. 12. We decline all responsibility.

EXERCISE 3. — *Use the right word* (*preposition or adverbial particle* : **up, out,** *etc.*) :

1. They opened ... a new market in the Near East. 2. Here is a statement of the amount spent by the Sales Manager ... entertainment. 3. Do you think the order will be placed ... Harper & Grant ? 4. A car will be put ... the visitor's disposal. 5. Has he gone ... John's report ? 6. We've been asked ... a quotation for a very large order. 7. He'll apply to the bank ... foreign exchange. 8. Their currency might be devalued in relation ... sterling. 9. He's responsible ... the production. 10. They supply us ... steel. 10. Can you find ... why there is a hold-up on delivery ? 11. They won't be able to cope ... the increase in production. 12. The minutes of the last meeting are taken ... read. 13. What are they arguing ... ? 14. Sally, could you get ... to our rep in Yorkshire ?

EXERCISE 4. — *Change as follows* :

I don't think it will be a fruitless visit →
It won't have been a fruitless visit

I don't think... 1. He will answer all your questions on the report. 2. He will give you an account of his visit in Abraca. 3. I shall have a discussion with him before I go to New York. 4. She will send the catalogues by Thursday. 5. He will make his report by Friday. 6. You will see all their models at the Exhibition. 7. You will find anything more troublesome in the accounts. 8. John will spend all his Abracan currency. 9. They will meet all their obligations to their shareholders.

EXERCISE 5. — *Change as follows* :

What kind of firm are we ? →
What kind of firm do you think we are ?

1. Where did Sally put those folders ? 2. When will the goods be delivered ? 3. How much did he spend on travelling ? 4. How many applications did we receive ? 5. Why did the boss want to see the shop steward ? 6. What did the Advertising Manager propose ? 7. What are those special

requirements of theirs ? 8. What did she find in the report ? 9. When will you go to Chicago again ? 10. What was our rep in Lancashire doing ? 11. What are our chances of getting the order ? 12. How could we convince the Chairman ? 13. What did he mean by that ? 14. How long did it take us ?

EXERCISE 6. — Use either a compound noun or the possessive case :

1. We did it during our drive for productivity. 2. This would increase the productivity of the firm. 3. Do you think we can get the support of the government ? 4. Do you think we could get a grant from the government ? 5. This wouldn't be the best scheme for re-organisation. 6. The enquiry came from a large company of computers. 7. We shall consider the complaint of the consumer. 8. Is this the new foreign policy of the Labour Party ? 9. The network of marketing of your company is envied by all our rivals. 10. The Managing Director of the company was against the scheme of profit sharing. 11. The enquiry of yesterday hasn't been dealt with. 12. Have you seen the figures of the membership of the union ? 13. This was part of a plan for rationalisation. 14. In theory the authority of the shareholders is supreme. 15. The strike of last Wednesday was only a token one.

EXERCISE 7. — You are making arrangements to order goods from Britain. On your first visit to see John Martin, the Sales Manager of Harper & Grant, you want to find out what the quotation he has given you includes. How would you ask the questions to get the following information which you need ? Please make a complete question each time.

1. You would like to know if the price of the goods is *to the ship*, *i.e.* one which includes transport from the factory to the docks (forwarding), the handling and shipping charges (which include wharfage, dock dues, port rates) but which does not include sea freight, insurance, and landing and delivery charges in your country. 2. You want the price of the goods to include all costs including the cost of loading and unloading at the ports, insurance, forwarding and shipping charges. 3. You have decided to ask John Martin to include *all* the charges (goods landed, duty paid, etc.), so that the goods arrive where you want to use them and no further payment will be involved. 4. You would like to know how the firm wish to be paid. 5. You want to know if the price will be lower if you place a large order.

EXERCISE 8. — Can you answer the following ? (Please answer with a complete sentence).

1. What sort of order would you place if you wanted to make it clear that it will not be changed or cancelled ? 2. An employee has been entertaining a foreign buyer with his own money. What does he do to be repaid by his firm ? 3. You are writing to a firm of suppliers and you want them to quote you a price which includes all costs until the goods arrive at a specified railway station. How do you phrase this ? 4. In order to guard against a loss owing to currency fluctuations, what rate of exchange is usually preferred ?

EXERCISE 9. — *Quickly improvise a comment on the following terms* :
1. the budget. 2. expenses.

EXERCISE 10. — *Translate into English* :

1. On nous a demandé nos prix pour une très grosse commande. 2. Nous avons déjà envoyé des factures fictives. 3. Ils veulent une réduction sur le prix unitaire par bureau pour une quantité plus importante. 4. Ce serait en plus du chiffre d'affaire prévu au budget pour l'année. 5. Cela conduira à d'autres commandes dans le pays. 6. Quelle est la méthode de paiement ? 7. Nous voulons une lettre de crédit irrévocable confirmée sur une banque londonienne. 8. Ont-ils fait un projet de programme de visite ? 9. Voilà un travail pour lequel vous pouvez vraiment être utile ! 10. Ne croyez-vous pas que ce serait pour nous une magnifique publicité ? 11. Il a dit qu'il ne nous avait pas engagés. 12. C'est peut-être quelque condition que nous ne pouvons satisfaire. 13. Est-ce que ce serait en plus du contrat principal ? 14. C'est une concession, et nous en avons évalué le prix. 15. N'oubliez pas que nous nous trouvons en face d'une grosse concurrence. 16. C'était le taux de change en vigueur au moment où nous avons donné les prix. 17. Plusieurs mois ont passé et nous n'avons reçu aucune commande. 18. Jetez un coup d'œil à l'analyse des frais généraux. 19. Je trouve que la somme que vous avez dépensé en représentation est trop élevée. 20. Avons-nous la capacité de production suffisante pour respecter les dates de livraison indiquées ?

UNIT 16

TRANSPORT PROBLEMS

PART 1 : INTRODUCTION

1. WORD STUDY

Vocabulary

alleged prétendu, allégué, soi-disant
assess évaluer, estimer
assumption hypothèse
bill note, facture
bulk masse ; global
catch up with rattraper
consumption consommation
contractor entrepreneur
cope with s'occuper de
depreciation amortissement
discount remise, rabais, escompte ; escompter, faire l'escompte de
docks port, quai
earn gagner, rapporter
fit out équiper, aménager
fixtures and fittings installation et agencement
fleet parc (*automobile*, etc)
forecast prévoir
gasoline essence
grant subvention, prêt
harm mal

hi-jack arraisonner, détourner
incentive stimulant
income revenu
inch pouce (2,54 cm)
liner transatlantique
lorry camion
lower abaisser
maintenance entretien
nominally de nom
obvious évident
offset compenser
operational d'exploitation
operating costs frais d'exploitation
operator (*ici*) gestionnaire
overnight (*adj*) de nuit
petrol essence
policy politique, tactique
put up augmenter
raise élever
rely compter (sur)
re-equip ré-équiper, renouveler les équipements
rail-end gare d'embarquement

road-worthiness bon état de
marche
search fouiller, inspecter
see off assister au départ de
spot check contrôle immédiat,
sondage
tailboard hayon, layon
traction unit élément tracteur

trade in reprendre (*voiture*)
trailer remorque
turn-round time temps d'immobilisation d'un véhicule avant le
retour, temps de livraison
upkeep entretien
worth-whileness opportunité,
validité

Phrases

It would work out more economically

cela serait plus économique

It works out twice as expensive

cela revient deux fois plus cher

Can you give me a lift?

pouvez-vous m'emmener dans votre
voiture ?

In the long run

à la longue

I don't hold out much hope

je n'ai pas grand espoir

I wish to heaven we had one!

ah ! si seulement nous en avions une !

On balance

tout bien pesé, à la réflexion

Explanations and Other Useful Terms

articulated vehicles
large trailer which is pulled by a traction unit and
can be dropped off a various points for loading and
unloading.

breakdown
here : failure, collapse. Usually refers to a car, lorry,
machine, etc. which ceases to function. (*compare*
breakdown in unit 15).

carriers
firms who transport goods. Some of these firms are
very large, like British Road Services, with depots
all round the country connected by trunk routes,
main roads. Some are small, and the owner drives
his own lorry.

contract hire
a transport contractor, like Andersons, would agree
to have a certain number of their vehicles at
Harper & Grant's disposal at fixed rates, plus
certain agreed extras.

— 251 —

depreciation	reduction in value owing to use. For example, the value of furniture, lamps, wall lights, etc. in a home (known as fixtures and fittings) depreciates in value every year.
dunnage	normally applies to pieces of wood and straw which are used to fill up gaps and pack goods tightly in a container or in the hold of a ship.
hi-jacked	to hi-jack is a slang word. Here, it means to seize a road vehicle in transit, and steal its load. Also used of the seizure and diversion of planes.
a lift	to give someone a lift (colloquial) is to transport without charges in a car or lorry a person who would otherwise have to use public transport, or go on foot. Most companies give strict instructions to their drivers that they may not give lifts, usually because they do not pay the extra insurance for passengers. However, this is often ignored.
to palletise	to load goods on to **pallets** (platforms) so that fork lift trucks can transport them from one point to another. If the goods lie flat on the ground, the lifting fork cannot pick them up. The pallet normally stays under the goods until they reach the final user.
road-worthiness	the fitness of a vehicle to be on a public highway or road. It must be in good mechanical order.
spot check	here, the detailed examination for road-worthiness of a vehicle selected at random, which could be carried out by the police anywhere and at any time. The phrase spot checking is generally used in the quality control of goods in production. A sample of goods, which might be typical of a large production batch, is selected for inspection.
traction unit	the front, motorised, part of an articulated vehicle, which does the pulling.
turn-round time	time from the arrival of a vehicle to when it starts its return journey. Time to turn round and face the homeward direction.

DO NOT CONFUSE :

economical	I'll never buy that kind of car again, it is not economical at all.
economic	This is due to the economic policy of the new government.

Pronunciation

1 — 1 - (- -) ánnual, balance, calculate, diesel, engine, income, interest, lorry, nominally, petrol, purchase, recently, regular, sensible, railboard, urgent, road-worthiness

- - (- -) accomplice, another, advantage, assess, articulate, capacity, contractor, control, defect, demand, employ, entirely, expenses, immediate, incentive, initial, inspector, invest, investment, original, rely

2 — '-ion : consumption, reduction, assumption, addition, operation, regulation, depreciation

3 — The = [ðə]   + lorry, driver, police, tunnel, charges

                + [ju:] unit, European market, United States

    [ði]   + order, airport, expenses, investment, enquiry, argument, equipment

    [ɔ]   lorry, obvious, offset, bother, problem, probable, Scotland

    [ou]   load, loan, road, own, flow, cope, lower, control, motor

    [ʌ]   up, bulk, pump, couple, double, trouble, tunnel, budget, worried

    [a:]   charge, grant, start, harm, can't, demand, transport

    [æ]   cash, tax, bank, can, café, hand, capital, contractor

    [ei]   tail, rail, same, able, space, raise, breakdown

    [i:]   be, see, meet, fleet, chief, diesel, least, technique, recently, immediate

4 — Compare : n. 'transport, v. to trans'port [træn-] *or* [tra:n]
able [eibl],   probable ['prɔbəbl],   probably ['prɔbəbli]
police [pə'li:s],   policy ['pɔlisi],   politics ['pɔlitiks],   political [pə'litikl]
economy [i:'kɔnəmi],   economist [i:'kɔnəmist],   economic(ally) [,i:kə'nɔmik(li)]
ad'vantage [ə'dva:ntidʒ],   advan'tageous [,ædvan'teidʒəs]
[ju:] assume, consume, resume ;   [ʌ] assumption, consumption, resumption

5 — Note : allege [ə'ledʒ],   gasoline ['gæsəli:n],   heaven ['hevən],   route [ru:t],   vehicle ['vi:ikl].

2. SUMMARY

The firm of Harper & Grant has a Transport Manager. His name is Bruce Hill. He is responsible for delivering goods. Some go by rail and some by road. For goods sent by road he uses a firm of contractors who supply him with lorries, on demand.

This morning he has just seen off a load of office desks and chairs 5
ordered for a new liner being fitted out on the River Clyde in Scotland. The tailboard, the back part of the lorry which can be raised and lowered, was only just able to be shut, as every inch of space was used; it was loaded to capacity. Bruce Hill is worried because he wants that same lorry back quickly for a regular south-west England delivery. He could 10
ask for another lorry from Andersons, the contractors, but they have recently put up the charges again for fuel consumption, driver's expenses and so on. It is difficult for him to keep to his budget. He has long been wanting a fleet of lorries of his own, because he is certain it would work out more economically for the firm in the long run. He goes to see his 15
immediate chief, Peter Wiles, to find out if Peter would put up the idea at the next Board Meeting. Peter is sure Hector Grant will reject the idea because of the initial expense. Bruce suggests that if they had their own fleet, or at least two lorries to start with, they could control some of the problems better. They could have their own fuel pump, which would 20
mean a reduction on bulk purchase of petrol. They would probably buy vehicles with diesel rather than petrol (gasoline) motors. The initial cost of a diesel vehicle is a lot higher than for one with a petrol engine, maintenance costs are usually higher too; but the operational costs are lower. Peter sees the advantages, but reminds Bruce that the new regula- 25
tions about the road-worthiness of goods vehicles are very strict. Police inspectors have the power to order spot checks, and they can order any vehicle with a defect off the road.

Surprisingly it is Hector Grant himself who proposes that the company should have their own transport. He asks Peter to prepare a D.C.F., 30
Discounted Cash Flow (see Unit 1). Discounted cash flow is a technique for assessing the profitability of a new investment. An investment is normally made on certain obvious assumptions, such as probable sales or operating costs. In addition, when buying two lorries, for instance, other factors should be considered, such as: (1) there will be an investment 35
grant, perhaps thirty per cent of cost, which is a government incentive for firms (who pay tax to the government on profits) to re-equip; (2) there will be a second-hand value on the lorries, when at the end of, say, five

years they are traded in and replaced by new ones; (3) during their
lifetime the lorries will represent money which, if left in the bank, would 40
have earned interest. The D.C.F. technique takes all such points into
consideration and discounts the annual forecast income on the investment
by a sum to repay net capital, pay interest and cover all operating costs
(wages, fuel and maintenance). The net discounted income related to the net
investment over the life of the investment indicates the degree of pro- 45
fitability or worth-whileness of the project. Neither the D.C.F. nor any other
technique can say whether the assumptions on which the investment is proposed are going to be right. Running a business means taking risks. It can,
however, say what the consequences will be if the assumptions are right.

But before Hector Grant makes a suggestion for a D.C.F. the driver of 50
Andersons' lorry, Ernie, on his way to Scotland, is asked for a lift by a
man he meets in a transport café, with rather unexpected results.

PART 2 : CONVERSATION AND DOCUMENTS

1. CONVERSATION

(Recorded Text)

(In Peter Wiles's office)

BRUCE HILL	**Peter? Can I trouble you?**
PETER WILES	**Is it urgent, Bruce? I'm up to my eyes in work this morning. You know H.G. likes you to cope with transport entirely. You're only nominally under me.**
HILL	**Yes, I know. But this is a policy matter. I think it's high time we had our own transport fleet. Every month it gets worse having to rely on outside contractors.**
PETER	**My dear Bruce, H.G. wouldn't hear of it. You know the new works extension is working out twice as expensive as we originally estimated. We're supposed to be making economies to offset the increase!**
HILL	**I don't think it would cost us so much ... in the long run.**
PETER	**There are a lot of arguments against having our own fleet. It's difficult to keep the lorries fully employed, and you've got to calculate depreciation.**
HILL	**I realise that. Of course the most efficient system would be to have articulated vehicles.**

5

10

15

PETER	Well, surely you have to be a very big operator to make that system economic. The traction units that do the pulling are very expensive. Anyway, what's wrong with the contractors who supply us with lorries?	20
HILL	They can't always let us have one when we want one. And then there's the cost. Andersons' bills get higher each time.	
PETER	They why don't you go to another contractor?	25
HILL	That's just it. We can't. We've been with Andersons so long we get a good discount. It's not the basic charge they increase, but the expenses: fuel consumption, alleged breakdown, driver's expenses on overnight stops and so on.	
PETER	If we had our own fleet there'd be similar problems and expenses.	30
HILL	But they'd be controllable. Turn-round time, for instance.	
PETER	How do you mean?	
HILL	I mean we can never really be sure of how long they'll take at the other end. This load that's just gone off today, for instance, taking those desks and chairs for the new ship at Clydebank. We need that lorry back here the day after tomorrow.	35
PETER	H'm. Well, I'll try to suggest to H.G. that we should have our own vehicles. But I don't hold out much hope . . .	40

(*The driver of Andersons' lorry, Ernie, has given a lift to a man he has met in a transport café*)

'FOXY' RUNCORN	It's good of you to give me a lift.
ERNIE	Well, here we go up Shap Fell. Two thousand feet of it. It's time they built a tunnel under this mountain.
'FOXY'	Turn off at the next road on the left, will you, Ernie?

(1) FOXY: Just be sensible, Ernie, and no harm will be done.'

— 256 —

ERNIE	**What? What did you say? Look here, what are you play-** 45 **ing at? I thought for a minute you'd got a gun in your hand.**
'FOXY'	**Yes, but it is a gun, Ernie. Just take the next turning on the left. Here it is.**
ERNIE	**But that's not a road, it's a private drive. What is this?** 50
'FOXY'	**Just be sensible, Ernie, and no harm will be done. If you do what I say, there'll be something in this for you....**

(Next day, Hector Grant rings his Transport Manager)

HECTOR GRANT	**Bruce? H.G. here. What on earth's happening in this place? I've just had a call from Scotland. They say that load of desks for the new liner never arrived. You're the** 55 **Transport Manager, you're supposed to deal with this sort of thing. I don't want to be bothered with it. What do I have a Transport Manager for? ... Yes ... find out, and deal with it.**

'They checked with a transport café near Carlisle and
he'd been there.'

(Twenty minutes later, Peter comes into H.G.'s office)

PETER	**H.G., I've just spoken to Bruce Hill. He's sure our load to** 60 **Clydeside has been hi-jacked.**
GRANT	**Hi-jacked? What on earth do you mean?**
PETER	**After you'd spoken to Bruce, he called the contractors. They've also been trying to contact their driver. They checked with a transport café near Carlisle and he'd been** 65 **there. After that, nothing. They've already been on to the police, who've searched the road and found nobody.**

GRANT	There must be some mistake. He must be somewhere between Carlisle and Scotland.
PETER	The police say they've checked the whole route. Apparently it's the third lorry to disappear in a week. They think it may be the same gang.
GRANT	Oh, damn it! It was a large order, wasn't it?
PETER	Yes. Sixty desks and the same number of chairs.
GRANT	Well, you'd better let the insurance company know. But I'm sure the police will catch up with them. It's funny the driver hasn't been found.
PETER	I suppose it's possible that the driver is an accomplice.
GRANT	These damned contractors. You never know where you are with them. How do we know the driver wasn't involved? I wish to heaven we had our own fleet!
PETER	What was that, H.G.?
GRANT	I think it's high time we had a couple of lorries of our own. Put up detailed proposals with a D.C.F. on the investment at the next Board Meeting, will you. You would be in favour, wouldn't you?
PETER	Er . . . yes, H.G. Yes, on balance I think I would. . . .

PRACTICE SENTENCES

Say the practice sentences on the record :

  i We ought to have our own transport fleet.

 ii There are a lot of arguments against it.

iii It's difficult to keep the lorries fully employed.

iv You've got to calculate depreciation.

 v The traction units are very expensive.

vi Why don't we go to another contractor ?

vii We've been with them so long we get a good discount.

viii Please put up detailed proposals al the next Board Meeting.

2. MEMO FROM THE TRANSPORT MANAGER

Bruce Hill, the Transport Manager, was later asked by Peter Wiles to write a memo putting down his reasons for recommending that Harper & Grant should have their own fleet of lorries to deliver their goods instead of hiring lorries from an outside firm.

From: The Transport Manager

date: 9th April, 197..

Subject: SUGGESTED PURCHASE OF TRANSPORT FLEET

To: The Managing Director.

During the last twelve months the volume of the company's home sales has increased by thirty per cent. The greater proportion has had to be delivered by road. There is every hope that this trend will continue and I would, therefore, like to suggest that deliveries could be made more economically if we owned a fleet of three or four lorries.

I have drawn up a chart, attached, indicating the trend in volume of deliveries by road (including deliveries to docks and rail-heads) over a period of eighteen months. From this it can be seen that the average volume of business would keep these lorries fully occupied. The table of expenses, also attached, shows the cost of hiring a lorry against the cost of using our own vehicles. It can be seen that, even allowing for the initial cost of the lorries, plus upkeep, fuel, etc., the net saving would be about twenty-five per cent.

(Bruce Hill)

PART 3 : NOTES AND PRACTICE

1. RAPPEL GRAMMATICAL

Summary :

6.   **Being fitted.** Le passif progressif rend compte ici que l'action est en cours. Comparons :

It was being fitted out	On était en train de l'aménager
It was fitted out	Il était aménagé (*c'était fini*)

— 259 —

13. La préposition **for** peut introduire des propositions infinitives pour introduire le complément d'un adjectif comme **difficult**, etc. ou après **enough too...** :

It will be easy for you to find out	Vous n'aurez pas de mal à le trouver
It's too short a notice for us to accept the order	C'est trop court pour que nous acceptions la commande
It was impossible for them to agree	Ils n'ont pas pu s'entendre
There's no need for you to ring the police	Il n'y a aucune raison que vous appeliez la police

14. **Of his own. Own** peut servir à renforcer l'idée de possession :

Mind your own business	Occupez-vous de vos propres affaires
They do their own advertising	Ils font leur publicité eux-mêmes

Le pronom possessif **mine, yours**, etc. peut être remplacé par l'adjectif possessif suivi de **own** (*sauf* : **its own, one's own**, où il n'y a que cette forme) :

Why should you take my dictating machine ? Haven't you got your own ?	Pourquoi prendrais-tu mon dictaphone ? N'as-tu pas le tien ?

Nous avons par ailleurs vu la construction avec le cas possessif :

A friend of Hector Grant's	Un ami d'Hector Grant

De même on dira :

A friend of mine	Un ami à moi, un de mes amis

Et :

The advertising Manager has a talent of her own	La Directrice du Service Publicité a un talent bien à elle
We have no fleet of our own	Nous n'avons pas de parc à nous

19. Ne pas confondre :

At least = au moins   **There are at least six of them**   ils sont au moins six
At last = enfin   **At last we were refunded**   on nous a enfin remboursés

39. Notons que dans la proposition subordonnée temporelle, on ne rencontre jamais **shall/will (should/would)**. Ainsi, on dira :

They will have a second-hand value when they are traded-in	Il auront une valeur d'occasion lorsqu'ils seront repris
He'll phone the Managing Director as soon as the goods are delivered	Ils téléphonera au Directeur dès qu'il saura que les marchandises seront livrées

47. **Whether** : la conjonction **whether** s'emploie lorsqu'il y a alternative, exprimée, ou sous-entendue, comme c'est le cas ici.

Conversation :

5-6. It's high time we had our own transport fleet. Had a la forme d'un prétérit, mais il s'agit d'un prétérit modal, c'est-à-dire que la notion de temps n'existe plus (on le voit, l'existence du parc est envisagée dans le futur, et non dans le passé, comme le temps pourrait l'indiquer), et que seule la notion de mode, c'est-à-dire une certaine attitude de l'esprit à l'égard de l'action envisagée, entre en considération. Ici, c'est, non pas *l'indicatif, mode de l'indication, du réel*, mais *l'hypothétique, l'irréel* qu'exprime cette forme. Le prétérit de tous les verbes a cette valeur modale :

It's high time you phoned him	Il est grand temps que vous lui téléphoniez

20. **The pulling.** Le gérondif est un nom verbal, qui a à la fois les caractéristiques d'un nom et celles d'un verbe.

Ainsi, comme un verbe, on peut le rencontrer au passé (**having pulled**), au passif (**being pulled**) avec un adverbe, et surtout, un sujet ou un complément :

Can you remember Sally putting away those files in the grey cupboard ?	Vous rappelez-vous que Sally ait rangés ces dossiers dans l'armoire grise ?

En tant que nom, il peut être accompagné d'un article, ce qui est le cas ici, d'un possessif - adjectif ou nom au cas possessif - ou d'un complément introduit par **of** :

Sally's typing is quite good	Sally est très bonne dactylo
Do you mind my smoking ?	Est-ce que cela vous dérange que je fume ?

En tant que nom, il peut avoir un sens général (**travelling** = les voyages) ou particulier (**What was all that shouting about this morning in H.G.'s office ?** = pourquoi tous ces grands cris dans le bureau de H.G. ce matin ?)

Les puristes voient une différence entre l'emploi du cas possessif (**Ernie's driving**) et la simple construction nom+gérondif (**Ernie driving**). Si le sens est *la manière de*, on aura le possessif ; s'il est *le fait de*, le possessif sera omis. Mais l'usage moderne tend de plus en plus à abandonner le cas possessif, et à remplacer l'adjectif possessif par le pronom personnel par ailleurs :

He objected to Elizabeth showing our visitor round the works	Il a fait objection à ce qu'Elizabeth fasse visiter l'usine à notre visiteur
I don't mind you doing it	Cela ne me dérange pas que vous le fassiez

(pour **Elizabeth's showing** et **your doing**)

23. Ne pas perdre de vue la construction :

They get higher and higher — Elles sont de plus en plus élevées

Our chairs are more and more comfortable — Nos sièges sont de plus en plus confortables

Notons que dans la langue économique, cette construction est moins fréquente que la suivante :

The procedure is increasingly complicated — La procédure est de plus en plus complexe

68. **There must be some mistake.** Rappelons que la négative serait :

There can't be any mistake — Il ne peut y avoir d'erreur

et que parlant du passé on dirait :

There must have been some mistake — Il y dû y avoir une erreur

81. **I wish we had our own fleet.** Quelle différence peut-on faire entre cette phrase et **I should like to have** ? Disons que la construction avec **wish** témoigne d'un regret de la part du sujet, et se situe dans un vague irréel. **I should like** n'est pas nuancé de regret. Il exprime un vœu, un désir que l'on juge peu réalisable.

Au passé, **wish** est un regret présent sur ce qui n'a pas eu lieu dans le passé, tandis que **I should have liked** exprime un désir passé qui n'a pas été satisfait dans le passé, mais pour lequel on peut très bien ne plus exprimer de regret :

I wish Joanna had dealt with that previous campaign — Ah ! Si Joanna s'était occupée de la précédente campagne !

I should have liked to have a more dynamic agent — J'aurais aimé avoir un agent commercial plus dynamique

Pour les souhaits encore réalisables avec **wish** on peut rencontrer les auxiliaires **would** (qui donne une idée de *consentement*) et **could** (qui évoque une *possibilité*). Le prétérit modal ne se rencontre guère qu'avec **to be, to have, can** et quelques rares verbes :

I wish you would do it now — J'aimerais que vous le fassiez maintenant

I wish Bruce could understand why we can't have a fleet now — J'aimerais que Bruce comprenne pourquoi nous ne pouvons avoir de parc en ce moment

I wish I knew where Andersons' driver is — Je voudrais bien savoir où se trouve le conducteur de chez Anderson

2. EXERCISES

EXERCISE 1. — *Change as follows* :

How long will it take ? → **we can't be sure how long it will take**

1. Who will be appointed ?   2. When will the store be opened ?   3. How would the commodities be distributed ?   4. At what time will the rep ring back ?   5. When will they launch a campaign ?   6. How long will the strike last ?   7. Who would he interview first ?   8. Where will the goods be stored ?   9. How would you reduce the costs ?   10. When will they publish the survey ?   11. Will they make a test ? (whether)   12. Can we rely on their driver ? (whether).

EXERCISE 2. — *Change as follows* :

Will they have their transport fleet ? → **it's high time they had their transport fleet**

1. Will Hector Grant make a decision ?   2. Will she send the remaining catalogues ?   3. Will they make economies ?   4. Shall we sell our products in supermarkets ?   5. Will the Manager deal with the question ?   6. Will you meet the architect ?   7. Will he cost the expenses ?   8. Will they think about giving me promotion ?   9. Will they build a by-pass ?   10. Will they pay their reps better ?   11. Will he come for the interview ?   12. Will you speak about it to the Personnel Manager ?

EXERCISE 3. — *Change as follows* :

There was a mistake → **there must have been a mistake**

1. The goods were sent by passenger-train.   2. Their offices closed on Wednesday afternoon.   3. The goods were awaiting collection at the station.   4. He was phoning from their head-office in London.   5. He received my telegram (by now)   6. The goods were dispatched on Monday last.   7. There were ten Directors on the Board.   8. The meeting broke up before 8.30.   9. He dealt with the question rapidly.

EXERCISE 4. — *Change as follows* :

a. **The bills get very high** → **the bills get higher and higher**
b. **Our seats are very comfortable** → **our seats are more and more comfortable**

1. TV commercials are stupid.   2. Their methods are efficient.   3. We obtain good results.   4. They yield high returns.   5. We make few profits.   6. The economic situation is bad.   6. The overheads are very heavy.   7. Her work is satisfactory.   8. Competition gets very tough.   9. The market is very competitive.   10. Tankers get very big.   11. They'll make drastic cuts.   12. Delays will be very short.   13. The situation is alarming.   14. Management techniques are very elaborate.

EXERCISE 5. — *Change as follows* :

They didn't find the driver → **it's funny the driver hasn't been found**

1. He didn't check the accounts. 2. She didn't sign a receipt. 3. They didn't adopt another policy. 4. They didn't take out an insurance policy. 5. They didn't deposit the money in the safe. 6. They didn't examine the articles thoroughly. 7. They didn't load the other crates on the lorry. 8. You didn't cancel the order. 9. You didn't ring up our forwarding agent. 10. She didn't duplicate the document.

EXERCISE 6. — *Change as follows* (*mind the tense*) :

They're fitting out a new liner → **a new liner is being fitted out**

1. They were packing the last crates. 2. They're checking all the accounts. 2. She is duplicating all the documents. 4. He is translating the folders into German and French. 5. They are unloading the tramper. 6. They are carrying on secret negotiations. 7. They are considering your proposals. 8. They were working overtime. 9. They are planning sweeping changes in their management techniques. 10. They are introducing a lot of innovations in all departments.

EXERCISE 7. — *Change to the future as follows* :

a. **We can reduce our profit margins** → **we'll be able to reduce our profit margins**

b. **We must take the sternest measures** → **we'll have to take the sternest measures**

1. They must borrow a larger sum. 2. We can order the goods in larger quantities. 3. You must grant them a discount. 4. Must we pay heavy duties ? 5. Can you reduce your profit margins ? 6. Can they use better techniques ? 7. They can pack these, can't they ? 8. She must sign the document. 9. The question must be examined again, mustn't it ? 10. They can make the necessary arrangements in advance, can't they ? 11. I think the Marketing Manager must resign. 12. Can they rationalise their production ? 13. All these goods must be thoroughly examined. 14. More profits must be ploughed back into the business.

EXERCISE 8. — *Change as follows* (*mind the tense*) :

a. **He can keep to his budget** → **it's easy for him to keep to his budget**

b. **He can't keep to his budget** → **it's difficult for him to keep to his budget**

1. You can do it more economically. 2. They won't be able to finish by Thursday. 3. We could (*conditional*) control some of the problems better. 4. Can you get a grant to re-equip the works ? 5. We'll be able to keep the lorries fully employed. 6. We could (*conditional*) increase our sales on the continent. 7. We shan't be able to deliver them until Tuesday 22 nd. 8. He was able to deal with the problem. 9. You could have analysed the situation. 10. He won't be able to pay his income tax. 11. They'll be able to send a statement of accounts every month.

EXERCISE 9. — *Please answer by giving a complete sentence.*

1. A load of desks, tables and chairs for office use has to be sent to Scotland. Can you supply the missing words ? The goods have to be ... into the lorry. When they arrive at their destination they have to be ... 2. What are the machines called which are used to lift goods and move them from one place to another ? 3. The crates containing the goods are also designed to enable the lifting mechanism to get underneath. Crates prepared in this way are said to be ... 4. Where do most lorry drivers go for their meals on their journeys ?

EXERCISE 10. — *Can you complete the following sentences ?*

1. Bruce Hill has to ... a budget. 2. I'm going to London. Can you ... me a lift ? 3. Bruce Hill thinks that their own fleet of lorries would ... more economically. 4. The police in Britain now have the power to ... a vehicle with a defect ... the road.

EXERCISE 11. — *Translate into English* :

1. Nous devrions avoir notre propre parc de transport. 2. Il y a beaucoup d'arguments défavorables. 3. Il est difficile d'utiliser à plein les camions. 4. Il faut que vous calculiez l'amortissement. 5. Les éléments tracteurs sont très chers. 6. Pourquoi n'allons-nous pas chez un autre entrepreneur ? 7. Cela fait si longtemps que nous sommes chez eux que nous recevons un bon rabais. 8. Veuillez présenter des propositions détaillées lors de la prochaine assemblée du Conseil. 9. Il a la responsabilité de la livraison des marchandises, n'est-ce pas ? 10. Veillez à ce que chaque centimètre carré d'espace soit utilisé, s'il vous plaît. 11. Ils viennent d'augmenter à nouveau les frais de consommation de carburant. 12. Cela reviendrait moins cher à la longue, n'est-ce pas ? 13. La police a procédé à une vérification et a exigé le retrait du véhicule défectueux. 14. Est-ce la bonne technique pour évaluer la rentabilité d'un investissement ? 15. Je me demande si on pourrait reprendre ces véhicules, ils ne valent rien sur le marché de l'occasion. 16. N'oubliez pas que gérer une entreprise comporte toujours des risques. 17. Cela revient à deux fois plus cher que nous avions escompté. 18. Nous sommes censés faire des économies pour compenser l'augmentation inattendue. 19. C'est le troisième camion qui disparaisse depuis huit jours. 20. Vous feriez mieux d'en aviser la compagnie d'assurances.

UNIT 17

THE NEW BOARD OF DIRECTORS

PART 1 : INTRODUCTION

1. WORDSTUDY

Vocabulary

accounting comptabilité
accurately   avec précision
act for représenter
actually en fait
attend assister à
balance équilibre(r)
breakdown répartir, ventiler
cost centre poste budgétaire
counter contrepoids
cut down réduire
director administrateur
draw up établir
financial year exercice
forecast prévoir; prévision
forward à terme
holding valeur, titre, avoir en
    portefeuille
    qualification holding actions de
    garantie
improve améliorer
income revenu
join entrer à
manage se débrouiller pour
monthly mensuel
neighbouring voisin
outline aperçu, grandes lignes

outlook point de vue
overweighted surchargé
own posséder
postpone différer
prevent empêcher
profit bénéfice
profitability rentabilité
put forward (a name) avancer
qualification cautionnement
Rules of Association statuts
sales turnover circulation,
    mouvement
sound (somebody) out sonder
state indiquer, préciser
stocks stocks
strengthen renforcer
support soutien, appui
table inscrire à l'ordre du jour
takeover prise de contrôle
trading exercice, exploitation
turnover chiffre d'affaires,
    roulement
unfortunate fâcheux
upset bouleverser
up-to-date à jour

Phrases

The firm will make it worth his while to stay	on le retiendra dans l'entreprise en lui offrant des avantages
He couldn't have everything his own way	il ne pouvait pas faire ce qu'il voulait
Mind you	notez bien, remarquez
I wanted to put you in the picture	je voulais vous mettre au courant
We can't afford to lose him	nous ne pouvons nous permettre de le perdre

Explanations and Comments

to break down   to divide into groups. For example, a company's proposed expenditure for the coming year can be broken down into the amounts spent on materials, overheads, salaries, advertising, etc. (*see* unit 15, breakdown).

budget   see unit 15.

budgetary control   a close watch over a company's performance, comparing it with budgetted performance and taking corrective action when necessary (*see* also Unit 1).

Company Secretary   every company has to appoint a secretary. He is legally responsible for giving information to the **Registrar (the Registrar of Companies**, a department of the Board of Trade) for seeing that the company's accounts are correctly kept, and for keeping the minute book, which is a record of all the company's meetings. A company secretary is often an accountant. Mr. Buckhurst is a **Fellow of the Institute of Chartered Accountants, F. C. A.**

cost centre   a business can be divided into cost centres for the purpose of collecting information on income and expenditure. These are the basis for budgetting (forward planning). Each department or cost centre is thus made responsible for its own financial planning and accountable for its actual performance.

draft   write, letter, minutes of a meeting, in rough form for final approval.

put (a name) forward   to propose that a person should be invited to join a board of directors, be elected to a society, etc.

Rules of Association see Articles of Association, Unit 13.

qualification holding in certain Articles of Association, it is made a regulation of the company that to qualify as a director a certain number of shares must be held (or owned).

to sound (someone) out to find out someone's opinion about a particular matter.

stocks supplies. Often broken down into raw stocks (raw materials), intermediate stocks, work-in progress and finished stocks.

to table (**a report, a motion**) : to put on record that a certain subject should be discussed at a future meeting.

Pronunciation

1 — 1 - (- -) accurately, balance, benefit, budget, budgetary, criticise, differ, everything, forecast, necessary, neighbouring, outline, outlook, period, purchase, (a) record, turnover

  - 2 (- -) advice, afraid, agenda, already, attent, ambitious, arrange, available, completely, control, director, discuss, elect, expect, financial, invite, to record, successful, support, suspect, tomorrow upset

2 — " *h* " *aspirate* : Harper, hundred, perhaps, handle, holding

[e]   set, death, next, friend, tempt, heavy, m*e*mber, n*e*phew, cl*e*ver, pr*e*sent, exp*e*ct

[ei] late, date, weight, make, great, greatly, neighbour, av*ai*lable

[eə] share, chairman, rarely, careful, vary

[iə] here, fear, year, dear, idea, p*e*riod, exp*e*rience

[æ]   act, plan, b*a*lance, mattress, factory, added

[ou] own, hold, hope, holding, contr*o*l, p*o*stpone

[ɔ:] ought, bought, board, course, forty, forward, quarterly, support, afford

[u:] do, move, lose, too, improve

[ju:] reduce, *u*nanimous

3 — Note : always ['ɔ:lwəz], annual ['ænjuəl], future ['fju:tʃə], picture ['piktʃə], postpone [poust'poun], F.C.A. ['ef'si:'ei].

2. SUMMARY

The death of the Chairman, Ambrose Harper, upset the balance of power on the Board of Directors of Harper & Grant Ltd. The next Chairman is Hector Grant, who, in Unit 13, postponed the possibility of a takeover by buying two hundred and fifty more shares in the company. The remaining two hundred and fifty were bought, as Hector feared they would be, by   5
Alfred Wentworth, the rather dynamic owner of a neighbouring mattress factory, and a friend of the late Ambrose Harper. He now owns such a large proportion of the shares that he will have to be asked to join the Board. The present members of the Board are: Hector Grant (Chairman and Managing Director), his nephew Peter Wiles (who was invited by the   10
Board to become a director on the death of Ambrose Harper), Peter Wiles's mother, Mrs. Margaret Wiles (who rarely attends Board meetings as she leaves Peter to act for her) and the Company Secretary, William Buckhurst (F.C.A.).

Peter thinks it is high time John Martin was made a director. He has   15
had a very successful year and has increased sales by almost forty per cent in the two years since he joined the firm. Peter wants him on the Board as an added support for himself. He feels the Board is already rather over-weighted with members like Hector Grant and William Buckhurst, whose outlook on business is not always up-to-date. He also   20
suspects that an ambitious young man like John Martin could easily be tempted away by another firm if Harper & Grant do not make it worth his while to stay.

At the Board Meeting the directors also discuss budgetary control,   25
and William Buckhurst, who has just attended a course on the subject, wants to introduce monthly accounting by cost centres. He wants the Board to have information about the company's trading position more accurately and more often than at present. A company's budget is the forward plan of what they expect to spend, to make and to sell during a specific period. Quarterly accounts, that is, a record of what has actually   30
been bought, sold and spent, are drawn up every three months in a financial year, but as Buckhurst explains, modern management needs to discover the profits and losses more often to keep a firmer control.

Peter talks about the Board to John while they are lunching together.

PART 2 : CONVERSATION AND DOCUMENTS

1. CONVERSATION

(Recorded Text)

PETER WILES   **I'm glad you could manage lunch today, John. I really wanted to sound you out about the future. Harper's death has caused a big change in the control of this company.**

JOHN MARTIN   **Yes, I realise that. He was a strong personality, wasn't he?**   5

PETER: 'Wentworth's a clever man, but I think we need to balance his power a bit, and that's why I want you, John, on the Board!'

PETER   **Yes, he was. H.G. couldn't have everything his own way while Harper was Chairman. Mind you, I'm not criticising my dear uncle. He's a clever man, but I think we need to balance his power a bit, and that's why I want you on the Board.**   10

JOHN   **You know, I've been hoping H.G. would put my name forward. But hasn't Alfred Wentworth been asked to join the Board now that he owns more shares?**

— 270 —

PETER	Yes, his name will be put forward at tomorrow's meeting. That's why I believe I've a chance to get you elected, because H.G. will want to strengthen his position in case old Wentworth tries to make things go his way.
JOHN	Wouldn't I have to own shares to become a director?
PETER	Yes, you would. But the Rules of Association drawn up by Harper and H.G.'s father state that the qualification holding is only two shares. So that's easily arranged. I hold two and my mother nine hundred and ninety-eight. Anyway, I wanted to put you in the picture. The next move is to get you made a director. I'll see what I can do.

(Next day, at the Board Meeting)

HECTOR GRANT	What's the next item on the agenda, William?
WILLIAM BUCKHURST	We've got this problem of Alfred Wentworth, of Wentworth & Company. He ought to be invited to join the Board.
GRANT	It's unfortunate, but I'm afraid he now owns so many shares that his election is inevitable. . . . Don't put that in the minutes, William!
PETER	I would like to propose that our Sales Manager, John Martin, should also be asked to join the Board. In the time he has been here he has greatly increased sales and done much to improve profits. I think if he was made a director his advice at board meetings would be invaluable.
GRANT	Well, perhaps next year. I . . .
PETER	Be careful, H.G. You don't want to lose him. There must be a lot of companies who'd be prepared to offer him a directorship. We can't afford to lose him.
GRANT	What do you think, William?
BUCKHURST	It might be a good idea to strengthen the support for yourself, H.G.
GRANT	Very well. As the character of the Board is changing so completely, this is probably the right moment . . . yes . . . I agree. John would be a useful counter to Wentworth. If everyone agrees . . .
PETER	Yes.
BUCKHURST	Agreed.
GRANT	William, will you draft suitable minutes about these two proposals then?

BUCKHURST	Yes, I will.
GRANT	Now the next item on the agenda is to consider a report with recommendations tabled by you, William, on budgetary control. Perhaps you'd like to give us an outline of your proposals. 55
BUCKHURST	As everyone here knows, I have just attended a course on financial control, and as a result I really do consider we should do the accounts more often than we do at present.
GRANT	At present the accounts are done every quarter. 60
BUCKHURST	Yes, but quarterly accounts don't allow us to keep a close enough control. If the company should suddenly make a heavy loss we ought to be able to act quickly. If we don't, it may be too late to prevent the loss getting larger still.
GRANT	Well, if sales go down, we reduce stocks, which means 65 cutting down purchases and, if necessary, we reduce personnel.
BUCKHURST	Yes, but we need the information faster than we're getting it at the moment. If profitability goes down—that is, profits in relation to sales turnover, or in relation to 70 capital employed—it may be necessary to increase prices, cut costs and so on. But the right information must be readily available.
GRANT	What do you propose?
BUCKHURST	What I would like to do is to break down the activities of 75 the company into cost centres.
GRANT	What does all this mean?
BUCKHURST	Each manager would be responsible for at least one cost centre. He would be required to forecast, well in advance, the income and expenditure of his centre. Then we put the 80 budgets from all the centres together. When they've been approved they become the annual budget, or plan, of the company. If the actual income or expenditure varies a lot from any budgeted figure, then that manager would be responsible and would have to explain why his actual figures 85 differed from his forecast, and take appropriate action.
GRANT	Will you let us have more details about this budgetary control, exactly how it would operate and so on?
BUCKHURST	Certainly.
GRANT	Now let's get on. The next item on the agenda is a recom- 90 mendation that we buy two lorries for the transport department. . . .

PRACTICE SENTENCES

Say the practice sentences on the record :

- i **What's the next item on the Agenda?**
- ii **He ought to be invited to join the Board.**
- iii **I'd like to propose that our Sales Manager should also be asked to join.**
- iv **We can't afford to lose him.**
- v **Perhaps you'd like to give us an outline of your proposals.**
- vi **At present the accounts are done every quarter.**
- vii **We need the information faster than we're getting it at the moment.**
- viii **The right information must be readily available.**

2. LETTERS FROM THE COMPANY SECRETARY

Great West Road
London W25
Telephone 01-567 1112
Telex 80153
Telegrams Harp LDN

Directors:
Ambrose Harper *(Chairman)*
Hector Grant *(Managing)*
William Buckhurst FCA *(Secretary)*
Margaret Wiles

Harper and Grant Limited

Alfred Wentworth, Esq.,
The Wentworth Mattress Co. Ltd.,
Great West Road,
London, W.25.

6th May, 197..

Dear Mr. Wentworth,

I have been directed by the Chairman to write and ask you if you would accept an invitation to join the Board of Directors of Harper & Grant Ltd.

As a shareholder you will already be aware of the changes on this Board caused by the death of the late chairman, Mr. Ambrose Harper. The Board were unanimous in hoping that you would consent to become a director and so benefit the company with your wide business abilities and experience.

Yours sincerely,

William Buckhurst
Company Secretary
HARPER & GRANT LTD.

As a result of the Board Meeting, the Company Secretary, William Buckhurst, wrote two letters, the first to Mr. Alfred Wentworth to ask him if he would like to join the Board, and the second, an official letter, confirming John Martin's appointment to the Board. For this second letter, even though Mr. Buckhurst knows John well enough to use his first name, he writes to him using his surname as it is an official letter for the records.

Great West Road
London W25
Telephone 01-567 1112
Telex 80153
Telegrams Harp LDN

Directors:
Ambrose Harper *(Chairman)*
Hector Grant *(Managing)*
William Buckhurst FCA *(Secretary)*
Margaret Wiles

Harper and Grant Limited

John Martin, Esq.,
41 Cherry Trees Road,
Marlow,
Bucks.   6th May, 197..

Dear Mr. Martin,

      I have been asked by Mr. Hector Grant to write to you to confirm your appointment to the Board of Directors of Harper & Grant Ltd. at a salary of £4,000 per annum.

      I should like to remind you that, as specified in the Articles of Association, a director must obtain the necessary share qualification within two months of appointment. As you know, arrangements are being made to enable you to make the necessary share purchase.

      I look forward with pleasure to our long and successful co-operation.

                          Yours sincerely,

                          William Buckhurst
                          Company Secretary
                          HARPER & GRANT LTD.

PART 3 : NOTES AND PRACTICE

1. RAPPEL GRAMMATICAL

Summary :

3. He postponed the possibility of a takeover by buying shares. Notons encore une fois cette construction avec préposition et la forme en -ing. Cf. p. 69, by + -ing.

6. rather dynamic : nous avons vu la différence entre **rather**, plutôt négatif, et **fairly**, qui est laudatif. On dirait de John Martin qu'il est **fairly dynamic**, il est même plus que **fairly dynamic**. Mais ici, il est évident que le dynamisme d'Alfred Wentworth inquiète les anciens de la Société Harper & Grant, comme en témoigne ce **rather**.

7-8. Such a large proportion : notons qu'avec **so** on aurait la construction

He owns so large a proportion	Il possède une part si grande

L'adjectif précède ainsi l'article indéfini après **how (ever)**, **as**, **so** et **too** :

How interesting a meeting it was !	Que la réunion était intéressante !
However clever he is, he couldn't prevent Mr. Wentworth buying the shares	Si habile qu'il soit, il n'a pu empêcher M. Wentworth d'acheter les actions
This is too good a report to be true	C'est un rapport trop beau pour être vrai

Quite et **rather** précèdent également, en général, l'article :

He joined the board quite a long time ago	Il est entré au Conseil il y a un bon bout de temps

16-17. By 40 %. La mesure d'une supériorité ou d'une infériorité s'exprime à l'aide de **by** :

The new method is by far the most accurate of all	La nouvelle méthode est de loin la plus précise
Alfred Wentworth is older than H. G. by six years	Alfred Wentworth est plus vieux que Hector Grant de six années

By sert également à indiquer la façon de compter ou de mesurer. Il est alors suivi de l'article défini **the** :

They are sold by the dozen	Ils se vendent à la douzaine

20. Whose. Il faut retenir que **whose** n'est jamais suivi de **the**, qu'il se rencontre en définitive assez rarement, et plus souvent dans la langue écrite que dans la langue parlée ; que le nom dont **whose** est le complément le suit immédiatement et ne peut en être séparé ; enfin, que bien qu'il soit le cas possessif de **who**, - pronom relatif ayant pour antécédent une personne - il a souvent, et de plus en plus, dans l'anglais d'aujourd'hui, pour antécédent un neutre - chose, entité, etc.

He is the man whose career impressed me most	C'est l'homme dont la carrière m'a le plus impressionné
The Managing Director, on whose behalf I am now speaking...	Le Président Directeur Général au nom de qui je parle...

Whose est également interrogatif :

Whose car is this ?	A qui est cette voiture ?

22-23. Worth while. L'adjectif **worth** se rencontre avec un nom, un pronom, ou un gérondif (qui peut avoir un sens passif) :

It's worth $ 500	Cela vaut 500 dollars
It's worth a lot of money	Cela vaut une fortune
Is it worth it (the trouble) ?	Cela en vaut-il la peine ?
His report is really worth reading	Son rapport vaut vraiment la peine d'être lu
William thinks it is worth doing	William estime que cela vaut la peine d'être fait

Worth peut se construire avec le nom **while**, suivi ou non d'un gérondif :

It will be worth your while	Cela vaudra la peine pour vous
Is it worth while going ?	Cela vaut-il la peine d'y aller ?

31. Every three months. Every sert à marquer la fréquence :

He used to come every four days	Il venait tous les quatre jours

C'est le seul cas où l'on rencontre un pluriel avec **every**. Ainsi :

He came every week	Il venait tous les huit jours

On peut rencontrer également **every** avec le numéral ordinal :

They're drawn up every third month	Ils sont établis tous les trois mois

Notons encore : **every other day** tous les deux jours, un jour sur deux.

Conversation :

14. Tomorrow's meeting. Cas possessif parce qu'il y a indication de temps.

16-17. In case old Wentworth tries to make things go his way. Pourquoi **in case** est-il ici suivi de l'indicatif, alors qu'à la ligne 62 : **if the company should make a heavy loss** nous avons **should** après **if** ? A la ligne 16, Peter est convaincu que M. Wentworth cherchera à tirer à lui la couverture, il emploie donc l'indicatif, mode de la certitude, qui inquiètera davantage son oncle qu'il cherche à convaincre. Dans le second cas, M. Buckhurst doit faire preuve de sa confiance en la société en employant le modal, qui indique qu'il n'évoque l'éventualité d'une mauvaise passe que d'une manière toute spéculative.

35-36. If he was made a director. Nous retrouvons la même nuance. **Was** est employé, et non **were**, parce que Peter est convaincu et de l'efficacité de John Martin, et de la nécessité de lui offrir un siège au Conseil.

64. Rappelons que **prevent** est ici suivi d'une forme en -**ing** directement parce qu'il s'agit d'empêcher qu'une chose n'arrive.

Si l'on agit sur une personne, **prevent** est suivi de **from** :

Do prevent him from saying that at the Board Meeting	Empêchez-le de dire cela à la réunion du Conseil, je vous en prie !

2. EXERCISES

EXERCISE 1. — Use the right preposition, if necessary :

1. He became a director ... the death of Ambrose Harper. 2. She leaves her son to act ... her. 3. Thanks to him, we increased sales ... 20 % 4. Everybody wants you ... the Board. 5. His outlook ... business isn't quite up-to-date. 6. I wanted to sound him out ... the future. 7. The actual figures didn't differ ... our forecasts. 8. They were unanimous ... hoping that you would join the Board. 9. He's attended a course ... budgetary control. 10. We can't prevent the shop steward ... speaking to the workmen as he pleases. 11. We must prevent the loss ... getting larger still. 12. Have you any information ... their financial position ? 13. What's the next item ... the agenda ? 14. His advice ... board meetings would be invaluable. 15. We'll break down the activities of the firm ... cost centres.

EXERCISE 2. — Use the right preposition, if necessary :

1. He postponed the possibility of a takeover ... buying 700 shares. 2. I saw their new model ... visiting the International Exhibition. 3. The Chairman died ... reading the minutes of the last meeting of the Board. 4. Hardiman always whistles ... working. 5. He burnt his fingers ... welding those sheets. 6. ... seeking a successor to the late Chairman, the shareholders will certainly prefer H.G. to Mr. Wentworth. 7. He rushed out of the store, ... shouting ' Fire ! ' 8. I read the whole of your report ... waiting for you. 9. I was surprised ... hearing the Marketing Manager had resigned. 10. Don't think you can appease the ill feeling ... proposing that profit sharing scheme of yours. 11. ...

hearing the Confidential file had probably been stolen, Sally burst into tears. 12. I spent the whole afternoon ... correcting spelling mistakes in the report she typed for me. 13. ... visiting the factory, I noticed there was no fire-extinguisher in the paint store. 14. ... explaining his project, the Secretary muddled up things. 15. ... looking up, I saw the men were using hooks to unload the crates.

EXERCISE 3. — *Use colloquial queries, as follows* :

a. **You can't have it your own way** → you can't have it your own way, can you ?

b. **He was a strong personality** → he was a strong personality, wasn't he ?

1. His salary will be £ 8,000 per annum. 2. It wasn't specified in the Articles of Association. 3. The other shareholders won't object to John's election. 4. Hector Grant has the largest holding. 5. The Company Secretary wrote an official letter to John yesterday. 6. The Sales Manager doesn't live in London. 7. You know the Advertising Manager well enough. 8. The figures can differ from the forecast. 9. The Board would have to invite him to join them. 10. Such a budget wouldn't be approved. 11. Our expenditures don't vary from the budgeted figures. 12. He said he would let us have more details. 13. They ought to break down the activities of the firm into cost centres. 14. They used to meet every other week. 15. We shall have to invite him to join the Board. 16. We couldn't afford to buy four lorries.

EXERCISE 4. — *Ask questions on the italicised words.*

the next Chairman is *Hector Grant* → **Who** *is the next Chairman* ?

1. He will succeed *his father-in-law* in the chair. 2. He avoided the risk of a takeover bid *by buying the shares*. 3. The Managing Director fears *a rival firm will buy the shares*. 4. Alfred Wentworth was the friend *of the late Chairman*. 5. I owned *only two* shares when I joined the Board. 6. *Peter Wiles* acts for the other important shareholder. 7. The meeting will take place *on 3rd April*. 8. He's been with us *for over ten years*. 9. He increased the sales *by 10 %*. 10. The extension will be built *between the Assembly Shop and the Delivery Bay*. 11. He didn't show the plans *because they are still confidential*. 12. They used to do the accounts *every third month*.

EXERCISE 5. — *Change as follows* :

He's been asked to join the Board → **hasn't he been asked to join the Board** ?

1. He asked very relevant questions. 2. He is criticising the Sales Manager. 3. You can have your own way in your own department. 4. They would put your name forward. 5. Hector Grant owns a lot more shares than old Wentworth. 6. John's presence will strengthen the Managing Director's position. 7. I shall have to buy the two shares within two months. 8. We must do it immediately.

EXERCISE 6. — *Use the possessive case or form a compound noun whenever it is possible :*

1. His name will be put forward at the meeting of tomorrow. 2. I shan't see him until the next meeting of the Board. 3. Can he make the necessary purchase of shares in due course ? 4. The brother of Mr. Wentworth is the Managing Director of a large factory of shoes. 5. What will be the new policy of the government concerning the maintenance of retail prices ? 6. The Rules of Association drawn up by the father of Mr. Grant state that the holding for qualification is only two shares. 7. The Secretary of the Company gave all the required information concerning the trading position of the company. 8. The subsidiary could make use of the world wide organisation of its parent company as regards marketing.

EXERCISE 7. — *Link up the following sentences with* **whose** :

1. Alfred Wentworth obtained 250 more shares ; Alfred Wentworth's holding was already large. 2. Peter and John are the two executives in Harper & Grant ; the firm now rests on their skills. 3. Mr. Buckhurst is to implement the reorganisation scheme as soon as possible ; Mr. Buckhurst's report impressed all the members of the Board. 4. There is the question of Mr. Hardiman ; his interests don't seem to have been taken into consideration. 5. You'd better ask John Martin ; his advice on such question is invaluable. 6. The new extension is to be erected on the site of the stores ; you can see their burnt-out ruins from the window of my office 7. Mr. Hardiman, here is a gentleman ; you owe your remaining in the firm to his support. 8. John Martin is the Sales Manager at Harper & Grant ; John Martin's father was a civil engineer. 9. Mr. Buckhurst is an F.C.A. ; we drove back in Mr. Buckhurst's car.

EXERCISE 8. — *Introduce a shade of doubt, indignation, surprise, etc., or express desire, will, etc., as follows :*

a. **foreigners keep deposits there, (it's natural)** →
     it's natural that foreigners should keep deposits there

b. **foreigners kept deposits there (it's natural)** →
     it's natural that foreigners should have kept deposits there

1. She forgot the appointment (I am surprised). 2. He'll get a salary of £ 5,000 per annum (I suggested). 3. Elizabeth took Mr. Duncan round the shops (he suggested). 4. We invited Mr. Wentworth to join the Board (it's natural). 5. He explained why his actual figures differed from his forecast (it's natural). 6. They refused to ask John to join the Board (it's shocking). 7. The Board will receive a grant (they recommended). 8. Workers are allowed to strike (it's quite natural). 9. You supported

such an unpopular measure (it's scandal). 10. H.G. spent a lot of money on entertainment (I'm quite surprised). 11. He acted quickly (they urged). 12. They made such a heavy loss in so short a time (it's incredible). 13. The Board will be consulted (John Martin insisted). 14. John has his say on how money should be spent (it's normal). 15. Every decision is based on a thorough analysis of all the alternatives (Mr. Buckhurst stressed). 16. New measures will enable the reps to get better compensation (they proposed).

EXERCISE 9. — *Complete the sentences, using the most appropriate word or phrase from the dialogue.*

1. John Martin had been hoping that H.G. would ... to join the Board. 2. The qualification ... for a director of Harper & Grant is two shares. 3. The next ... to be discussed is budgetary control. 4. H.G. asked William to ... suitable minutes about the new appointments so the Board. 5. Peter thought that there was a danger that another company might offer John Martin a ... 6. William said he would like to ... the activities of the company into cost centres.

EXERCISE 10. — *Can you act as the Company Secretary and draft the minutes of the meeting which has just taken place? The minutes are a record of the points discussed and the decisions taken. You will have to invent what was finally decided about buying two lorries for the firm. If you need a guide as to the way minutes are written, look at Unit 5.*

EXERCISE 11. — *Translate into English :*

1. Quel est le point suivant inscrit à l'ordre du jour? 2. On devrait l'inviter à entrer au Conseil. 3. Je voudrais suggérer qu'on demande également à notre Directeur des Ventes d'y entrer. 4. On ne peut pas se permettre de le perdre. 5. Peut-être voudrez-vous bien nous donner un aperçu de vos suggestions. 6. A l'heure actuelle, nos comptes sont faits tous les trimestres. 7. Il nous faut les renseignements plus vite que nous les obtenons à présent. 8. Il faut que nous disposions facilement des informations voulues. 9. C'est un rapport trop long pour que je le lise à présent. 10. Vous voulez retourner à Djemsa, mais est-ce que cela en vaut la peine? 11. Il possède une participation si importante qu'il devient extrêmement dangereux. 12. La méthode préconisée par William Buckhurst est de loin la meilleure. 13. Mr. Grant m'a prié de vous écrire pour vous confirmer votre nomination. 14. Vous êtes peut-être au courant des changements occasionnés par la mort du Président du Conseil d'Administration. 15. Il faut prendre les mesures qui s'imposent dès que possible. 16. Voulez-vous rédiger un procès-verbal convenable au sujet de ces deux propositions? 17. Si les ventes diminuent, nous réduirons les stocks, ce qui entraîne une réduction des achats. 18. Je crois que le Directeur Gérant à l'intention de vous sonder à propos de l'avenir de votre service. 19. Quels sont les autres noms qui ont été avancés? 20. A l'avance, je me fais un plaisir d'une longue et heureuse collaboration.

UNIT 18

THE TRIALS

OF A SALES REPRESENTATIVE

PART 1 : INTRODUCTION

1. WORDSTUDY

Vocabulary

align aligner
anvil enclume(tte)
apologise s'excuser
appointment rendez-vous
area secteur
batch fournée
bent courbé
circularise envoyer une circulaire
   (à)
clip agrafe ; agrafer
competitive concurrentiel
confidence confiance
congratulations félicitations
demand exiger
diagram schéma, croquis
draughtsman dessinateur
finish fini
inconvenience inconvénient,
   dérangement

layout disposition
long-lasting durable
magazine magasin, chargeur
manage arriver à
properly correctement
quotation prix, devis
receiver combiné, récepteur
replacement article en remplacement
rep, representative représentant
report signaler
slightly légèrement
stain-proof intachable
staple agrafe
stapler agrafeuse
summon convoquer
tough dur
traveller voyageur, représentant
wonder se demander
work marcher, fonctionner

Phrases

He's run into a bad patch	il traverse une mauvaise passe
They're in the process of...	ils sont en train de...
Umpteen times	trente-six fois, des tas de fois
See you later	à tout à l'heure ! à plus tard
More fools they !	ils n'en sont que plus idiots !
Come on !	allons ! allons !

Explanations and Other Useful Terms

batch
a number of things in a group, e.g. a batch of letters to answer.

to canvass
in business, to call on a person or firm in the hope of receiving an order.

circularise
send the same letter, printed or duplicated, to a number of different people.

commission
a fee paid for transacting business.

to cover an area
to call on clients in this territory with a view to getting order.

demand
what people want to buy, or are likely to buy. For example, if there is a cold winter there will be a big demand for heating appliances.

design service
in the case of Harper & Grant, the service is to propose a complete office plan. If accepted, Harper & Grant would buy carpets, curtains, etc. from other firms, and charge their clients for a package deal (the complete arrangements).

discount
a reduction given to a customer on the normal price. **Trade discount** is the reduction in price given by the manufacturer to the wholesaler, or the wholesaler to the retailer, so that each may make their profit. **Cash discount** is a reward for paying promptly.

distributor
the agent of a manufacturer who keeps a stock of goods to distribute or resell over a certain area. Can also mean the wholesaler.

finish
the result of the extra care given in the final stages of production of an article.

— 282 —

goodwill	the good reputation which has been developed by a business. If the business is sold, it becomes part of the value of the business which must be paid for.
merchandise	goods available for sale.
middleman	someone who deals between producer and consumer, i.e. a wholesaler.
prospect	a potential buyer.
representative (rep.)	(**salesman** or **traveller**). One who **represents**, or acts for, his firm. His main job is to promote sales but he may also be responsible for dealing with complaints, servicing new machines, assisting with the assembly of machinery, gathering market information, collecting payments, etc. (See also Unit 7).
sale or return	arrangement by which goods not sold may be returned without charge.
sales resistance	lack of interest in buying the goods.
sample	specimen, example, of the goods offered.
stain-proof	material so treated it will resist stains, or marks. Sometimes called stain-resistant.
sub-contract	if Harper & Grant contract to furnish an office, they sub-contract to firms who manufacture goods which they do not make themselves.
terms	conditions under which a business transaction is offered or accepted.

Pronunciation

1 — 1 - (- -) absolutely, anvil, area, catalogue, circularise, confidence, cover, curtain, customer, dignified, effort, figure, modify, notice, season, traveller

- 2 (- -) afraid, appointment, assemble, campaign, competitive, complaint, correctly, design, discover, enough, equip, executive, however, particular, perhaps, per cent, responsible, supply

- - 3 (-) inefficiency, representative

— 283 —

2 — *Pronounce* [-r] *between the two words* :

cheaper equipment... I'm not sure about that... they're in the process... before anything else... I wonder if... the buyer of the firm... Harper and Grant... a particular area... the idea of quality... for a meeting.

3 — *ch* = [tʃ] cheap, much ; *ch* = [ʃ] machine ; *ch* = [k] chemicals, technique ; *gh* = [f] tough, rough, enough, draughtsman

[ə:] firm, heard, service, furnish, curtain
[ə] per cent, perhaps, correct, supply, effort, fig*u*re, Yorkshire
[ai] height, r*i*val, cr*i*sis, al*i*gn, des*i*gn, arr*i*ve, adv*i*ce, adv*i*se, dignif*i*ed
[i] off*i*ce, serv*i*ce, art*i*cle, carp*e*t, curt*ai*n, b*u*sy, worried, because, b*ui*lding, conf*i*dence
[ʌ] umpteen, other, s*u*mmon, cover, London, discuss, wonder, worried, something, enough, tough, dozen
[aiə] fire, hire, diary, diagram, trial, buyer

4 — Compare : a rep [rep], a representative [ˌrepriˈzentativ]
a contract [ˈkɔntrækt], to contract [kənˈtrækt]
to hear [hiə] (*past*) I heard [hə:d]

5 — Note : properly [ˈprɔpəli], sub-contract [ˈsʌb-kənˈtrækt], Yorkshire [ˈjɔ:kʃə].

2. SUMMARY

Harper & Grant have Sales Representatives to do the selling for them. Each 'rep.' is responsible for covering a particular area. Mr. Shuttleworth is the representative for North Yorkshire. He has not been doing too well lately, and John Martin has summoned him to London for a meeting to discuss his latest figures. At the last meeting of representatives 5 in London three months ago John Martin asked all of them to make big efforts to increase sales by twenty per cent. Most of the reps. have managed to do this, but Mr. Shuttleworth has had a bad season, and his figures for this quarter are lower than the last quarter's. John Martin wonders if Shuttleworth is worried about something, or is in need of a 10 change. Or perhaps it is because he doesn't go out enough on the road, but spends too much time in his garden. Or then, again, he may have run into a bad patch because he has lost some of his confidence.

On the way to London Mr. Shuttleworth calls in to see the buyer of a big chemical firm who has given him small orders in the past. He has 15 heard that they are expanding and are in the process of building a big new office block. Mr. Shuttleworth wants to get the order to furnish all the new offices. Harper & Grant run an office design service : as well as supplying furniture they also plan the office layout, and sub-contract to curtain, carpet and light-fitting firms. However, this particular buyer is a 20 tough customer. He is interested in prices before anything else. Mr. Shuttleworth confesses to his wife, on the morning he leaves for the appointment, that he has not much hope. This buyer is the sort of man who will choose something because it is sixpence cheaper than the next article. The idea of quality does not come into it. 25

While he is with the buyer, Mr. Gorgondale, he is upset to discover that a number of staplers which have just arrived from the Harper & Grant factory do not work. A stapler is a small machine which fastens together, with metal clips, several sheets of paper. The anvil on to which the staples are pressed was not assembled correctly. When Mr. Shuttle- 30 worth gets to London he finds John Martin in the middle of a crisis. Complaints are coming in from all over Britain about these new stapling machines. Several angry firms have returned the staplers and demanded their money back. It is not a very good moment for Mr. Shuttleworth's interview. 35

PART 2 : CONVERSATION AND DOCUMENTS

1. CONVERSATION

(Recorded Text)

(Mr. Shuttleworth calls on Mr. Gorgondale of the Crucible Chemical Company)

SECRETARY	**Harper & Grant's traveller to see you. Would you please go in now, Mr. Shuttleworth.**
MR. SHUTTLEWORTH	**Good morning, Mr. Gorgondale. Good of you to see me in the middle of your busy morning.**
MR. GORGONDALE	**I'm afraid I can only spare you a few minutes, Mr. Shuttle- 5 worth. Now what did you want to see me about?**

SHUTTLEWORTH	Well, this new office block of yours on the other side of town. Have you had time to consider furnishing yet? You know, as well as supplying office furniture we also run a special service to design and equip offices: curtains, carpets and all that. We can also advise on office layouts, to save time and avoid inefficiency....
GORGONDALE	We have already planned the new offices.
SHUTTLEWORTH	You mean ... you've already obtained quotations from other firms?
GORGONDALE	Yes.
SHUTTLEWORTH	I see. Well, I'm sure you'd like to see our latest range. It's called the 'Standfirm'. It had a huge success at the recent business exhibition in London. This is the catalogue. Here you have the top executive desk, for people like yourself. Very imposing and dignified, don't you think?
GORGONDALE	It's big enough, certainly.
SHUTTLEWORTH	Then we have this smaller desk. They're all made of this new, absolutely stain-proof material. It will go on looking like a new piece of furniture when your grandchildren are running the business.
GORGONDALE	I am not married, Mr. Shuttleworth.
SHUTTLEWORTH	Oh well ... er ... plenty of time for that. ... And this, as you see, is the typist's desk; this one a draughtsman's desk, and so on. All of them are the same height, and you can use them separately or grouped together.
GORGONDALE	Hmm. Very nice, I'm sure. But your prices, Mr. Shuttleworth. That's what interests me.
SHUTTLEWORTH	Ah! Our prices are most reasonable. You can't find this long-lasting furniture at cheap prices. There is certainly cheaper office equipment on the market. But when you look at the quality and the finish I think we have no rivals.
GORGONDALE	Quite so, quite so. All very interesting, I'm sure. But cost, Mr. Shuttleworth. Your prices are much too high. Look at these wastepaper bins—twice what I'd pay for them elsewhere. They're just not competitive.
SHUTTLEWORTH	Oh, but they're highly competitive when you consider quality....
GORGONDALE	Well, you talk of quality. I'm not even sure about that. Those dozen staplers we ordered from you the other week: they arrived this morning and half of them don't work properly.
SHUTTLEWORTH	Really? I can't believe it. They are the very latest design.

GORGONDALE   Here you are. Here's one of them. Try it yourself. You
             see, it clips two or three pages all right and then the metal
             staple falls out, all bent.   50
SHUTTLEWORTH Yes, you're right. There is something wrong. But it can't
             be anything serious. Let me see now. Here it is. Very
             simple. This anvil on to which the staples are pressed is
             wrongly placed, and so when the staples are pressed from
             the magazine they don't hold properly. I'm very sorry, 55
             Mr. Gorgondale. I'll report it immediately. If you'll let me
             have the others I'll correct them at once.

SHUTTLEWORTH: 'Yes, you're right.
There is something wrong. But it can't
be anything serious.'

(When Mr. Shuttleworth gets to London, he goes to see John Martin)

JOHN MARTIN   Oh, hello, Shuttleworth, come in.
SHUTTLEWORTH Hello, Mr. Martin.
JOHN   Sit down. I'm just trying to get Mr. Wiles on the phone.   60
              Hello? Yes, good. Peter, any more news ... what? Oh,
              no! Sixty this morning! That makes about three hundred
              staplers sent back this week. There must be something
              really wrong. I know they were tested umpteen times.
              Yes ... all right. See you later. (*He puts the receiver*   65
              down.) Troubles never stop in this place. I sometimes
              wonder why I'm still here.
SHUTTLEWORTH I heard that you've been made a director, Mr. Martin.
              Congratulations.
JOHN   Thanks very much. Now, Walter, I'm really sorry to get   70
              you down here, but even Mr. Grant's worried about your
              area. I know your difficulties, but we've got to do some-
              thing to increase sales. What about that chemical firm?
              Did you do anything with them?

SHUTTLEWORTH	No. Not a thing. It's the price, Mr. Martin. They just won't listen to the quality argument.	7
JOHN	More fools they! But what are we going to do? Are you getting a bit discouraged? Perhaps we ought to move you to another area? The trouble is, it's not a very good moment to go into details. We're in the middle of a crisis.	8
SHUTTLEWORTH	What's the trouble, Mr. Martin?	
JOHN	Those new staplers. Mr. Wiles has just told me we've had another sixty complaints today. I can't think what's gone wrong. The Lord knows how much we'll lose if we have to take them all back and modify the design.	8
SHUTTLEWORTH	I think I know what's wrong with them. That chemical firm had a bad batch. I examined one and noticed that it's the anvil. It's wrongly placed.	
JOHN	Really? Are you sure that's what it is? Can the customer put it right?	9
SHUTTLEWORTH	Yes. We can circularise all the customers who've ordered the staplers with a simple explanation and diagram. You've got one here. This one's all right. The anvil is correctly aligned.	
JOHN	Walter, you're a genius! You ought to be in the design department.	9
SHUTTLEWORTH	I might do better there than in sales.	
JOHN	Oh, come on, Walter. A pessimistic salesman never sells anything! Let's get together and plan a new campaign for your area. . . .	10

PRACTICE SENTENCES

Say the practice sentences on the record :

  i I'm sure you'd like to see our latest range.

  ii This is the catalogue.

  iii Our prices are most reasonable.

  iv Your prices are much too high.

  v They're the very latest design.

  vi We've got to do something to increase sales.

  vii Let's get together and plan a new campaign for your area.

2. A CIRCULAR AND A COMPLAINT

Here is the circular letter which was written to all the customers of Harper & Grant's who had bought this new model stapler.

Harper and Grant Limited

Great West Road
London W25
Telephone 01-567 1112
Telex 80153
Telegrams Harp LDN

Directors:
Hector Grant (Chairman & Managing Director)
William Buckhurst FCA (Secretary)
John Martin
Alfred Wentworth
Margaret Wiles
Peter Wiles

19th July, 197..

Dear Sirs,

We have been informed that a batch of our new Mark 6B staplers, of which you have recently taken a delivery, have caused some trouble. On investigation we find that a number of staplers were faultily assembled, the anvil being slightly out of alignment. If you do have any trouble, we are confident that the enclosed diagram will make it clear how the error can be corrected.

We apologise for any inconvenience you may have been caused.

Yours faithfully,

John Martin
Sales Manager
HARPER & GRANT LTD.

And here is a complaint letter from one of the angry customers:

John Martin, Esq.,
Sales Manager,
Harper & Grant Ltd.,
Great West Road,
London, W.25.   21st July, 197..

Dear Sir,

      Exactly ten days ago I returned a dozen staplers to you
because they did not work.   I fully expected to be sent replacements,
an apology, or even my money back.   Instead I received this morning
a diagram instructing me how to repair the staplers myself.   I should
be glad to know how I can do this when I no longer have the staplers.

      Kindly send me, by return, twelve staplers which work
efficiently.

      With thanks,

                  Yours faithfully,

                  Philip Goswind

PART 3 : NOTES AND PRACTICE

1. RAPPEL GRAMMATICAL

Summary :

2.   **Each.** On dirait : **each rep is responsible for his (or her) area,** tandis
qu'avec **every,** on pourra rencontrer : **every rep is responsible for their
areas** ou **for his (or her) area.**

5.   **Latest** et **last : latest** indique le plus récent, **last** le dernier de la série.
Latest s'emploie lorsque la série est inachevée : **their latest catalogue,
your latest figures, the latest developments. Last** s'emploie pour le dernier
de la série achevée :

    They have gone bankrupt : this   Ils ont fait faillite : cela aura été
    will have been their last   leur dernier catalogue
    catalogue

On emploie **last** avec les indications de jours, mois, etc. et tout ce qui équivaut à une date : **last week, last Thursday, last meeting** (bien que la série des assemblées ne soit pas close, on rencontre ici **last**).

9. **The last quarter's** : on aurait pu dire : **those of the last quarter.** (Jamais **these**, qui est une faute fréquente de francophone).

13. **He may have run into a bad patch** : les francophones ont parfois du mal à faire la distinction entre **may**, *éventualité*, et **must** dans sa valeur de *quasi-certitude*. Il y a pourtant dans ce cas en anglais exactement la même différence de certitude qu'en français entre *pouvoir* et *devoir* :

He may have made an error in his forecasts	Il a pu se tromper dans ses prévisions
He must have made a mistake in his accounts	Il a dû se tromper dans ses comptes

Conversation :

8. Notons cette structure complexe : **What did you want to see me about ?**

On peut en rencontrer de plus complexes pour un francophone :

What did he say he would do ?	Qu'a-t-il dit qu'il ferait ?
When do you say he will come ?	Quand dites-vous qu'il viendra ?
Why do you think we couldn't succeed ?	Pourquoi croyez-vous que nous ne pourrions pas réussir ?
Where did he say he met you ?	Où dit-il vous avoir rencontré ?

8. Comparons ici **consider furnishing** avec la première phrase du **Summary**, qui contient un emploi du gérondif avec **the** : **Sales Representatives do the selling.** Pourquoi pas d'article défini dans le premier cas, et un article dans ce dernier ? **Furnishing** — sans article, est aux yeux de M. Shuttleworth encore une éventualité, une virtualité, donc une abstraction. Il n'emploie pas d'article. Tandis que **the selling** est la réalité concrète et quotidienne du représentant pour sa maison. D'où l'article.

25-26. **When your grandchildren are running the business.** Dans la subordonnée temporelle, on ne rencontre pas **shall/will - should/would.** Il faut s'habituer à la petite gymnastique qui porte sur quatre temps :

— *présent* (lorsque le français emploie le *futur*)

— *present perfect* (lorsque le français emploie le *futur antérieur*)

— *prétérit* (lorsque le français emploie le *futur du passé*, c'est-à-dire le temps qui a la même forme que le conditionnel et qu'on nomme traditionnellement conditionnel)

— *plu-perfect* (lorsque le français a le *futur antérieur du passé*, c'est-à-dire le « conditionnel passé ») :

I'll complain when I see their representative	Je ferai une réclamation quand je verrai leur représentant
I'll repair them when I've received their diagram	Je les réparerai quand j'aurai reçu leur schéma
He said he would complain when he saw Mr. Shuttleworth	Il a dit qu'il se plaindrait quand il verrait M. Shuttleworth
He said he'd repair them when he'd received our diagram	Il a dit qu'il les réparerait quand il aurait reçu notre schéma

Bien entendu, ce système de concordance n'est valable que dans la proposition subordonnée temporelle. Il ne faut pas confondre **when** conjonction de temps — ci-dessus — avec **when** interrogatif :

| When will their rep call again ? | Quand leur représentant passera-t-il à nouveau ? |
| I wonder when we shall receive the goods | Je me demande quand nous recevrons les marchandises |

When est également relatif (**the day when** = le jour où) et il est dans ce cas suivi de **shall/will** :

| I'm looking forward to the day when we shall meet again | J'attends avec plaisir le jour où nous nous rencontrerons à nouveau |

30. **The same height.** La mesure s'exprime sans préposition :

They are the same colour	Ils sont de la même couleur
They are not the same length	Ils n'ont pas la même longueur
I am your age	Je suis de votre âge
Can't they make them the same width ?	Ne peuvent-ils pas les faire de la même largeur

35. **Long-lasting.** Adjectif composé formé d'un adverbe et d'un participe.

On peut trouver les combinaisons suivantes :

— *le 2ᵉ terme est un adjectif* :

| The new range is sky-blue | La nouvelle série est bleu-ciel |
| Hardiman is over-scrupulous | Hardiman est scrupuleux à l'excès |

— *le 2ᵉ terme est un participe présent* :

| Shuttleworth was an easy-going fellow | Shuttleworth était un homme insouciant |
| These are long-lasting pieces of furniture | Ce sont des meubles inusables |

— *le deuxième terme est un participe passé* :

| Who would choose that worm-eaten furniture ? | Qui choisirait ce mobilier mangé aux vers ? |

— le deuxième terme est un nom à imitation de participe passé (en -ed) :

Dans ce cas, l'adjectif composé peut désigner les parties du corps (**dark-haired**), les vêtements (**blue-uniformed air-hostesses**), les parties d'un objet (**a four-storeyed building**) ou des qualités abstraites :

Hector Grant isn't narrow-minded	Hector Grant n'est pas borné
His nephew is a quick-witted young executive	Son neveu est un jeune cadre à l'esprit vif

Dans la langue contemporaine, c'est-à-dire notamment celle de l'économie, des affaires, etc, on trouve des formations diverses :

We booked Mr. Mahawi into a first-rate hotel	Nous avons installé M. Mahawi dans un hôtel de premier ordre
Second-hand lorries are traded in at a very low price	Les camions d'occasion sont repris à très bas prix
They scored an unheard-of success in Abraca	Ils ont eu un succès inouï en Abraca
John took the 9.12 plane to New York	John a pris l'avion de 9 h 12 pour New York
This is where your couldn't-care-less attitude has led you, Walter	Voilà où votre je-m'en fichisme vous a entraîné, Walter
This is no longer up-to-date	Ce n'est plus à la page

51-52. **It can't be anything serious.** Quel serait l'affirmative ?

It must be something serious   Cela doit être quelque chose de grave

63-64. **There must be something wrong.** Quel serait la négative ?

There can't be anything wrong   Il ne peut rien avoir d'anormal

77. **More fools they.** Explorons un peu davantage cette construction, qu'illustre cet exemple un peu condensé :

Dans ce type de construction, **the**, placé devant la forme comparative, est en fait un adverbe modifiant l'adjectif et ayant le sens de *d'autant*. Cette construction peut avoir une subordonnée complétive, qui est en général introduite par **as** (ou **since**, ou **because**) ; ou par un complément introduit par **for**, comme dans l'exemple ci-dessus. Voyons quelques applications :

We'll break into the market all the more easily as we really have no serious competitors	Nous pénétrons sur ce marché d'autant plus facilement que nous n'avons pas vraiment de concurrents sérieux

Sally was all the more worried as her signature was on the receipt	Sally était d'autant plus tracassée que sa signature figurait sur le bon d'enlèvement
Walter felt all the more depressed as Gorgondale had proved to him that he lacked dynamism in business	Walter était d'autant plus déprimé que Gorgondale lui avait prouvé son manque de dynamisme en affaires
We'll lose this customer	Nous allons perdre ce client
We'll be none the poorer for it !	Nous n'en serons pas plus pauvres !
So much the better if you could repair them on the spot	Tant mieux si vous avez pu les réparer sur place
So much the worse for you	Tant pis pour vous
All the more reason for moving Shuttleworth to another area	Raison de plus pour transférer Shuttleworth dans un autre secteur

Complaint

I fully expected to be sent a replacement. Notons que dans ce passif (*infinitif ici*) de verbe du type **show, send, give, teach,** etc... le sujet de la construction passive est la personne, et l'objet la chose. Bien que l'actif ait deux compléments directs, on ne trouve que la construction passive avec sujet de la personne :

I was shown into a large, newly-decorated and gorgeously-furnished office	On m'introduit dans un vaste bureau, nouvellement tapissé, et somptueusement meublé
They'll be sent our latest catalogue, anyway	On leur enverra notre dernier catalogue, de toute façon
She was taught Spanish in Spain	On lui a appris l'espagnol en Espagne
We were given a bonus	On nous a donné une prime

2. EXERCISES

EXERCISE 1. — Change as follows :

    a. maybe he ran into a bad patch →
                he may have run into a bad patch
    b. he certainly ran into a bad patch →
                he must have run into a bad patch

1. Maybe he costed the expenditure. 2. It certainly cost you a great deal of money. 3. Maybe they received our brochure. 4. He certainly stopped in that transport café. 5. He certainly wrote his report on Saturday. 6. Maybe he met the buyer of Crucible Chemicals. 7. Maybe they chose another article. 8. He certainly found John at his office. 9. Maybe there was a mistake in his accounts.

EXERCISE 2. — *Say the contrary as follows* :

it must be serious   →   **it can't be serious**
it can't be wrong   →   **it must be wrong**

1. There must be a mistake. 2. It can't be anything serious. 3. He must have sold the bad staplers. 4. She can't have put the invoice in the wrong envelope. 5. Their prices can't be lower than yours. 6. There must be a cheaper article on the market. 7. He must have lost confidence. 8. He can't have heard we were doing research on this new material.

EXERCISE 3. — *Build sentences as suggested here* :

They'll send me replacements (I expected so) →
I expected to be sent replacements

1. They'll send him a price list with the old prices (he expected so). 2. They'll ask him to join the Board (he hoped so). 3. They'll show me their new lines (I expected so). 4. They'll send Gorgondale another batch of staplers (he hoped so). 5. They'll allot new shares to the shareholders (they hope so). 6. They'll teach you salesmanship in colleges (don't expect so). 7. They'll tell me what do do (I don't expect so). 8. They'll give the customers the opportunity of returning the goods (they expect so). 9. They'll grant you a favourable discount (do you hope so ?). 10. They'll give him compensation for the damage (he had expected so).

EXERCISE 4. — *Try and form compound adjectives* :

1. Motor industries that are owned by the state. 2. A scheme that has been sponsored by the trade-unions. 3. Our committee is not a body that makes decisions. 4. They are industries that are orientated towards the market. 5. They produce the same goods in subsidiaries that are based abroad (in foreign countries). 6. Components built in America are assembled locally. 7. France is lagging behind in industries based on science. 8. There was no slump as usual after the war, but a boom instead.

EXERCISE 5. — *Change as follows* :

Your prices are high ; our prices are not →
Your prices are much higher than ours

1. Their lines look modern ; your lines don't. 2. Your representatives are well-paid ; my representatives are not. 3. This desk is imposing and dignified ; your desk is not. 4. Our articles are cheap ; their articles are not. 5. Our position is bad ; their position is not. 6. Their growth has been fast ; our growth has not.

EXERCISE 6. — *Change as follows* :

   a. **I'll see Walter when he comes back** →
     He said he'd see Walter when he came back

   b. **I'll see Walter when he's seen Gorgondale** →
     He said he'd see Walter when he'd seen Gorgondale

1. I'll pay the difference when all the staplers have been replaced. 2. I'll have a word with Jack Green when he arrives at the works. 3. I'll see the Transport Manager when all the lorries have been loaded. 4. I'll type the report only when Mr. Grant has read over the draft. 5. I'll tell him when he returns from Scotland. 6. I'll place an order when I've visited your stand at the exhibition.

EXERCISE 7. — *Change as follows* :

   Our competitors have no experience ; therefore it will be easy for us
     → **it will be all the easier for us as our competitors have no experience**

1. The lighting was remarkable ; so the display of goods was very effective. 2. The staff got no Xmas bonus, so they are very angry . 3. These mills are too small and conventional, so they are less profitable. 4. We had little experience, so the venture was unsuccessful. 5. The shop switched to self-service, so the scale of pilfering has become dramatic. 6. If the town is big, small dealers are vulnerable to competition. 7. It demands constant maintenance, so it is very costly. 8. The workers aren't used to taking precautions, so these new machines are very dangerous.

EXERCISE 8. — *Ask questions as follows* :

   They'll meet on Monday 17th (when) →
     When did you say they would meet ?

1. The question of redundancies will be tackled at the next meeting (what). 2. They will accept the French scheme (whose). 3. The Benelux countries will accept the British proposals (who). 4. The cheque is payable on presentation (how). 5. The extension is to be built across the road (where). 6. The shares were quoted at £ 1.65 p. yesterday (how much).

EXERCISE 9. — *What expressions would be used in the following situations ? Please answer with complete sentences ; begin with ' we '.*

1. You want to assure a possible buyer of your merchandise that your prices compare well with similar goods manufactured by other firms. 2. You want to send a letter round to a number of clients who have bought faulty staplers. 3. The design of a new product is not good ; you think it would be improved if it were changed slightly and made simpler.

EXERCISE 10. — *Translate into English* :

1. Je suis sûr que vous aimeriez voir notre dernière collection. 2. Voici le catalogue. 3. Nos prix sont des plus raisonnables. 4. Vos prix sont beaucoup trop élevés. 5. Ils sont du tout dernier modèle. 6. Il faut qu'on fasse quelque chose pour augmenter les ventes. 7. Essayons de faire un nouveau plan de campagne pour votre secteur. 8. Je crains de ne pouvoir vous accorder que quelques minutes. 9. On a envoyé une mauvaise fournée d'agrafeuses à la société chimique. 10. Nous avons un service spécial pour la conception et l'équipement complet des bureaux. 11. Je m'attendais à recevoir des excuses, ou qu'on me retourne mon argent. 12. Nous vous prions de nous excuser pour tout dérangement que nous avons pu vous causer. 13. Félicitations ! j'ai appris que vous étiez entré au Conseil d'Administration ! 14. Dieu sait combien nous allons perdre si nous devons modifier le modèle. 15. Je vais le signaler immédiatement à notre bureau des études. 16. Est-ce que tous vos modèles sont de la même hauteur ? 17. Eh bien, à quel sujet vouliez-vous me voir ? 18. Je l'ai convoqué ici à Londres pour discuter un peu de ses derniers chiffres. 19. La plupart des représentants ont fait une très mauvaise saison. 20. Ils ne font pas tout eux-mêmes, ils sous-traitent avec d'autres entreprises.

UNIT 19

AUDITING THE ACCOUNTS

PART 1 : INTRODUCTION

1. WORD STUDY

Vocabulary

account compte
accounts comptabilité
  trading and profit and loss account
    compte d'exploitation et de
    profits et pertes
assets actif
  current assets actif liquide,
    disponible et réalisable
audit apurer, vérifier
auditor commissaire aux comptes
balance sheet bilan
cash caisse ; argent liquide ;
  encaisser
capital capitaux ; fonds
  authorised capital capital
    social
  share capital capital actions
cheat fraude ; frauder
commodities denrées, marchandises
clerk employé de bureau
compilation présentation,
  compilation
current courant

daily quotidien(nement)
deduct déduire
depreciation amortissement
director administrateur
  Directors' Report Rapport de
    Gestion
dismiss licencier, congédier
dividend dividende
draw out retirer, sortir (argent)
earnings gains
  retained earnings bénéfices non
    distribués
ensure s'assurer
exempt from dispensé de, non
  soumis à
fees honoraires
fixed assets immobilisations,
  actif immobilisé
fiddle « tripatouillage », fraude
finished stock stock fini
formal officiel
further promouvoir
furthermore en outre

— 298 —

goods paid for marchandises payées
handwriting écriture
hourly d'heure en heure
income revenu(s)
investments investissements,
    placements
issue émission ; émettre
item article, écriture
ledger grand livre
liabilities passif
  current liabilities exigibilités,
    passif exigible à court terme
list dresser la liste
make out (a cheque) faire, établir
make up constituer
market value valeur marchande
notice remarquer
pay back rembourser, restituer
pay in verser, faire encaisser
paying-in voucher bordereau de
    versement
plant matériel, machines,
    équipements
practice cabinet
privately-owned privé, personnel
profitable rentable
profit statement compte de profits
prove s'avérer
query mettre en doute

reserves réserves
retain retenir
sales ventes, chiffre d'affaires
  net sales chiffre d'affaires net
satisfy convaincre, assurer
son-in-law gendre
staff personnel
statement relevé de comptes ;
    état, solde, bilan
steal voler
stocks approvisionnements, stocks
straight away immédiatement
supplier fournisseur
surplus excédent, plus-value
  trading surplus résultat
    d'exploitation
total up faire l'addition
trading account compte
    d'exploitation
valuation évaluation, estimation
  stock valuation inventaire
voucher bordereau
  paying-in voucher bordereau de
    versement
work in progress travaux en cours
whichever quel qu'il soit
withdraw retirer
withdrawal retrait

Phrases

They act on behalf of... ils agissent pour le compte de...
They must judge for themselves ils doivent juger par eux-mêmes
He is in private practice il a un cabinet particulier
In no way nullement
If they get away with it s'ils y arrivent, s'ils s'en sortent
On a larger scale dans des proportions plus grandes
On a sale or return basis (*marchandises prises*) en dépôt,
    à condition

When do you think you'll be finished ?	quand pensez-vous en avoir terminé ?
I'll be through by the end of the month	j'aurai fini d'ici la fin du mois

Explanations and Other Useful Terms

accounts	the detailed record of a firm's business transactions. **Nominal accounts** usually refer to the record of the various kinds of expense (rent, wages and salaries, advertising, etc.) income, profit or loss, or to the general division of accounts into separate groups. **Real accounts** relate to tangible things, i. e. land, buildings, machinery, furniture, vehicles, cash. **Personal accounts** are the record of business with firms or people, i.e. the suppliers (who are called **creditors**) and the customers (or **debtors**).
assets	*here*, property, stock, cash-in-hand.
auditors	qualified accountants who are called in on behalf of the members (shareholders) of a limited company to examine and report upon the accounts of the company.
auditors' report	a report from the auditors to the members of a company stating that they have examined the accounts, and that in their opinion the company's balance sheet has been properly prepared and gives a true and fair state of affairs, at the date on which the accounting period has ended and of the profit for that period.
Balance Sheet	a statement of the company's position on a certain date. It shows the **assets** (*see above*) and the **liabilities** (*see below*) and the **capital** on that date.
bank statement	information on all transactions of a person or firm with a bank. It is a record of the amounts paid in and drawn out (**deposits** and **withdrawals**) showing the balance.
book-keeper	the person responsible for keeping the records day by day.
book-keeping system	the way in which the details of all business transactions are recorded (*see* : **single entry** and **double entry**).
cash book	where all cash transactions are recorded.
credit	**items** (also called **entries**) made in an account book recording payments, liabilities, profits and income. These entries are written on the right hand side.

credit note	a summary of a credit which the supplier agrees a customer is entitled to. The most frequent reason would be return of goods which the supplier sent in error. The value of a credit note is credited to the customer's account with the supplier.
creditors	people, or companies to whom you, or your company, owe money. Creditors are a current liability in the balance sheet.
debit	items recorded in an account book, on the left hand side, recording receipts, assets, losses and expenses.
debtors	people, or companies who owe you, or your company, money. These are a current asset in the balance sheet.
Directors' Report	this comments on the profit or loss made during the accounting period and makes recommendations on the dividend to be paid. This has to be approved at the annual general meeting of the shareholders. Following recent legislation in Great Britain, it will now be necessary for details of shares held by the directors to be disclosed in the annual report. Certain information on salaries paid to directors also now has to be given.
dividend	the sum distributed to the members of a company out of profits of the company.
double entry	a method of showing that every business transaction has two aspects, i.e. materials or goods purchased on credit are a liability on the firm to pay the suppliers later, but at the same time they are an asset as at some time the materials will be used for manufacture and then sold, or the goods purchased will be resold.
draw out (money)	to take money out of an account at a bank.
float	here, a sum of money which is kept on hand, easily available.
ledger	the most important account book, since all transactions are recorded in it. It is often divided for the sake of convenience into :
	— **a sales ledger**, list of goods or services supplied ;
	— **a bought ledger**, list of goods or services purchased ;

	— **a general ledger**, list of property, such as machinery, vehicles buildings, etc. (real accounts) and expenses, income, etc. (nominal accounts) ; and
	— **a private ledger**, which is confidential and records items such as capital, loans, mortgages, directors' salaries and awards, etc.
liabilities	money owed, debts, i.e. what one is liable to pay.
paying-in vouchers	paying in slips : see Unit 13.
petty cash book	the record of payments made from a small cash float, which is used to pay for such items as stationery, stamps, cleaning, taxis, etc.
to post	in book-keeping to post means to transfer items from subsidiary account books to the ledger or ledgers.
Profit Statement	**(trading and profit and loss account)** : a summary of all the income and expense accounts **(nominal accounts)** at the end of the accounting period. The balance of this account represents the **net profit** *or* **loss** for the period.
single entry	a record of only one side of a business transaction, as used in day books, sales books, etc., showing the single item of debit or credit.
valuation	process of deciding the value of something. Here, the value of the store of goods available for sale.

Pronunciation

1 — 1 - (- -) assets, audit, auditor, capital, fluctuate, honesty, income, period, practice, satisfied, summarise, volume.

- 2 (- -) account, affair, anomaly, behalf, cashier, commodities, connected, consider, consist, deduct, derive, director, dishonesty, efficiently, ensure, equivalent, exempt, extent, immediately, intend, investment, machinery, publicity, reserve, retain, until, withdraw, withdrawal.

- - 3 (-) independent, individual, satisfactory, understandable, liability.

2 — - ' - my'self, your'self, him'self, her'self, our'selves, your'selves, them'selves.
  -'ier, -'eer : cashier, engineer

3 — [a:] ask, clerk, staff, charge, plant, department, behalf

[æ] cash, act, bad, slang, bank, handle, balance, satisfied

[ɔ:] law, talk, source, fault, audit, report, August, always

[ɔ] not, loss, stock, what, want, often, column, copper, problem, commodities

[ʌ] son, funds, must, judge, publish, summarise, fluctuate

[ju:] use, usually, value, future, produce, duty

[ju] 'fluctuate, 'volume, 'regular, indi'vidual, 'valuation

[ai] try, lie, lying, find, item, private, precisely, satisfied

[i] efficient, listed, capital, fiddle, notice, direct, director, practice

4 — Compare : plus [plʌs], surplus ['sə:pləs]

divide [di'vaid], dividend ['dividənd]

compile [kəm'pail], compilation [ˌkɔmpi'leiʃən]

value ['vælju:], valuation [ˌvælju'eiʃən]

5 — Note : cheat [tʃi:t], column ['kɔləm], debt [det], depreciation [diˌpri:ʃi'eiʃən], ensure [in'ʃuə], issue ['iʃu:, 'isju:, 'iʃju:], query ['kwiəri], voucher ['vautʃə].

2. SUMMARY

Every year the accounts of a limited company must be approved by auditors. They act on behalf of the shareholders. Their duty is to ensure that the directors are reporting correctly on the state of affairs of the company. They do not judge whether the directors are managing the company efficiently or not. That is something the shareholders must judge for themselves.   5

Until recently, the accounts of Harper & Grant have been audited by Hector Grant's son-in-law, who is in private practice as an accountant. A new firm of auditors has now been appointed. A privately owned limited company is now no longer exempt from having to publish its accounts. It was therefore considered necessary to have the accounts audited by independent auditors 10 in no way connected with Harper & Grant.

William Buckhurst, as Company Secretary, is responsible for seeing that the books and records for the period in question are ready for checking. It could make a bad impression if the accounts department was not able to supply immediately any information wanted by the auditors.   15

What precisely do the auditors check? They have to be satisfied that everything which goes into making up the Profit Statement, the Balance Sheet and the Directors' Report is correct. The Profit Statement (sometimes called a Trading and Profit and Loss Account) shows how the profit for the year is arrived at. It starts with net sales or income, and deducts 20 the cost of materials, work and overhead charges. This leaves a trading surplus, from which charges, such as depreciation on plant and buildings, auditors' fees, and administration and selling costs must be deducted to produce the net profit (or loss). The Balance Sheet is a summarised statement showing the amount of funds employed in the business and the 25 sources from which these funds are derived. On one side is listed the capital employed, which usually consists of the issued share capital plus reserves and retained earnings. You will remember from Unit 13 that the share capital of Harper & Grant consisted of five thousand £1 shares, with a total market value of five hundred thousand pounds. In other 30 words, there are four hundred and ninety-five thousand pounds in reserves and retained earnings. This starts with the total cost of its fixed assets (land, buildings and machinery) and any trade investments (interests in other companies), followed by a breakdown of net current assets (that is, cash and stocks, plus what the firm is owed by its 35 customers, less its liabilities, or what it owes to others). The Wentworth Mattress Company owns shares in Harper & Grant, so this would be shown as a trade investment in Wentworth's Balance Sheet. The totals on the two sides of the Balance Sheet must agree; that is, come to the same figure. The total dividend to be paid for the year is a current liability, and 40 is therefore an item in the compilation of net current assets.

One of the most difficult jobs in preparing accounts is stock valuation ; that is, putting a value on all goods in the hands of the company. It may seem easy, as goods could be counted, and then the price paid for them could be checked against the suppliers' invoices. But the value of commodities (*e.g.* 45 copper) often fluctuates. Furthermore, much of a company's stock will consist of work in progress or finished stock, and the volume of all stock is changing daily, if not hourly. The rule for stock valuation is that it should be taken at cost price or market price, whichever is the lower.

So far we have seen only one case of dishonesty in Harper & Grant, 50 when a clerk in the Sales Department took some cash left lying on a desk. Unfortunately, there is always a temptation to people handling money all the time to attempt, in a weak moment, *a fiddle* (a slang term for a small cheat or dishonest action) which they feel will not be noticed. If they get away with it, are successful, they may well be tempted to do it again, or make a regular practice of it, perhaps on a larger scale.

PART 2 : CONVERSATION AND DOCUMENTS

1. CONVERSATION

(Recorded Text)

(William Buckhurst goes into the Accounts Office to speak to the chief auditor)

WILLIAM
BUCKHURST **Well, Mr. Brent, you've had three hours at those books. What about some lunch?**

MR. BRENT **That would be very welcome.**

BUCKHURST **No problems?**

BRENT **Er ... yes, Mr. Buckhurst. One or two small things.** 5
Would you like to go into them now, or after lunch?

BUCKHURST **Well, perhaps we might do it now, so that I can try and get the information straight away.**

BRENT **The first is this figure here in the stock valuation. This figure for paint. I suppose you have this paint in stock. It's listed** 10
as goods paid for, but I can find no record of payment.

BUCKHURST **Ah, I know what that is. There won't be a cheque for the total amount. We always buy paint on a sale or return basis and pay for it each quarter as we use it. I'm afraid that's my fault. I accepted the figure in the stock depart-** 15
ment. We forgot the sale or return arrangement and put the paint in the wrong column.

BUCKHURST: 'You've had three hours
at those books. What about some lunch?'

BRENT	Very understandable. This sort of thing often happens.
BUCKHURST	What's the other anomaly?
BRENT	Well, these cheques made out to members of the staff. 20 Could you tell me something about them?
BUCKHURST	Certainly. We often cash cheques for staff as a service. The cheques are made out to the company by the individuals. The cashier then totals up the value of the cheques, comes to me for a company cheque for the same 25 sum, and then goes to the bank. He pays in the staff members' cheques and draws out an equivalent sum of cash with the company cheque.
BRENT	But I notice from the bank statement that the amount paid in is less than the amount drawn out. Here are the 30 paying-in vouchers. This was the sum paid in to the bank, but this was the amount drawn out.
BUCKHURST	Oh dear . . . yes. It does seem to be different. A difference of fifteen pounds. I don't like the look of that one. Will you leave it with me and I'll look into it this afternoon, 35 and come and talk to you again.

(*Later Mr. Buckhurst looks in on Mr. Brent again*)

BUCKHURST	I've found out the reason for the difference in those two amounts.
BRENT	Oh?
BUCKHURST	I'm afraid it was a fiddle. It can only have been 40 Donald Kennet, the clerk who always goes to the bank. I'm very upset about it. We've never had a thing like this before.
BRENT	I wonder what he'll have to say for himself.
BUCKHURST	Yes. I'm just going to see him now. He's waiting in 45 my office. . . .

(*In Mr. Buckhurst's office*)

BUCKHURST	Ah, Donald.
DONALD KENNET	You wanted to see me, Mr. Buckhurst?
BUCKHURST	Yes, Donald. We have a problem here which the auditors have raised. Perhaps you can help. 50
KENNET	Oh, yes. I certainly will if I can, sir.
BUCKHURST	You usually go to the bank on Fridays to cash staff cheques, don't you?

KENNET	Yes, Mr. Buckhurst.
BUCKHURST	Can you remember any occasions in the last few months 55 when you have not gone?
KENNET	Er . . . I was away for my holidays in the summer. I think that was the only time I didn't go.
BUCKHURST	Yes, that was in August, wasn't it? Well, this figure he's querying was in October . . . and there was another occa- 60 sion in . . . in . . . er . . . June.
KENNET	What occasion do you mean? What are you referring to?
BUCKHURST	The auditor has found that on these two occasions more was drawn out from the bank than was paid in. Can you 65 explain the reason for that?
KENNET	Er . . . I'm sure I don't know why the amounts should be different. They should be exactly the same. Can I look at the bank statements?
BUCKHURST	Certainly. Here they are. 70
KENNET	Thank you.
BUCKHURST	And here are the two paying-in vouchers for the two dates; both in your handwriting, I think?
KENNET	Yes . . . but I don't understand . . .
BUCKHURST	The withdrawal on the bank statement here must be the 75 cash for the staff, because on both days it is the only amount drawn. You don't think you could somehow have lost one of the cheques you were paying in?
KENNET	Look, I'm sorry, Mr. Buckhurst. I can explain it. I really was going to pay it back later. You see I . . . my mother 80 was ill and . . .
BUCKHURST	Why didn't you come and ask me for help if you were in trouble? Or you could have seen the Personnel Manager. We might have arranged for you to draw your pay in advance. But this . . . this is stealing. 85
KENNET	I didn't mean to steal it. I was going to pay it back. I intended to pay it back. I didn't mean to be dishonest, really I didn't. . . .

(*Later*)

BUCKHURST	Well, Mr. Brent, when do you think you'll be finished?
BRENT	Oh, I think I should be through by the end of the month. 90 But now I've seen the extent of the work, I'll bring in two of the others to help me.

BUCKHURST	No more problems so far?	
BRENT	No, I don't think so. It all seems to be in order.	
BUCKHURST	Thanks. By the way, that clerk was responsible.	95
BRENT	Oh dear! Poor fellow. You'll have to dismiss him, I suppose.	
BUCKHURST	Yes, we may have to. It's a pity. He works hard and he's been satisfactory in every way, apart from this.	
BRENT	Well, I'm sorry to have been the cause of such an unhappy discovery.	100
BUCKHURST	We're very glad you did discover it. You have probably saved the company from an even bigger loss.	

PRACTICE SENTENCES

Say the practice sentences on the record :

  i I can find no record of payment.
  ii We always buy it on a sale or return basis.
  iii We pay for it each quarter, as we use it.
  iv We often cash cheques for staff as a service.
  v The cheques are made out to the company.
  vi The cashier totals up the value of the cheques.
  vii Here are the paying-in vouchers.

2. THE DIRECTORS' REPORT

When Harper & Grant's Profit and Loss Account and the Balance Sheet were approved, they were sent to all shareholders with the Directors' Report on the year's business. The shareholders were then invited to attend the Annual General Meeting, or A.G.M. In a public company the Directors' Report is often printed in the newspapers, as it can be excellent publicity if the firm is doing well. It is also useful if the company wishes to raise further capital with a new issue of shares.

Here is part of the Directors' Report:

The process of expansion has continued throughout the past year. Market research in connection with new products was carried out, budgetary control and work study developed and a programme of management training introduced.

Work on the new factory extension was begun, and a training programme instituted for the extra personnel who will be required. The new extension will greatly increase the volume of our production. The machinery we have installed is of the very latest design. We are confident that we shall increase the quality of our products, as well as the quantity. It is hoped that, following the formal opening, the new extension will be in full operation.

We are pursuing an active export policy, and we hope that future plans in this direction will prove profitable. To further future expansion, your directors are proposing, for passing at the A.G.M., the necessary resolution to increase our authorised capital and to become a public company. We look forward to a year of vigorous and successful trading.

PART 3 : NOTES AND PRACTICE

1. RAPPEL GRAMMATICAL

Summary

1. **The accounts must be approved.** Il est important à ce stade de pouvoir dans la conversation, spontanément, donner toutes les variations des équivalents des défectifs. Exemple :

They had had to be approved	On avait dû les approuver
They ought to have been approved	On aurait dû les approuver

4. **Whether.** Dans la langue écrite, introduit une alternative. Dans la langue parlée, on entend de plus en plus **if**.

9. **They are no longer exempt from it.** Comparons cette phrase avec celle de la ligne 93 de la conversation : **no more problems so far ?**

L'idée de *ne plus se* rend pas **no longer** s'il y a une idée de *temps*, et **no more** s'il y a une idée de *quantité* :

John is no longer in his office	John n'est plus dans son bureau
They didn't order any more staplers	Ils n'ont plus commandé d'agrafeuses

17. **Everything which.** Variante possible : **all that.**

20. **How the profit is arrived at.** Notons la place de la préposition. Ainsi :

What is Shuttleworth waiting for ?	Qu'est-ce qu'attend Shuttleworth ?
Show me the design you were looking at	Montrez-moi le modèle que vous regardiez à l'instant
Who was Brent speaking with ?	Avec qui Brent parlait-il ?

55. Veut-on relever tous les nombreux passifs de ce texte, qui prouvent l'extrême importance de cette construction (cf. ci-dessus 1. 1) :

-6	**The accounts have been audited**	La comptabilité a été apurée
-7-8	**A new firm has been appointed**	On a désigné un nouveau cabinet
-9-10	**It was considered necessary to have the accounts audited...**	On a jugé nécessaire de faire apurer les comptes...
-16	**They have to be satisfied that...**	Ils doivent s'assurer que...
-19-20	**It shows how the profit for the year is arrived at**	Il fait apparaître la manière dont on est arrivé aux bénéfices pour l'année
-22-23	**Charges must be deducted**	Il faut déduire les frais
-26-27	**On one side is listed the capital employed**	D'un côté apparaît le capital employé
-35-36	**What the firm is owed by its customers**	Ce que les clients doivent à l'entreprise
-37-38	**This would be shown as a trade investment**	Ceci apparaîtrait à la rubrique des placements
-40	**The total dividend to be paid for the year**	Le dividende global à payer pour l'année
-43-44	**It seems easy, as goods could be counted...**	Cela semble facile, car apparemment les marchandises peuvent se compter...
-48-49	**It should be taken at cost price**	On doit le prendre au prix de revient
-54	**A cheat they feel will not be noticed**	Une fraude dont ils pensent qu'on ne la remarquera pas
-55	**They may be tempted to do it again**	Ils peuvent avoir la tentation de recommencer

Conversation :

11. **I can find no record of payment.** Variante : **I can't find any record.**

12. There won't be a cheque for the total amount. Le défectif **will** peut exprimer la *probabilité*, la *quasi-certitude* :

The phone's ringing !	Le téléphone sonne !
— **It will be our rep from Yorkshire**	Cela doit être notre représentant du Yorkshire
— **Gorgondale said he couldn't afford our desks**	Gorgondale a dit qu'il ne pouvait pas s'offrir nos bureaux
— **He would !**	C'était à prévoir
You won't find him at the office, it's too late	Vous avez peu de chances de le trouver au bureau, il est trop tard

40. It can only have been Kennet. Can a ici également la nuance de quasi-certitude. On voit donc que les défectifs anglais sont riches de nuances.

44. I wonder what he'll have to say. Ici, **'ll** donne une idée d'*éventualité*.

52. On Fridays. Distinguer **on Fridays** : *tous* les vendredis, de **on Friday** : ce vendredi-ci (*dernier*, ou *prochain*).

67-68. Continuons cette exploration des défectifs par une comparaison de ces deux **should** :

a. **I don't know why they should be different.**
b. **They should be exactly the same.**

Dans a., **should** introduit une nuance de *doute* et *d'indignation*.

Dans b., **should** indique une idée de *ce qui devrait être*.

83-84. Terminons cette exploration des défectifs par ces deux phrases :
a. **You could have seen the Personnel Manager**
b. **We might have arranged for you to draw your pay in advance.**

a. contient une idée de *possibilité matérielle* qui ne s'est pas réalisée.

b. évoque une *éventualité* qui aurait pu alors se faire.

102. Il faut savoir manier la forme emphatique à bon escient, sans trop en abuser. Bien écouter à chaque fois les intonations de phrase.

2. EXERCISES

EXERCISE 1. — Put the right preposition or adverbial particle :

1. Each rep is responsible ... covering a particular area. 2. We must increase sales ... 10 %. 3. I called ... to see their Sales Manager.
4. They subcontract ... six or seven other firms. 5. I'm interested ...

prices, not .. quality. 6. They've already got quotations .. our competitors. 7. They're the cheapest ... the market. 8. It's twice what I pay ... them elsewhere. 9. The accounts were approved ... the auditors. 10. A bank statement is a record of the amounts paid ... and drawn .... 11. We buy our paint ... a sale or return basis. 12. The amount has not been credited ... your account. 13. It was purchased ... credit. 14. The cashier totalled ... the value of the cheques. 15. These ranges are not available ... sale at the moment. 16. They must report correctly ... the state of affairs of the company. 17. The shareholders will judge ... themselves. 18. They're no longer exempt ... having to publish their accounts. 19. Are these books ready ... checking? 20. Would you like to go ... these details now?

EXERCISE 2. — *Complete with question-tags, as follows :*

a. **You usually go to the bank on Fridays,...** → **..., don't you?**

b. **He doesn't go the the bank on Tuesdays,...** → **..., does he?**

1. Smith was rather late yesterday morning, ... 2. We'll have to phone him back, ... 3. Shuttleworth didn't look very cheerful, ... 4. The black chairs haven't yet been mended ... 5. There won't be enough paint, ... 6. It could be done in the same afternoon, ... 7. He made her type the letter again, ... 8. I'm in the red again, Mr. Brewer, ... 9. We ought to ring him back? ... 10. You hadn't noticed the fiddle, ... 11. There aren't any problems so far, ... 12. You can get the information straight away, ...

EXERCISE 3. — *Change as follows :*

We are glad you discovered it → **we're glad you did discover it**

We're glad 1. you sold him the Standfirm model. 2. he placed the order with us after all. 3. he told you about it. 4. he made out the cheque to you. 5. you saw Gorgondale just in time. 6. Donald went to the bank straight away. 7. You left it in the hands of the legal department. 8. she found out the reason for the difference.

EXERCISE 4. — *Change as follows :*

a. **we must do it on Tuesday** → **we'll have to do it on Tuesday**

b. **we can do it on Tuesday** → **we'll be able to do it on Tuesday**

1. She must sell all her shares. 2. Can you get any information about his financial standing? 3. You must modify the new design. 4. We can't do it without a computer, can we? 5. Can't they make other arrangements for the delivery? 6. We must adopt another marketing policy. 7. Donald Kennet must provide a specimen of his signature. 8. Can't they pay a higher dividend? 9. You can find other outlets, can't you? 10. Must I fill in all these forms? 11. They can't pay us, can they? 12. Tell him he must promise delivery by June 10th at the latest.

EXERCISE 5. — Change as follows :

a. we must do it on Wednesday → we ought to have done it on Wednesday

b. we can do it on Wednesday → we could have done it on Wednesday

1. We must invest in another company. 2. Can they refund the money by February 1st ? 3. You must pay more attention to the loading of the lorries. 4. You can't share the commission with him, anyway. 5. Must they tackle the problem of redundancies first ? 6. You must take the risk of inflation into account. 7. It can give you greater control over the market. 8. We must build the new extension across the road. 9. You must have a look at the classified advertisements. 10. We can get a better discount, can't we ? 11. We must return them a copy of the contract. 12. Can't you improve productivity ?

EXERCISE 6. — Change as follows :

The man to whom I spoke was their buyer → The man I spoke to was their buyer .

1. You can see the sources from which these funds are derived. 2. The job for which I applied was given to a young graduate of Manchester Business School. 3. This is not the area for which Shuttleworth is responsible. 4. The diagram to which he referred is in the green folder on my desk. 5. The memo on which he commented so sarcastically had been drawn up by H.G. himself. 6. This enables one to calculate the credit to which the customer is entitled. 7. Here is the list of the customers to whom invitations have been distributed. 8. The method upon which William reported required the use of a computer.

EXERCISE 7. — A passive medley ! Change as follows :

They applied for an I.D.C. → An I.D.C. was applied for

1. He attended to this customer. 2. They would have cashed the cheque earlier. 3. We can't hand the documents to the bank now. 4. They ought to have forbidden the use of hooks. 5. Could they supply larger quantities from stock ? 6. They might have opened all the cases at the customs. 7. Can't they cut the manufacturing costs ? 8. We could apply the American lesson in our firm. 9. They are negotiating other contracts at the moment. 10. They made use of the latest data processing techniques. 11. We are now examining Mr. Buckhurst's latest proposals. 12. If you withdraw your order, you forfeit your deposit.

EXERCISE 8. — A passive medley, N° 2 ! Change as follows, using **by** *and an agent :*

**The auditors will have to approve the accounts →
the accounts will have to be approved by the auditors**

1. H.G.'s son-in-law has audited the accounts for 10 years. 2. This is the amount for the company to pay. 3. They must now get an independent

firm to audit the accounts. 4. The auditors will have noticed the fiddle.
5. The bank sends a statement of account to each customer. 6. The
Board had rejected the older candidate for the post. 7. The shop-assistant
couldn't have repaired the apparatus. 8. The T.U.C. could certainly
not have supported such a strike. 9. French firms are missing extraordinary export opportunities. 10. The chartered accountant didn't check
all the entries, did he ? 11. Mr. Buckhurst will give all the documents
to your cashier. 12. We suppose Barclays Bank will grant them the loan.

EXERCISE 9. — *Complete the sentences, choosing the appropriate*
alternative from the words in brackets.

1. The history of a firm's business transactions is recorded by using the
(*double entry | single entry*) system of book-keeping. 2. Money owed by a
firm for goods purchased is a (*liability | asset*). 3. An audit is usually
carried out (*bi-annually | annually*). 4. Daily records of sales, purchases,
etc. must be (*written up | posted*) in a ledger. 5. Profit made would be
entered on the (*credit | debit*) side of the accounts.

EXERCISE 10. — *Complete the following passage using the most*
appropriate word or words.

A ... is responsible for the day-to-day work of recording business by
making entries, posting the books and making the accounts balance.
An ..., who may also do the work just mentioned, is qualified to 'close
the books' and complete the record of the year's trading. He has to
prepare a ... Account and a ... Every year, a firm's books must be
examined by an independent firm of ... These will be members of a
professional accounting body such as ... When they have examined
a firm's ... they give an undertaking in the form of a ... that they
consider the figures are correct.

EXERCISE 11. — *Translate into English* :

1. Je ne trouve pas de preuve du paiement. 2. Nous l'achetons toujours
en dépôt (*à condition*). 3. Nous le payons chaque trimestre, selon utili-
sation. 4. Nous encaissons souvent des chèques pour le personnel pour
leur rendre service. 5. Les chèques sont établis au nom de la société.
6. Le caissier fait le total de la valeur des chèques. 7. Voici les bordereaux
de versement. 8. Ils agissent pour le compte des actionnaires. 9. Le
Directeur du Personnel appréciera lui-même. 10. Il a un cabinet particulier
de comptable. 11. Cela aurait pu faire une mauvaise impression sur les
actionnaires. 12. L'amortissement n'a pas été déduit. 13. La valeur des
marchandises est en variation fréquente. 14. Je ne suis pas d'accord
avec les chiffres de l'inventaire. 15. Le montant versé est inférieur à la
somme retirée. 16. Cela ne me plaît pas du tout ! 17. Le chiffre que le
commissaire met en cause concerne le mois de mars. 18. On a retiré
davantage de la banque qu'on a versé. 19. Je crois que j'en aurai terminé
d'ici la fin mai. 20. Le contrôle budgétaire a été mis sur pied, et l'on
a introduit un programme de formation à la gestion.

UNIT 20

IMPROVING METHODS OF TRAINING

PART 1 : INTRODUCTION

1. WORD STUDY

Vocabulary

Act (of Parliament) loi
apprentice apprenti
apprenticeship apprentissage
assume supposer
attend (*trans.*) assister à, suivre
award attribution
charge faire payer
chart diagramme, courbe,
    mesurer, figurer
chief principal
college institut universitaire
costing évaluation
come under relever de, dépendre
craft artisanat, métier manuel
day release jour de congé
facilities facilités, installations
feature aspect, trait
grant subvention
graph courbe
guilty coupable
hand over remettre
improve améliorer
incentive stimulant

inefficient inefficace
instructor moniteur, instructeur
labour main d'œuvre
levy taxe, impôt
link up être en liaison
make up compenser
marker marqueur
nominal fictif, insignifiant
outright direct ; d'emblée
payroll salaires (*feuille de*)
peel off enlever, détacher
premises locaux
put up installer
qualify prétendre au titre de
qualified qualifié
rate taux
restrictive practices entraves à la
    liberté (*du travail, du commerce,*
    etc...)
sandwich course cours théorique
    avec formation pratique
    intégrée
savings économies

serve one's apprenticeship   faire
    son apprentissage
set up installer, créer
skill compétence
skilled spécialisé
standard norme requise
stick on coller
strip bande
syllabus programme

trade métier
training formation (*professionnelle*)
turnover mouvement, rotation
unplanned non-planifié, inorganisé
up-to-date moderne, à jour
wage salaire
wasteful dispendieux
work flow acheminement

Phrases

They have one day off	ils ont un jour de congé
They must take a test	ils doivent passer un examen
We take advantage of the benefits	nous profitons des avantages
They're trained on the shop floor	ils sont formés sur le tas
It's not up to standard	ce n'est pas à la hauteur
It would go a long way towards paying for it	cela couvrirait une bonne partie des frais

Explanations

cost breakdown   the division of the total cost of making or doing something into its component parts (*see* breakdown, Unit 15). For example, the cost of making a table could be broken down into materials, labour and overheads. If materials represented eighty per cent of the cost it would become obvious that a reduction in labour costs would not have a significant effect on total cost.

day release   a system whereby a trainee may be released for a day a week from the firm where he is learning a trade or skill in order to study at another establishment such as a technical college.

grant   a sum of money given by an organisation, such as one of the Industrial Training Boards, to a particular firm (or person, as in the case of a university grant) The government gives grants of many kinds, especially in the field of education.

graph   a symbolic diagram expressing a system of mathematical connections between various quantities.

incentive	something that encourages a particular activity, e.g. more money for greater output is to many people an incentive to work harder.
levy	a tax.
nominal wage	a small wage, one very much below the normal wage, a token wage.
payroll	the total amount paid out by a firm in salaries and wages.
qualify	here, to have reached the required standard in order to begin to practise a job or profession.
restrictive practices	any activity which hinders (holds up *or* stops) maximum production. For example, the insistence by a trade union that only a certain group of employees may be used for a particular job, which does not normally require skill, might be considered by the management as a 'restrictive practice'.
Training Boards	authorities set up by the government to administer and encourage all types of training programmes in industry.
training facilities	a facility is anything which makes it possible or easier to do something. A training workshop is a training facility. A factory football field would be a recreational facility.
wage rate	the amount of wages per hour or per week : or, by another system, the amount calculated according to output, (production).
wall chart	a diagram for display on a wall which shows some aspect of a business (e.g. a chart might indicate weekly output by means of a graph).

Pronunciation

1 — 1 - (- -) annual, benefit, complex, enterprise, nominal, operative, object, payroll, syllabus, technical, vacancy

   - 2 (- - -) advantage, affect, apprentice, appreciate, appropriate, arrangement, assume, award, concern, consult, develop, encourage, establish, expect, extort, facilities, finance, imagine, incentive, include, occur, opinion, propose, relate, release, respect, restrictive, surprise

   - - 3 (-) engineering, comprehensive, university

2 — [θ] thing, think, thought, through, path, method
   [ð] this, within, without, though, therefore, whether
   [s] release, insist, consider, syllabus, purpose, premises, promise, adhesive
   [z] tradesman, enterprise, means, organisation
   [ei] trade, train, wage, labour, waste
   [e] method, levy, measure, benefit, any
   [ɔ] object, (noun) offer, involve, promise, operative
   [ə:] earn, learn, firm, terms, serve, workshop, purpose

3 — Compare : 'object, 'subject ; ob'jective, sub'jective ; to ob'ject
   apprentice [ə'prentis], apprenticeship [ə'prentiʃip]
   to examine [ig'zæmin], examination [ig,zæmi'neiʃən]
   to argue ['a:gju:], an argument ['a:gjumənt]
   to refer [ri'fə:], a reference ['ref(ə)rəns]
   a 'benefit ; be'nefic ; 'benefice ; ,bene'ficial ; ,bene'ficiary

4 — Note : adhesive [əd'hi:siv], college ['kɔlidʒ], feature ['fi:tʃə], guilty ['gilti], persuade [pə'sweid], premises ['premisiz], re-distributed ['ri:-dis'tribjutid], standard ['stændəd], separate (adj.) ['seprit].

2. SUMMARY

A recent Government Act established a number of Training Boards for different industry groups. Every firm comes under a Board: Harper & Grant come under the Engineering Board. The object of the Act is to improve the amount and standard of all types of training, so that industry in Britain will have people with the right sort of skills.   5

Each Board charges a levy on its members to finance its schemes, in this case two and a half per cent of the total annual payroll. The money is then redistributed to help pay for all types of training within the industry, including William Buckhurst's recent course. A firm therefore has an incentive, an award to encourage it to develop good training schemes and 10 get back the money paid into the training board.

A good example of the improvement in training facilities is one which concerns *apprentices*, young people who learn a particular trade while working. They get a nominal wage while serving their apprenticeship. Until recently, when an apprentice had served his time he was automati- 15

cally considered to be a qualified tradesman and could earn the appropriate wage rate for skilled men. Now the Boards insist on the apprentices following a specially planned course with a syllabus. They must take a test, or examination, before they can qualify. All craft apprentices must have one day off a week, called day release, to attend a course at a techni- 20
cal college, which relates to the practical work they do in the workshop.

The larger a firm, the more complex and comprehensive its arrangements tend to be for in-company training of management in modern techniques. In some firms training of managers is done by sending them to courses run by various colleges and consulting organisations. Most firms 25
are prepared to take on students who are on *sandwich courses*. These are courses, including such subjects as Export Marketing and Management Accountancy, run by the newer universities and some technical colleges. The student normally spends two years in college, followed by one year's practical experience working in a company, ending up with another year 30
in college and his final exams. (See Unit 11.)

Today, Peter Wiles goes along to the Personnel Manager's office because he has heard that Ian Hampden has put up a new kind of wall chart and graph. These are very easy to use because they have plastic markers on adhesive strips which can be peeled off and stuck on again 35
without leaving a mark. These graphs are used to chart, or measure, many things, for example, the labour turnover in each department. Peter wants to be able to show a *work flow* diagram, that is, a plan of the movement of items in the process of being manufactured.

While in the Personnel Office, Ian asks Peter for his opinion about the 40
suggestion that Harper & Grant should have their own apprentices' workshop. Peter thinks Ian has not a hope of persuading Hector Grant to spend money on a scheme like this. But Ian feels deeply about the subject of training and later, to his surprise, finds that he has got his own way.

PART 2 : CONVERSATION AND DOCUMENTS

1. CONVERSATION

(Recorded Text)

IAN HAMPDEN **O.K., Peter, I'll send you some charts like these if you'd like them. They're very easy to use.**

PETER WILES	Thanks, Ian. These wall charts are just what I need.
IAN	Don't go for a moment. I'd like your advice.
PETER	What's the problem? 5
IAN	It's the apprentices' workshop. I'm seeing H.G. this afternoon. He's given me half an hour to convince him that we need a workshop of our own for training purposes.
PETER	I bet you won't do it!
IAN	Thanks for the encouragement. I'll take your bet, though. 10 Five pounds if I persuade H.G.? I need an incentive.
PETER	Done! Though I must say, this is one bet I hope I lose. The present training method is primitive. And we can get any money we spend on the workshop from the Engineering Board, can't we? Won't they give an outright 15 cash grant for training facilities like this?
IAN	Yes. We pay a levy of two and a half per cent of our annual payroll by law, and we aren't taking advantage of the benefits it offers. That'll be my chief argument.
PETER	You'd better get your sums right. You know H.G. sees 20 everything in terms of figures. His dreams are probably in figures!
IAN	I expect you're right.

(*Ian goes along for his interview with Hector Grant*)

HECTOR GRANT	Well, Ian, what do you want?
IAN	Er . . . The training programme. We . . . er . . . 25
GRANT	I thought that we'd agreed to discuss it tomorrow?
IAN	Er . . . no. Three o'clock today.
GRANT	Oh, very well then. Though I can't say I'm in the mood for any discussions. I've just had an awful lunch with Alfred Wentworth. He will insist on telling me how to run 30 my own business.
IAN	I'm sorry, H.G. I . . . er . . .
GRANT	Well, don't let's waste time. What is it you wanted to see me about?
IAN	I think we really need to rethink our entire training pro- 35 gramme. In my opinion, our present apprentice training system is inefficient and wasteful.

IAN: 'They are trained on the shop floor, when and where the foreman and skilled operatives can spare the time.'

GRANT	What's wrong with it?
IAN	It's unplanned. Each year we take on a couple of tool-maker or sheet-metal worker apprentices. They are 40 trained on the shop floor, when and where the foreman and skilled operatives can spare the time. Of course, we try to keep them busy, but inevitably while they are learning they make mistakes. The quality of their work is not up to standard. We lose time and material. And the 45 apprentices aren't efficiently trained.
GRANT	They also go to the local technical college for training, don't they?
IAN	Yes, they do. By the rules of the national scheme we have to release them one day a week to attend courses, and 50 those link up with the practical work they do with us. This wouldn't be affected by what I am proposing. What I propose has to do with our training programme, here, on the premises.
GRANT	Well, what do you propose? 55
IAN	Well, I ... er ... I think we need a separate apprentices' workshop with full-time instructors.
GRANT	That's out of the question. It would cost far too much.

IAN	Are we right in assuming that? We should save on time. The training would be concentrated; we'd cut out the waste of time and material on the shop floor....
GRANT	Have you thought of what it would involve, setting up and equipping such a workshop? It's out of the question.
IAN	Yes, but you know we can get a grant from the Engineering Board?
GRANT	Of course I know that! But what kind of grant is it going to be? Do you really imagine it would be enough to cover such a scheme as yours?
IAN	Not completely, no. But it would go a long way towards paying for it. The Board make outright cash grants for new training facilities of this kind.
GRANT	I know damned well it wouldn't be enough! Well now, look, I'm rather busy now. If that's all ...
IAN	With due respect, H.G., it isn't all. I don't think you have given this very serious matter enough of your attention.
GRANT	Oh, indeed?
IAN	I consider this to be a matter absolutely vital to the future of the firm. The purpose of the Government in setting up this scheme, and extorting the cash from industry to run it, was to give us the incentive to get most of it back by good up-to-date training. In my view they were completely right, and any firm that doesn't take advantage of it is guilty of restrictive practices.
GRANT	These are very strong words, Ian.
IAN	I mean what I say. And I've done quite a detailed costing. I think we've a chance of getting a good three-quarters of the money we'd need from the Board. The remaining twenty-five per cent would be more than made up by the savings effected by not having apprentices on the shop floor.
GRANT	I see. Well, Ian, I must say you have put your case with ... er ... vigour. Well, I suppose I must give your proposal a little more thought. Yes ... er ... leave me your cost breakdown. I don't promise anything, but I'll look into it.
IAN	Thank you, H.G. I hoped you would.

60

65

70

75

80

85

90

95

(*Later on, Ian sees Peter*)

IAN	Oh, Peter, did you get those wall charts you wanted?
PETER	Yes, I did, thanks. Now we've got the great job of redoing all the production charts and the work flow diagram. Marvellous fun. By the way, here you are. Five lovely 100 pounds, dear boy. I'm forced to hand them over.
IAN	Why, what's this?
PETER	H.G. had me in this morning and told me a lot of stuff about how all modern firms were determined to improve the quality and quantity of their training. How did you do 105 it?

PRACTICE SENTENCES

Say the practice sentences on the record :

i We pay a levy of two and a half per cent of our annual payroll.

ii We need to rethink our entire training programme.

iii We need a separate apprentices' workshop with full-time instructors.

iv The Engineering Board makes cash grants for new training facilities.

v The remaining twenty-five per cent would be more than made up by the savings effected.

vi I don't think you've given this very serious matter enough of your attention.

2. DOCUMENTS

APPLYING FOR A GRANT

As soon as Mr. Grant gave his permission, Ian Hampden wrote to the District Office of the Engineering Training Board.

Harper and Grant Limited

Great West Road
London W25
Telephone 01-567 1112
Telex 80153
Telegrams Harp LDN

Directors:
Hector Grant (*Chairman & Managing Director*)
William Buckhurst FCA (*Secretary*)
John Martin
Alfred Wentworth
Margaret Wiles
Peter Wiles

                                              3rd October, 197..

Dear Sirs,

          As you know, we are a limited liability company
manufacturing and marketing office furniture. We employ about
five hundred people and contributed in the last year £16,000 in
levies to the Training Board. We are at present considering a
further development of our training scheme, the major feature of
which would be the setting up of a separate apprentices' workshop.

          Would you please advise how to apply for a grant towards
such an enterprise and the conditions which you would require.

                                   Yours faithfully,

                                   Ian Hampden
                                   Personnel Manager
                                   HARPER & GRANT LTD.

Applying for a Job

Here is a letter which Ian Hampden received on the same day:

                                        The Firs,
                                        Long Lane,
                                        Bickley,   Surrey.

The Personnel Manager,
Harper & Grant Ltd.,
Great West Road,
London, W.25.   1st October, 197..

Dear Sir,

          I am writing to ask you if you have a vacancy on your staff
for an assistant accountant.

          I am twenty-two years of age and have been working in the
costing department of the Bedford Furnishing Company, Bedford House,
London, E.C.1., for the past two years. I am studying Accountancy
and Business Management at the Polytechnic and wish to complete my
course there, which has another two years to run.

          The only reason for my seeking new employment is that Bedford
Furnishing is moving shortly to a development area in the north-west,
where its main works is already located.

          If there is some chance of a vacancy occurring in the near
future, I would greatly appreciate being given an interview. My
present employers would gladly give a reference.

                                   Yours faithfully,

                                   Simon Deeds.

PART 3 : NOTES AND PRACTICE

1. RAPPEL GRAMMATICAL

Summary :

18. Ici, le gérondif est entièrement traité comme verbe : il est précédé d'un *sujet* (non d'un possesseur au cas possessif) et suivi d'un *complément* d'objet.

22. **The larger a firm, the more complex its arrangements...** La variation parallèle (ou inverse) se forme à l'aide du comparatif précédé de **the**, qui est ici adverbe. Il faut noter la construction, où l'adjectif est en tête de chaque proposition :

The better I know Joanna, the more I appreciate her skill as an Advertising Manager	Mieux je connais Joanna, plus j'apprécie sa compétence comme chef de publicité
The older the boss gets, the less aware he is of these requirements	Plus le patron vieillit, moins il est conscient de ces besoins
The sooner the better	Le plus tôt sera le mieux

28. **The newer universities.** Le comparatif s'emploie en anglais lorsqu'il y a comparaison implicite. Les universités nouvelles ne sont nouvelles que comparativement à d'autres plus anciennes, qui du même coup sont elles mêmes **the older** universities.

29. Notons le possessif avec l'appréciation de temps : **one year's experience**

39. **Being manufactured.** Comparons le passif progressif avec la simple construction be + participe passé :

They are being manufactured	On est en train de les fabriquer
They are manufactured	Ils sont fabriqués (*c'est fait*)

Conversation :

4. **Advice.** Advice est un nom de sens collectif, qui s'accorde au singulier. De même : **information**, des renseignements, et souvent : **progress**, des progrès, **knowledge**, des connaissances. On dira :

I gave him a piece of advice   je lui ai donné *un* conseil

6. **I'm seeing H. G. this afternoon.** La forme progressive a une valeur de futur proche. **See** n'est pas ici le verbe de perception *voir* - on sait que les verbes de perception, **see, hear, feel,** ne se rencontrent pas à la forme progressive - mais à la valeur du verbe **meet,** *rencontrer.*

8. **Need**, on se le rappelle, peut être un verbe ordinaire ou un modal (défectif). Revoyons ses valeurs à l'aide de quelques petits exemples simples :

H. G. needed the money badly	H. G. avait un besoin terrible de l'argent
We don't need such a workshop, do we ?	Nous n'avons pas besoin d'un semblable atelier, si ?
You needn't worry, Mr. Hampden, you'll have your workshop	Il n'y a pas lieu de vous en faire Mr. Hampden, vous aurez votre atelier
You needn't have seen him after I'd given him my report	Il n'y avait pas lieu que vous le voyiez après que je lui ai eu remis mon rapport
Need you see him now ?	Faut-il que vous le voyez maintenant ?
That's all that need be said **That's all that needs to be said**	C'est tout ce qu'il y a à dire

Lorsque **need** a un nom complément, il ne peut être employé que comme un verbe ordinaire (-s à la 3e personne du singulier du présent de l'indicatif, **do** à l'interrogative et à la négative, tous les temps). Lorsqu'il a pour complément un verbe, on peut peut-être constater que :

— il s'emploie comme *verbe ordinaire* s'il y a une *idée de besoin associée avec le sujet*

— il s'emploie comme *défectif* lorsqu'il y a une *idée de besoin associée avec les circonstances*. Ainsi :

John doesn't need to be told	John n'a pas besoin qu'on lui en parle (il est déjà au courant)
We needn't tell him	Il n'y a pas lieu de lui en parler
Ian didn't need to be reminded of it	Ian n'avait pas besoin qu'on le lui rappelle (il y pensait)

La forme modale (=défective) **need** s'emploie sans changement avec une valeur de passé dans une subordonnée régie par une principale au passé :

I assured Ian that he needn't worry about the scheme	J'ai assuré Ian qu'il n'avait pas lieu de s'inquiéter à propos du projet

30. **He will insist on telling me how to run my business. Will** n'est nullement ici auxiliaire du futur. Il exprime une attitude du sujet qui est réprouvée dans le contexte :

He will meddle with things that don't concern him at all	Il faut toujours qu'il se mêle de choses qui ne le regardent absolument pas

43. **Try.** Rappelons :

I'll try to back you up, Ian	J'essayerai de vous soutenir, Ian

Ici, **try** est suivi de **to**, ce qui donne le sens de *s'efforcer de, tenter de*. **Try** +
gérondif donne une idée d'*essayer à titre d'expérience*. Comparer :

I tried writing to Gorgondale, but he didn't reply	J'ai essayé d'écrire à Gorgondale, mais il n'a pas répondu
I tried to write my report at the office, but there was too much noise	J'ai essayé d'écrire mon rapport au bureau, mais il y avait trop de bruit

Dans le premier cas, la lettre est bien partie, mais c'est une expérience
qui a échoué. Dans le second cas, le rapport n'a pas été écrit.

86. A good three quarters. Il n'y a pas à être surpris de rencontrer cet
article singulier avec un pluriel. **Three quarters** est considéré comme une
quantité, un tout neutre, et non pas une somme de plusieurs éléments
considérés isolément. Ainsi :

You'll have to wait another three months	Il va falloir que vous attendiez encore trois mois
I made a nice £500 out of it.	Cela m'a rapporté la coquette somme de £500.

Documents :

Reason peut se construire comme ici (**the reason for my seeking...**) ou bien :

The reason why I am seeking new employment	La raison pour laquelle je cherche un nouvel emploi

2. EXERCISES

EXERCISE 1. — Turn into the plural whenever possible :

1. He considers buying our equipment. 2. A shop steward draws no
salary from his union. 3. This domestic appliance is imported from
Japan. 4. Each case has to be examined on its merits. 5. The employer
earns a bigger profit. 6. Each firm pays a 2.5 % levy on its payroll.
7. Such a price is likely to involve a capital loss. 8. The country is lacking
in heavy industry. 9. Does he want the technical information straight
away ? 10. He aims at protecting himself against price fluctuation of
this commodity. 11. He's lucky he hasn't been made redundant.

EXERCISE 2. — Turn into the singular whenever possible :

1. Do they know of these techniques ? 2. Those systems are not necessarily more satisfactory. 3. Explanations have been given by American
economists. 4. The confidential designs were not to be found in the files
on your desk. 5. What do these figures on the chart indicate ? 6. These
techniques offer few economic advantages. 7. The taxes are being levied
at all stages of the manufacture. 8. New discoveries have revolutionised
those techniques. 9. Are there any specific measures we could adopt as
regards redundancies ? 10. They want to pay for the reservations in
advance, don't they ? 11. The shipping companies are making heavy
losses on these routes.

EXERCISE 3. — Turn into the passive :

1. They are building these models in their Belgian subsidiary. 2. They are considering the Secretary's proposals. 3. They are manufacturing these items in Italy under licence. 4. Are they launching a campaign for their new detergent ? 5. Are they changing the commission scheme for their reps ? 6. We are narrowing the gap between America and ourselves. 7. They are introducing a lot of managerial innovations.

EXERCISE 4. — Change as follows :

When a firm is large, its arrangements for training are complex →
the larger a firm, the more complex its arrangements for training

1. If you buy a great quantity, the discount is large. 2. If the number of sales is great, the profit will be high. 3. If we achieve a great number of sales, we can afford a narrow margin. 4. If competition is intense, the need for research is great. 5. If we have few stocks, we'll have little trouble. 6. If you do it slowly, it will work well. 7. If the depression is deep, it will be bad for agriculture. 8. If the firm grows big, the problems of running it are complex. 9. If we have few shopwalkers, shoplifting will become dramatic. 10. If the industry is big, it can operate efficiently.

EXERCISE 5. — Change as follows, choosing the right form for the present (either simple or continuous present) :

a. **this is the reason for my seeking new employment** →
        this is the reason why I'm seeking new employment
b. **this was the reason for my seeking employment** →
        this is the reason why I sought employment

1. This is the reason for Mr. Hampden's wanting an apprentices' workshop. 2. This was the reason for the government's establishing Training Boards. 3. This was the reason for John's costing all the expenditures. 4. This is the reason for her inserting an advertisement in the trade press. 5. This was the reason for our sending the goods per passenger train. 6. This is the reason for the apprentices wasting so much time. 7. This was the reason for the firm's losing so much money. 8. This was the reason for my giving them a day off. 9. This was the reason for the service costing so much.

EXERCISE 6. — Change as follows :

a. **the City won't lose its place in world finance** →
        there's no reason why the City should lose its place...
b. **the City didn't lose its place in world finance** →
        there's no reason why the City should have lost its place...

1. I won't register the letter. 2. The goods weren't delivered so late. 3. They won't buy lorries for the Transport Department. 4. The General Manager won't make a fuss about it. 5. There weren't very heavy duties on office equipment. 6. I didn't write my report during the week-end. 7. The Board won't examine such problems.

EXERCISE 7. — Change as follows :
a. **I shan't register the letter** → **there's no reason why I should register the letter**
b. **I'll find a solution** → **there's no reason why I shouldn't find a solution**

1. He'll show you round the shops.   2. He won't send them an apology.
3. The firm will have its own workshop.   4. We'll do the servicing on the premises.   5. We shan't employ a man with such references.   6. The tool-makers won't work overtime.   7. You'll see their agent about it.
8. I shan't be moved to another area.   9. We'll get some of our money back.   10. We'll have those wall charts in our office as well.

EXERCISE 8. — Here are some questions on the apprenticeship system in Britain. Please answer with complete sentences.

1. What is an apprentice ?   2. Are apprentices paid during their apprenticeship ?   3. What condition must the modern engineering apprentice fulfil, in contrast with his predecessors ?   4. What is day release?

EXERCISE 9. — And now some on Training Boards :

1. How were Training Boards set up in Britain ?   2. What kind of Board would Harper & Grant belong to ?   3. What is the responsibility of these Boards ?   4. How are these Boards financed ?

EXERCISE 10. — Here is a longer exercise. To answer it, look back at the episode, or listen to it again on the record.

Summarise Ian Hampden's arguments for persuading Hector Grant to start an apprentices' workshop (give a numbered list of points).

EXERCISE 11. — Translate into English :

1. Nous payons une taxe de 2,50 % sur l'ensemble des salaires annuels.
2. Il faut que nous repensions tout notre programme de formation professionnelle.   3. Nous avons besoin d'un atelier d'apprentissage avec des moniteurs à plein temps.   4. La Commission des Industries mécaniques accorde des subventions pour de nouvelles installations de formation professionnelle.   5. Les 25 % qui restent seraient plus que couverts par les économies effectuées.   6. Je ne crois pas que vous ayez prêté assez de votre attention à cette grave question.   7. Ils ont un poste libre dans leur personnel pour un aide-comptable.   8. Je vous serais très obligé si vous acceptiez de m'accorder un entretien.   9. Mes employeurs se feraient un plaisir de témoigner pour moi.   10. Je dois dire qu'il a exposé son problème avec force.   11. Je ne vous promets rien, mais j'étudierai la question.   12. Toutes les entreprises modernes sont résolues à améliorer la formation professionnelle qualitativement et quantitativement.   13. Cela couvrirait une bonne partie de nos frais.   14. Vous admettrez que ce sont des entraves à la liberté du travail.   15. Il n'en est pas question, cela coûterait bien trop cher !   16. Avez-vous réfléchi à ce que cela impliquerait d'installer cet atelier ?   17. Nous perdons du temps à former nos apprentis sur le tas.   18. La qualité de leur travail n'est pas ce qu'il faudrait.   19. L'étudiant suit un cours théorique avec stage intégré.
20. J'ai un jour de congé hebdomadaire pour suivre des cours à l'université.

UNIT 21

DEBTORS AND CREDITORS

PART 1 : INTRODUCTION

1. WORD STUDY

Vocabulary

accordingly en conséquence
amazing surprenant
bookshop librairie
chase up poursuivre
chap type, gars
collect recouvrer
debt dette, créance
  bad debt créance douteuse
  debt collector agent de
    recouvrement
debtor débiteur
default faire défaut
defer ajourner, différer
discount rabais, escompte
drive campagne, effort
drastic énergique
due dû, échu
graded gradué ; progressif (*ou*
  dégressif)
inducement encouragement
insolvent insolvable

keep up to se tenir à
nearby non loin de
notice remarquer
outstanding arriéré, en souffrance
overdue en retard, arriéré
quota contingent
receipt reçu
retail business commerce de détail
rumour bruit qui court
salary scheme système de
  rémunérations
serial number numéro de série
slightly légèrement
supplement compléter, ajouter à
supply fournir
third party tiers
terms conditions
trainee stagiaire
wholesale business commerce de
  gros
within en moins de (*temps*)

Phrases

It is done on a cash basis	il se fait au comptant
It is done on credit	il se fait à crédit
To use legal pressure	recourir à la loi
They've gone bankrupt	ils ont fait faillite
It will work out better	cela marchera mieux
They've been done out of payment	ils ont été refaits

Explanations and Notes

bankrupt	a business, or a person is said to go bankrupt when it or he cannot continue trading through lack of funds. A firm is declared bankrupt and an official **receiver** takes charge of any remaining assets. Creditors are sometimes paid a proportion of the money owing to them when the firm's affairs are finally settled.
basic salary	(salary ; see Unit 12). Here, salary without commission ; or salary without extra payment for special work, overtime, etc.
credit	to give credit is to give a time allowance before payment is due. — **long credit**, *or* **long-term credit** : bills need not be paid for a certain period of time. — **short credit**, *or* **short-term credit** : bills must be paid very soon after receipt of goods.
debt collector	a professional who collects debts on a commission basis.
defer payment	to put off, postpone, paying until later.
default	fail to perform a duty, or, as here, fail to pay a debt.
insolvent	without sufficient funds to continue doing business.
outstanding accounts	money which has been owed to a firm, or a person, for a long time.
retail	trade between supplier and customer.
serial number	a number forming a series, for classification purposes.
wholesale	trade between manufacturer and supplier or retailer.

Pronunciation

1 — 1 - (- -) agency, common, creditor, difficult, interest, legal, recognise, reference, retail, salary, supplement

- 2 (- -) address, affair, accordingly, amazing, collect, collector, decide, default, defer, dishonest, explain, inform, insolvent, original, outstanding, prefer, present, pretend, professional, receive, receipt, reply, research, today, trainee

- - 3 (-) individual, reputation, conversation, recommend

2 — *w is not pronounced in :* who, whom, whose, whole, wholesale, answer
[s]   chase, case, basis, basic, disagree, dishonest, research
[ŋ]   long, bring, collecting, studying
[ŋk]   bank, thank, link, think
[r]   really, region, salary, different, reference, interest, operate, area, grant, growth, credit, pressure, graded, strange
[ou]   owe, show, low, know, notice, wholesale, overdue
[au]   pound, south, count, account, discount, amount

3 — finance [fai'næns],   financial [fai'nænʃəl, fi'nænʃəl]
retail (n.) ['ri:teil] (v.) [ri:'teil],   retailer [ri:'teilə]
a supplement ['sʌpləmənt],   to supplement ['sʌpliment]

4 — cp. to defer [di'fə:], to differ ['difə]

5 — Note : debt [det], default [di'fɔ:lt], quota ['kwoutə], region ['ri:dʒən], rumour ['ru:mə], serial ['siərjəl], several ['sevrəl].

2. SUMMARY

We are back in the Accounts Department today. Christopher Thorn, the Management Trainee, is studying the work in the Accounts Department. Mr. Buckhurst, the Chief Accountant, has decided to chase up some *bad debts*, that is, money which has been owing to the firm for a long time. Collecting bad debts is often a difficult affair. Retail business is usually ⁅5⁆ done on a cash basis, and wholesale business is done on credit. Harper & Grant mainly do business on wholesale terms: they have to give credit, that is, shops or stores can have the goods they want and defer payment. But credit is usually only given for thirty days. For each individual sale an invoice is sent to the customer, that is a list of the goods delivered and the ⁅10⁆ amount due, owed, on that particular transaction. At the end of the month each customer is sent an account, which shows the total amount due.

Any company likes to receive long credit from its suppliers and would like to give short credit to its customers. It is fairly common to offer an inducement to customers to pay earlier than they need by offering a small 15 discount; that is, the customer pays slightly less if he pays within, say, ten days of the date of invoice.

Sometimes, of course, a debtor cannot pay; for example, it may happen that a firm never gets its money because another firm whom they supplied with goods has become insolvent. In some cases a firm does not pay 20 because the people who run it are dishonest.

Accounts not paid in time are called overdue accounts. Very often a sales representative has to call and collect the money or make enquiries. Sometimes, in very difficult cases, a firm employs a professional debt collector. No company wants to get a reputation for being a bad payer. It 25 may then be difficult to get supplies on credit. There are agencies which will give information about the financial situation of almost any company, so that suppliers can judge whether they are a good credit risk. Many buyers will suggest that a supplier writes to their bank for a reference.

Luckily, Harper & Grant always mark their goods with a serial 30 number. Some firms do this, others do not. In this case, it turns out to be very useful indeed.

PART 2 : CONVERSATION AND DOCUMENTS

1. CONVERSATION

(Recorded Text)

(*In the Accounts Department*)

CHRISTOPHER THORN	**Good morning, Mr. Buckhurst.**
WILLIAM BUCKHURST	**Morning. We've got a drive on today to try and get payment on one or two of these long outstanding accounts.**
THORN	**Yes, I noticed yesterday that there were several bad debts. I thought we only gave credit for thirty days?** 5
BUCKHURST	**Yes, that's correct. It's supposed to mean that payment may be deferred until the end of the month following that**

	in which the goods were delivered. But ... er .. look at this! This retailer, Bush & Green, has owed us seven hundred pounds for office furniture for over nine months. 10
THORN	How often do you send out the accounts?
BUCKHURST	At the end of every month. Really we must do something drastic about this lot. There's a great deal of money owing to us on these overdue accounts. We don't want any of them to default. I think I'll get our rep. in the north on to 15 this one. You know Mr. Shuttleworth? That's his area.
THORN	I thought there was a rumour that Mr. Shuttleworth was going to a different region?
BUCKHURST	Yes, he's going to the south-west, but he doesn't know it yet. 20
THORN	About those debts. Can't we put a professional debt collector on to collect some of them?
BUCKHURST	Yes, we can. But I'm against doing that until we've done everything we can do ourselves to get the money. To bring in a third party, or to use legal pressure, is a sure way to 25 lose a customer.
THORN	I see a couple of rather strong letters have been sent to this firm with no reply. Have they gone bankrupt ?
BUCKHURST	I hope not. H'm. I'll get Shuttleworth on to that one right away. What time is it? Nine o'clock. He may not have left 30 home yet. I'll ring him at once.

(*A week later Mr. Shuttleworth is in London. He goes to see Mr. Buckhurst in his office*)

BUCKHURST	Come along in, Mr. Shuttleworth. Have you seen Mr. Martin yet?
SHUTTLEWORTH	Yes, I have, Mr. Buckhurst. He's just told me about my new area. He told me to come and see you about the new 35 salary scheme.
BUCKHURST	Did he explain it to you?
SHUTTLEWORTH	Not really.
BUCKHURST	Well, as you know, our representatives have up till now been paid a basic salary supplemented by a commission 40 on sales. The new system will be a graded salary based on sales quotas.
SHUTTLEWORTH	What really interests me is whether I shall earn more money or less!

BUCKHURST	I think you'll find it will work out better. All the districts 45 have been carefully researched and an estimate has been made of the probable volume of sales and your salary graded accordingly. All you've got to do is to keep up to the quota, or better, surpass it. But in simple terms, it means that you can count on a much higher basic salary. 50
SHUTTLEWORTH	I see.
BUCKHURST	We're gradually introducing this system, and we find that the reps. prefer it. What do you feel about going to the south-west?
SHUTTLEWORTH	Oh, I'm very pleased. I think it's about time I had a new 55 area.
BUCKHURST	You did very well about that matter of the bad debt. We didn't even know that Bush & Green had moved. How did you find out what had happened?
SHUTTLEWORTH	Oh, an amazing bit of luck, really. I made enquiries about 60 Bush & Green in several shops near their old address. There's a café at that address now. I suspected the people who run the café, because they acted strangely when I asked them what they did with any letters that came for Bush & Green. The chap hesitated quite a long time 65 before he said that he sent them all back to the Post Office. I was sure he was lying.
BUCKHURST	What was the bit of luck?
SHUTTLEWORTH	Well, I thought I'd try one more place, and I got into conversation with the chap who owns the bookshop next 70 door. While I was talking to him I noticed his office door was open, and inside I could see what looked very like one of our filing cabinets. He said he'd bought it in Wilminster, that's a little market town near by. Well, I took the serial number and I telephoned to Mr. Martin. 75 He checked that it was one of the filing cabinets we'd supplied to Bush & Green. Then I got the bookshop owner to give me his receipt. He'd bought the cabinet from a firm who called themselves Windel & Riddel. Windel & Riddel indeed! Huh! 80
BUCKHURST	What did you do next? You realise, of course, that Bush & Green might have sold the cabinet first to this firm?
SHUTTLEWORTH	I didn't think so. I was sure it was the same people operating under a different name.

BUCKHURST	Did you go and see them?	85
SHUTTLEWORTH	I certainly did. And I presented our bill to them. They pretended they didn't know anything about it. But then the boss came in, and he recognised me. I'd taken the order from him originally. He went at once to write out the cheque, and he asked me to keep quiet about it. What do you think we ought to do?	90
BUCKHURST	Well, we've got our cheque, but there are probably a lot of other people who have been done out of payment in the same way. I think it's our duty to inform the police. And ... er ... Shuttleworth, we must take more care in the future before we recommend supplying on credit.	95

SHUTTLEWORTH: '. . . I got into conversation with the chap who owns the bookshop next door.'

PRACTICE SENTENCES

Say the practice sentences on the record :

i We send out the accounts at the end of every month.

ii There's a great deal of money owing to us on these overdue accounts.

iii We don't want any of them to default.

iv Some rather strong letters have been sent to this firm.

v Have they gone bankrupt?

2. DEMANDS FOR PAYMENT

Another of Harper & Grant's bad debts was a firm called Crosby & Turner Ltd. Here are three letters which were sent to them at different times, each one a little sterner than the last.

Harper and Grant Limited

Great West Road
London W25
Telephone 01-567 1112
Telex 80153
Telegrams Harp LDN

Directors:
Hector Grant *(Chairman & Managing Director)*
William Buckhurst FCA *(Secretary)*
John Martin
Alfred Wentworth
Margaret Wiles
Peter Wiles

Crosby & Turner Ltd.,
114 Hedge Lane,
Willowhampton.

15th December, 197..

Dear Sirs,

We enclose a statement of account up to 30th November, from which you will see that you owe us £247 for goods delivered in October. As you will know, our conditions of sale stipulate payment as net thirty days.

An early settlement would be appreciated.

Yours faithfully,

Michael Williamson
for Chief Accountant
HARPER & GRANT LTD.

Crosby & Turner Ltd.,
114 Hedge Lane,
Willowhampton.

9th January, 197..

Dear Sirs,

      We have had no reply from you concerning the statement of
account sent on 15th December, and conclude that our letter of that
date must have gone astray.   We enclose a duplicate of our letter,
and statement to which we ask you to give your earliest attention.

Yours faithfully,

Michael Williamson
for Chief Accountant
HARPER & GRANT LTD.

Crosby & Turner Ltd.,
114 Hedge Lane,
Willowhampton.

3rd February, 197..

Dear Sirs,

      We have not yet received payment of your outstanding balance
of £247, neither have we received a written acknowledgement of our
letters of 15th December and 9th January.   On 20th January your
Chief Buyer, Mr. J. Hamilton, gave a verbal assurance to our salesman,
Mr. B.K. Higgins, that a cheque would be posted to us that day.

      We should like to draw your attention to the fact that you
have considerably exceeded the term of credit usually allowed.   We
must, therefore, insist on receiving payment by 10th February.
Failing this, we shall have no alternative but to refer the matter to
our solicitors.

Yours faithfully,

William Buckhurst
Company Secretary
HARPER & GRANT LTD.

PART 3 : NOTES AND PRACTICE

1. RAPPEL GRAMMATICAL

Summary :

4. **Owing.** Notons que cet adjectif employé comme attribut est la forme en -ing du verbe **owe.** *devoir*, employée avec un sens passif. Il ne faut pas dire **owed,** dans ce cas (forme verbale, participe passé), mais **owing.**

11. **The amount due.** Due est attribut (**the amount that is due**), d'où sa place après **amount.**

16. **Within.** Comparons cette préposition avec **by :**

It is to be paid within three months	C'est payable sous trois mois
It is to be paid by September 10th	C'est payable d'ici le 10 septembre

Conversation :

10. **Over nine months.** Variante : **more than nine months.**

43. **More money or less.** On suppose que le maniement des comparatifs est au point :

This is more efficient than in the past	C'est plus efficace qu'autrefois (*supériorité*)
It isn't so regular as it used to be	Ce n'est pas aussi régulier qu'autrefois (*égalité*)
They're less aggressive in their advertising now	Ils sont moins aggressifs dans leur publicité, désormais (*infériorité*)
Each letter was a little sterner than the previous one	Chaque lettre était un peu plus ferme que la précédente

Documents :

3e lettre. **Neither have we received.** Rappelons l'emploi de **either** et **neither :**

They haven't phoned ; neither have they written	Ils n'ont pas téléphoné ; pas plus qu'ils n'ont écrit
They haven't phoned ; and they haven't written either	Ils n'ont pas téléphoné ; et ils n'ont pas écrit non plus

L'emploi suivant est également connu :

He isn't rich ; neither am I	Il n'est pas riche, moi non plus

— 339 —

Comparer :

He is clever ; so is Shuttleworth   Il est habile ; Shuttleworth aussi

Bref rappel grammatical... Temps de plus pour pratiquer oralement les structures de cette unité.

2. EXERCISES

EXERCISE 1. — Put the right preposition :

1. It has been owing ... the firm for a long time.   2. He received a long-term credit ... his suppliers.   3. We'll have to pay ... ten days of the date of invoice.   4. They supplied the government ... office furniture. 5. They have a reputation ... being bad payers.   6. We got these articles ... credit.   7. I thought you gave credit ... 30 days.   8. Can't we put a professional debt collector ... collecting some of these debts ?   9. You can't count ... a much higher basic salary.

EXERCISE 2. — Use either **for** *or* **since** :

1. We haven't seen your rep ... the whole season.   2. It's money that has been owing to the firm ... a long time.   3. They'd been partners ... 1948. 4. They've owed us £700 ... over nine months.   5. The boss has been away ... Monday last.   6. He stayed in the Near East ... six years. 7. He's been on the Board ... I was elected myself.   8. We've been increasing our sales ... John joined the company.   9. They've been carrying out research ... two months.

EXERCISE 3. — Change as follows :

**Bush & Green have paid us (Crosby & Turner) →
Bush & Green have paid us ; so have Crosby & Turner**

1. Bush & Green owe us over £600 (Crosby & Turner).   2. Shuttleworth was working in the North (Ogden).   3. Lawson & Fraser may go bankrupt (String & Thomas).   4. Brent sent us his invoice (Cruttwell).   5. We'll send them a reminder (Wentworths).   6. We should inform the police about their dealings (you).

EXERCISE 4. — Change as follows :

**Bush & Green haven't paid us (Crosby & Turner) →
Bush & Green haven't paid us ; neither have Crosby & Turner**

1. These letters haven't been properly filed (those documents).   2. We can't do anything about this bad debt (a debt collector).   3. John didn't find out what had happened (the Chief Accountant).   4. We wouldn't give them a reference (the bank).   5. The Secretary won't recommend credit (1).   6. Your secretary isn't in my office (mine).

EXERCISE 5. — Change as follows :

Burns paid us (Turnbull) → **Burns paid us, so did Turnbull**

Wolfe hasn't paid us (Crawley) →
   Wolfe hasn't paid us, neither has Crawley

1. Richards didn't reply to our offer (Sumner).   2. The bank won't recommend credit to them (Andersons).   3. Elizabeth can use a tape-recorder (Sally).   4. We couldn't grant such a discount (our competitors).   5. We sold them office equipment (Windel & Riddle).   6. They'll present their bill to Charlton & Dudley (we).   7. Hector Grant mustn't be told about it (Peter Wiles).   8. The girls in the General Office would refuse to work so late (the chaps in the press-shop).

EXERCISE 6. — Change as follows :

They haven't come ; neither have they phoned →
   they haven't come ; and they haven't phoned either

1. They haven't sent the staples ; neither have they sent the staplers. 2. They haven't paid Harper & Grant ; neither have they paid Wentworths. 3. That Thomson bill hasn't been paid ; neither has Riddett's invoice. 4. I won't work overtime ; neither will Jack Green.   5. I didn't see the Managing Director ; neither have I seen their buyer.   6. I didn't lose any money ; neither did I make any profit.   7. He didn't surpass his quotas ; neither did he keep up to them.

EXERCISE 7. — Ask questions as suggested here :

We ought to see a debt collector (*what*) →
   what do you think we ought to do ?

1. He bought the duplicator in Wilminster (*where*).   2. He'll send them a strong reminder (*what*).   3. They owe us over £600 (*how much*).   4. They'll deliver the goods by November 20th (*when*).   5. He went to see the Personnel Manager concerning the clocking in (*what ... for*).   6. John Martin bought the remaining 50 shares (*who*).

EXERCISE 8. — Change as follows :

He gave me his receipt → **I got him to give me his receipt**

1. He saw a firm of consultants about it.   2. The Sales Manager made a speech.   3. He had the old shed pulled down.   4. He wrote a memo about safety measures.   5. He introduced this new graded salary scheme. 6. She went to see the boss about it.

EXERCISE 9. — *Change the sentence without changing the meaning as follows* :

In our firm, engineering is unfortunately more important than marketing →
in our firm, marketing is unfortunately not so important as engineering

1. The mail order system is more popular in the USA than in Britain.
2. TV advertising is noisier in the USA than in Britain. 3. It's easier to stop a recession than an inflation. 4. Coal is more important in this region than textiles. 5. The consumer demand for durables is higher than 10 years ago. 6. Your figures are more reliable than the accountant's.
7. Our furniture is better than that of our competitors.

EXERCISE 10. — *Complete the following sentences* :

1. A firm which cannot pay its debts may have to be declared ... 2. Bills which have not been paid for a period over the usual thirty days are called ... 3. A firm may write to someone who owes them money asking for ... of the account. 4. The money earned by an employee, before extras such as overtime, increments, etc. are added, is called a ... 5. Many firms mark their goods with a ...

EXERCISE 11. — *Translate into English* :

1. Nous envoyons les relevés de comptes à la fin de chaque mois. 2. On nous doit beaucoup d'argent dans ces arriérés. 3. Nous ne voulons pas qu'aucun d'entre eux fasse défaut. 4. On a envoyé certaines lettres énergiques à cette entreprise. 5. Ont-ils fait faillite ? 6. Le paiement doit être effectué avant la fin du mois. 7. On envoie toujours une facture avec les marchandises. 8. On peut parfois recouvrer des créances douteuses en menaçant de poursuites. 9. On peut ajourner le paiement à la fin de mois. 10. Nous n'avons pas reçu d'accusé de réception de notre lettre du 9 janvier. 11. Nous voudrions attirer votre attention sur le fait que vous avez largement dépassé les délais de paiement habituellement accordés. 12. Nous n'aurons pas d'autre solution que de mettre l'affaire entre les mains de notre contentieux. 13. C'est une chance que j'aie pu retrouver le numéro de série. 14. Est-ce que cela vous plaît d'aller dans un autre secteur ? 15. Je ne suis pas partisan de recourir à un tiers. 16. On les payait jusqu'ici sur la base d'un fixe auquel s'ajoutait une commission sur les ventes. 17. C'est le meilleur moyen de perdre un bon client. 18. Nous devons faire quelque chose d'énergique à propos de ces créances douteuses. 19. Ils auront du mal à trouver des fournitures à crédit. 20. L'agence pourra vous renseigner sur la solvabilité de Thurloe & Marvell.

UNIT 22

PATENTS AND TRADE - MARKS

PART 1 : INTRODUCTION

1. WORD STUDY

Vocabulary

apply for faire une demande
authority autorité, autorisation
average moyenne
box file classeur, boîtier
break into the market pénétrer sur le marché
carry out effectuer
clip agrafe, fermoir
come up with réaliser, inventer
device système
dial cadran ; composer un numéro
fee taxe, droit, honoraire
file classeur ; classer, enregistrer, déposer une demande
funny drôle
gross brut
lapse devenir périmé, caduc, tomber en désuétude
margin marge (*bénéficiaire*)
marketing report étude de marché
off en dessous de, inférieur à
pass off faire passer
patent brevet d'invention

Patent Office bureau des brevets
patent agents agents en brevets
patent fee taxe de droit de brevet
patentee titulaire d'un brevet
paper holder pince, attache
photostat photocopie
prospects perspectives
provisional provisoire
run diriger, gérer
record enregistrer
register enregistrer, déposer
right droit
shake secouer, faire trembler
sole exclusif, seul
static statique, stable, stagnant
stationery papeterie
specification mémoire descriptif, description
terms of reference attributions
trade-mark marque de fabrique
    registred trade-mark marque déposée

Note : *une patente* = a license

il paie patente = he is duly licensed

Phrases

It remains in force	il reste valable, en vigueur
To bring someone up to date	mettre quelqu'un au courant
I'm all set to see your firm	je suis impatient de voir votre usine
Good Gracious !	Mon Dieu ! Bon sang de bonsoir !

Explanations and Other Useful Terms

box file a file in the form of a kind of box, in which papers and documents are kept in position by a metal clip

lapse to be allowed to go out of date, in this case, through failure to continue payment

market leaders firms which do the most business in a particular field and 'set the pace' on design and price.

market research an investigation of a market for a product ; to discover, for example, who are the leading producers, what type of customers they appeal to, what are the present sales figures, whether a new manufacturer could successfully enter the market, what type of advertising would be required, etc. (*see* also Unit 2)

marketing report details collected by a team of researchers of all the information required on a certain market, for example, the number of firms supplying the market.

photostat a copy of a document or drawing made by photographic processes.

specification details of, and instructions for, the design and materials of something which is to be made.

static not moving. When applied to a market it means that demand remains at the same level, neither rising nor falling.

Patent Office — **patent** : the grant of sole right to make or sell an invention. If a patented invention is copied without authority, the **patentee** can bring a legal action against the person or company **infringing** the patent.

— **Patent Office** : where inventions, etc. are registered or patented and thus protected from imitation.

register   here to fill out the necessary documents required by the Patent Office.

terms of reference   the details of a job which are referred to a person or an organisation. For instance, John Martin asked Smith-Weston to report on whether the market for box-files is growing or contracting ; which firms met the demand ; the market share enjoyed by each major supplier ; price levels and methods of distribution. He did not invite comments on his own sales organisation. The consultants had to restrict their activities to their terms of reference.

trade-mark   a device, e.g. a name, design, etc. adopted by a manufacturer exclusively, and market on his goods to show that they are made by him.

Pronunciation

1 — 1 - (- -) average, Manchester, necessary, a patent, a project, a prospect, register

- 2 (- -) authority, apparently, conclusion, contain, to contract, decide, device, existence, expense, extremely, forget, original, produce, provisional, success

2 — [a:] mark, last, start, chance, market, rather, margin, pass off
[æ] fact, chap, lapse, average, static, contract
[ou] show, grow, gross, close, both, sole, holder, project, photostat
[ɔ:] ought, force, launch, overall, report, important
[ɔ] copy, sorry, profit, prospect

3 — Compare : a contract ['kɔntrækt], to contract [kən'trækt]
a patent ['peitənt], the Patent Office ['peitənt] or [ˌpætənt'ɔfis]
a patentee [ˌpeitən'ti:] or [ˌpætən'ti:]
to apply [ə'plai], an application [ˌæpli kei ʃən], an applicant ['æplikənt]

4 — Note : dial [daiəl], good gracious [ˌgud' grei ʃəs], otherwise ['ʌðəwaiz], stationery ['stei ʃənəri], urgent ['ə:dʒənt].

2. SUMMARY

Harper & Grant are hoping to enter the box-file market. Their research department has come up with a very new, simple and quick device to hold papers together in a box file. Before the Sales Manager, John Martin, can get the authority to spend money on a new project like this he has to find out the chances of success. He therefore asked a firm of Market 5 Research consultants to examine the prospects, that is, report on the size of the present market for this type of file. The firm of consultants who have carried out the market research were first given terms of reference, that is, they were asked to supply particular information. John Martin wanted to know if the market was growing or contracting, getting smaller. 10

When the marketing report comes in, it shows that there is a growing interest in box files. The report also gives details of all the other firms who produce box files; the ones who do the most business are called the market leaders. When Mr. Grant sees the report he wants to know what the average price was to the user or buyer. In this case the average price 15 was ten shillings each file. The wholesale price, the price paid by the retailer, is twenty-five to thirty-five per cent off the retail price. This is the gross margin the retailer makes, out of which he must pay all expenses and make a profit.

When launching a new invention it is vitally important to register the new idea with the Patent Office. A patent gives the patentee the sole right, 20 the only right, to make, use or sell his invention during the time the patent remains in force, that is, as long as the annual patent fee is paid. It can be up to sixteen years. After that anyone can use the idea. If the fees are not paid, then the patent is said to have lapsed.

The next important step is to register the file and decide on a trade-mark for it. John Martin goes along to Hector Grant's office to bring 25 him up to date on the box file situation so far.

PART 2 : CONVERSATION AND DOCUMENTS

1. CONVERSATION
(Recorded Text)

JOHN MARTIN **Good morning, H.G. Are you free?**
HECTOR GRANT **Yes, come in, John. I've just got a quarter of an hour before Alfred Wentworth arrives to see over the factory.**

	You said you'd got that marketing report on the box files. Let's get on with it. What do they say?	5
JOHN	As you know, I asked Smith-Weston Consultants to do us a brief marketing report on box files. . . .	
GRANT	Well?	
JOHN	Here's their report. Apparently the market for box files was static for a number of years, but it's growing now. There are eight firms in the business, and one of them Maynard & Company, has about forty per cent of the market.	10
GRANT	What's the average retail price for this type of file?	
JOHN	About ten shillings per file.	15
GRANT	What are the wholesale prices?	
JOHN	Wholesale prices range from twenty-five to thirty-five per cent off retail prices.	
GRANT	H'm. Maynards, you say. They run office-stationery shops all over the country. Did you find out about the patent?	20
JOHN	Yes. I asked Wainright & Hansford, the patent agents, to see if our new design can be patented.	
GRANT	And can it? Is it a new idea, or have dozens of other people thought of it first?	25
JOHN	Apparently this type of steel and suction clip inside the file is a completely new idea. The agents suggest we should patent it at once. We can put in a provisional specification now—that records the invention with the Patent Office—and then we've got twelve months to file the complete specification.	30
GRANT	What about a trade-mark for it?	
JOHN	The agents suggest we should put in an application to register the file at once. Otherwise a rival firm could pass off their files as being made by us.	35

(*The telephone rings*)

GRANT	Hello? Yes? Oh, Mr. Wentworth's on his way up now, is he? Thank you. . . . H'm, he's early. Elizabeth, ask Mr. Wentworth to come straight in, will you?	
ELIZABETH	Oh, he's here now, Mr. Grant. Would you go in, please, Mr. Wentworth.	40
WENTWORTH	Morning, morning. Well, Hector, my boy, I'm all set to see the famous Harper & Grant factory. I've sat looking	

	at it long enough from across the road. Always thought I'd like to have a closer look.
GRANT	For goodness sake, sit down Alfred. The floor shakes 45 when you walk about like that. . . . What do you think of this? Not bad, eh? We're applying for a patent for this new paper holder inside the file. It works by suction. I'll bet you've never seen anything like this before.
WENTWORTH	What? How does it work? Ah, I see. Well, you know, 50 that's funny. I have seen one rather like this. Chap I know in Manchester. I saw one like this, in fact, last week.
GRANT	What!
JOHN	It can't be the same!
GRANT	It's not possible! 55
JOHN	Are you sure?
WENTWORTH	Of course I'm sure. I said I'd buy some for my various offices when he'd started to market them.
GRANT	Now look here, Alfred, who was this man? This is extremely serious. We're just about to apply for a patent for 60 this.
WENTWORTH	Well, you'd better be quick, or you'll find someone else has got there first.
JOHN	What's the name of this man's firm?
WENTWORTH	Oh, he's one of the sales boys for Maynards. . . . Robin- 65 son, I think his name is.
JOHN	Oh Lord! It couldn't be worse. We were hoping to break into the market with this.
WENTWORTH	Well, I should get your application in to the Patent Office. 70
JOHN	But, Mr. Wentworth, we've only just had the report in today from the patent agents.
GRANT	Well, you'd better get our application in today, John.
JOHN	Right, H.G. May I use your phone?
GRANT	Yes, yes. 75
JOHN	(*He picks up phone and dials.*) Sally? The new box file paper holder . . . I want the second copy of the specification, and the photostat of the drawing. Let me have them straight away, will you? I'm in the Chairman's office. What? You sent them to Birmingham? Both copies of the 80 drawing! Oh, good gracious. What on earth did you do that for? Can't the Design Department let us have another copy? . . . Yes, ask them.

GRANT	What's the trouble?	
JOHN	Apparently Sally sent off both copies we had of the drawing to the Birmingham factory who are making the file for us. She forgot to check whether they were, in fact, the only two copies in existence.	85
GRANT	What time does the Patent Office close?	
WENTWORTH	Six o'clock. You ought to know that, Hector.	90

(*The internal phone rings*)

GRANT	Yes? Oh. John? It's your secretary.	
JOHN	What? They can't find them? Well, it's too late now to be sorry.	
GRANT	What's happened?	
JOHN	The Design Department can't find the original designs.	95
GRANT	Do we need drawings for the Patent Office?	
JOHN ₁	In some cases it's not necessary to supply drawings for a provisional specification, but in this case, apparently, we must include them.	
WENTWORTH	Well, get on to Birmingham. What's the time now? Twelve twenty. If they put them on the next train to London you could have them collected at the station and taken straight round to the Patent Office.	100
GRANT	(*Speaking into phone.*) Get me Mr. Clark, of the Kitson Board Company, Birmingham, will you. It's urgent.	105
JOHN	One of my sales clerks has got a motor bike. I'll send him to collect the drawings and he can take them straight to the Patent Office. I'll get on to him. . . .	

PRACTICE SENTENCES

Say the practice sentences on the record :
  i What's the average retail price for this type of file?
 ii Wholesale prices are about twenty-five per cent off retail prices.
iii The agents suggest we should patent it at once.
 iv We're applying for a patent.
  v We're hoping to break into the market.
 vi We've had the report in from the patent agents.

2. MARKET RESEARCH

Here is a letter which Smith-Weston, the firm of consultants, sent to John Martin with their marketing report. It contains a brief general statement which gives their main conclusions.

SMITH-WESTON CONSULTANTS
Industrial Consultants
Market Research & Production Engineering

John Martin, Esq.,
Sales Manager,
Harper & Grant Ltd.,
Great West Road,
London, W.25.   9th March, 197..

Dear Mr. Martin,

        We now have pleasure in presenting the results of our researches into the box file market. You will recall that in your terms of reference you instructed us to report on three main subjects: on the overall size of the market, its trend, and the firms which are at present supplying it.

        In general terms we find that, though static for several years, the market is now expanding. There are eight major firms in the business, one of which holds forty per cent of the trade. The average retail price is approximately ten shillings per file, while wholesale prices range between sixty-five to seventy-five per cent of the retail price.

        Our recommendation is that you should enter the market by selling directly to the large users through your existing sales force. We consider that your particular product has every chance of success. Attached you will find a detailed account of our researches.

Yours sincerely,

O. Morgan,

Oswald Morgan
SMITH-WESTON CONSULTANTS

PART 3 : NOTES AND PRACTICE

1. RAPPEL GRAMMATICAL

Summary :

13. **The ones who.** Variante : **those who**

18. **The margin the retailer makes.** Notons le relatif zéro.

Conversation :

10. **The market was static.** Notons cet emploi des temps - *simple past* et *perfect* dans cet épisode. Le prétérit indique que l'action est révolue :

He asked them to examine the prospects	Il leur a demandé d'étudier les perspectives

Par contre, le *perfect* indique que l'action continue dans le présent, ou que c'est à son résultat présent qu'on s'intéresse :

They've been on the market for six or seven years	Ils sont sur le marché depuis six ou sept ans
They've carried out the market research	Ils ont effectué l'étude de marché

L'emploi du prétérit dans **the market was static for a number of years, but it's growing now** peut d'abord surprendre, puisque c'est jusqu'à ce jour qu'il est resté stable. Mais justement, John veut souligner que cette situation est bien révolue, et qu'une nouvelle tendance est amorcée.

Et plus bas, lignes 51 et 52 :

I've seen one rather like this	J'en ai vu un assez semblable à celui-ci
I saw one like this last week	J'en ai vu un dans la semaine dernière

Dans le premier cas, A. Wentworth annonce le résultat présent de quelque chose de passé. Ce qui compte, c'est que pour l'instant il l'ait vu. Dans sa confirmation, ce qu'il précise c'est la date, et nous avons cette fois le prétérit.

47. **We're applying for a patent.** Le progressif a ici une valeur de futur proche.

57. **I said I'd buy some...** Qu'a-t-il dit (*discours direct*) :

I'll buy some when you've started to market them	Je vous en achèterai quand vous aurez commencé à les distribuer

60. We're just about to apply. Variante : **we're going to apply**, et nous avons vu plus haut : **we're applying**...

Le passé récent par contre peut s'exprimer de deux manières différentes (notons les temps) :

I've just seen the agent	
I saw the agent just now	Je viens de voir le concessionnaire

73. You'd better get our application in today. N'oublions pas la construction du passé :

You'd better have seen to that matter yourself	Vous auriez mieux fait de vous occuper de cette question vous-même

2. EXERCISES

EXERCISE 1. — *Sax the following sentences, beginning with* **if** *and changing the sentence as necessary, as follows* :

To safeguard a new invention, an inventor must patent it. →
If **an inventor wants to safeguard a new invention, he must patent it.**

1. Wishing to patent a new invention, an inventor must register it at the Patent Office. 2. Unless the annual patent fee is paid, the patent will lapse. 3. Selling a product without a trade-mark means that it can be copied by rival firms. 4. To get information about the chances of selling a new stapling machine, Harper & Grant must ask for a market report.

EXERCISE 2. — *Make questions to which the following sentences can be answers* :

1. It (*the new box file*) works like this. 2. Yes, I have seen something like this before. 3. Yes, he (*Mr. Wentworth*) is here now. 4. You can apply to the Patent Office to register it (*a new invention*). 5. You can get them (*drawings*) photostated.

EXERCISE 3. — *Change as follows* :

I have just bought some → **I bought some just now**

1. I've just seen the agent. 2. I've just sent them the 3 copies. 3. The oven has just broken down. 4. He's just met one of their salesmen. 5. Smith-Weston have just rung up. 6. The boss has just read their marketing report.

EXERCISE 4. — *Change as follows* :

You say you've got the marketing report →
you said you'd got the marketing report

1. I know you've been working overtime. 2. I expect they won't claim compensation. 3. I can see she's worried about the loss. 4. She claims she can do it while you're away. 5. I think I'll have a closer look into she matter. 6. He pretends he's known about your project all the time.

EXERCISE 5. — *Express anxiousness, concern, impatience, etc. as follows* :

I must see if our new design can be patented. — Oh it can, can't it ?

I must see if... 1. that firm in Birmingham can let us have the documents back. 2. Sally will accept working overtime once more. 3. The Sales Assistant would go and fetch them at the airport. 4. John left a message for you before going to Clarkson & Strand. 5. The other two men have finished unloading the crates. 6. Westminster Bank can grant us an overdraft.

EXERCISE 6. — *Change as follows* :

a. **it must be the same** → **it can't be the same**
b. **you must do it at once** → **you needn't do it at once**

1. She must have lost it. 2. You must go to Andersons immediately. 3. The market must be very tough at the moment. 4. There must be serious drawbacks with this method. 5. I must phone Kitson today, mustn't I ? 6. You must have sent the wrong drawing. 7. They must be worried about the loss. 8. The firm must file in the application today.

EXERCISE 7. — *Change as follows* :

The patent lapsed (they said) → **it is said to have lapsed**

1. Windel & Riddel went bankrupt (they assumed). 2. My secretary made three copies (I expected her to). 3. The men in the design department kept a copy of this file (we suppose so). 4. The box file market was very buoyant (they reported). 5. Mr. Shuttleworth ran into a bad patch (they say). 6. The rep spoke about the project to one of his colleagues from a rival firm (we suppose so). 7. Crosby & Turner are insolvent (people say).

EXERCISE 8. — *Change as follows* :

You'd better (not) register it at once → **you'd better (not) have registered it at once**

You'd better... 1. take Duncan round the shops yourself. 2. put the documents in the safe. 3. not leave the money on your desk. 4. go to the Design Department before 12. 5. not bring in a third party concerning those overdue accounts. 6. not take the documents away home. 7. apply to the Patent Office as soon as you have the drawings.

EXERCISE 9. — *Change as follows* :

I'll speak to Mr. Clark when I see him →
        he said he'd speak to Mr. Clark when he saw him

1. I'll phone them when I have read your report. 2. I'll report on it as soon as I see their new models. 3. I'll celebrate as soon as John gets back with his patent. 4. I'll tell you more about it when the figures are published. 5. We'll show the model to the press when Joanna gives it the go-ahead. 6. I'll buy some when you've started to market them.

EXERCISE 10. — *Change as follows* (*mind the tense*) :

Are these the only copies (She forgot to check it)
→ **she forgot to check whether these were the only copies**

1. Is the gross profit 25 or 30 % ? (he says he can't remember). 2. Have they got the right information about the market ? (I doubt it) 3. Would the Patent Office accept the application without the drawings ? (he isn't sure) 4. Can the goods be delivered in the first week of December ? (I couldn't be certain) 5. Can they grant us a 5 % discount for larger quantities (you ought to ask them). 6. Have our competitors carried out a similar research (they couldn't say). 7. Did Robinson intend to apply for a patent as well (Wentworth doesn't know). 8. Have they got accurate figures concerning Maynard's turnover last year ? (you ought have checked with them).

EXERCISE 11. — *Translate into English* :

1. Quel est le prix moyen de détail pour ce type de dossier ? 2. Les prix de gros sont de l'ordre de 25 % en dessous des prix de détail. 3. L'agence en brevets nous conseille de le faire breveter tout de suite. 4. Nous déposons une demande de brevet. 5. Nous espérons pénétrer sur le marché. 6. Nous avons reçu le rapport des agents en brevets. 7. Ce sont ceux qui font le plus gros bénéfice. 8. Leur rapport concerne la configuration du marché, les tendances, et les entreprises qui l'alimentent actuellement. 9. L'une des huit entreprises principales fait 35 % des affaires. 10. Nous vendrons directement aux usagers importants grâce à notre équipe actuelle de vendeurs. 11. Veuillez trouver ci-joint le compte-rendu détaillé de nos recherches. 12. Le Bureau des Etudes n'arrive pas à retrouver les plans originaux. 13. Il n'est pas nécessaire de fournir les plans pour un mémoire descriptif provisoire. 14. Vous pourriez les faire prendre à la gare, n'est-ce pas ? 15. Voulez-vous me passer M. Weston de Smith-Weston, c'est urgent. 16. J'ai besoin d'une photocopie de trois premières pages de ce catalogue. 17. Je parie que vous n'avez rien vu de semblable auparavant. 18. Vous feriez bien de vous dépêcher, sinon quelqu'un arrivera avant vous. 19. Est-ce qu'il s'agit d'une marque déposée ? 20. Ils viennent de trouver un système nouveau, simple et rapide ; ils devraient le faire breveter.

UNIT 23

INSURANCE

PART 1 : INTRODUCTION

1. WORD STUDY

Vocabulary

Act of God cas de force majeure
adjuster expert en assurances, répartiteur d'avaries
all-risks policy assurance tous risques
assess évaluer, estimer
blanket insurance assurance générale, tous risques
brake frein
broker courtier en assurances
burglary vol, cambriolage
claim (*ici*) déclaration de sinistre
  put in a claim établir une déclaration de sinistre
  meet a claim satisfaire une demande de dommages
comprehensive policy assurance tous risques
cover couvrir, assurer, garantir
damage dégâts, avarie
damp humidité
dent coup, bosse

depreciate se dévaluer
development événement, suite
exception réserve
hill colline
hire louer
hold détenir, retenir
huge énorme
injure léser
  injured party la victime
insure assurer
investigate faire une enquête
jam se bloquer, se coincer
knock out débosseler
liable redevable, responsable, passible de
loss perte
number plate plaque de police d'un véhicule
outbreak of war déclaration de guerre
pay up payer intégralement
policy police, assurance

premium   prime
put in (a claim)   faire une déclaration de sinistre
puzzle   intriguer
raid   faire une descente de police
release   lâcher, libérer
re-spray   repeindre
robbery   vol à main armée
salvage   récupérer
spoiled   gâté, endommagé
stick   coller
strip down   démonter

syndicate   syndicat, consortium
  d'assurances
take place   se produire, avoir lieu
theft   vol
tip off   donner un tuyau
underwrite   souscrire
underwriter   assureur, souscripteur
windscreen   pare-brise
within   au sein de
wreck   épave
write off   épave ;   véhicule
  irrécupérable

Phrase

To give a lift   monter quelqu'un en voiture

Explanations and Other Useful Terms

actuary
professional expert who works out the average expectation of life, on which life insurance premiums are based.

adjusters
an independent firm who assess the damage to property.

all risks policy
a policy which covers all possible normal dangers with the exception of war, Act of God, etc.

assure, assurance
the words assure, assurance, etc... are the older forms of **insurance, insure**, etc. and are now used only - but not exclusively - for **life** and **marine insurance.**

cover
to have cover = to be insured.

disclaim all liability
to refuse to be responsible. Perhaps a false claim has been made for damage by fire ; the insurance company discovers that it was a case of **arson** (deliberately setting fire to something) and they therefore disclaim all liability, they refuse to pay the claim.

endowment
insurance combined with a **saving plan.** When the insured reaches a certain age a **lump sum** (one large amount) is paid.

insurance brokers
brokers act as agents between the client and the insurance company.

meet a claim
pay the amount asked for.

— 356 —

premium	rate payable for an insurance policy.
salvage	to rescue something which has been damaged because of an accident, e.g. to salvage material from a sunken ship, from a fire, etc.
syndicate	a group of people working together and pooling their resources ; in this case a group of insurance underwriters.
third party	cover against a claim made by a third person, that is, someone other than the insured or the insurer. In Britain, it is a criminal offence to drive a car without third party insurance.
underwriter	insurer. **Underwriter** is the more specific and professional term ; **insurer** the looser and wider term. Underwriters are people who take the risks of insurance. If there are no claims they make a profit. If there are a large number of claims, they make a loss.
write-off	something which can no longer be considered to have any value. Here, a vehicle which has been so badly damaged that it can be written off.

Pronunciation

1 — 1 - (- -) accident, damage, negligence, ordinary, syndicate, underwriter

  - 2 (- -) abandoned, adjuster, approach, arrange, arrest, assess, belong, concern, development, entire, impossible, inform, insurance, insure, inspect, investigate

  - - 3 (-) comprehensive, independently, represent

2 — [ə:] firm, further, furniture
    [ɔ:] all, warn, course, normal, inform
    [ɔ] loss, job, policy, property, problem
    [ʌ] sum, month, once, puzzle, adjust
    [ou] load, road, total, broker, almost, although, approach
    [æ] damp, happen, damage, value, blanket, transit, transport
    [dʒ] jam, salvage, damage, huge, arrange, hi-jack

3 — Compare : depreciate [di'pri:ʃieit], depreciation [di,pri:ʃi'eiʃən]

4 — Note : grouped [gru:pt], huge [hju:dʒ], offence [ə'fens], outbreak ['autbreik], salvage ['sælvidʒ], theft [θeft], valuable ['væljuəbl], vehicle ['vi:ikl].

2. SUMMARY

Some weeks ago a lorry carrying Harper & Grant's goods was hi-jacked on the road. Now there is a further development of this which concerns the insurance. Every firm insures itself against loss or damage to its property. Harper & Grant's insurance brokers had arranged a blanket insurance with a syndicate of Lloyds underwriters. *Blanket insurance* 5 means insurance which covers everything, a comprehensive policy. Harper & Grant make a statement at the end of an accounting period (say once a month or once a quarter) of the total value of all goods handled. The premium is then paid as a percentage of the total value of goods. Lloyds, of course, is a huge insurance organisation in London. Within this 10 organisation, underwriters, or insurers, work independently, although they are grouped in syndicates. When the lorry was found abandoned, with its spoiled load of office furniture, the adjusters came in. The underwriters employ a firm of adjusters whose job is to assess or value the loss or damage. The sum they give will not usually be as much as the full 15 insured value of the goods or property. They will take into account, among other things, the depreciated value: for example, the value of the lorry has gone down, depreciated, because it is two years old. However, in this case the lorry is a write-off, a total wreck and impossible to repair. But this does not concern Harper & Grant, because the lorry 20 belonged to Andersons, the transport company from whom they hire vehicles. But the load of office furniture does concern them. They have already had to replace the load, which was wanted urgently in Scotland.

When a company, or a person, takes out an insurance policy it is very often an all-risks policy, that is, it insures the goods or property against 25 almost anything that could happen. But most insurance companies put in some exceptions, like outbreak of war or Act of God (something out of the ordinary which cannot be considered a normal risk). When an accident or robbery takes place the injured party puts in a claim to the insurance company. If the insurance company agrees to pay it is 30 said to meet the claim. Notice, first you *take out* a policy, then you *put in* a claim, and the insurance company, you hope, agrees *to meet* the claim.

About two weeks after the following incident Mr. Buckhurst received a telephone call from the police in Carlisle. Thanks to the driver's descrip- 35 tion of the man who asked him for a lift, the police were able to arrest the entire gang. They discovered them in Carlisle, where they were busy changing number plates and respraying two stolen lorries, so they will not be doing any more hi-jacking, for the time being, anyway.

1. CONVERSATION

(Recorded Text)

WILLIAM BUCKHURST	Hello, Peter. Are you looking for me?
PETER WILES	Yes, as a matter of fact I am. Have you heard any more about the missing lorry while I've been away?
BUCKHURST	Yes, we have. Andersons have just been on to me. The vehicle insurers say the lorry is a complete write-off. 5
PETER	I hope we're covered all right.
BUCKHURST	Yes, we are.
PETER	What puzzles me is why they stole office furniture.
BUCKHURST	Well, apparently, it seems that the gang had been tipped off that a lorry belonging to Andersons would be coming 10 through that way with a valuable load of cigarettes.
PETER	Ah, that sounds more like it!
BUCKHURST	When Andersons' driver was approached by a man in the transport café he was asked what he was carrying. He said it was a load of office desks and filing cabinets, but 15 they must have thought he was lying for some reason.
PETER	What happened to the driver?
BUCKHURST	It seems he was taken to a farm a long way from the main road and held there for several hours before the gang released him. Then he had to walk six miles before he 20 found a telephone and was able to get hold of the police.
PETER	Did the police raid the farm?
BUCKHURST	Yes, they did. But by that time, of course, the gang had left. 25
PETER	What did they do with the lorry?
BUCKHURST	They took the brake off and let it go over the side of a steep hill! It's a total wreck.
PETER	What about our desks?
BUCKHURST	Well, now, apparently the insurance of the load is not so 30 simple. I informed our insurance brokers as soon as the theft was reported. As you know, all goods delivered for

	us within the United Kingdom are covered by a blanket insurance policy.	
PETER	Who underwrote the policy? Lloyds, wasn't it?	35
BUCKHURST	Yes, we're insured with a syndicate of Lloyds underwriters. Someone from a firm of adjusters is going up to inspect the damaged goods tomorrow to give an opinion about their value.	
PETER	Well ... what's the problem? They won't make any difficulty about paying up, surely?	40
BUCKHURST	Well, it could be difficult. Our insurers seem to think the desks and chairs may not be too badly damaged.	
PETER	I think someone from the firm ought to go up and give us an opinion of the damage. I'd like to go up there myself and have a look.	45
BUCKHURST	Oh, but it's miles from a main road. It's right up in the Moorland Valley.	
PETER	Well, I can't go, anyway. I've got too much to do at the moment. I'll get Christopher Thorn to go up; he's got a car he can easily go ...	50

(*Christopher Thorn gets to Moorland Valley*)

CHRISTOPHER THORN	Good morning. Nice morning for a country drive, isn't it? Oh, what a mess that lorry's in.	
MR. ROBERTS	May I ask who you are and what your business is up here?	55
CHRISTOPHER	Well, I might ask you the same question.	
ROBERTS	My name is Roberts. I represent Brown & Johnson, Insurance Adjusters. I've been asked to investigate the damage to the load which this lorry was carrying.	
CHRISTOPHER	Ah, how do you do. My name is Thorn, I work for Harper & Grant.	60
ROBERTS	Oh, yes, your firm is making the claim.	
CHRISTOPHER	Well, let's have a look. I was warned that the lorry doors might have jammed.	
ROBERTS	I don't think these filing cabinets are too badly damaged. I think it should be possible to salvage the lot. These dents could be quite easily knocked out, and these desks could be repainted.	65
CHRISTOPHER	Oh, I don't think I agree, Mr. Roberts. Look at this chair, it's a complete write-off. We'd never be able to repair that.	70

And the filing cabinets. Look at them! They must have been under water for some time. They would have to be stripped down and completely repainted.

ROBERTS: 'These dents could be quite easily knocked out . . .'

ROBERTS   **H'm, well, I think I might recommend payment of . . . seventy-five per cent of the insured value. . . . Hello! 75 What's this piece of paper?**

CHRISTOPHER   **I should think it used to be stuck on the windscreen; it's come unstuck with the damp and . . . What does it say?**

ROBERTS	'Drivers are warned that it is a serious offence against 80 company regulations, as agreed with the General Workers' Union, to give lifts in this vehicle to any person not being an employee of Andersons Transport Company.' You realise what this means?
CHRISTOPHER	Sorry, no, I don't. 85
ROBERTS	Didn't the driver inform the police that he gave a lift to this man in the transport café?
CHRISTOPHER	Yes, I believe he did. But I don't see . . .
ROBERTS	I think your company will find, Mr. Thorn, that Andersons, the carriers, should be held responsible for 90 any damage to their customers' goods in transit if the damage is caused by negligence on the part of the driver. Of course, it will depend on the contract your firm has with Andersons, but I don't think your insurers need be liable at all. 95

PRACTICE SENTENCES

Say the practice sentences on the record :

 i The vehicle insurers say the lorry is a complete write-off.
 ii All goods delivered for us within the country are covered by a blanket insurance policy.
 iii We're insured with a syndicate of Lloyds underwriters.
 iv Someone from a firm of adjusters is going to inspect the damaged goods tomorrow.
 v I represent Brown & Johnson, Insurance Adjusters.
 vi We might recommend payment of seventy-five per cent of the insured value.

2. APPLYING FOR COVER

Here is a letter written by William Buckhurst, the Company Secretary, asking the insurance brokers to arrange cover for the new extension to the factory, which is almost finished.

Harper and Grant Limited

Great West Road
London W25
Telephone 01-567 1112
Telex 80153
Telegrams Harp LDN

Directors:
Hector Grant *(Chairman & Managing Director)*
William Buckhurst FCA *(Secretary)*
John Martin
Alfred Wentworth
Margaret Wiles
Peter Wiles

The Everest Insurance Co. Ltd.,
Buxton Avenue,
London, E.C.1.   12th April, 197..

Dear Sirs,

    We would like you to arrange the necessary insurance covers for the new extension which has been built on to our existing factory. The builders inform us that the work should be finished by 9th July, and we would like you to arrange for us to be covered from that date.

    Will you please, therefore, send us quotations for the following insurances in order to bring the new building into line with the rest of our insurance.

Risk	Amount of insurance	Premises and Property
Fire	£60,000	Factory extension.
Fire	£50,000	Factory extension contents including machinery.
Burglary	£15,000	Additional stores in new building.

    We presume that for staff working in the new extension, the insurance we already have covers all risks to personnel. We should be glad, however, to have confirmation that the present policy can be adjusted to apply to the additional premises.

    We should be glad if you could let us have the quotations as soon as possible.

Yours faithfully,

William Buckhurst
Company Secretary
HARPER & GRANT LTD.

PART 3 : NOTES AND PRACTICE

1. RAPPEL GRAMMATICAL

Summary :

1. **Some weeks ago.** Rappelons que **ago** s'emploie avec un prétérit seulement :

I discussed the terms with them a fortnight ago	J'ai discuté des conditions avec eux il y a quinze jours

Pour indiquer le temps passé depuis la fin d'une action dans une proposition au *plu-perfect*, on rencontre **before** :

I had seen the broker a few days before	Il y avait quelque jours que j'avais vu le courtier

15. **as much... as.** Le comparatif d'égalité avec un adjectif ou un adverbe s'exprime à l'aide de **as... as** :

It's as efficient as your system	C'est aussi efficace que votre système

Avec un verbe, un participe, un nom singulier, on rencontre : **as much... as** :

He doesn't work as (so) much as he used to	Il ne travaille pas autant qu'autrefois
We could make as much profit	Nous pourrions faire autant de bénéfice

Avec un nom pluriel, on dit : **as many... as** :

There will be as many workers in the new extension as in the old works	Il y aura autant d'ouvriers dans la nouvelle extension que dans les anciens ateliers

23. **They have already had to replace the load.** Cet Unit est riche en défectifs et leurs équivalents. Bonne occasion d'en finir avec les dernières hésitations sur leur maniement :

26. **anything that could happen. Could** a ici la valeur de **might.** Il est modal (perspective hypothétique). L'hypothèse au passé serait ?...

Burglars might have broken into the office	Des cambrioleurs auraient pu pénétrer dans le bureau par effraction

28. **it cannot be considered a normal risk. Can** a ici encore une valeur d'*éventualité* en même temps que de *possibilité*.

Conversation :

Poursuivons la prospection des défectifs dans la conversation :

16. **They must have thought he was lying.** Forte supposition portant sur le passé.

20. **He had to walk six miles.** Equivalent de **must** au prétérit. Quelques variations :

We'll have to insure the staff	Nous devrons assurer le personnel
They would have had to work overtime	Il aurait fallu qu'ils fassent des heures supplémentaires
Wouldn't be obliged to pay up ?	Ne devraient-ils pas payer intégralement ?

21. **Before he was able to get hold of the police.** Equivalent de **can** au prétérit. Quelques variations :

Would they be able to respray all these cabinets ?	Pourraient-ils repeindre tous ces meubles ?
The night-watchman had been able to give a full description of his attacker	Le veilleur de nuit avait pu donner un signalement complet de son agresseur

42. **It could be difficult = It might be difficult.** Dans la conversation courante, **can/could** l'emporte de plus en plus sur **may/might**.

43. **They may not be damaged too badly.** *Eventualité.* A propos de **may**, ne pas oublier que la nuance *d'autorisation* ne se rencontre en fait qu'à l'interrogative du présent, et ses corollaires, c'est-à-dire le discours indirect et la réponse :

May I smoke in the paint store ?	Puis-je fumer dans l'entrepôt des peintures ?
- No, you may not	Non
He asked if he might smoke	Il a demandé s'il pouvait fumer

Une interdiction sera communiquée de la manière suivante :

You are not supposed to smoke in the fuel store	On ne peut pas fumer dans l'entrepôt des carburants

Variante : **you are not expected... you are not to... it is forbidden to... you should not... you must not... people are not allowed...**

44. **someone ought to go up.** Le regret s'exprimerait ainsi :

Someone ought to have accompanied Christopher Thorn	Quelqu'un aurait dû accompagner Christopher Thorn

54. May I ask you... ? Exemple typique de la valeur de permission de **may** dans une interrogative au présent.

56. I might ask you the same question. Au contraire ici, **might** a la valeur d'éventualité, comme en 64 : **the door might have jammed.**

66. It should be possible to salvage the lot. Combinaison de **should** avec l'équivalent de **can** (be possible to). **Should** indique l'idée que cela *devrait* se faire ; **Can** admet par ailleurs bien des constructions équivalentes, en dehors de **to be able to** :

They were not in a position to send someone to Scotland	Ils ne pouvaient pas (n'étaient pas en mesure d') envoyer quelqu'un en Ecosse
He was incapable of explaining this to the adjuster	Il n'a pas pu expliquer cela à l'expert
Would it be possible for you to hand me your report by the end of the week ?	Vous serait-il possible (=pourriez-vous) de me remettre votre rapport d'ici la fin de la semaine

67. could be knocked out... repainted... *Possibilité matérielle.*

70. We'd never be able to repair that. *Possibilité matérielle* à nouveau. Variante possible : **we could never reapir that.**

71. The must have been under water for some time. *Quasi-certitude, forte probabilité.*

72. They would have to be stripped. Equivalent de **must** dans une construction passive. Mettons à l'actif :

We should have to strip them down ⎫ Il faudrait que nous les démon-
We'd be obliged to strip them down ⎭ tions complètement

90. Should be held responsible. Ce qui s'impose.

77. It used to be stuck on the windscreen. On dit que **used to** est la *forme fréquentative,* c'est-à-dire un type de construction qui s'emploie lorsqu'une action se répétait avec une certaine fréquence dans le passé. Mais en fait ce **used to** a d'autres valeurs que la fréquence dans le passé.

Rappelons que **used to** n'a pas de présent, que l'interrogative et la négative emploient en général l'auxiliaire **do** :

He used to work at the office every day after the staff had left	Il travaillait au bureau tous les jours après le départ du personnel
Did they use to send circulars in this case ?	Envoyaient-ils des circulaires dans ce cas ?
He used to be accompanied by a policeman, didn't he ?	Il était habituellement accompagné d'un agent, n'est-ce pas ?

Par extension, **used to** s'emploie souvent pour indiquer la différence entre ce qui était dans le passé et qui n'est plus, comme c'est le cas ligne 77 :

There used to be a fire-extingui-sher in this corner	Il y avait un extincteur dans ce coin
Photocopiers used to be a rarity a few years ago	Les photocopieurs étaient rares il y a quelques années

2. EXERCISES

EXERCISE 1. — Complete the following sentences using **how, what, where, why, when,** *as follows* :

Andersons' driver was approached in the transport café and asked ... he was carrying →

Andersons' driver was approached in the transport café and asked what he was carrying.

1. The driver of the hi-jacked lorry was taken to a remote farm ... he could not easily be found.   2. The police raided the farm ... they received the description from the driver.   3. Peter could not understand ... the gang had hi-jacked a load of office furniture.   4. At first, no one knew ... had happened to the driver.   5. Before an insurance claim is met, the insurance company must first see ... damage has been done.

EXERCISE 2. — Please supply the missing words. Give a complete sentence for your answer :

1. It's a good idea to ... a life insurance policy.   2. If you lose something which is insured you must ... a claim.   3. Andersons' lorry was so badly damaged that is was a complete ...   4. The adjuster, Mr. Roberts, thought it ought to be possible to ... the office furniture.

EXERCISE 3. — Change as follows :

a. **Sally types faster than Elizabeth → Sally types as fast as Elizabeth**

b. **John spent more on entertainment than H.G. →**
   John spent as much on entertainment as H.G.

c. **Shuttleworth sold more desks than John →**
   Shuttleworth sold as many desks as John

1. We sold more desks at the exhibition this year than last year.   2. The new method is more efficient and faster than the old one.   3. There is more traffic on the high road than on the motor-way.   4. We'll have to pay more for the new premium than for the old one.   5. It would be

cheaper and more useful than anything else.   6. They sent more goods by plane than by rail.   7. The secretary does more work than the boss. 8. French businessmen are more enterprising than American ones.   9. He bought more shares than Alfred Wentworth.   10. They obtain a higher yield than their competitors.   11. The European labour-force is more adaptable than the American one.   12. The index of production covers a greater part of g.n.p. than in America.

EXERCISE 4. — Change as follows :

Who are you ?   →   **May I ask you who you are ?**

1. What did you see at the exhibition ?   2. What did you find in the adjuster's report ? 3. What was Sally doing in the delivery bay ?   4. When will the problem be examined by the Board ?   5. Why did he go to the bank with Mr. Buckhurst ?   6. When can I have a word with you concerning the training programme ?   7. How will these cabinets be repaired ? 8. How much did you pay for the repair ?   9. How many applicants did you see for the post ?

EXERCISE 5. — Change as follows :

a. **they're under water (a week)**   →   **they must have been under water for a week**

b. **he's in Abraca (October 20th)**   →   **he must have been in Abraca since October 20 th**

1. They're working here (a month).   2. Hardiman is out of work (three months).   3. They are carrying on secret negotiations (the last strike). 4. He is reading your report (an hour).   5. He's canvassing his new area (January 10th).   6. Donald is fiddling the accounts (Mr. Buckhurst let him go alone to the bank).

EXERCISE 6. — Change as follows :

a. **they can calculate the amount of the premium** →
    they'd be able to calculate the amount of the premium

b. **they must pay the full insured value of the goods** →
    they'd be obliged to pay the full insured value of the goods

1. He can draw up his tax declaration by himself.   2. He must work 20 miles away from home.   3. The US can't maintain the dollar exchange rate.   4. You must replace all these parts as soon as possible.   5. Must I make the remittance through a London bank ?   6. Can't they forward the goods within a week ?   7. You must send the spare parts by plane. 8. You must apply to the head office, mustn't you ?   9. He can't set up in business as a chartered accountant, can he ?

EXERCISE 7. — *Change as follows, using* **have** **to** *with things, and* **be obliged to** *with persons* :

a. **you must take the sternest measures** →
> **you'll be obliged to take the sternest measures**
b. **the industry must become more dynamic** →
> **the industry will have to become more dynamic**

1. We must stop work for a whole day to repair the oven. 2. The railway system must be streamlined. 3. The firm must adopt a new approach to customer requirements. 4. The management must meet all the claims of the workers. 5. The industry must diversify at any cost. 6. The American supplier must withdraw from the market. 7. The various operations must be synchronized more accurately. 8. The supermarket industry must re-appraise its pricing policy. 9. You must pay all outstanding premiums first.

EXERCISE 8. — *Change as follows* :

1. **They could cut the expenditure by 20 %** →
> **they were able to cut the expenditure by 20 %**
b. **He couldn't explain what had happened** →
> **he was unable to explain what had happened**

1. His partner could bring the necessary capital. 2. They couldn't raise the necessary funds. 3. Sally couldn't find a copy of the Auditors' report. 4. We could always forecast the sales with great accuracy. 5. We couldn't trace receiving their payment. 6. We could make full use of our computer from the very start. 7. Unfortunately, they could neither concentrate nor disperse their resources. 8. The unions couldn't work out a long-term strategy.

EXERCISE 9. — *Change as follow* :

a **They could have met your requirements** →
> **they would have been capable of meeting**
b. **They couldn't have met your requirements** →
> **they would have been incapable of meeting your requirements**

1. British industry couldn't have sold enough abroad. 2. Joanna could have translated the catalogue into Spanish. 3. The men couldn't have seen the advantages of the profit sharing scheme. 4. They couldn't have kept the wages in step with increases in productivity. 5. Perhaps another government could have persuaded industrialists to build factories in those areas. 6. A firm like Harper & Grant could have successfully competed with the Americans on the market. 7. Mr. Windsmore couldn't have carried out the advertising campaign. 8. They could have achieved substantial reductions in production costs. 9. French firms couldn't have survived intense American competition. 10. Peter Wiles could have solved this problem of distribution more satisfactorily. 11. I couldn't have made such a survey by myself. 12. They could have set up a training programme on the new premises.

1. Les assureurs du véhicule disent que la camion n'est plus qu'une épave.
2. Toutes les marchandises livrées pour nous dans le pays sont garanties
par une assurance tous risques. 3. Nous sommes assurés auprès d'une
agence du Groupe Lloyds. 4. Quelqu'un d'une agence d'experts en
assurances va examiner les dégâts demain. 5. Je représente Brown &
Johnson, les Experts en Assurance. 6. Nous pourrions recommander
le remboursement de 75 % de la valeur assurée. 7. La prime représente
un pourcentage de la valeur assurée. 8. Les experts doivent tenir compte
de l'amortissement. 9. J'ai avisé nos assureurs dès que le vol a été signalé.
10. Ils ne vont pas faire de difficulté pour payer intégralement, non ?
11. Je crois que quelqu'un de la maison devrait aller voir les experts.
12. L'expert estime qu'on devrait pouvoir récupérer la totalité des marchandises. 13. Il faudrait qu'on démonte les classeurs et qu'on les
repeigne complètement. 14. C'est une infraction grave aux règlements de
la société. 15. Les transporteurs doivent être tenus responsables pour
tous dégâts survenus en transit. 16. Tout dépendra du contrat qui vous
lie avec l'entreprise de transport. 17. Nous voudrions que la garantie
parte du 10 novembre. 18. La police couvre déjà tous les risques concernant le personnel. 19. Auprès de qui l'assurance est-elle souscrite ?
Lloyd's, n'est-ce pas ? 20. Nous vous serions obligés de nous envoyer
les tarifs dès que possible.

UNIT 24

THE FIRM EXPANDS

PART 1 : INTRODUCTION

1. WORD STUDY

Vocabulary

adjourn lever la séance
allotment attribution, répartition (*d'actions*)
arise provenir de
articles statuts
authorised (capital) social
available disponible
canteen cantine
clerical (staff) (*personnel*) de bureau
complaint plainte, réclamation
counter comptoir
debenture obligation
display exposer, étaler
endeavour effort
equity (shares) actions ordinaires
extensive approfondie
fair juste
fitter ajusteur
football pitch terrain de football
level niveler
mention mentionner
miss manquer

open (market) (*marché*) libre
ordinary shares actions ordinaires
old-fashioned démodé, suranné
over-subscribed sursouscrit
perform exécuter, célébrer
preference shares actions privilégiées
put forward proposer
rate rythme
resolution résolution, motion, vœu
silly sot, stupide
speed up accélérer
stride aller à grands pas
substantial important
undertake se charger de
unfair injuste
unlike à la différence de
welfare committee comité d'entreprise
well-being bien-être
wind up liquider
wisdom sagesse

Phrases

It was discussed at some length	on en a parlé assez abondamment
The meeting is brought to an early close	la séance est levée assez rapidement
The company is going public	la maison entre « en société »
There isn't much point in...	il n'y a pas lieu vraiment de...
We can take a ballot	on peut passer aux votes
To vote by proxy	voter par procuration
At a premium, at par, at a discount	à prime, au pair, à perte

Explanations and Other Useful Terms

adjourn postpone, put off the discussions until the next meeting.

ballot *here*, a secret vote.

go public to change from a private company, where the shares cannot be freely bought and sold, to a public company where the shares can be purchased by anyone (cf. pp 204, 205).

ordinary shares the holders of ordinary shares may, in a good year, receive a large dividend which is paid out of the profits once the preference shareholders have been paid. In a bad year, the directors may recommend no payment of ordinary dividend, or a small payment out of retained profits.

preference shares shares which have a fixed rate of **dividend** (interest paid per year). If a company does well, holders do not receive an additional dividend over this rate. Holders of preference shares do not usually have voting rights, which means that they cannot vote at general meetings. However, dividends are paid first to owners of preference shares before any profits are distributed in the form of dividends to the holders of ordinary shares.

take the minutes as read *see* Unit 5.

welfare concerned with making better conditions for everyone. Here, it includes anything to do with the health, safety and leisure of the employees. A **Welfare Committee** will concern itself with working conditions, sports facilities, etc.

Pronunciation

1 — 1 - (- -) attitude, ballot, ceremony, clerical, fashion, level, ordinary, participate, robbery, subject, voluntary, welfare

    - 2 (- -) adventurous, attach, available, canteen, committee, complaint, compulsory, concern, conservative, debenture, discuss, display, eleven, facilities, official, preliminary, provide, responsible

    - - 3 employee, resolution, undertake

2 — [εə] share, chair, fair, there, m*a*yor, v*a*rious, *a*rea, unf*air*, welf*are*
   [iə] here, hear, ar*ea*, id*ea*, s*e*rious
   [ei] they, raise, great, s*a*fety, av*ai*lable
   [e] health, cheque, m*e*mber, cl*e*rical, inst*ea*d, end*ea*vour

3 — Compare : equal ['i:kwəl], equity ['ekwiti], various ['vɛərjəs], variety [və'raiəti], office ['ɔfis], offical [ə'fiʃəl], major, minor ['meidʒə, 'mainə], majority, minority [mə'dʒɔriti, mai'nɔriti] *or* [mi' -, mə'], a woman ['wumen], women ['wimin],

   [en] s*e*nd, b*e*nd, *e*nding, dep*e*nd, deb*e*nture, m*e*ntion, exp*e*nse
   [aen] s*a*nd, b*a*nk, h*a*ndle, subst*a*ntial, b*a*nkrupt, m*a*nsion, exp*a*nd

4 — Note : adjourn [ə'dʒə:n], favourite ['feivrit], mayor [mɛə].

2. SUMMARY

In this episode there is a meeting of the Welfare Committee. On this Committee sit representatives of the various departments in the company. A maintenance fitter, Roy Biggs, speaks for the men employees; the women who work on the shop floor are represented by Miss Tappett, and Miss Prince speaks for the clerical staff. The Personnel Manager is the 5 Chairman of the Committee. The Company Secretary, Mr. William Buckhurst, is also a member of the committee, but, as we hear, he is unable to be present today.

The Welfare Committee looks after anything which concerns the well-being and the health or safety of employees. Today the Welfare 10 Committee discuss a variety of subjects, the first being the reactions of the staff to the new canteen. This has reorganised its serving counters (where the food is displayed) so that they serve a greater number of people more efficiently. Then the Committee discusses a suggestion that wages should be paid by cheque and not in cash. The idea is to avoid drawing large 15 sums of money every week from a bank, with the possible danger of robbery. The next item, which is discussed at some length, is what to do with an area of land behind the factory which could be used for sports facilities, as a place to play games, such as football. The meeting is then brought to an early close because the members of the Committee want to 20 be present at the official opening of the new factory extension. This is going to be opened by the Mayor.

In Hector Grant's speech, which he makes before introducing the Mayor, he mentions ways of raising money. When a company goes public it raises more capital by selling shares to anyone who wishes to buy them. The 25 shares are usually of two kinds: preference shares and ordinary shares.

The meeting of the Welfare Committee is just about to begin.

PART 2 : CONVERSATION AND DOCUMENTS

1. CONVERSATION

(Recorded Text)

(Ian Hampden, Personnel Manager, is president of the Welfare Committee Meeting)

IAN HAMPDEN	**Miss Prince, Miss Tappett, Mr. Biggs ... Well, I think everyone's here, except the Company Secretary, Mr. Buckhurst. I'm afraid he can't join us this morning because he has to meet the Mayor for the opening of the new factory extension. By the way, we'll have to be fairly brief if we're to be down there before eleven. We don't want to miss the official opening, do we?** 5
ROY BIGGS	**No, we don't.**
IAN	**Good. Well, let's take the minutes of the last meeting as read, if you agree?** (*Murmurs of assent.*) **Now the first item on today's agenda arises out of the last meeting. It was agreed by the Committee to collect reactions from the staff to the new canteen and the new serving counters, which were designed to speed up the rate of service. Miss Tappett, you undertook to find out about this.** 10 15

IAN: 'Miss Prince, Miss Tappett, Mr. Biggs... Well, I think everyone's here...'

MISS TAPPETT	Everyone seemed to be very satisfied, Mr. Hampden.
IAN	Are there any complaints?
MISS TAPPETT	Oh, there were a few silly ones, but nothing serious. Most people think it's a great improvement on the old canteen. 20
IAN	Good. Next, the suggestion was made that all wages should in future be paid by cheque instead of in cash. Mr. Biggs undertook to enquire into this. Well, Roy?
BIGGS	I made quite extensive enquiries, Mr. Hampden. Some people didn't object to the idea. They understood the 25 point about safety. But the majority of people, especially the male staff, didn't want to hear about it. They like to see their money. Most of them asked when they'd have time to go to a bank.
MISS PRINCE	Their wives could draw the money from the bank. 30
BIGGS	Most men prefer to handle their own money, Miss Prince.
MISS PRINCE	In my view that is a very old-fashioned attitude.
BIGGS	Maybe, but that is the majority opinion.
IAN	Well, I gather there's not much point in pursuing this matter, anyway for the time being. 35
BIGGS	No, not really.
IAN	Well, next we come to the question of sports facilities, and I'd first like to make a statement about this. As you know, the management is seriously interested in using the area of land beyond the new extension. One suggestion is that 40 some form of sports ground be provided. They ask the

	Welfare Committee to make recommendations. As a
	preliminary I think we should put forward our own views
	on the matter. Roy, perhaps we could start with your
	opinion. 45
BIGGS	I think, if there's enough money that the land should be
	levelled and made into a football field. The majority of
	employees are men, and football is their favourite sport. I
	strongly recommend a football pitch.
MISS PRINCE	It's true, Mr. Biggs, that there are more male than female 50
	employees in this firm, but still, there are a lot of women.
	I think it would be most unfair if the men were given
	special treatment in this way.
IAN	What do you think, Miss Tappett?
MISS TAPPETT	Me? Oh, I really don't know. Well, speaking for myself, I 55
	rather like things as they are. It's nice, with the trees and
	the grass at lunch-time.
BIGGS	I think we should ask for suggestions from everyone first.
	Then we can take a ballot.
MISS PRINCE	But if there's a ballot, the majority wins. I think more 60
	interest should be taken in minority opinions.
IAN	Maybe we can do that, depending on the cash available.
	But the first thing is to get information. Roy, would you
	be willing to make yourself responsible for getting sug-
	gestions from the staff? 65
BIGGS	Yes, all right.
IAN	Fine. Oh, look, it's ten to eleven. I think we'll have to
	adjourn if we want to hear the speeches. I think we've
	settled most of the business. Now we'd better fix the date
	of the next meeting. . . . 70

(At the official opening of the new factory extension)

HECTOR GRANT	Mr. Mayor, ladies and gentlemen. You all know what this
	little ceremony is about; to launch this new extension. But
	before I call upon the Mayor, Alderman Ridley, to per-
	form the ceremony, I would like to tell you something
	about the state of our company and what we hope to do in 75
	the future. It's sixty years ago to the day that the late Mr.
	Harper and my father first started. . . . (*Mr. Grant's
	speech continues*) . . . At the annual general meeting of
	Harper & Grant, held this morning, the necessary resolu-
	tions were passed to allow a substantial increase in our 80
	authorised capital and to change the articles so that the

shares of the company may be freely bought and sold on the open market.... We're going public.

VOICE   What about the workers?

HECTOR GRANT   Anyone will be able to buy Harper & Grant shares. But   85
we are proposing to issue a special class of share, with all
the rights attaching to the ordinary shares, which can be
bought and sold by employees only, at a price below the
open-market value. We want all employees to have the
chance to participate in what we are all sure will be the   90
successful future of their company. As we continue to
stride forward, we must keep a fair balance between the
perhaps somewhat conservative wisdom and care for
detail that comes with experience, and the adventurous
spirit of high endeavour. With your help, success will be   95
assured. (*Applause.*)

PRACTICE SENTENCES

Say the practice sentences on the record :

  i The first item on today's agenda arises out of the last meeting.
 ii The management asks the Welfare Committee to make recommendations.
iii We must try to decide today what method we should adopt.
 iv I think we'll have to adjourn.
  v We'd better fix the date of the next meeting.
 vi We're proposing to issue a special class of share.

2. COMPANIES IN ENGLAND

Application and allotment: anyone who wishes to buy new issue shares in a company can fill in (complete) an application form, which is sometimes part of an advertisement offering the shares or which can be obtained from the issuing house which is handling the shares required. Sometimes an issue of shares is *over-subscribed*, that is, there are not enough shares to go round, as too many people want them. In this case the would-be purchaser may receive only a proportion of the shares he wanted, or in some cases he may not receive any; this happens if the number of people wanting shares is so great that a ballot is held. In this case a ballot does not mean a vote. It means that lots are drawn. If the purchaser is lucky and gets some shares he will be sent a letter of allotment, and this will be replaced later by a share certificate.

Voting rights: the holders of ordinary shares (the equity holders) have the right to vote at the annual general meeting of a company or any extraordinary meeting of shareholders which may be called. They vote on the appointment of auditors, elect directors and can pass or reject resolutions coming from the floor of the meeting or put forward by the directors. A resolution put forward by the directors would call for approval of the accounts and the directors' report of the year's trading. Each share carries one vote.

In most companies shareholders have the right to vote by *proxy*, that is, they appoint someone to vote for them by signing a form. The person who votes for them may be a director of the company or another shareholder. A share is said to be *at a premium* when it costs more than its *face value*, its actual denomination. If the share is at its face value it is said to be *at par*. If it can be bought for less, it is said to be *at a discount*.

Debentures, unlike shares, are loans to a company with a fixed rate of interest. This interest has to be paid before any dividends (preference or ordinary) are paid.

If a company fails or goes out of business it can be brought to an end by either *voluntary* or *compulsory liquidation*. With the first, the shareholders pass a resolution to wind up the business, thereby putting the company into liquidation. A liquidator is appointed who sells the assets of the company, pays all debts, etc. Sometimes compulsory liquidation is ordered because a company has not obeyed the rules laid down by the Companies Act (an Act of Parliament) or because a creditor has asked a court for a *winding-up order* (the company has refused to pay, and this seems to be the only way of obtaining some, at least, of the money he is owed). If this order is granted, the directors are deposed and the business is stopped. The claims of all creditors are then paid when the assets of the company have been sold. If there is any money left this is then divided among the shareholders according to the shares they hold.

(See also pp 204, 205)

THE NEW BRITISH CURRENCY

In February, 1971, a new decimal system of currency replaced the old system. It has two units: the pound (£) and the penny (p), each pound consisting of 100 pence. The new coins are:

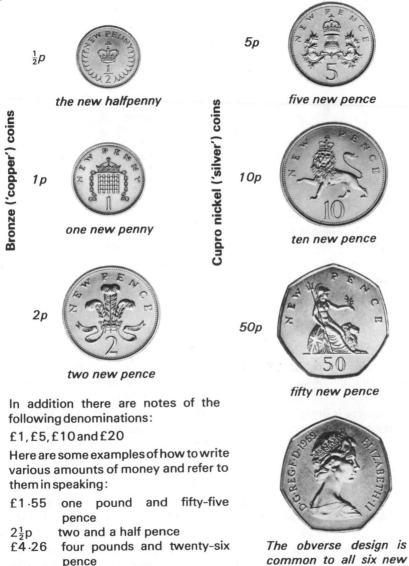

Bronze ('copper') coins

½p — the new halfpenny

1p — one new penny

2p — two new pence

Cupro nickel ('silver') coins

5p — five new pence

10p — ten new pence

50p — fifty new pence

In addition there are notes of the following denominations:

£1, £5, £10 and £20

Here are some examples of how to write various amounts of money and refer to them in speaking:

£1·55   one pound and fifty-five pence
2½p   two and a half pence
£4·26   four pounds and twenty-six pence
48p   forty-eight pence

The obverse design is common to all six new coins.

— 379 —

PART 3 : NOTES AND PRACTICE

1. RAPPEL GRAMMATICAL

Summary :

Rappelons que le futur proche se forme soit par **be going to**, soit par **be about to,** comme nous en avons deux exemples ici :

22. **It is going to be opened by the Mayor**   Il va être inauguré par le Maire

27. **The meeting is just about to begin**   La réunion est sur le point de commencer

Signalons que dans la langue des affaires, de l'économie, etc. la notion de futur est souvent évoquée à l'aide de constructions qui font la part de l'hypothèse.

Ainsi, la notion d'éventualité future pourra être évoquée à l'aide de **to be expected to** :

Business is expected to maintain its level of last year   On estime que les affaires se maintiendront au niveau de l'an dernier

The annual meeting is expected to be rather stormy   On s'attend à une assemblée générale annuelle plutôt orageuse

Une construction extrêmement fréquente pour évoquer le futur emploie **likely** de la manière suivante :

The programme is likely to entail a drastic reduction in manning   Le programme risque d'entraîner une importante réduction de main-d'œuvre

The Ministry is likely to impose an import levy on overseas cereals   On s'attend à ce que le Ministère impose une taxe à l'importation des céréales en provenance de l'étranger

La négative se formera par **not likely** ou **unlikely to** :

They're unlikely to solve the problem of redundancy   Il y a peu de chances qu'ils résolvent le problème du chômage technologique

They're unlikely to call for another debate on the question   Il est peu vraisemblable qu'ils provoquent une seconde réunion sur cette question

Conversation :

6. **We have to be there before eleven.** Notons à propos de **before** dans cette affirmative que les phrases négatives correspondantes se construisent en général avec **until** :

> **They won't be despatched until**   Elles ne seront pas expédiées avant
> **the end of the week**   la fin de la semaine

40. **One suggestion is that some form of sports ground be provided. Be** est ici le subjonctif présent de **to be**. Il se rencontre encore dans le style administratif, juridique, etc. On peut l'entendre dans des circonstances comme celle-ci, où l'orateur peut chercher à parler dans une langue un peu plus guindée. Cet usage après des verbes indiquant la proposition, la suggestion, la volonté, etc. est plus fréquent en américain qu'en anglais.

2. EXERCISES

EXERCISE 1. — Put in the missing preposition, etc. :

1. Miss Prince speaks ... the clerical staff.   2. The Welfare Committee looks ... all that concerns the well-being, health and safety of employees. 3. What were the reactions of the staff ... the profit sharing scheme ? 4. Wages should be paid ... cheque not ... cash .   5. The next item has been discussed ... some length.   6. Let's take the minutes of the last meeting ... read.   7. It's a great improvement ... the old system. 8. Some people didn't object ... the idea.   9. There's not much point ... pursuing the matter.   10. We could start ... the opinion of the Personnel Manager.   11. Everything will depend ... the cash available.

EXERCISE 2. — Read aloud the following sentences as fast as possible... You should not hesitate when reading the figures !

1. Hire purchase credit on cars fell by 23 % in the 2nd half of 1970.   2. The growth rate is expected to fall by 2.5 % by 1980.   3. The new plant will employ 1,867 workers against the present figure of 2,692.   4. £18,986 were distributed last year to preference shareholders.   5. The percentage of sales spent on research went from 0.8 % to 2.6 %.   6. Between 1938 and 1956 average earnings rose by 245 %.   7. Their invoice amounted to £1,874.   8. 60 days after sight pay to our order £2,693 for value received. 9. The rate of purchase tax rose from 27 ½ % to 33 ½ %.   10. There are only 20 % of the whole capital of £3m in 5.50 % preference shares.   11. The company's total earnings last year were a mere $ 3,632,000.   12. Is their phone number 286.99.07 or 286.90.97 ?

EXERCISE 3. — Change as follows :

all the goods may be damaged → all the goods might have been damaged

1. The insurance premium may be raised by 5 %.   2. Such a case may not be covered by the guarantee.   3. We may hire a safe at the bank.   4. They may allow you an overdraft.   5. The lease may be cancelled at any time.

6. Your decision may lead the firm to disaster. 7. Half of the workers may lose their jobs within a year. 8. You may make a very bad bargain. 9. Deliveries may be delayed by the bad weather.

EXERCISE 4. — *Change as follows* :

Have they given a new order to the firm →
they are expected to give a new order to the firm

1. Have exports fallen by more than 5 % ? 2. Have there been further levies on goods purchased abroad ? 3. Has the American firm set up an assembly plant in Europe ? 4. Has the government made cuts in the rate of interest ? 5. Has the company given the go-ahead for the merger ? 6. Have the sales risen according to your forecasts ?

EXERCISE 5. — *Change as follows* :

a. **such investors will be attracted by Harper & Grant shares** →
such investors are likely to be attracted by H. & G. shares
b. **Hector Grant won't lose the confidence of his employers** →
Hector Grant is unlikely to lose the confidence of his employees

1. A reasonably stable industry will be more efficient. 2. The savings will be offset by increased social costs. 3. The engineer won't admit he has failed. 4. They won't solve the problem of redundancy. 5. Inefficient enterprises will be closed down. 6. The government won't impose a wage freeze. 7. Negotiations will begin next February. 8. All the workers will get a 5 % rise. 9. Delivery times won't be shortened. 10. There will be another devaluation. 11. The local authorities won't refuse them money. 12. The Board will recommend a reduction in current spending.

EXERCISE 6. — *Turn into the singular whenever it is possible* :

1. These systems are not necessarily more satisfactory. 2. They want to pay for these items in advance. 3. What if the directors clash with their most loyal supporters ? 4. The cards were not in those files, were they ? 5. They put themselves forward for their workmates' grievances. 6. These means of conveyance are finally cheaper than the others. 7. Payments to foreign owners of British-based firms are invisible imports.

EXERCISE 7. — *Turn into the plural whenever it is possible* :

1. Every institution functions as a broker. 2. The small dealer is unable to exploit this modern method of distribution. 3. This has been a very lucrative transaction. 4. The profit margin in that transaction was very low. 5. Every branch sends a daily statement to its customers. 6. This figure doesn't compare with that of the previous month, does it ?

EXERCISE 8. — *Change as follows* :

a. **we draw large sums every week from a bank ; we must avoid it** →
we must avoid drawing large sums every week from a bank
b. **most men handle their own money ; this is what they prefer** →
most men prefer to handle their own money

1. They have to publish their accounts ; they are no longer exempt from it.   2. He sees that the books are ready for checking ; he is responsible for it.   3. He made himself responsible for getting suggestions from the staff ; he was willing...   4. He'll tell me how to run my business ; he insists on that.   5. They'll leave the job to be done by outsiders ; there's a strong objection to it.   6. They didn't collaborate in the policy of wage-restraint, they refused.   7. They didn't pursue the matter ; there was no point in it.   8. We shall meet your representative ; we're looking forward to it.   9. The government won't impose import duties in defence of its agriculture ; it is reluctant to.   10. The information section keeps a sharp eye on competitors ; it's its duty.

EXERCISE 9. — *Please complete the following with the correct word or phrase* :

1. At the beginning of a meeting, the chairman may ask if the minutes of the last meeting ...   2. A private company which wants to enlarge its share capital by attracting outsiders to take shares will have to ...   3. A firm which cannot pay its outstanding debts and is losing trade may have to go into ...   4. A shareholder who cannot attend an Annual General Meeting may appoint someone to vote for him ...

EXERCISE 10. — *Write a report for the staff magazine of what Hector Grant said in his speech* :

Example of the first sentence : At the official opening of the new factory extension last Thursday, the Chairman, Mr. Hector Grant, after welcoming the mayor, announced that Harper & Grant would shortly become a public company.

Note : The wording can be changed and modified a little, if you wish, as long as the essential points he makes in his speech are reported. *Useful link phrases* : ' He said that ... ' ; ' He pointed out that ... ' ; ' He went on to say that ... ' ; ' He continued by saying that ... ' ; ' He added that ... ' ; ' He finished by saying that ... '.

EXERCISE 11. — *Translate into English* :

1. Le premier point à l'ordre du jour émane de la dernière réunion.   2. La direction demande au comité d'entreprise d'émettre des vœux.   3. Nous devons essayer de décider aujourd'hui de la méthode que nous devons adopter.   4. Je crois que nous allons devoir lever la séance.   5. Nous ferions bien de fixer la date de la prochaine séance.   6. Nous envisageons d'émettre une catégorie spéciale d'actions.   7. On estime que les affaires se maintiendront au même niveau que l'an dernier.   8. Notre Directeur des ventes est absent depuis huit jours.   9. Il ne rentrera pas avant le 22.   10. Les actionnaires ont voté une résolution pour liquider l'affaire.   11. Avez-vous le droit de vote à l'assemblée générale annuelle des actionnaires ?   12. Les actionnaires ont le droit de voter par procuration.   13. Harper & Grant va devenir une société anonyme.   14. Il y aura une augmentation importante du capital social.   15. Peter et John critiquent souvent ce qu'ils appellent la sagesse un peu conservatrice de Hector Grant.   16. Il y a plus d'employés que d'employées dans l'entreprise.   17. Je crois qu'on devrait tenir compte davantage des avis de la minorité.   18. A mon avis, c'est une attitude bien dépassée.   19. Au préalable, je crois que nous devrions donner notre avis sur la question.   20. Grâce à votre soutien, le succès sera assuré.

VERBES IRRÉGULIERS

to arise, arose, arisen
to bear, bore, born
to become, became, become
to begin, began, begun
to bid[1], bade, bidden
to bid[2], bid, bid (n. a bid)
to bind, bound, bound
to break, broke, broken
to bring, brought, brought
to build, built, built
to buy, bought, bought
to cast[3], cast, cast
to catch, caught, caught
to choose, chose, chosen
    (n. a choice)
to come, came, come
to cost[4], cost, cost
to cut, cut, cut
to deal, dealt, dealt
to do, did, done
to draw, drew, drawn
to drive, drove, driven
to fall, fell, fallen
to feed, fed, fed
to feel, felt, felt
to fight, fought, fought
to find, found, found
to fly, flew, flown
to forbid, forbade, forbidden
to forget, forgot, forgotten
to forgive, forgave, forgiven
to freeze, froze, frozen
to get, got, got
to give, gave, given (n. a gift)
to go, went, gone
to grow, grew, grown (n. growth)
to hang, hung, hung
to hear, heard, heard
to hide, hid, hid
to hit, hit, hit
to hold, held, held
to keep, kept, kept
to know, knew, known
to lay, laid, laid
to learn, learnt, learnt
to let, let, let
to leave, left, left
to lend, lent, lent

to lie, lay, lain
to light, lit, lit
to lose, lost, lost (n. a loss)
to make, made, made
to mean, meant, meant
to meet, met, met
to overcome, overcame, overcome
to pay, paid, paid
to put, put, put
to read, read, read
to ring, rang, rung
to rise[5], rose, risen
to say, said, said
to see, saw, seen
to seek, sought, sought
to sell, sold, sold (n. a sale)
to send, sent, sent
to set, set, set
to shake, shook, shaken
to show, showed, shown
to shut, shut, shut
to sink, sank, sunk
to sit, sat, sat
to speak, spoke, spoken
to speed, sped, sped
to spend, spent, spent
to spoil, spoilt, spoilt
to spread, spread, spread
to spring, sprang, sprung
to stand, stood, stood
to steal, stole, stolen
to stick, stuck, stuck
to strike, struck, struck
to strive, strove, striven
to swear, swore, sworn
to take, took, taken
to teach, taught, taught
to tell, told, told
to think, thought, thought
to thrive, throve, thriven
to throw, threw, thrown
to understand, understood,
    understood
to win, won, won
to withdraw, withdrew, withdrawn
to withhold, withheld, withheld
to withstand, withstood, withstood
to write, wrote, written

Notes : bid 1 : *ordonner* ; bid 2 : *enchérir* ; *id.* outbid, overbid
cast 3 : to cast, cast, cast, *mais* ; to broadcast, broadcasted, broadcast(ed) ;
     to forecast, forecast (ed), forecast(ed)
cost 1 : cost, cost, cost = *coûter* ; cost, costed, costed = *évaluer le coût.*
rise 5 : to rise : *s'élever, monter, augmenter* ; to raise (*rég.*) : *augmenter, élever* ;
    n. a pay rise : *une augmentation* ; *U.S.A.* a raise : *une augmentation*

GLOSSAIRE

A

account [ə'kaunt] compte 6, 14
  close an account [klouz ən —] fermer un compte 13
  bank account ['bæŋk —] compte en banque 13
  current account ['kʌrənt —] compte courant 13
  deposit account [di'pɔzit —] compte de dépôt à terme ou à préavis 13
  nominal accounts ['nɔminl —] compte de choses 19
  personal accounts ['pə:sənl] comptes de personnes 19
  real accounts [riəl —] comptes de valeurs, d'exploitation 19
  account executive [— ig'zekjutiv] chef de publicité 6
  account group [— gru:p] équipe publicitaire 14
  accounts comptabilité 19
  account payee only [— pei'i: 'ounli] non négociable 13
accountancy [ə'kauntənsi] comptabilité 19
accountant [ə'kauntənt] comptable 17
achieve [ə't ʃi:v] réaliser 17
acknowledge [ək'nɔlidʒ] accuser réception 3
acknowledgement [ək'nɔlidʒmənt] accusé de réception 3
actuary ['æktjuəri] actuaire 23
adjourn [ə'dʒə:n] lever la séance 24
adjusters [ə'dʒʌstəz] experts, répartiteurs d'avarie 23
administrative department [əd'ministrətiv di'pa:tmənt] services administratifs 2
advertise ['ædvətaiz] faire de la publicité 6
  advertisement [əd'və:tismənt] publicité 6, 14
  classified ad. ['klæsifaid 'æd] petite annonce 14
  advertising agency ['ædvətaiziŋ 'eidʒənsi] agence de publicité 6

advertising campaign [— kæm'pein] campagne publicitaire 6
advertising manager [— 'mænidʒə] directeur de la publicité 6
afford [ə'fɔ:d] pouvoir s'offrir 1
agenda [ə'dʒəndə] ordre du jour 5
  item on the agenda ['aitəm] question à l'ordre du jour 5
agent ['eidʒənt] agent commercial, concessionnaire 1
  sole agent [soul] concessionnaire exclusif 3
  clearing agent ['kliəriŋ —] 3
  forwarding agent ['fɔ:wədiŋ —] transitaire 3
agitate ['ædʒiteit] faire de l'agitation 12
analyse a job ['ænəlaiz] étudier un travail 9
and Company (& Co.) [ən'kʌmpəni ən 'kou] et Cie 13
apply for [ə'plai fə] faire acte de candidature pour... 22
applicant ['æplikənt] candidat 6
application and allotment (of shares) [æpli'keiʃən ən ə'lɔtmənt] souscription et attribution (d'actions) 24
  get an application in faire une demande
appoint [ə'pɔint] nommer, désigner 1
appointment [ə'pɔintmənt] rendez-vous 2
apprentice [ə'prentis] apprenti 20
apprentice ship [ə'prentiʃip] apprentissage 20
appropriation [ə,proupri'eiʃən] affectation, imputation, répartition 14
approve [ə'pru:v] approuver 5
arson ['a:sən] incendie volontaire 23
articles ['a:tiklz] articles, clauses 10,13
  Articles of Association [— əv æ,sou si'eiʃən] statuts 13
apologize [ə'pɔlədʒaiz] s'excuser 7
assemble [ə'sembl] monter 2, 7
  assembly [ə'sembli] montage 7
  assembly shop [— ʃɔp] atelier de montage 2

assess [ə'ses] faire une estimation, évaluer 16

assessment estimation, expertise 16

assets ['æsets] biens, avoir-actif 19

assistant [ə'sistənt] sous —, vendeur 11

assurance [ə'ʃuərəns] assurance 23

attend [ə'tend] assister à 23

auditors ['ɔ:ditəz] commissaires aux comptes 19

authorized capital capital social 13

automatic [,ɔ:tə'mætik] automatique 1

automation [,ɔ:tə'meiʃən] automation 1

avoid [ə'vɔid] éviter 5

B

back up ['bæk 'ʌp] soutenir 1

balance sheet ['bæləns] bilan 19

ballot ['bælət] vote ; tirage au sort 24

bank [bæŋk] banque

    bank charges [— 'tʃa:dʒiz] frais de banque 13

    bank rate [— reit] taux d'escompte de la Banque (d'Angleterre etc.) 13

    bank statement [— 'steitmənt] relevé de compte 13, 19

bankers' draft ['bæŋkəz 'dra:ft] traite bancaire 13

bankrupt ['bæŋkrʌpt] en faillite 21

    declared bankrupt [di'klɛəd —] déclaré en faillite 21

    go bankrupt ['gou —] faire faillite 21

batch [bætʃ] fournée 18

bay [bei] hall 5

beneficiary ['beni'fiʃəri] bénéficiaire 15

benefits ['benifits] avantages 9

bill of exchange ['bil əv iks'tʃeindʒ] lettre de change 3

bill of lading ['bilev 'leidiŋ] connaissement 3, 15

blanket insurance ['blæŋkit in'ʃuərəns] assurance générale 23

blanking ['blæŋkiŋ] découpage à la presse 2

blotter ['blɔtə] sous-main 14

blotting paper ['blɔtiŋ peipə] buvard 14

board (cardboard) [bɔ:d, 'ka:dbɔ:d] carton 7

board conseil d'administration 5

    board meeting ['bɔ:d mi:tiŋ] séance du conseil 1

    board room [— rum] salle du conseil 6

bonus ['bounəs] prime 5

book [buk] réserve 9

book-keeping system ['buk-ki:piŋ 'sistəm] comptabilité 19

book-keeper ['buk-'ki:pə] comptable 19

boss [bɔs] patron 2

bounce [bauns] être sans provision (*chèque*) 13

box file ['bɔks-fail] dossier, classeur fermant 22

branch [bra:ntʃ] succursale ; agence 13

brand [brænd] marque 14

    Brand Manager ['brænd 'mænidʒə] directeur de la marque 14

break into a market ['breik intu ə 'ma:kit] pénétrer un marché 22

break [breik] casser

    break down ['breik 'daun] tomber en panne ; ventiler, ventilation 17, 16, 15

    broken down ['broukən 'daun] en panne 17

brief-case ['bri:f-keis] porte-documents 3

bring it (*a subject*) **up** ['briŋ it ʌp] mettre une question sur le tapis 12

brochure ['brouʃjuə] brochure 6

budget ['bʌdʒit] budget 15, 17

    budgetary control ['bʌdʒitəri 'kən'troul] contrôle budgétaire 1, 17

building ['bildiŋ] bâtiment

    building inspector [— in'spektə] Inspecteur de l'Urbanisme et de l'Equipement 5

    building society [— sə'saiəti] Société de Prêt Immobilier 13

    building bye-law [— bai lɔ:] arrêté municipal sur la construction 5

built up ['bilt 'ʌp] tout monté 7

bulk order ['bʌlk 'ɔ:də] commande en gros 15

Buying Department ['baiiŋ di'pa:tment] Service Achats 4

bye-law ['bai lɔ:] décret d'une autorité locale 5

C

call back ['kɔ:l 'bæk] rappeler 7

campaign [kæm'pein] campagne 7

    teaser campaign ['ti:zə —] campagne mystère 14

cancel ['kænsl] annuler 4

canteen [kæn'ti:n] cantine 24

canvass ['kænvəs] prospecter, faire une tournée 18

carriers ['kæriəz] transporteurs 16

carry a vote ['kæri ə 'vòut] donne le droit de vote 13

cash [kæʃ] comptant ; liquide, espèces, trésorerie

    cash against documents [— ə'genst 'dɔkjumənts] comptant contre documents 15

    cash book ['kæʃ buk] livre de caisse 19

cash flow [ˈkæʃ ˈflou] capacité de financement 2,5
catalogue [ˈkætələg] catalogue 1
circulate [ˈsəːkjuleit] faire circuler, communiquer 11
  limited circulation [ˈlimitid ˌsəːkjuˈlei ʃən] diffusion restreinte 11
chair [tʃɛə] fauteuil, chaise, siège 1
  chairman [ˈtʃɛəmən] président 1
chargehand [ˈtʃaːdʒhænd] chef d'équipe 8
cheque [tʃek] chèque 11, 13
  crossed cheque [ˈkrɔst —] chèque barré 11, 13
circularise [ˈsəːkjuləraiz] envoyer en circulaire 18
civil court [ˈsivil ˈkɔːt] tribunal civil 8
claim [kleim] réclamation, revendication, demande 4, 8
clear [kliə] dédouaner 3
  clearing house [ˈkliəriŋ haus] chambre de compensation 13
clearance [ˈkliərəns] expédition en douane ; dédouanement 3
  date of clearance [ˈdeit əv ˈkliərəns] date de sortie (du port) 3
clerk [klaːk] employé de bureau 11
clinch a deal [klintʃ ə diːl] conclure une affaire 15
clock in [ˈklɔkˈin] pointer 12
come up with [ˈkʌm ˈʌp wið] produire 22
commercial bank [keˈməːʃl ˈbæŋk] banque d'affaires 23
commission [kəˈmiʃən] commission 1
company [ˈkʌmpəni] société 1
  Company Secretary [— ˈsekrətri] secrétaire général 1, 17
compensate [ˈkɔmpenseit] indemniser 10
  compensation [ˌkɔmpenˈseiʃən] réparation civile 4, 8
competition [ˌkɔmpiˈtiʃən] concurrence 4, 8
competitive [kəmˈpetitiv] concurrentiel 18
complain [kəmˈplein] se plaindre, réclamer 7
complaint [— t] réclamation 7
component [kəmˈpounənt] pièce, élément 7
  component part — [ˈpaːt] pièce détachée, élément 2
computerize [kəmˈpjuːtəraiz] passer sur ordinateur 4
confidential [ˌkɔnfidenʃəl] confidentiel 11
consign [kenˈsain] envoyer, expédier 3
  consignee [ˌkɔnsaiˈniː] destinataire 15
  consignor [kənˈsainə] expéditeur 15
console (*control panel*) [ˈkɔnsoul] console 4
consultants [kənˈsʌltənts] organisateurs, conseils 9

consumer [kənˈsjuːmə] consommateur 1
  consumer goods [— ˈgudz] biens de consommation 14
  consumer survey [— ˈsəːvei] étude de marché 14
container [kənˈteinə] container, conteneur 3, 7
contract [ə ˈkɔntrækt ; tə kenˈtrækt] contrat ; établir un contrat 18
  contract hire [— ˈhaiə] louer sous contrat 16
  contractors [kənˈtræktəz] entrepreneurs 5, 16
  honour a contract [ˈɔnə] honorer un contrat 4
  sub-contract [ˈsʌb —] sous-traiter 18
contribute [kənˈtribjuːt] contribuer ; cotiser 10
contribution [ˌkɔntriˈbjuːʃən] cotisation 10
controller [kənˈtroulə] contrôleur 14
controlling interest [kənˈtrouliŋ ˈintrist] intérêt prédominant 13
conveyor belt [kənˈveiə ˈbelt] chaîne, bande porteuse 2
cope with [ˈkoup ˈwið] être aux prises (avec) 3
copy [ˈkɔpi] copie, exemplaire 6
copywriter [ˈkɔpi-raitə] rédacteur publicitaire 6
corporate planning [ˈkɔːprit ˈplæniŋ] planification concertée 9
cost [kɔst] coût, frais ; évaluer le coût de... 15
  cost breakdown [— ˈbreikdaun] ventilation des frais 20
  cost centre [— ˈsentə] poste budgétaire 17
  cost, insurance and freight (*c.i.f.*) [ˈkɔst inˈʃuərəns ən ˈfreit] [ˈsiː ˈai ˈef] coût, assurance, frêt, C.A.F. 15
  direct cost [diˈrekt —] frais directs 15
  fixed costs [fikst] frais fixes 15
  marginal cost [ˈmaːdʒinl] frais marginaux 15
counterfoil [ˈkauntəfɔil] souche, talon 13
cover [ˈkʌvə] couvrir 23, 18
  to have cover être couvert 23
  covering [ˈkʌvəriŋ] couverture 18
craftsman [ˈkraːftsmən] artisan 10
crate [kreit] caisse à claire-voie 3, 7
credit [ˈkredit] crédit 19
  to credit créditer 19
  credit note [— nout] note de crédit 19
  long credit, long term credit [ˈlɔŋ —, ˈlɔŋ təːm —] crédit long 21

short credit, short term credit ['ʃɔ:t —, 'ʃɔ:t tə:m —] crédit court   21
creditor ['kreditə] créditeur   19
Critical Path Analysis (**C.P.A.**) ['kritikl pa:θ ə'nælisis ; 'si: 'pi: 'ei] recherche opérationnelle, méthode du chemin critique   1, 9

D

damaged ['dæmidʒd] endommagé, avarié   7
damages ['dæmidʒiz] dommages et intérêts   7
day release ['dei-ri'li:s] jour de congé   20
deadline ['dedlain] limite ultime   2
deal with ['di:l wiθ] traiter de, avec   3
debenture [di'bentʃə] obligation   24
debit ['debit] débit   19
debt [det] dette   19
debt collector ['det kə'lektə] agent de recouvrement   21
debtor ['detə] débiteur   19
deed [di:d] acte   10
default [di'fɔ:lt] manquement ; faire défaut   21
defer payment [di'fə: 'peimənt] remettre le paiement à une date ultérieure 21
delay [di'lei] retard ; retarder   5
deliver [di'livə] livrer   21
delivery [di'livəri] livraison   21
delivery bank [— bæŋk] quai de déchargement   2
delivery bay [— bei] hall de livraison 2
delivery charge [— tʃa:dʒ] frais de livraison   2
delivery date [— deit] date de livraison   1
meet a delivery date ['mi:t —] respecter les délais de livraison   4
demand [di'ma:nd] la demande   18
demurrage [di'mʌridʒ] surestaries   15
deposit [di'pɔzit] dépôt ; déposer   19
depreciation [di'pri:ʃi'eiʃən] amortissement   16
design ['di'zain] dessein ; projet, étude
design department [— di'pa:tmənt] bureau des études   11
design service [— 'sə:vis] services d'études   18
designer [di'zaiə] graphiste   7
despatch [dis'pætʃ] expédier   7
despatch case [— keis] porte-documents   3
diagram ['daiəgræm] diagramme   18
dial [daiəl] cadran ; composer un numéro   4
diary ['daiəri] agenda   9

dictating machine [dik'teitiŋ mə'ʃi:n] dictaphone   4
direct mail advertising [di'rekt 'meil 'ædvətaiziŋ], **direct mail shot** [— 'ʃɔt] publicité directe par correspondance   14
director [di'rektə] administrateur
Directors' Report [di'rektəz ri'pɔ:t] rapport de gestion   19
disclaim all liability [dis'kleim 'ɔ:l laiə'biliti] rejeter toute responsabilité   23
discount [dis'kaunt] escompte, rabais 18
cash discount ['kæʃ —] escompte de caisse   18
trade discount ['treid —] remise sur les marchandises, sur facture, d'usage 18
at a discount [ət ə —] à perte   24
Discounted Cash Flow (**D.C.F.**) — id 'kæʃ 'flou] flux de disponibilité bancaire à court terme   1
dishonoured [dis'ɔnəd] protesté ; non accepté   13
dismiss [dis'mis] renvoyer   10
disown [dis'aun] désavouer   9
display [dis'plei] exposer   14
distribute [dis'tribju:t] distribuer   18
distributor [dis'tribjutə] distributeur 18
channel of distribution ['tʃænl əv ˌdistri'bju:ʃən] canaux de distribution   1
District Organiser ['distrikt 'ɔ:gənaizə] 12 délégué régional   18
dividend ['dividənd] dividende   19
dock dues ['dɔk 'dju:z] droits de bassin 1
double entry ['dʌbl 'entri] partie double 19
draft [dra:ft] traite, effet, lettre de change   17
draughtsman [dra:ftsmən] dessinateur 18
draw out (**money**) ['drɔ: 'aut] sortir, retirer   19
drawn on ['drɔ:n 'ɔn] tiré sur   13
drawee [drɔ:'i:] tiré, payeur   13
drawer ['drɔ:ə] tireur, souscripteur 13
drill [dril] forer, fraiseuse   2
drive [draiv] campagne, effort   2
dunnage ['dʌnidʒ] fardage, calage, grenier   16
duplicate ['dju:plikeit] duplicata, double ; faire en double   3
duplicating machine [— iŋ mə'ʃi:n] duplicateur   3
duty ['dju:ti] taxe, droit   1
duty paid ['dju:ti 'peid] droits acquittés   15

E

eager ['i:gə] avide, désireux, impatient 14
efficiency [i'fiʃənsi] rendement 1
efficient [i'fiʃənt] efficace 1
Electronic Data Processing (E.D.P.)
[elik'trɔnik 'deitə prou'sesiŋ],
[i:, di: 'pi:] informatique 1
endorse [in'dɔ:s] endosser, avaliser 13
endorsement [in'dɔ:smənt] endos(sement) 13
endowment [in'daumənt] dotation 23
enforce [in'fɔ:s] appliquer, mettre en vigueur 8
engineered by [endʒi'niəd bai] monté, manigancé par... 12
entail [in'teil] entraîner 4
entitled (to) [in'taitld] qui a droit à 8
estimate [æn'estimit, tə 'estimeit] devis, estimation ; faire une estimation 5
executive [ig'zekjutiv] cadre 6
exhibition [,eksi'biʃən] exposition 14
expedite ['ekspidait] presser, activer 4
expenses [iks'pensiz] dépenses, frais 15
entertainment expenses [,entə'teinmənt —] frais de représentation 15
expired [iks'paiəd] périmé 15
extension [ik'stenʃən] extension 5

F

face value ['feis 'vælju:] valeur nominale 24
facility [fə'siliti] installation 20
factory ['fæktəri] usine 4
factory inspector inspecteur du travail 8
fatal (*accident*) ['feitl] mortel 9
faulty ['fɔ:lti] défectueux 7
fiddle (*slang*) [fidl] tripotage, fraude, trafic 19
field survey étude de marché 1
file [fail] dossier, chemise ; classer 1
filing cabinet ['failiŋ kæbinit] classeur 1
finish ['finiʃ] fini 18
fire (*slang = dismiss*) [faiə] saquer, renvoyer 10
firm [fə:m] entreprise ; ferme 1, 15
firm order [— 'ɔ:də] commande ferme 15
fitters' shop ['fitəz 'ʃɔp] atelier d'ajustage 8
fix an appointment fixer un rendez-vous 2
fixtures and fittings ['fikstʃəz ən 'fitiŋs] installations et agencements 4
flimsy ['flimzi] papier pelure 3
float [flout] capitaux circulants, roulants 19

F (continued)

folder ['fouldə] chemise, dossier 5
foreman [fɔ:mən] contremaître, agent de maîtrise 8, 12
formal [fɔ:ml] officiel 5
forthcoming ['fɔ:θ'kʌmiŋ] prochain, futur 2
forward-looking ['fɔ:wəd-lukiŋ] tourné vers l'avenir 2
foundations [faun'deiʃənz] fondations 5
franco dom ['fræŋkou 'dɔm] franco domicile 15
frank [fræŋk] affranchir, oblitérer 3
franking machine [— iŋ mə'ʃi:n] machine à affranchir 3
free on board (f.o.b.) ['fri: ɔn 'bɔ:d, 'ef ou 'bi:] franco bord 15
free on rail (f.o.r.) ['fri: ɔn 'reil, 'ef ou 'a:] franco wagon 15
freight [freit] frêt, chargement 3
full-time [ful-taim] à plein temps 8
fund [fʌnd] fonds, caisse 10

G

get on to ['get 'ɔn tu] appeler au téléphone 3
get through ['get 'θru:] avoir la communication 3
goggles ['gɔglz] lunettes de protection 8
goods [gudz] marchandises
goodwill ['gud'wil] clientèle ; pas de porte 18
grant [gra:nt] subvention, allocation 20
graph [græf] graphique, diagramme 20
grievance ['gri:vəns] grief 12
grinder, grinding machine ['graində] rectifieuse 8
group rates ['gru:p 'reits] cadences de groupe 9
growth [grouθ] croissance, expansion 1

H

halve [ha:v] réduire de moitié 5
handle ['hændl] manipuler ; avoir en main, traiter 3
handling ['hændliŋ] manutention 1
head office ['hed-'ɔfis] siège social 7
hectic ['hektik] changé, affolant 3
hi-jack ['hai-dʒæk] détourner 16
hire [haiə] engager 1
hire purchase, H.P. ['haiə 'pə:tʃis, 'eitʃ 'pi:] vente à tempérament 1
hoarding ['hɔ:diŋ] panneau d'affichage 6
holding ['houldiŋ] participation, portefeuille 13, 17
hold-up ['hould ʌp] bloquer, arrêter, retarder 3
hook [huk] crochet 7

I

import [ən 'impɔ:t, tu im'pɔ:t] importation ; importer

import licence ['impɔ:t 'laisəns] licence d'importation, permis d'entrée 1

incentive [in'sentiv] stimulant 20

income ['inkʌm] revenu 1

  income per capita [— pə 'kæpitə] revenu par tête 1

incoming ['in'kʌmiŋ] arrivée 3

indent [in'dent] ordre d'achat, bon de commande (commerce extérieur) 15

industrial accident [in'dʌstriəl 'æksidənt] accident du travail 8

Industrial Development Certificate (I.D.C.) [in'dʌstriəl di'veləpmənt sə'tifikit, 'ai di: 'si] permis de construire industriel 5

insolvent [in'sɔlvənt] insolvable 21

inspect [in'spekt] inspecter 7

  inspection records [— ʃən 'rekɔ:dz] archives d'inspection 7

institute proceedings ['institju:t prə'sidiŋz] poursuivre en justice, engager une procédure 8

insurance [in'ʃuərəns] assurance 23

  insurance broker [— 'broukə] courtier d'assurance 23

insure [in'ʃuə] assurer

interest ['intrist] intérêt 13

internal phone [in'tə:nl 'foun] téléphone intérieur 4

International Subscriber Dialling (I.S.D.) ['intə'næ ʃənl səb'skraibə 'daiəliŋ, 'ai es 'di:] Système Téléphonique Internat¹ Automatique 3

intake ['inteik] arrivée, entrée 3

involve [in'vɔlv] entraîner, impliquer

inter-office communication system ['intə'rɔfis kəm'juni'keiʃən sistəm] interphone 14

investigate [in'vestigeit] chercher, enquêter 9

investigator [in'vestigeitə] enquêteur 9

invoice ['invɔis] facture ; facturer 15

  pro forma invoice [prou 'fɔ:mə] facture simulée 15

issue ['isju:] émettre 12

item ['aitəm] article, point, question 5

itinerary [ai'tinrəri] itinéraire 1, 15

K

keep up (with) ['ki:p 'ʌp wið] se tenir à jour 2

knocked down (K.D.) ['nɔkt'down, 'kei 'di:] démonté, en pièces détachées 7

L

labour turnoyer ['leibə 'tə:nouvə] mobilité de la main-d'œuvre 12

lack [læk] manque ; manquer 1

lapse [læps] tomber en désuétude, devenir caduc 22

lathe [leið] tour 8

layout ['leiaut] mise en page ; disposition, implantation 6

leaflet ['li:flit] prospectus, imprimé 6

ledger ['ledʒə] grand livre 19 -

  bought ledger ['bɔ:t —] grand livre d'achats 19

  general ledger ['dʒenrəl —] grand livre général 19

  private ledger ['praivit —] grand livre privé 19

  sales ledger ['seilz —] grand livre des ventes 19

letter ['letə] lettre

  letter of credit [— rəv 'kredit] lettre de crédit 3, 15

  irrevocable letter of credit [,iri'voukəbl —] lettre de crédit irrévocable 3, 15

  transferable letter of credit ['trænsfərəbl —] négociable, cessible 15

letterhead ['letəhed] entête 3, 4

levy ['levi] impôt, taxe ; imposer, taxer 18, 15

liabilities [,laiə'bilitiz] passif 19

liable ['laiəbl] **to** : passible de ; **for** : soumis à 2

fork lift ['fɔ:k 'lift] gerbeuse 16

limited to ['limitid tə] limité à 11

  Limited (Ltd.) ['limitid] 1

  limited company [— 'kʌmpəni] société anonyme 1, 13

  limited liability company S.A.R.L. 1, 13

line [lain] ligne ; chaîne ; article 2, etc.

  new line ['nju: —] nouvel article 2

  along the line [ə'lɔŋ ðə —] dans le circuit 3

liquidate ['likwideit] liquider

liquidation [,likwi'deiʃən] liquidation

  compulsory liquidation [kəm'pʌlsəri —] liquidation forcée 24

  voluntary liquidation ['vɔləntəri —] liquidation volontaire 24

load [loud] charger 7

  loading bank ['loudiŋ bæŋk] quai de chargement 7

loan [loun] prêt, emprunt 13

  short-term loan ['ʃɔ:t tə:m —] prêt à court terme 13

long [lɔŋ] long

  in the long run [in ðə 'lɔŋ 'rʌn] à la longue 16

long-term assessment [ˈlɔŋ-təːm əˈsesmənt] évaluation à long terme 3

lump sum [ˈlʌmp ˈsʌm] somme forfaitaire, prix global 23

M

machine [məˈʃiːn]
  machine layout [— ˈleiaut] implantation 5
  machine tool [— ˈtuːl] machine outil 8

mail [meil] courrier 3
  sort the mail [ˈsɔːt —] trier le courrier 9

maintenance fitter [ˈmeintinəns ˈfitə] ajusteur, ouvrier de l'entretien 24

manage [ˈmænidʒ] gérer, diriger, arriver à

management [ˈmænidʒmənt] gestion, direction

management trainee [— treiˈniː] stagiaire 11

manager [ˈmænidʒə] directeur, gérant, chef

Managing Director [ˈmænidʒiŋ diˈrektə] administrateur délégué, P.D.G. 1

market [ˈmaːkit] marché 1
  open up a new market [ˈoupən ʌp ə ˈnjuː ˈmaːkit] créer un marché 1
  market leaders [— ˈliːdəz] chefs de file 22
  marketing budget [ˈmaːkitiŋ ˈbʌdʒit] budget marketing 14
  Marketing Manager [— ˈmænidʒə] directeur du marketing 14
  marketing report [— riˈpɔːt] rapport de marketing 22
  marketing research [— riˈsəːtʃ] étude de marché 2, 22

medium (media) [ˈmiːdjəm, ˈmiːdjə] support publicitaire 6

meet a claim [ˈmiːt ə ˈkleim] donner suite à une déclaration de sinistre 23

meeting [ˈmiːtiŋ] réunion, assemblée 1, etc.

memorandum (memo) [ˌmeməˈrændəm, ˈmemou] note de service, circulaire 3
  Memorandum of Association [— əv æˌsousiˈeiʃən] acte constitutif de société, statuts 13

merchandise [ˈməːtʃəndaiz] marchandises 18

middleman [ˈmidlmæn] intermédiaire 18

milling machine [ˈmiliŋ maˈʃiːn] fraiseuse 8

minutes [ˈminits] procès-verbal 5
  minute book [ˈminit buk] registre des délibérations 17

take the minutes as read [ˈteik ðə əz ˈred] considérer le procès-verbal de la dernière assemblée comme lu et approuvé 5, 24

mishandling [ˈmisˈhændliŋ] faute de manutention 7

modify [ˈmɔdifai] modifier 18

money on deposit [ˈmʌni ɔn diˈpɔzit] agent en dépôt 13

mortgage [ˈmɔːgidʒ] hypothèque; hypothéquer 13

N

National Health Service [ˈnæʃnl ˈhelθ ˈsəːvis] sécurité sociale 8

negligence [ˈneglidʒəns] négligence 8

net price [ˈnet ˈprais] prix net 15

night safe [ˈnait ˈseif] coffre de nuit 13

nominal wage [ˈnɔminəl ˈweidʒ] salaire insignifiant 20

nominally [ˈnɔminəli] nominalement 16

not negotiable [ˈnɔt niˈgouʃjəbl] non négociable 13

O

office block [ˈɔfis blɔk] bâtiment administratif 2

official [əˈfiʃəl] official 15

official receiver [— riˈsiːvə] administrateur sequestre, syndic de faillite 21

offset [ˈɔfset] compenser 4, 16

open an account [ˈoupən ən əˈkaunt] ouvrir un compte 13

operate [ˈɔpəreit] faire marcher 1
  Operational Research (O.R.) [ˈɔpəˈreiʃnl riˈsəːtʃ-ˈou ˈaː] recherche opérationnelle 1

operator [ˈɔpəreitə] celui qui agit, fait marcher 9

operative [ˈɔpərətiv] ouvrier 12

order [ˈɔːdə] commande ; commander 7
  place an order [ˈpleis ən —] passer une commande 7
  order number [— ˈnʌmbə] numéro de de commande 7
  winding-up order [ˈwaindiŋ-ˈʌp —] ordre de liquidation 24

order in bulk [ˈɔːdər inˈbʌlk] commande en gros 15

outgoing [ˈautˈgouiŋ] sortie 3

outlook [ˈautluk] conceptions 1

out-of-date [ˈautəvˈdeit] dépassé, démodé 3

outpace [autˈpeis] distancer, dépasser 1

output [ˈautput] production
  double the output [ˈdʌbl ði —] doubler la production 2

outstanding accounts [aut'stændiŋ ə'kaunts] arriérés, comptes en souffrance 21
outvote [aut'vout] mettre en minorité 13
overdraft ['ouvədra:ft] découvert 13
overdue ['ouvədju:] arriéré, en retard 4
overheads ['ouvəhedz] frais généraux 15
over-subscribed ['ouvə-səb'skraibd] sursouscrit 24
overtime ['ouvətaim] heures supplémentaires 4, 12
owe [ou] devoir 16
owing ['ouiŋ] dû 16
ownership ['ounəʃip] propriété 10

P

pack ['pæk] emballer 7
packing and despatch department service emballages et expéditions 7
package deal ['pækidʒ 'di:l] concession, compromis 15, 18
packaging conditionnement
palletise ['pælitaiz] palettiser 16
pallets ['pælits] palettes 16
part-time ['pa:t-'taim] à mi-temps, à temps partiel 8
pay [pei] payer
pay in ['pei 'in] verser, déposer 19
pay in cash ['pei in 'kæʃ] payer en espèces 11
payee [pei'i:] bénéficiaire, preneur] 13
paying-in slips ['peiiŋ-'in 'slips] ; paying-in vouchers [— 'vautʃəz] bordereaux de versement 13, 19
pay piece rates [— 'pi:s reits] payer à la tâche 9
get pay docked ['get 'pei 'dɔkt] se faire rogner son salaire, avoir un 'rabat de col' 12
payroll ['peiroul] bulletin de paie 20
par [pa:] pair
at par [ət 'pa:] au pair 24
patent ['peitənt, 'pætənt] brevet 22
Patent Office ['pætənt' ɔfis] bureau des brevets 22
penalty clause ['penalti 'klɔ:z] clause pénale 4
pending ['pendiŋ] en attente 1
pension ['penʃən] pension, retraite 10
personnel [,pə:sə'nel] personnel 5
Personnel Department [— di'pa:tmənt] Service du Personnel 2
Personnel Manager [— 'mænidʒə] Directeur du Personnel 12
petty cash ['peti 'kæʃ] petite caisse 19
photostat ['foutoustæt] photocopie 22

plane [plein] rabot 8
plant [pla:nt] matériel, machine ; usine 4
policy ['pɔlisi] police ; politique, ligne de conduite
all risks policy ['ɔ:l 'risks 'pɔlisi] police d'assurance tous risques 23
port rates ['pɔ:t 'reits] droits de port 1
post [poust] porter, passer (une écriture) 19
precedent noun : 'presidənt ; adj. : pri'si:dent] précédent 10
premium ['pri:mjəm] prime 23
be at a premium [ət ə —] faire prime 24
president ['prezidənt] président ; U.S. directeur général 1
press [pres] presse ; emboutir 2, 12
pressing ['presiŋ] emboutissage 2
private company ['praivit —] société privée ; (équivalent de) S.A.R.L. 13
probe [proub] sonder ; essai 1
produce [prə'dju:s] produire
product ['prɔdʌkt] produit
launch a product ['lɔ:ntʃ] lancer un produit 11
production [prə'dʌkʃən] production
production line [— lain] chaîne de production 4
keep the production line clear [— kliə] tenir la chaîne de production disponible 4
re-schedule a production line ['ri:-'ʃedju:l] réorganiser la chaîne de — 4
Production Manager Directeur de la Production, chef de l'ordonnancement 1, 4
productivity ['prɔdʌk'tiviti] productivité 9
profit ['prɔfit] profit, bénéfice
profit margin [— 'ma:dʒin] marge bénéficiaire 15
profit sharing scheme [— ʃɛəriŋ 'ski:m] projet d'intéressement, de participation 12
profit statement [— 'steitmənt] compte de profits et pertes 19
(trading and profit and loss account)
profitable ['prɔfitəbl] rentable 1
Project Evaluation and Review Technique (P.E.R.T.) ['prɔdʒikt i'vælju'eiʃən ən ri'vju: tek'ni:k pə:t] méthode PERT 1
proofs [pru:fs] épreuves
check proofs ['tʃek —] relire les épreuves 6
prospect [ə'prɔspekt] client éventuel 18

— 392 —

provisions [prə'viʒənz] clauses, dispositions 8
proxy ['prɔksi] procuration 24
profitability [ˌprɔfitə'biliti] rentabilité
public ['pʌblik] public
  public address (system) [— ə'dres] système d'appel général 4
  public company [— 'kʌmpəni] S.A. 13
  go public [gou —] se mettre en société, devenir une société anonyme 24
  public relations [— ri'leiʃənz] relations publiques 6
put in a claim ['put in ə 'kleim] présenter une réclamation, faire une déclaration de sinistre 23
put (a name) forward ['put — 'fɔ:wəd] proposer un candidat 17
put (someone) in the picture ['put in ðə 'piktʃə] mettre au courant 17

Q

qualification ['kwɔlifi'keiʃən] cautionnement
  qualification holding [— 'houldiŋ] actions de garantie 17
qualify ['kwɔlifai] donner qualité, prétendre 20
  qualify for a pension [— fər ə 'penʃən] faire valoir ses droits à la retraite 10
quarterly ['kwɔ:təli] trimestriel 15
query ['kwiəri] contester 19
quote [kwout] coter ; indiquer un prix 2
  quotation [kwou'teiʃən] cotation ; prix 2, 15

R

raise a loan ['reiz ə 'loun] émettre un emprunt 13
range [reindʒ] gamme 11
rate [reit] taux, cours, tarif, cadence
  rate (someone) as sound [əz saund] juger solvable, sain 3
  rate of interest [— əv 'intrest] taux d'intérêt 13
rationalisation [ˌræʃənəlai'zeiʃən] rationalisation 9
record [ə 'rekɔ:d, tə ri'kɔ:d] record, archive ; enregistrer
  break a record ['breik —] battre un record 8
red tape ['red'teip] paperasserie, routine 1
be in the red [in ðə 'red] être à découvert, " fauché " 13
redundant [ri'dʌndənt] au chômage, de trop 10
reference ['refrəns] référence 12
register ['redʒistə] enregistrer, recommander 22

registrar ['redʒistə] directeur des enregistrements de sociétés 24
release [ri'li:s] communiqué de presse 14
report [ri'pɔ:t] rapport 7
represent [repri'zent] représenter 18
rep [rep] **sales representative** ['seilz repri'zentativ] représentant 7, 18
requirement [ri'kwaiə] besoin, exigence 2
respray ['ri:'sprei] repeindre 7
restrictive practice [ris'triktiv 'præktis] entrave à la liberté du commerce, etc... 20
retail [n. 'ri:teil, v. ri:'teil] détail, vendre au détail 21
retailer [ri'teilə] détaillant 1
retire [ri'taiə] prendre sa retraite 10
revoke [ri'vouk] révoquer, annuler 15
road [roud] route
  road-worthiness ['roud-wə:ðinis] bon état de marche 16
  be on the road [bi: ɔn ðə 'roud] être en tournée 7
roll off ['roul'ɔ:f] tirer (des stencils) 3
Rules of Association ['ru:lz əv ə'sousi'ei ʃən] statuts 17, (see also 13)
run out of ['rʌn aut əv] manquer de, être à court de 2

S

sacked [sækt] licencié, renvoyé 10
safe [seif] coffre-fort 11
  safety measure ['seifti 'meʒə] mesure de sécurité 8
salary ['sæləri] traitement, appointement 12, 21
  basic salary ['beisik] fixe 21
sales [seilz] ventes, chiffre d'affaire 11
  sales-assistant 11
  salesman ['seilzmən] } vendeur 18
  sales figures [— 'figəz] chiffre d'affaires 11
  Sales Manager [— 'mænidʒə] Directeur des Ventes 1
  sale or return ['seil ɔ: ri'tə:n] en dépôt, à condition 18
  sales resistance [— ri'zistəns] résistance à la vente 18
salvage ['sælvidʒ] récupérer 23
sample [sa:mpl] échantillon, témoin 18
sandwich course ['sændwitʃ 'kɔ:s] cours avec stage intégré 11, 20
saving plan ['seiviŋ 'plæn] plan d'épargne 23
schedule ['ʃedju:l] horaire, plan de travail 14
  ahead of schedule [ə'hed əv —] en avance 14

behind schedule [bi'haind —] en
retard 14
on schedule [ɔn —] à l'heure, dans les
temps 14
scheduled ['ʃedju:ld] prévu 14
scheme [ski:m] projet, plan 10
a bonus scheme ['bounəs —] système
de prime 9
incentive payments scheme [in'sentiv
'peimənts —] système d'encouragement à la production 9
pension scheme ['penʃən] système
de retraite 10
security [si'kjuəriti] garantie, nantissement 13
Security Officer [— 'ɔfisə] Responsable
de la Sécurité 11
see over (a place) ['si:'ouvə] visiter 2
selection [si'lekʃən] sélection 12
send round ['send 'raund] envoyer,
diffuser 3
serial number ['siərjəl 'nʌmbə] numéro
de série 21
set out ['set 'aut] présenter 3
share [ʃɛə] action 10
ordinary share ['ɔ:dinəri] action
ordinaire 24
preference share ['prefrəns] action
privilégiée 24
share-capital capital actions 13
shareholder ['ʃɛəhouldə] actionnaire
13, 19
ship [ʃip] bateau, expédier
shipping charges ['ʃipiŋ 'tʃa:dʒiz]
frais d'expédition maritime 15
ship's manifest [— s 'mænifest] manifeste, déclaration d'expédition 15
shop (in a factory) [ʃɔp] atelier 2, 8
closed shop ['klouzd —] usine dans
laquelle la direction fait de la
discrimination syndicale 12
shop floor ['ʃɔp 'flɔ:] le tas, l'usine,
la base 12
shop steward [— 'stju:əd] délégué
syndical 8, 12
shorthand ['ʃɔ:thænd] sténographie 3
short list ['ʃɔ:t list] liste courte 6
sick-pay scheme ['sik-pei 'ski:m] allocation maladie 8
sight draft ['sait 'dra:ft] traite à vue 3
single entry ['siŋgl 'entri] partie simple 19
skilled worker ['skild 'wə:kə] ouvrier
spécialisé 5
slogan ['slougən] slogan 14
solicitor [sə'lisitə] chef du contentieux 2
specification ['spesifi'keiʃən] norme ;
description 2, 22

sort [sɔ:t] sorte, espèce
sort out ['sɔ:t 'aut] tirer 3
to sound (someone) out ['saund 'aut]
sonder 17
spot check ['spɔt 'tʃek] **spot checking**
['spɔt 'tʃekiŋ] contrôle de police
routière 16
spray [sprei] vaporiser, peindre au
pistolet 7
stain-proof ['stein-pru:f], **stain-resistant**
['stein-ri'zistənt] intachable 18
sophisticated [sə'fistikeitid] compliqué 1
stand (exhibition) [stænd] stand 14
'dry' stand ['drai —] stand où l'on ne
sert pas de boisson 14
standardize ['stændədaiz] standardiser,
unifier, normaliser 9
staple [steipl] agrafe 18
stapler ['steiplə] agrafeuse 18
static ['stætik] statique 22
stationery ['steiʃənəri] papeterie 3
statutory ['stætjutəri] prévu par la loi 8
steel filings ['sti:l 'failiŋz] limaille 8
stencil ['stensil] stencil 3
cut a stencil ['kʌt ə 'stensil] faire un
stencil 3
stock [stɔk] stock, provision, valeur 2
stocks [stɔks] stocks, approvisionne-
ment 17
in stock [in —] en stock, en magasin 2
out of stock ['aut əv —] épuisé] 2
stock item (line) ['stɔk 'aitəm, 'lain]
article de production courante 2
non-stock item ['nɔn-'stɔk —] article
de production extraordinaire 2
streamline ['stri:mlain] rénover, ration-
naliser, moderniser 9
strike [straik] grève 12
to strike se mettre en grève 12
to be on strike être en grève 12
official strike [ə'fiʃəl —] grève offi-
cielle 12
'wild cat' strike ['waild kæt —] grève
officieuse, sauvage 12
study ['stʌdi] étudier ; étude
sample study ['sa:mpl —] étude
témoin 9
time study ['taim —] étude des
temps 9
time and motion study ['taim ən
'mouʃən —] étude des temps et des
mouvements 9
work study ['wə:k 'stʌdi] étude de
postes 9
stuff (*slang* = **material**) [stʌf] truc,
machin 7
subsidiary [səb'sidjəri] filiale 11

sue poursuivre (en justice)   8
supervisor ['sjupəvaizə] responsable   8
supplement [ə 'sʌpləmənt, tə 'sʌpliment] ajouter   21
survey [*n.* 'sə:vei, *v.* sə'vei] étudier ; étude   9
  desk survey ['desk 'sə:vei] étude théorique   1
  field survey ['fi:ld —] étude de marché 1
syndicate ['sindikit] syndicat, consortium   23
swarf [swɔ:f] limaille, boue de meule   8

T

table [teibl] mettre à l'ordre du jour   17
take [teik] prendre
  take as read [— əz 'red] considérer comme lu et approuvé   5
  take out (a policy) ['teik aut ə 'pɔlisi] prendre une assurance   23
  take over ['teik 'ouvə] succéder ; absorber   10
takeover ['teikouvə] prise de contrôle   10
  takeover bid offre publique d'achat   10
tape recorder ['teip ri'kɔ:də] magnétophone   4
tariff ['tærif] tarif, droits   1
technical college ['teknikl 'kɔlidʒ] collège technique   20
telex ['teleks] télétype   1
terms [tə:mz] conditions   18
  terms of payment [— 'peimənt] — de paiement   15, 22
third party ['θə:d 'pa:ti] tiers   23
time [taim] temps
  time and a half ['taim ənd ə 'ha:f] (payer) à 50 % au-dessus du tarif   12
  double time ['dʌbl 'taim] (payer) au tarif double   4
  time clock ['taim 'klɔk] horloge pointeuse   12
tip off ['tip 'ɔf] donner un tuyau   23
tool room ['tu:l rum] salle d'outillage   8
traction unit ['trækʃen ju:nit] élément tracteur   16
trade [treid] commerce, affaires
  trade-mark ['treid-ma:k] marque de fabrique   22
  registered trade-mark ['redʒistəd —] marque déposée   22
  trade press ['treid 'pres] presse professionnelle   14
  tradesman ['treidzmən] marchand, fournisseur   5
  trade union ['treid 'ju:njən] syndicat 12

training ['treiniŋ] formation professionnelle
  Training Board ['treiniŋ 'bɔ:d] Commission de la F.P. (Ministère du Travail)   20
  training facilities [—fə'silitiz] installation de F.P.   20
  training programme [— 'prougræm] programme de F.P.   5
transit ['trænzit] transit
  in transit en transit   7
transport cafe ['trænspɔ:t 'kæfei] restaurant routier   16
trans-ship [træns-'ʃip] transborder   1
traveller (salesman) ['trævlə] voyageur de commerce, représentant   18
treble [trebl] tripler   1
trust [trʌst] trust, fideicommis   10
turn-round time ['tə:n-raund 'taim] temps d'immobilisation à la livraison   16
turnover ['tə:nouvə] chiffre d'affaire ; roulement ; mouvement du personnel   15
  budgeted turnover ['bʌdʒitid 'tə:nouvə] prévisions de chiffres d'affaires   15
typographer [tai'pɔgrəfə] typographe   6

U

umpteen ['ʌmpti:n] des tas de...   18
unassembled ['ʌnə'sembld] non monté, en pièces détachées   7
union ['ju:njən] syndicat
  union dues [— 'dju:z] cotisation syndicale   12
  union rules [— 'ru:lz] règlement syndical   12
unload ['ʌn'loud] décharger
  unloading bank [—iŋ bæŋk] quai de déchargement   7
  unloader ['ʌn'loudə] débardeur, manutentionnaire   7
underwriters ['ʌndəraitəz] assureurs   23
unsecured ['ʌnsi'kjuəd] sans garantie   13

V

vacant ['veikənt] libre (*situation*)   6
valuation [vælju'eiʃən] évaluation, inventaire   19
visualiser ['vizjuəlaizə] coalisateur publicitaire   6
voting rights ['voutiŋ raits] droit de vote   24
vested ['vestid] dévolu, assigné   11

W

wage [weidʒ] salaire
  wage claim [— 'kleim] revendication de salaire   12
  wage rate [— 'reit] taux de salaire   20
  wages ['weidʒiz] salaire   12
walk out ['wɔ:k aut] débrayage, grève   12
wall chart ['wɔ:l tʃa:t] tableau, graphique   20
warehouse ['wɛəhaus] entrepôt, magasin 2
  bonded warehouse ['bɔndid —] magasins généraux, entrepôt en douanes   15
  ex warehouse ['eks —] départ entrepôt   15
wâybill ['weibil] lettre de voiture ; feuille de route   3, 15
welder ['weldə] soudeur   2
  spot welding ['spɔt weldiŋ] soudure par points   2
welfare ['welfɛə] bien-être   24
  welfare department service social
  welfare committee comité d'entreprise

wharfage ['wɔ:fidʒ] droits de quai   15
wholesale ['houlseil] gros, en gros   21
  wholesaler ['houlseilə] grossiste   1
withdraw [wið'drɔ:] retirer   13
  withdrawal [wið'drɔ:əl] retrait   19
work [wə:k] travail, travailler
  work flow ['wə:k flou] acheminement   20
  works [wə:ks] usine   4, 9
  ex works [eks —] départ usine   4
Workers' Compensation Act loi sur les accidents du travail
write [rait] écrite
  write-off [— ɔ:f] amortir, annuler   23
  write off épave   23
  write-up [— ʌp] rédiger ; faire du battage   14

Y

year [jiə] année
  financial year [fai'nænʃl 'jiə] exercice   17

COMMON ABBREVIATIONS USED
IN BUSINESS AND COMMERCE

A

a.a.	always afloat
a.a.r.	against all risks
A.B.C.C.	Association of British Chambers of Commerce
A.l	fist class
A/C	account
acc.	acceptance, accepted
acct.	account
ad., advt	advertisement
a/d	after date
a.f.	advance freight
a.f.b.	air freight bill
Agt	agent
amt	amount
a/o	account of
A.R.	accounts receivable
A/R, a/r	all risks (insurance)
arr., arrd.	arrival, arrived
a/s	after sight ; alongside
A.S.	account sales
A/V	ad valorem (according to value)
av., avg.	average

B

B/	bag or bale
bal.	balance
B/D	bank draft
B/E, b/e	bill of exchange
b/f	brought forward
B.I.S.	Bank for International Settlements
Bk	bank or book
B/L	bill of lading
b/o	brought over
B.O.T.	Board of Trade
B.P.	bills payable
b.p.	by proxy, by procuration
Bros.	Brothers
B/S	balance sheet ; bill of sale
b.t.	berth terms
bt	bought

C

c	cent
c/	coupon
C.A.	chartered accountant
C/A	capital account
C.A.D.	cash against documents
c & f	cost and freight
C.B.	cash book
c.b.d., C.B.D.	cash before delivery
c.f.	carried forward
cge pd.	carriage paid
c.i.f.	cost, insurance, freight
Co.	company
c/o	care of
C.O.D.	cash on delivery
col.	column
con., consol.	consolidated
contd	continued
corp., cpn.	corporation
C.P.	carriage paid
C/P	charter-party
C.R.	company's risk
Cr.	credit, creditor
c.w.o., C.W.O.	cash with order
cwt	hundredweight

D

d	penny, pence ; discount ; dividend
D/A	documents against acceptance ; deposit account
d/d	days after date
dd	delivered
dept.	department
d.f.	dead freight
dft	draft
D/O	delivery order
do	ditto
dol(s)	dollar(s)
doz.	dozen
Dr.	debit, debtor
d.s.	days after sight

— 397 —

E

E & O E	errors and omissions excepted
E.C.S.C.	European Coal and Steel Community
E.E.C.	European Economic Community
E.F.T.A.	European Free Trade Association
e.g.	for instance
encl.	enclosed, enclosure
Ex.	exchange
ex whf.	ex wharf
ex whse.	ex warehouse

F

f.a.q.	fair average quality; free alongside quay
f.a.s.	free along side ship
F.B.I.	Federation of British Industries
F.C.A.	Fellow of the Institute of Chartered Accountants
F.D.	free delivery to dock
fd	forward
F.O.	Foreign Office
f.o.b.	free on board
f.o.c.	free of charge
f.o.q.	free on quay
f.o.r.	free on rail
f.o.t.	free on truck
f.o.w.	free on wharf/waggon
f.p.	fully paid
frt.	freight
ft.	foot, feet
fwd.	forward

G

g.a., G.A.	general average
gal.	gallon
G.A.T.T.	General Agreement of Tariffs and Trade
G.B.	Great Britain
gov., govt.	government
G.P.O.	General Post Office
gr. wt.	gross weight
gtd., guar.	guaranteed
g.n.p.	gross national product

H

H.M.C.	Her (His) Majesty's Customs
H.O.	Head Office
H.P.	hire purchase; horse power

I

I.C.C.	International Chamber of Commerce
id.	idem, the same
i.e.	*id est*, that is
I.M.F.	International Monetary Fund
in. ins.	inch, inches
Inc.	incorporated
incl.	inclusive
ins.	insurance
inst.	instant, present month
int.	interest
inv.	invoice
I.O.U.	I owe you
I.R.	Inland Revenue

J

Jr	junior

L

£	pound (sterling)
Lb	pound (weight)
L/C	letter of credit
£.s.d.	pounds, shillings, pence
Ltd	limited
L.I.P.	life insurance policy

M

m.	month; mile; million
memo	memorandum
Messrs.	Messieurs
mixt	mixed
M.O.	money order
M/V	motor vessel

N

No	number
N.Y.S.E.	New York Stock Exchange

O

o/a.	on account
o.b.	on board
o/d	overdraft
O.E.C.D.	Organisation for Economic Cooperation et Development
O.H.M.S.	On Her Majesty's Service
O.P.	open policy (insurance)
O.R.	owner's risk (insurance)
oz	ounce

P

p.	new pence
P.A.	particular average
p.a.	per annum
p.c.	per cent
pd.	paid
per pro., p.p.	*per procurationem*, by proxy
pkg.	package
P. & L.	profit and loss
P.L.A.	Port of London Authority
P.N.	promissory note
P.O.	Post Office ; postal order
P.O.B.	post-office box
p.p.	*per procurationem*, by proxy
ppd.	prepaid
prox.	proximo, next
p.t.o., P.T.O.	please turn over

Q

Qlty	quality
Qnty	quantity

R

R/D	refer to drawer
re.	in re, relating to, regarding
rec., recd.	receipt ; received
ref.	reference
reg.	registered
retd.	returned
Rly, Ry	railway

S

s , /	shilling
$	dollar
S.E.	Stock Exchange
S/N.	shipping note
sec.	secretary
sen.	senior
sgd.	signed
shipt.	shipment

SS, S.S.	steamship
sq	square
st.	stone, street
std.	standard

T

t.	ton
tfr.	transfer
T.L. (t.l.)	total loss
T.N., tel No	telephone number
T.U.C.	Trade Union Congress

U

U.K.	United Kingdom
ult.	ultimo, last month
UNCTAD.	The United Nations Conference on Trade and Development
U/W	underwriter

V

V.A.T.	value added tax
viz.	*videlicet*, namely
vs.	versus
vol.	volume

W

W.B.	waybill
whf.	wharf
whse.	warehouse
wt.	weight

X

X-wks	ex works
x. whf.	ex wharf
x. whse.	ex warehouse

Y

yd(s)	yard(s)

ACHEVÉ D'IMPRIMER
SUR LES PRESSES DE
L'IMPRIMERIE CHIRAT
42540 ST-JUST-LA-PENDUE
EN OCTOBRE 1992
DÉPÔT LÉGAL 1992 N° 7229

IMPRIMÉ EN FRANCE